BATTERING
and
Family Therapy

To the two men whose support,
love, respect, and appreciation
of these two strong women
facilitated our creative process

A Feminist Perspective

Marsali Hansen & Michèle Harway
Editors

SAGE Publications
International Educational and Professional Publisher
Newbury Park London New Delhi

For information address:

SAGE Publications, Inc.
2455 Teller Road
Newbury Park, California 91320

SAGE Publications Ltd.
6 Bonhill Street
London EC2A 4PU
United Kingdom

SAGE Publications India Pvt. Ltd.
M-32 Market
Greater Kailash I
New Delhi 110 048 India

Printed in the United States of America

Library of Congress Cataloging-in-Publication Data

Main entry under title:

Battering and family therapy: a feminist perspective / edited by
Marsali Hansen, Michèle Harway.
p. cm.
Includes bibliographical references and index.
ISBN 0-8039-4320-2 (cl).—ISBN 0-8039-4321-0 (pb)
1. Family violence. 2. Wife abuse. 3. Family psychotherapy.
4. Feminist therapy. I. Hansen, Marsali. II. Harway, Michèle.
RC569.5.F3B38 1993
616.85′822—dc20 92-42025
CIP

93 94 95 96 10 9 8 7 6 5 4 3 2

Sage Production Editor: Judith L. Hunter

Contents

Foreword

Violence against women has been part of everyday life since the beginning of recorded history. For centuries it was so normative that no sanctions existed against it. Men enjoyed safety from societal intrusion within their homes, which were seen as their castles. Men's patriarchy over their families was purchased at the expense of an invisible horde of women who were beaten in their homes. The primary response of a battered woman during these times was to attempt to minimize violence by catering to the every mood and whim of her partner. Often, however, violence occurred repeatedly, leading the woman to realize how illusory was the belief that she could control her husband's behavior. But there were virtually no resources that would permit escape, and the social sanctioning of male violence left the battered woman without even the hope of support or validation from family and friends. Formal questioning of the appropriateness of men's beating their wives began only within this century. Prevalence data revealing the enormous proportions of the problem have been available for fewer than 20 years.

Today, behavioral scientists recognize the gendered nature of the violence in women's everyday lives. The victims of male violence are made vulnerable to abuse primarily because they are women. Naming the types of violence by creating such terms as *battering, acquaintance rape,* and *workplace harassment* has validated women's experiences and empowered them to speak of those experiences. However, the terms also may have impeded scholarly development, because they divided researchers into tiny camps, obscured the multiple, different victimizations sustained by many women, and discouraged a conceptualization of male violence that recognizes its common causal pathways.

Contemporary policy-making has been characterized by a perceptual blackout about violence in the family. Recognition of the true scope of battering has been precluded, because to do so would contradict prevailing idealizations of the traditional American family. Naturally, without accurate description of the size of the problem, institutional responses were inadequate. Nevertheless, the past several years have seen one formal system after the next—mental health, criminal justice, and medicine—step forward to assert what it could contribute to the victim of domestic violence. There have been many gains, such as the creation of protection orders and mandatory arrest policies, inclusion of violence considerations into custody decisions, and implementation of emergency room protocols. All too often, however, these resources are more illusory than real, because practitioners fail to incorporate practice standards promoted by professional associations and because the services cannot be accessed by women who lack financial resources. Psychological treatment of batterers and their partners from a family therapy model also has been sharply criticized. Practitioners have often failed to detect battering, and, even when they have identified it, they have proceeded with treatment plans that ignored the violence.

On October 20, 1992, the Association of American Medical Colleges (AAMC) communicated to its Council of Deans the urgent need to include education on domestic violence in medical training at all levels, from undergraduate through residency and continuing education. This communication concerning voluntary compliance was prompted by proposed legislation, H.R. 4846, introduced by Representative Ron Wyden (D-OR), that would have mandated inclusion of "significant training in identifying victims of domestic violence and in providing treatment for medical conditions arising from such violence" as a condition for an institution's receiving federal funds from the Public Health Service. The AAMC and other medical organizations have historically opposed curriculum mandates, and their strategy to head off this one is to revise the curriculum proactively. There is an important message in this for those who train health care practitioners of every type. It is time to get serious about domestic violence.

This book is about three "F"s: family violence, family therapy, and feminist thinking. Both feminism and family therapy incorporate concepts of power, but the conceptualization from the latter perspective is male defined, and male dominance is typically taken for granted. Some writers have questioned the fruitfulness of attempting to integrate feminism with family systems therapy because of the two perspectives' fundamental incompatibility in understandings of power (Bograd, 1988). Without major restructuring, attempting to integrate feminism and family therapy may be a case of rearranging deck chairs on the *Titanic*. Feminists have questioned the appropriateness of family therapy for domestic violence because application of this conceptual framework to battering implies the wife's coresponsibility for the violence. Harway and Hansen acknowledge that the contemporary family is a system in which the balance of power is inherently unequal. Consequently, with certain well-described exceptions, the chapter authors assume an individual approach to treatment. Although therapy might sometimes be conducted in groups, such groups would not mix perpetrators and victims.

The contributors to this volume are experts in the field of family violence. They consider family violence from theoretical, empirical, legal, and treatment vantage points. The theoretical material includes discussion and critique of various models of family violence, including the feminist model. Legal scholars address judicial options for the battered woman and delineate therapists' ethical duties when treating violent families. The impact of domestic violence on child custody decisions is also addressed, as is the use of the battered woman syndrome in legal arguments for self-defense in cases where victims are accused of killing their partners. Several contributors review the meager body of scholarship in this field to date and observe that little of it has been notably feminist in theoretical underpinnings. Among the topics that have been studied are the psychological impact of battering on victims and their children, and violence in lesbian relationships. Contributors offer useful suggestions for obtaining relevant information about ongoing violence without involving the victim in the treatment of the batterer in ways that could make her vulnerable to retaliation. Also discussed is the triaging of cases in which both domestic violence and alcoholism are present. Finally, in recognition that the cause of family violence is the batterer, the editors have included material on the characteristics of offenders and their treatment.

For me, the most troubling material in this book is the information provided on current practice standards for violent families, as reflected by surveys of family counselors and psychotherapists. These data suggest to me that the concern of medical educators to include domestic violence in their curricula should be extended to the other helping professions as well.

Mary P. Koss, Ph.D.

Acknowledgments

There are a number of people to whom we owe our appreciation. The completion of the manuscript would not have been so smooth without them. These include Nancy Zemirah, for her assistance in background research; Jody Borelli, for hours in the library researching the literature and for her analysis of the data; Sally Peace, for typing up chapter drafts; Max Frankl, for coordination of the final manuscript; Jan Panet, for help with data analyses; Scott Hampton, Jay Mills, and Michele Thomas, for helpful suggestions in editing; and Bob Geffner and Herb Goldenberg, for their ideas, which greatly improved our thinking. In addition, Marsali Hansen would like to thank Leon VanderCreek for his support of her work and Ginger Brown and the Indiana University of Pennsylvania Graduate School for funding parts of the research. Michèle Harway would like to thank Edwin S. Cox for his gracious support and the California Family Study Center for its funding. We would both like to thank Chapman University for contribution to early stages of the research and Nancyann Cervantes for her coauthoring of those studies.

Finally, we need to give special thanks to Terry Hendrix, wonderful editor and friend, and to Lenore Walker for her exuberance, support, and encouragement, and her belief that this book was needed.

Marsali Hansen
Michèle Harway

POSTSCRIPT: The order of the editors' names was determined by a flip of a coin.

1

An Overview of Domestic Violence

MICHÈLE HARWAY
MARSALI HANSEN

Prevalence of Domestic Violence

"You are more likely to be physically assaulted, beaten, and killed in your own home at the hands of a loved one than anyplace else, or by anyone else in our society" (Gelles & Straus, 1989, p. 18). This statement by two of the most respected researchers in the field of family violence reflects the findings of numerous studies of the prevalence of domestic violence in our society. Gelles and Straus's 1975 First National Family Violence Survey (cited in Gelles & Straus, 1989) indicated that 1 out of every 6 wives reported that she had been hit by her husband at some point in her marriage. This study, based on interviews with a national sample of more than 2,000 families, also indicated that about 1 woman in 22 (3.8%) is the victim of physically abusive violence each year, with the average battered wife being attacked three times each year. Attacks take the form of severe beatings in 6 cases out of 1,000 and involve the use of guns or knives in 2 cases out of 1,000.

Gelles and Straus's Second National Family Violence Survey (including interviews with an additional 6,000 families) indicated again that 1 out of 6 American couples experienced an incident involving a physical assault during 1985 (cited in Gelles & Straus, 1989). Projections have been made that 8.7 million couples experienced at least one assault during that year. Most of these assaults involved "minor" violence (e.g., pushing, slapping, shoving, or throwing things); however, in a projected 3.4 million households the violence had a high risk of causing injury. Straus and Gelles

(1988) suggest that these numbers probably underestimate the correct incidence of domestic violence, and that true rates could be as high as twice those reported to them. Other researchers also point to the serious underestimation of the prevalence of domestic violence from these figures: for example, Steinmetz (1977) estimates that fewer than 1 of every 250 spouse assaults is reported.

Gelles and Straus's study results are consistent with those coming from government studies. A U.S. Department of Justice study of "intimate victims" involving interviews of 136,000 Americans found 3.8 million incidents of violence among intimates during a four-year period. A third of these incidents took place between relatives, and more than half were between spouses or ex-spouses (Lentzer, 1980).

By contrast, the National Crime Survey of 60,000 households reports dramatically lower rates than those of the National Family Violence Survey (2.2/1,000, in contrast to 116/1,000). The difference in reporting may be an artifact of the method used in collecting the data: The National Crime Survey was presented to respondents as a study of crime, whereas the Family Violence Survey was presented as a study of family problems. Most people do not think of family violence as a crime, thus fewer incidents of domestic battery may have been reported (Gaquin, 1977-1978). In an overview of a number of studies using the Conflict Tactics Scale (an instrument used to document frequency and severity of conjugal conflict, including incidents of domestic violence), Straus and Gelles examined data from 12 studies (conducted mainly by other researchers). The number of violent episodes reported in these studies ranged from 121 per 1,000 couples to 510 per 1,000 couples. The rate of 510 was for assaults experienced by battered wives when they were dating their husbands.

That conjugal violence is not restricted to married or cohabiting couples is supported by other data: Straus and Gelles's surveys indicate that between 22% and 67% of dating relationships involve some kind of violence.

Seriousness of Domestic Violence

Conjugal assaults tend to have more serious consequences than other types of assaults. The National Crime Survey indicated that conjugal assaults accounted for 12% of assaults ending in serious injury, 16% of assaults requiring medical care, and 18% of assaults requiring victims to miss at least one day's work (while constituting only 5% of total reported assaults). Thus serious injury as a result of domestic violence is highly likely.

Okun (1986) studied 300 residents of a battered women's shelter in Michigan. For these women, an average interval of almost five years had elapsed from time of first assault in the relationship until arrival at the shelter. Shelter residents had endured an average of 59 assaults each. Prior to intake, each woman had, on the average, experienced more than 5 assaults every four weeks, for an annualized frequency rate of more than 65 conjugal assaults per year. More than 20% stated that they were being assaulted twice or more per week. Of the women who had ever been pregnant during their abusive relationships, 62% had been assaulted during a pregnancy. Two-thirds of the sample had experienced at least one assault in which they were extensively beaten up or worse. One in 6 had been threatened with a knife or gun by her partner and 1 in 30 had actually been attacked with a knife or gun. These 300 women reported on intake 28 fractures (most commonly of the nose or jaw) and 22 serious injuries not involving fractures (chronic back injuries, torn ligaments, dislocations, ruptured eardrums, broken teeth, lacerations, stab wounds, bullet wounds). These injuries included only those that were sustained at the time of intake, not previous injuries. Of this group, only 24% had ever received medical treatment for injuries sustained during conjugal assaults. The remainder had wanted medical treatment but were prevented by their partners from obtaining it. Some 69% of these women had experienced at least one assault that resulted in police intervention, and more than 17% had received multiple visits from the police.

In many cases, domestic violence is extreme enough to result in murder, with lethality in cases of wife battering most likely to occur when the woman tries to leave. Dobash and Dobash (1977-1978) report that 70-80% of women who are murdered are killed by their husbands, other members of their families, or close male friends. Straus and Gelles's (1988) data also support these findings, indicating that women are seldom murder victims outside of the home. Women constitute only 21% of stranger homicide victims, but 76% of spouse murder victims. At the same time, women themselves commit only one-tenth of the nonspouse murders in the United States, but commit nearly half (48%) of the murders of spouses or close friends.

Both Walker's work (see Chapter 16, this volume) and that of Gelles and Straus suggest that women who murder their spouses most often do so in self-defense after years of physical abuse: "Human beings can absorb outrageous violence over long periods of time with barely a whimper and rarely a cry for help. Every one of the women we have met who has slain her husband did so after years of cruel physical and mental punishment" (Gelles & Straus, 1989, p. 19). Okun's (1986) data indicate that 54% of the battered women he interviewed had forcibly retaliated in self-defense on at least one occasion, and 37% said that they did so sometimes, often, or usually. Women's violence is usually in self-defense, and is less likely to inflict damage because women are smaller and less aggressive (Gelles & Straus, 1989). Women who murder have often been recipients of more serious battering than women who do not (Browne, 1987; Walker, 1989b). Most of these women had sought help repeatedly prior to acting.

Impact of Prevalence and Seriousness of Domestic Violence on Clinical Practice

The data reported above confirm that domestic violence is widespread and has the potential for being quite serious. Data from national surveys indicate that psychotherapists who are working with violent families need a comprehensive understanding of wife battering because of the likelihood that at some time during their clinical practice they will have to treat a violent couple, or someone involved in a violent relationship, even if they do not specialize in the treatment of violent families. Because violence is underreported and the seriousness of violent episodes may be understated, it is particularly important that psychotherapists be skilled in recognizing violence and in intervening appropriately.

This book focuses on critical concerns involved in the treatment of violent couples. The authors agree with the feminist perspective that a social and physical power differential exists between men and women and that therapists need to acknowledge this social reality in their assessment of couples. It is our intention to bring together in this volume three issues of importance to mental health practitioners: family violence, family therapy, and feminist thinking. These issues are considered from empirical, theoretical, legal, and practical viewpoints by chapter authors who are experts in their fields and whose work appears together in one volume for the first time.

Social and Historical Context

The position of women throughout history has been well documented (Hilton, 1989). Women were regarded as property, and laws were directed toward their protection as property, throughout England and America until well into the nineteenth century. Within this perspective, the severity of wife beating was restricted only by the customs of the community in which it occurred (Dobash & Dobash, 1977-1978). The severity of violence, therefore, has long been dictated by community attitudes, and women who were beaten by their husbands have been recipients of a standard that was not applied to other crimes. The standard that husbands were allowed to "chastise" their wives with "a whip or rattan no bigger than the thumb" was practiced by the courts well into the last century (Saunders, 1977). Though wife abuse became illegal in two states in 1871 (Dobash & Dobash, 1977-1978), it was not until the temperance movement began to focus on women battered by drunken husbands that spouse abuse was carefully examined. Likewise, it was only when women won the right to vote that the property standard became an issue. Even with these reforms, wife abuse has been tolerated by the courts to a far greater degree than have other forms of assault; police are reluctant to arrest, prosecutors are unwilling to prosecute, and judges hesitate to convict (Archer, 1989; Meier, 1987). Only with the increased strength of the women's movement in the 1960s, 1970s, and 1980s has the outrage over battering returned, and states have begun to revise their legal codes regarding domestic violence (Caringella-MacDonald, 1988).

Several serious concerns arise in the identification of the social perspective on spouse abuse. First, because spouse abuse is often viewed as a private concern by both the community and the agencies assigned to protect members of the community (Archer, 1989; Mugford, Mugford, & Easteal, 1989), battering may not be recognized and intervened in as quickly as other crimes. Mugford et al. (1989), for example, indicate that one-third of respondents they surveyed believe that domestic violence is a private matter.

An additional concern is the prevalence of the perception that spouse abuse is justifiable under certain circumstances (Dobash & Dobash, 1977-1978; Mugford et al., 1989). Such a perspective can result in the oft-cited "bitch deserved it defense" used by some men who kill their wives. Defending themselves with the argument that any man would have responded in a similar manner given the extreme provocation of living with such a woman, some men who have killed their wives have been reported to receive lighter sentences than those found guilty of other homicides (Goodman, 1989).

Sociological theory suggests that battering is used as a means of control in the marital relationship—a means through which men assert their patriarchal authority. Dobash and Dobash (1977-1978) refer to their own research to support this perception by documenting the direction of assaults. In their sample of 3,020 cases, husbands were rarely assaulted by their wives (1.1%); women were attacked in 75% of the cases, and only 15% of attacks on women occurred outside the home. General acceptance of battering is supported by both legal and case data; wife abuse is viewed and responded to with less outrage and milder consequences than is violence committed against other identified groups.

Causes of Violence

Several psychological and sociological theories have attempted to explain the violent family, including descriptions of what types of individuals are violent or victims of violence and descriptions of what conditions result in violence in families. Approaches that explain an individual's predisposition to be violent or to submit to violence as related to personality factors have led to psychiatric diagnoses and explanations for domestic violence that include a description of the battered woman's personality as deficient (as critiqued in L. S. Brown, 1991; Walker, 1991), a view that has been challenged by feminists and other theorists. Other theoretical approaches have explained the behavior of battered women as arising out of learned helplessness (Walker, 1984a), as normal reactions to pathological situations (Root, 1992), as arising out of traumatic bonding (Painter & Dutton, 1985), and as the result of power imbalances over time (Dutton & Painter, 1981). Batterers have been described as sexually aggressive, as alcoholics, and as having violence-prone personalities (Hotaling & Sugarman, 1986; Walker, 1984a). Other theories have described violence as arising out of dysfunctional relationships in which the violence is mutually caused (Giles-Sims, 1983). Sociological theories describe violence as occurring because of cultural norms that permit and, in some subgroups, encourage violent behavior, and because of the very nature of the family itself, which is conflict ridden and has high potential for violence (Straus, 1980).

Context Within Which Battering Occurs

"Men who assault their wives are actually living up to cultural prescriptions that are cherished in Western society—aggressiveness, male dominance and female subordination—and they are using physical force as a means to enforce that dominance," assert Dobash and Dobash (1979, p. 24). Because this feminist view suggests that battering is neither unusual in our society nor pathological, no book on domestic violence informed by a feminist perspective would be complete without a consideration of the social context within which violence occurs. For this reason, we comment here on some sex role stereotypes that may maintain battering as the societal problem it is today.

The traditional family is a system in which the balance of power is inherently unequal, mimicking other relationships of men and women, where men have usually held the power and women have been subservient to those in power over them. Frieze, Parsons, Johnson, Ruble, and Zellman

(1978) discuss one of the effects of power imbalance: that the woman, as the less powerful member of the family, learns to be more accommodating and also to tune in more to the needs of her spouse. Clinicians working with battered women have noted the complacency that many battered women exhibit, their difficulty in leaving the abusive situation, and their tendency to placate their abusers so as to avoid repetition of violent episodes (Painter & Dutton, 1985; Walker, 1984a).

Another gender-related stereotype that is supported by much research is that females are more emotionally expressive than males (see Sade & Notarius, 1985, for a review of these studies). Thus women are seen as emotional (equated with irrationality) and men as nonexpressive (equated with rationality). At the same time, however, the expression of aggressiveness (which is more characteristic of males) is not typically labeled as an expression of emotion or as an irrational act (Frieze et al., 1978). Thus it is easy to see how society fails to condemn aggression by a batterer toward his wife (even that stemming from a loss of control) because it is congruent with the male role, whereas fighting back (usually in self-defense) by the wife may be condemned because it is incongruent with the female role.

Practice of Family Therapy

Therapists' perceptions and treatment approaches are a concern of researchers. Goodstein and Page (1981) indicate that women seen in emergency rooms for the treatment of injuries resulting from battering often report histories of prior counseling. However, these women indicate that counseling consisted of a single session and they never returned for additional treatment because the therapists failed to address the violence. An accurate assessment of whether violence is a factor when women or couples present for psychotherapy is critical, as is appropriate and immediate intervention.

Couples counseling and family therapy are both currently often used in the treatment of domestic violence. However, these modalities have been widely criticized for failing to detect battering accurately and, when they do detect battering, for intervening in ways that do not effectively address the violence. Family therapy has also been criticized because it considers violence from a systemic perspective that serves to obscure the seriousness of the physical abuse (Bograd, 1984; Pressman, 1989). Feminist writers have gone so far as to question the appropriateness of family therapy for treatment of couples involved in domestic violence because its focu the couple defuses the batterer's responsibility for his actions Frantz-Cook, 1984). Treatment of the couple together has be as implicitly agreeing with the batterer's belief in his wife's "coresponsibility" for his actions. In addition, family therapy often focuses on the transactional and reciprocal sequences of behavior that are observed in the couple's interactions, with battering seen as the result of an escalating sequence of reciprocal interactions that ultimately leads to violence that functionally diffuses the tension in the relationship. New ways of intervening with this population are needed.

Recent research on the perceptions of therapists raises serious questions as to their ability to assess accurately the seriousness of domestic violence and to intervene in a way that will provide protection for the victim (Hansen, Harway, & Cervantes, 1991; Harway & Hansen, 1990a, 1990b).

Overview of Current Therapeutic Practices in Intervening With Violent Families

Many different approaches have been suggested for working with violent families. In this volume, we critique some common theories and practices while suggesting others as more appropriate. Here we provide a brief overview of common therapeutic approaches to working with domestic violence. One of the controversies addressed in this volume is whether conjoint counseling is an appropriate modality for working with violent couples or families. Much of the literature suggests that it is not. Assuming an individual therapy approach, we discuss separately possible interventions for the battered and for the batterer.

WORKING WITH THE BATTERED WOMAN

First, it must be emphasized that many battered women do not seek individual counseling, and many others seek therapy for some other problem, perhaps not letting on that they are victims of violence. Therefore, the initial dilemma for a concerned psychotherapist is twofold: (a) how to provide therapeutic support for women who do not present to the formal mental health system (but who may seek medical treatment, legal assistance, or help from public agencies) and (b) how to recognize the existence of violence in the life of a client seeking therapy for some other presenting problem. Only when these dilemmas are solved can the issue of how to intervene be properly addressed. In addition to practicing individual psychotherapy, a therapist may be involved in a consulting capacity with other organizations providing services to this population: battered women's shelters, special domestic violence intervention programs, battered women's support groups, law enforcement agencies, substance abuse or eating disorder programs (where many battered women may first present), social service programs that work with victims of violent crimes, and other community agencies.

Appropriate interventions in cases of violence include (but are not limited to) the following:

1. doing a careful assessment, such as assessing for safety, identifying the client's coping skills, determining whether there is a history of the client's having been abused as a child, and assessing for multiple presenting problems (e.g., sexuality issues, drug and alcohol abuse, eating disorders)
2. doing crisis intervention, that is, providing immediate protection to the victim (working with violent families often requires going beyond the purely therapeutic into many other arenas, including the legal)
3. providing education, such as information about battering and the effects of victimization as well as about parenting, health care, and general skills development
4. providing referrals for advocacy and other needed services (e.g., to shelters, support groups, and batterers' groups, as well as welfare agencies and legal protection)
5. working psychotherapeutically: providing emotional support for a woman who usually is isolated from others, validating feelings and experiences that the battered woman may minimize or discount, helping her work through her anger and rage, doing grief and loss work (for the loss of the actual relationship or the idealized relationship that never was), doing self-esteem and self-nurturing work, working on developing assertiveness skills, exploring options and choices for life-styles, assisting in gathering information about healthy, nonviolent relationships and teaching the client how to feel deserving of these, and (much later) exploring termination issues to learn about positive ways of leaving

WORKING WITH THE BATTERER

Most of the interventions described in the literature are intended to help the battered woman; much less has been written about how to work with the batterer. In many cases, the batterer will not be receptive to being helped, especially given that many perpetrators believe that hitting one's wife is a normal part of the marital relationship. Thaxton (1985) indicates that batterers most often agree to counseling as a ploy to maintain their marriages. Court-referred cases account for the majority of other counseling referrals.

Interventions with batterers frequently take the form of batterers' groups. Often these are operated in conjunction with battered women's services. A common theme is anger management and "fair fighting." Some groups focus on educating batterers about sex role stereotypes. One approach that appears to be exceedingly effective brings together in a single group both male and female batterers. Much of the work focuses on exploring sex role stereotyping. The simple contact between male and female perpetrators of violence in a therapeutic context seems to be particularly effective at exploding defenses and defusing cross-sex anger (Richardson, 1990).

When women are encouraged to leave their batterers but the behavior of the latter is not addressed and changed, this simply encourages a "cycling through" of women victims. Thus it is critical that more focus be put on intervening with batterers.

Overview of This Volume

A review of the current literature identifies a need for the integration of research on battering with current approaches toward treatment. Practitioners could benefit from clearly presented formulations of issues critical in the evaluation, assessment, and treatment of battering. The chapters in this book present specific areas of concern to practitioners and provide recommendations for sound intervention.

In Chapter 2, Hart places wife abuse in the legal context. She presents a brief history of the legal status of battered women and then provides descriptions of current laws governing family violence. She also explores the historical development of the current legal structure and reports on recent legal developments.

Harway, in Chapter 3, describes the violent family, with a focus on the battered woman, based on the work of Walker and others. She presents explanatory theories about violent families, debunks myths about battered women and their batterers, and reviews the relationship issues that characterize a violent couple.

In Chapter 4, we present the results of our recent national surveys of therapists' awareness of family violence. Our data suggest that, when presented with actual cases of family violence, therapists fail to attend to the potential seriousness of the circumstances, either by ignoring the indices of violence or by minimizing them. Additionally, therapists continue to have difficulty in formulating appropriate interventions even when presented with the lethal outcome of the case. We close the chapter with a discussion of concerns regarding therapists' case formulations and knowledge of appropriate interventions.

McHugh, in Chapter 5, examines from a feminist perspective some concerns about the methodology employed in the study of battering. She draws attention to specific methodological issues that flaw much current research. Some of the concerns McHugh addresses involve the documentation of the incidence of violence, whether the focus of research ought to be on the victim or on the perpetrator, and the appropriateness of current interventions.

In Chapter 6, Hansen critiques family systems approaches to battering, arguing that the more traditional of these approaches to treating abusive relationships result in victim blaming or in perceptions of coresponsibility or no responsibility for the violence. She challenges these approaches as excusing the batterer and often making his victim responsible for her own predicament. Hansen then examines the application of feminist therapy to current approaches.

In Chapter 7, Hansen and Goldenberg describe the conditions under which a couple might be treated within the context of family therapy and how this treatment modality might best be applied. They provide a description of the type of couple who might be most appropriate for this kind of intervention. These authors also address the desires of many women to remain in their relationships, and explore specific concerns involving the wife's need for empowerment within the context of the relationship.

Register, in Chapter 8, examines therapeutic approaches that focus on individual work with victims of family violence as an alternative to the family systems approach. She presents specific steps for treatment.

In Chapter 9, Gondolf reviews treatment approaches that focus on the batterer, presenting such programs as a feminist alternative to the criticism of coresponsibility inherent in the family systems approach. He reports on research that supports his proposition that treating the batterer is the most effective approach to the problem.

Goodwin addresses specific training considerations in Chapter 10. Recognizing child abuse is a skill that therapists have only recently acquired, and recognizing family violence is not yet a proficiency. Goodwin proposes specific guidelines for training new therapists and supervising current practitioners.

In Chapter 11, Berman reviews the psychological and social impacts of family violence on children, describing both short- and long-term consequences for children of viewing violent interactions between parents. Her discussion emphasizes treatment issues.

Cervantes presents specific legal and ethical considerations for therapists in Chapter 12. She notes that because legal and ethical standards are complex and ever changing, therapists must be well versed in this area.

In Chapter 13, Cervantes and Cervantes address the specific concerns of culturally diverse populations faced with domestic violence, discussing the special needs of women from identifiable ethnic minority backgrounds.

Child custody is often an arena of continued conflict that is especially perilous in the case of abusive relationships. In Chapter 14, Liss and Stahly discuss legal and psychological factors relating to these special cases.

Women in same-sex relationships are not immune from family violence. Special issues that affect lesbian relationships are considered by Renzetti in Chapter 15.

Walker, in Chapter 16, documents the psychological characteristics of women who murder their abusive husbands. She summarizes the results of her work with these women and provides guidelines for therapists who may be required to provide legal testimony.

Alcohol abuse and family violence have been linked by many researchers. In Chapter 17, Cooley addresses the specific concerns of therapists who may need to treat both problems simultaneously. She discusses the difficulties inherent in current theoretical formulations employed by popular approaches to the treatment of drug and alcohol abuse and presents more useful conceptualizations, including recommendations for treatment.

Finally, in Chapter 18 we summarize the salient characteristics that lead to appropriate intervention in professional treatment for the victims of family violence. We conclude with a presentation of models of assessment and intervention for new generations of therapists.

2

The Legal Road to Freedom

BARBARA J. HART

The search for freedom from domestic violence is often a long and arduous process, and it cannot occur until battering and terrorism cease. Even then, it is obstructed unless the battered woman can achieve autonomy and self-determination. The law is a tool that can facilitate the search for safety and freedom. Historically, however, the law has protected perpetrators. This chapter first presents a brief history of the evolving law on domestic violence. It then examines the phenomenon of domestic violence and its impact on battered women and children. Finally, it provides an overview of the legal strategies now available in most states that may put an end to the violence, afford battered women safeguards against future abuse, mandate compensation for the losses imposed by the abuse, and offer resources essential for independence and safety.

History of Law on Domestic Violence

Violence against wives is a right men exercised with impunity for centuries. This prerogative of men has been articulated in the precepts of religion, philosophy, and law throughout the Northern Hemisphere. Physical violence against wives was deemed necessary for the "well-being" of women. It was couched in terms of corrective discipline and chastisement of erring wives (Davis, 1972). A medieval Christian scholar propagated "Rules of Marriage" in the late fifteenth century:

> When you see your wife commit an offense, don't rush at her with insults and violent blows. . . . Scold her sharply, bully and terrify her. And if this doesn't

> work . . . take up a stick and beat her soundly, for it is better to punish the body and correct the soul than to damage the soul and spare the body. . . . Then readily beat her, not in rage but out of charity and concern for her soul, so that the beating will redound to your merit and her good. (quoted in Davidson, 1978, p. 99)

British common law later embraced, but limited, the husband's authority to assault wives by adopting the "rule of thumb," which permitted a man to beat his wife with a "rod not thicker than his thumb" (Davidson, 1977).

Jurists and legislators in the United States followed in the tradition of the European clergy and lawmakers and approved the use of men's violence against their wives:

> In 1824 the Mississippi Supreme Court in *Bradley v. State* voiced approval of the husband's role as disciplinarian and stated its belief that the law should not disturb that role: Let the husband be permitted to exercise the right of moderate chastisement, in cases of great emergency, and use salutary restraints in every case of misbehaviour, without being subjected to vexatious prosecutions, resulting in the mutual discredit and shame of all parties concerned. *Bradley v. State,* 1 Miss. 156 (1824). (U.S. Commission on Civil Rights, 1982, p. 2)

Not until 1871 did a court in this country rescind the legal right of men to beat their wives.

> The privilege, ancient though it be, to beat [one's wife] with a stick, to pull her hair, choke her, spit in her face or kick her about the floor, or to inflict upon her like indignities, is not now acknowledged by our law. . . . in person, the wife is entitled to the same protection of the law that the husband can invoke for himself. . . . All stand upon the same footing before the law "as citizens of Alabama, possessing equal civil and political rights and public privileges." *Fulgham v. State,* 46 Ala. 146-47 (1871). (U.S. Commission on Civil Rights, 1982, p. 2)

But the highest court of another state subsequently disagreed and endorsed a limited right of violence against wives:

> If no permanent injury has been inflicted, nor malice, cruelty nor dangerous violence shown by the husband, it is better to draw the curtain, shut out the public gaze, and leave the parties to forget and forgive. *State v. Oliver,* 70 N.C. 60, 61-62 (1874). (U.S. Commission on Civil Rights, 1982, p. 2)

In 1882, Maryland was the first state to pass a law that made wife beating a crime, punishable by 40 lashes or a year in jail (Davidson, 1977). Nonetheless, over the course of the ensuing century, men's use of violence went basically unfettered. Although technically no jurisdiction in this country now permits a husband to strike his wife or a man to assault his partner (U.S. Commission on Civil Rights, 1982), the reality is that men still use violence against wives without fear of reprisal in many jurisdictions.

Issues Addressed in Recent Legal Reform

It was not until the late 1970s that the law started to become an ally of battered women. The women's liberation movement of the late 1960s gave birth to women's support centers and telephone crisis lines. Battered women quickly responded, identified their plight, and sought assistance. Women's advocates and attorneys heard stories of domestic terrorism that had been unspoken (Schechter, 1982). The secret about violence against women in intimate relationships covered domestic brutality of astounding proportions. Advocates, lawyers, and legislators began to look for legal solutions based in the experience of battered women, not based in common misconceptions about women's masochism, men's passion, or marital dysfunction.

The task of fashioning statutory law to confront domestic violence and to sustain its victims has not been an easy one. The web of control and terror woven by batterers is not readily unraveled. It is complex and pervasive. Those crafting domestic violence law in the past two decades have recognized that the law must address several critical issues to provide effective relief. Some of these pivotal issues are discussed below.

Batterers use violence as a tool to achieve power and control over their partners and children (Bowker, Arbitell, & McFerron, 1988; Dobash & Dobash, 1979; Ellis, 1987; Hart, 1988b; Pence & Paymar, 1986; Schechter, 1982).

> Batterers believe they are entitled to the obedience, services, loyalty, and the exclusive intimacy of battered women. They fancy themselves entitled to the control of their mates and have learned they will not suffer adverse consequences if they employ violence as a tactic to achieve or sustain power over their female partners; most batterers view the subservience of women as right and good—in effect, normal (Hart, 1988; Pence & Paymar, 1986; Dobash & Dobash, 1983; Rich, 1979). The wife who disagrees with her battering husband or fails to defer to his preferences risks retaliatory violence (Adams, 1988; Ptacek, 1988; Dobash & Dobash, 1983). (Hart, 1990a, p. 319)

The risk of violent assault on a battered woman increases when the woman challenges the batterer's control over her, when she takes action on her own behalf that may set back his interests, and when she acts in a way that clearly advises him that she contemplates a future life without him (Ellis, 1987).

Batterers often increase the severity of violence toward partners at the time of separation. Many people, including clinicians, believe that battered women will be safe once they separate from their batterers. They also believe that women are free to leave abusers at any time. However, leaving does not usually put an end to the violence. A batterer may, in fact, escalate his violence to coerce a battered woman into "reconciliation" or to retaliate for the battered woman's abandonment of the batterer. Men who believe they are entitled to ongoing relationships with their partners, or that they "own" their partners, view the women's departure as ultimate betrayal that justifies retaliation (Bernard, Vera, Vera, & Newman, 1982; Dutton, 1988a; Saunders & Browne, 1990).

Evidence of the gravity of separation violence is overwhelming. Up to three-fourths of domestic assaults reported to law enforcement agencies may be inflicted after separation of the couple (U.S. Department of Justice, 1983). One study revealed that 73% of the battered women seeking emergency medical services sustained injuries after leaving the batterers (Stark et al., 1981). Women are most likely to be murdered when attempting to report abuse or to leave abusive relationships (Browne, 1987; Sonkin, Martin, & Walker, 1985).

The fact that leaving may be dangerous does not mean that the battered woman should stay or is safer remaining with the batterer. Cohabiting with a batterer is highly dangerous, because violence usually increases in frequency and severity over time and because a batterer may engage in preemptive strikes, fearing abandonment or anticipating separation even before the battered woman reaches such a decision (Browne, 1987; Hart, 1990a; Walker, 1984a). Many batterers who kill their female partners acknowledge that they did so because the woman stated that she no longer loved or trusted the violent partner (Hart, 1991a). Although leaving may pose additional hazards, ultimately a battered woman may best achieve safety and freedom apart from the batterer (Bowker, 1983).

Men who batter their wives/partners often endanger and abuse their children. Most children of battered women witness the violence of their fathers against their mothers, and some experience symptoms equivalent to those of children who have themselves been severely abused (Pagelow, 1989). Boys who witness their fathers' abuse of their mothers are more likely to inflict severe violence against intimates as adults than are those who grow up in homes free of abuse (Hotaling & Sugarman, 1986). Data suggest that girls who witness maternal abuse may tolerate abuse as adults more than girls who do not (Hotaling & Sugarman, 1986).

Between 50% and 70% of the men who batter their wives also abuse their children (Pagelow, 1989; Walker, 1982). Severe child abuse usually occurs in the context of domestic violence, and the onset of child abuse usually postdates abuse of the mother (Stark & Flitcraft, 1985). The more grievous the abuse of the mother, the greater the likelihood that child abuse will be severe (Bowker et al., 1988).

> Abuse of children by batterers may be more likely when the marriage is dissolving, the couple has separated, and the husband and father is highly committed to continued dominance and control of the mother and children (Bowker, Arbitell & McFerron, 1988). Since . . . abuse by husbands and fathers is instrumental, directed at subjugating, controlling and isolating, when a woman has separated from her batterer and is seeking to establish autonomy and independence from him, his struggle to . . . dominate her may increase and he may turn to abuse and subjugation of the children as a tactic of . . . control of their mother (Stark & Flitcraft, 1988b; Bowker, Arbitell & McFerron, 1988). (Hart, 1990a, p. 322)

Battering men also use custodial interference as a tool to terrorize battered women or to retaliate for the women's terminating the relationship (Hart, 1990a). About 40.4 children are abducted by a parent each hour in this country. About half of the abductions are short-term manipulations around custody orders, but the other half involve concealing the whereabouts of the child for longer periods of time or taking the child out of state (Finkelhor, Hotaling, & Sedlak, 1990). Intervention to stop the violence and safeguard victims can enable children from violent homes to avoid these risks and achieve nonabusive adult relationships (Browne, 1991; Jaffe, Wolfe, & Wilson, 1990).

Battered women and their dependent children are often economically compelled back into relationships with batterers. Women and children suffer substantial economic losses upon separation and divorce in this country. One study discovered that the standard of living of women plunged 73% after divorce, whereas that of divorcing men increased by 42% in the same time frame (Weitzman, 1985). Many women who establish households independent of battering husbands/partners find themselves in poverty. The number of female-headed households living below the poverty line has nearly doubled since 1970. Two out of three adults living in poverty are women. A recent Philadelphia study discovered that one-third of all children in the United States are living below the poverty level; for black children the poverty rate is a staggering 60% (Henninger, 1986).

In 1987, only 42.8% of all fathers ordered to pay child support fully complied with the court orders; 21.4% made partial payment and 35.7%

paid nothing. The average award was only $2,710 per year per family (U.S. Department of Commerce, 1987). The 1986 Philadelphia divorce study found that men who batter are less likely to pay support than are men who do not use violence toward their intimates (45%, compared with 76%), and batterers are less likely to comply fully with child support orders (28.3%, compared with 49%) (Kurz & Coughey, 1989).

Economic viability appears to be a critical factor in the decision making of battered women considering separation from the batterer (Aguirre, 1985; Strube & Barbour, 1983). The most likely predictor of whether a battered woman will permanently separate from her abuser is whether she has the economic resources to survive without him (Gondolf & Fisher, 1988; Okun, 1986). Three critical ingredients of economic independence for battered women include income from a source other than the batterer, adequate transportation, and sufficient child-care arrangements (Gondolf & Fisher, 1988).

Domestic violence is costly, as are its remedies. Former Surgeon General C. Everett Koop identified violence against women by their partners as the number one health problem for women in the United States. Domestic violence causes more injuries to women than automobile accidents, muggings, and rapes combined (Koop, 1989). The severity of injuries sustained in domestic violence assaults is significantly greater than that sustained in stranger assaults (Finesmith, 1983). "Injuries inflicted in domestic violence incidents are as serious as, or more serious than, injuries inflicted in 90% of all violent felonies" (Attorney General's Family Violence Task Force, 1989, p. 5). More than $50 million is paid in medical costs related to abuse of intimate adult partners in the United States each year. Yet the emotional and psychological abuse inflicted by batterers may be even more costly than the physical injuries (Straus, 1987).

Batterers universally destroy family property: Telephones, televisions, cars, walls, children's favorite toys, and the clothing of battered women are frequently targeted by the batterer (Fortune, 1981; Ganley, 1981). The financial cost of this destruction is substantial, and although national data are not available, battered women seeking shelter in domestic violence programs report that the losses sustained through batterer property destruction prior to separation average $10,000 per perpetrator (Hart, 1991b). Battered women's service providers report that the cost of relocation for battered women displaced by domestic violence is a minimum of $5,000 per relocation (Hart, 1991b).

The adverse consequences of domestic violence must be substantial for perpetrators to cease their acts of terrorism. Research demonstrates that men stop battering women partners to the extent that they perceive that penalties for further violence will be both certain and severe (Carmody &

Williams, 1987; Jaffe, Wolfe, Telford, & Austin, 1986). It appears that most batterers engage in a cost-benefit analysis in electing to continue or terminate their violent assaults on wives or women partners. In those jurisdictions where the courts and the criminal justice system respond to domestic violence as serious criminal conduct and impose sanctions accordingly, the cost-benefit balance tips in favor of desistance (Attorney General's Family Violence Task Force, 1989; Hart, 1990b).

A leading study demonstrates that where police arrest perpetrators of domestic violence, rather than separate the couple or mediate between the victim and the offender, the arrested perpetrators are significantly less likely to recidivate within six months than are those offenders with whom the police conciliate or take no action (Sherman & Berk, 1984).

Preliminary data suggest that court-mandated treatment following arrest and prosecution for domestic assaults may substantially contribute to the reduction in severe violence by batterers (Dutton, 1986; Jaffe et al., 1986). Those completing court-mandated treatment appear less likely to recidivate than do those terminating before completion (Edleson & Grusznski, 1988).

All of the above is relatively new knowledge, gleaned from the experiences of battered women, practitioners, and research inquiries. Much of it differs sharply from strongly held cultural beliefs about marital relationships and about the experience of adults and children in families. It suggests a need for reformulating strategies, both legal and clinical, for intervention in domestic violence. Collectively, it has given clear direction to those setting about the task of legal reform.

Recent Developments in the Law

Hearing from divorcing women that they were not able to escape the violence even after separation—that women were literally hostages of violent husbands—and that current law failed to protect them from the abuse and actually impeded escape from batterers, legal services attorneys and advocates began in 1975 to fashion statutory law to remedy the problems arising from domestic violence (Fields, 1978a). Drafters early recognized that statutory relief would fail to serve battered women if it merely punished batterers for their violence rather than seeking to prevent future violence and to safeguard victims (Finn & Colson, 1990). Testimony offered before legislators and public policymakers demonstrated that batterers are resistant to change—unwilling to stop coercive violence, to relinquish the stranglehold of control they exert over the lives of their partners, to allow battered women to establish safe and independent households, and to undertake cooperative and nonabusive parenting (U.S. Commission on Civil Rights, 1982). As a consequence, the legislatures in most states have undertaken comprehensive statutory revisions of civil and criminal law to put an end to intimate violence and to enhance the recovery of its survivors. The most effective legislative initiatives forged over the past 16 years are described below.

CIVIL PROTECTION ORDERS

The grandmother of domestic violence law is the civil protection order. It was first adopted in 1976, and within 13 years all 50 states and the District of Columbia passed similar legislation. Initially, in most statutes only married people or individuals living in committed relationships were eligible to petition for relief. Now, however, in most jurisdictions the class of eligible victims is much broader, including the victim who is divorced, who is a current or former family or household member of the perpetrator, who is related by blood or marriage to the batterer, who is the parent of a child of the abuser, and who has been sexually or otherwise intimate with the abuser. Gay and lesbian people in intimate relationships are eligible for relief in about half of the states (Finn & Colson, 1990).

All the statutes authorize relief where the adult partner has been abused. More than half also permit an adult household member to seek an order on behalf of a child who alone is the target of abuse (Finn & Colson, 1990). *Abuse* is usually defined as physical assault, threatened or attempted physical assault, or acts of physical menace that instill fear of or risk serious bodily injury. In more than half of the states abuse also includes sexual assault of the battered adult, and almost as many states define abuse to include the sexual assault of children. False imprisonment, burglary, and property destruction are contained within the scope of abuse in several states (Finn & Colson, 1990).

Statutes permit broad relief. Most include restraining orders, eviction of the perpetrator from the residence of the abused, no-contact or stay-away mandates, child and spousal support awards, child custody provisions, and counseling and attorney's fees and other costs. Some statutes also provide for relocation costs, restitution, mandated counseling of perpetrators, and orders enjoining the abuser from disposing of the property of the abused or the couple (Finn & Colson, 1990).

Most state statutes provide that only the perpetrator can be compelled to action or restrained by the protection order. Thus counseling, drug and alcohol treatment, and other rehabilitation mandates are directed at abusers. Legislators were intentional in this limitation; they recognized that abusers are solely responsible for the violence and that battered persons should not be subject to penalties for failure to comply with the course of treatment prescribed by the judiciary (Finn & Colson, 1990; Herrell & Hofford, 1990, p. 25).

In half the states the maximum duration of a protection order is one year. California permits orders for three years, Indiana for only five days, and there is substantial variability in the remaining states (Finn & Colson, 1990).

Civil protection orders may be the most immediate and accessible relief available to victims of crime. In almost half the states victims have access to the courts around the clock. In California, the police can obtain a protection order on behalf of the victim by telephone. Immediate relief can be awarded upon the filing of the petition in all jurisdictions. In half the states there are no filing fees and in the rest the fees may be waived for indigent victims. In almost two-thirds of the states a victim need not be represented by an attorney, and applicants can obtain assistance from the court in completing petitions (Finn & Colson, 1990).

Civil protection orders can be effective in eliminating or reducing domestic violence when orders are properly issued and enforced. The utility of protection orders seems to depend both on the specificity of the relief ordered and the enforcement practices of the police and the courts. Providing precise conditions of relief makes the offender aware of the specific behavior prohibited. "A *high degree of specificity* also makes it easier for police officers and other judges to determine later whether the [perpetrator] has violated the order" (Finn & Colson, 1990, p. 2). For orders to be effective, they must be comprehensive; courts should tailor comprehensive relief to the particular safety needs of the victim in each case (Herrell & Hofford, 1990). Legal and personal safety are advanced when battered women can acquire protection orders that confront the coercive controls and violence imposed by batterers, afford battered women and children safe housing and economic support, and exact swift and certain penalties for violation of any provision.

DOMESTIC VIOLENCE ARREST STATUTES

Police have historically had the right to make a warrantless arrest of any suspect they believe has committed a felony even though the police have not observed the commission of the crime (Goolkasian, 1986). While police in most jurisdictions also have had the power to make a warrantless arrest when they witness a misdemeanor, in some states a warrant had to be obtained if the misdemeanor did not occur in the presence of the officer. This has changed dramatically in the past 10 years; now state statutes enable police to arrest without a warrant absent observation in specific domestic violence misdemeanors, and in 15 states the codes *require* police to make an arrest when they determine a domestic violence crime has been committed (Lerman & Livingston, 1983; Zorza, 1991). Statutes in at least 25 states permit police to make a warrantless arrest if they determine that a civil protection order has been violated. Codes of another 13 states *require* police to make an arrest where they determine that the perpetrator has violated a civil protection order (Finn & Colson, 1990).

The advantages of warrantless arrests are several. It is easier to take a suspect into custody at the scene than to locate him after obtaining a warrant from the court. Police are more likely to initiate prosecution if they can arrest at the time they respond to the domestic violence call; thus the perpetrator may be introduced into the criminal justice system earlier and begin the process of desistance before victims are irreparably harmed and perpetrators firmly committed to domestic violence. Offenders more often admit their culpability in the immediacy of an arrest at the scene of the crime. Victims are better protected by prompt arrest, arraignment, and the imposition of special bail conditions or criminal protective orders (Hart, Stubbling, & Stuehling, 1990).

Most domestic crimes involving injury should be classified as felonies, given that injuries produced by domestic violence are as serious as those inflicted in 90% of all violent felonies (Attorney General's Family Violence Task Force, 1989; Goolkasian, 1986). Nonetheless, police still identify most domestic violence assaults as misdemeanors. Thus the expansion of arrest authority to include domestic violence crimes has given law enforcement a powerful tool for intervention in situations in which they previously concluded (erroneously or otherwise) that they had no authority to act.

Once a police officer concludes that there is probable cause to believe that a domestic violence crime has been committed, the officer should effect an arrest. No state statute permits victims or perpetrators to compel or restrain an officer in his or her decision about arrest. Clinicians may find it appropriate to advise clients, whether survivors or perpetrators, of the fact that they cannot exercise control over this decision in most jurisdictions.

Litigation in the past 10 years has exerted additional pressure on law enforcement to act diligently to protect the victims of domestic violence. Several police departments across the country that failed to protect battered women have been found liable and have had large damages assessed against them (Carrington, 1989).

DOMESTIC VIOLENCE CUSTODY STATUTES

A majority of the states have adopted statutes requiring courts to consider domestic violence as a factor in custody and visitation determinations. In Washington State if the court concludes that a parent has engaged in child abuse or domestic violence, it is precluded from awarding joint legal custody and it may limit unsupervised residential time of the offending parent with the child. In Arizona, North Dakota, Oklahoma, and Wyoming, domestic violence is presumed to be contrary to the best interests of the child and any award of visitation must be designed to best protect the child and the abused parent from further harm. In California, the courts must consider awards of supervised visitation when there is a finding of domestic violence. In Pennsylvania, Montana, and Minnesota, statutes provide that if a parent is convicted of certain enumerated violent crimes, the court must find that the offending parent does not pose a threat of harm to the child or that it is in the best interests of the child before making an award of custody or visitation to the offending parent. The Pennsylvania custody statute requires the court to take testimony about specialized domestic violence counseling received by the offending parent and about any continuing risk of harm to the child before issuing any order of custody to a parent convicted of specific enumerated crimes. The California Code specifies that both parents and the child may be required to participate in counseling when there is a custody dispute but that the counseling of the parents should be separate and at separate times if the abused person so requests. Prior to the adoption of these provisions, custody judges routinely concluded that the abuse of a parent by the other was irrelevant in custody proceedings, that violence toward a spouse/partner had nothing to do with one's ability to parent adequately (New York Task Force on Women in the Courts, 1987).

Some civil protection order statutes direct courts to craft specific provisions in temporary custody awards to safeguard the battered adult and children. As a consequence, advocates for battered women have begun to engage in safety planning with battered women and children to identify the special needs of abused adults and children when the abuser is allowed custodial access (Hart, 1991c). The safety planning process, coupled with the court's approval of the safety conditions recommended by the child, has provided essential safeguards and has been a great source of empowerment of children.

MANDATORY CUSTODY MEDIATION

Data from the National Center for State Courts reveal that only a handful of states mandate custody mediation by statute. In about one-third of the states, various judicial districts mandate custody mediation by local court rule (Myers, Gelles, Hanson, & Keilitz, 1988). In several states, mediation of custody disputes may not be compelled by the courts in the context of domestic violence.

Feminist scholars and advocates for battered women strongly oppose the imposition of mediation in the resolution of custody disputes (Bruch, 1988; Lefcourt, 1989). The only research that squarely addresses the question of whether victims are better protected from future violence by adversarial rather than mediation divorce processes demonstrates that battering men inflict less postseparation violence if the divorce proceedings are based in advocacy rather than in conciliation (Ellis, 1987, 1989; Ellis & Wight-Peasley, 1986).

The process of mediation requires cooperation, honest communication, equivalent power, similar investment in the outcomes, voluntary participation, and an environment of safety. No matter how skillful the mediator, batterers cannot be quickly transformed so that the mediation process can proceed with integrity (Hart, 1990a; Pagelow, 1990). Custody mediation is not a legal tool that enhances custody outcomes for battered women and children (Bruch, 1988; Sun & Thomas, 1987).

EXPERT TESTIMONY ON THE EXPERIENCE OF BATTERED WOMEN

Many appellate courts across the country have generated case law that permits the defense to offer expert testimony on the perceptions, beliefs, and experiences of battered women defendants in criminal trials where battered women are charged with killing or assaulting their battering partners. A handful of state legislatures have revised state codes to affirmatively permit this expert testimony. Courts have been receptive to expert testimony by forensic specialists, clinicians, and, to a lesser extent, battered women's advocates.

Law reform in this area has been partially a consequence of judicial education about the counterintuitive realities of domestic violence. Appellate courts in a significant number of states have concluded that jurors and judges both harbor misconceptions about battering; often they hold strong beliefs that blame victims and exonerate batterers. The judiciary has concluded that if these critical actors in the justice system are not cognizant of the terror imposed and manipulated by batterers, they cannot fairly evaluate the evidence presented at trial without assistance from expert witnesses.

The governors of Ohio and Maryland recently granted clemency to battered women who were convicted without the benefit of adequate expert testimony about the phenomenon of domestic violence and the impact of batterer violence upon the battered woman defendant. In its most recent session, the legislature in Texas passed a resolution that requires a review of all the sentences of incarcerated persons who were victims of domestic violence.

VICTIMS' RIGHTS STATUTES

Since 1965, crime victim reform measures have become an important part of legislative activity in most states. From 1981 through the first quarter of 1983, 74 new victims' rights statutes were enacted across the country (Hudson, 1984). This chapter cannot describe all of these initiatives, but those that have been most helpful to battered women are described below.

Victim confidentiality statutes. The Victims of Crime Act of 1984 (VOCA) prohibits recipients of VOCA grants from disclosing any information about any victim of crime served without the consent of the victim (42 U.S.C. 10604[d]). More than a third of the states have enacted even broader privilege provisions concerning confidential communications between battered women and counselors in domestic violence programs. Some statutes specify that communications that occur within counseling groups in domestic violence centers are likewise covered by the privilege (Marks, 1986; Post, 1991). Several states have adopted statutes that provide for the confidentiality of the addresses of both domestic violence programs and battered women who are seeking to reside at undisclosed locations (Marks, 1986). Beyond this, in California the legislature recently adopted a statute that provides similar protection to the communications between crime victims and victim/witness advocates (10.35 and 10.37 California Evidence Code). The communications privilege accorded battered women in domestic violence programs is not applicable to clinicians working with survivors in other arenas. Many states have adopted clinical privileges for psychologists and psychiatrists, and a lesser number have enacted social worker privilege statutes (Marks, 1986; Post, 1991).

Police notification laws. Law enforcement officers in many states are now required by statute to inform battered adults of the availability of civil and criminal protection orders, of crime victims compensation, and of domestic violence services (see Fl. Statutes, 1987 S. 960.001; 18 Pa.C.S. 2711).

Victim impact statements. Victims may submit victim impact statements to the court supporting or opposing proposed plea bargains in many jurisdictions (Hudson, 1984). Victims also have the right to submit impact statements in the sentencing phase of criminal matters, including hearings on the death penalty (*Payne v. Tennessee,* June 1991). In many states victims can provide either statements or testimony before parole boards on the question of discharge from incarceration.

Victim intimidation statutes. Many states have adopted legislation to protect victims and witnesses during the pendency of criminal matters.

These statutes are often called victim intimidation laws, criminal protective order statutes, or criminal stay-away provisions. These orders may be issued against the defendant or any other person who attempts to interfere with a victim's or a witness's participation in any stage of a criminal matter.

Research demonstrates the effectiveness of victim intimidation protective orders issued in pretrial criminal proceedings (Goolkasian, 1986). Although these orders are typically not as broad as the civil protection order, they do usually require the defendant to stay away from the victim or witness and to refrain from any harassment or intimidation. Battered women are generally more cooperative with prosecution when they do not have to live with defendants prior to trial. The reluctance of a battered woman to participate in the prosecution process may be reduced when she is free from the threats of her partner, or those of his family and friends, attempting to dissuade her from testifying or cooperating with prosecution.

Crime victim compensation. In 1988, the U.S. Congress amended the Victims of Crime Act, requiring state victim compensation programs to make awards to victims of domestic violence. States no longer may deny compensation to a battered woman because of her familial relationship to the offender or because she is sharing a residence with him; the exception to this rule is made where it appears that the offender would reap unjust enrichment as a result of an award.

Most statutes permit recovery for medical and treatment costs resulting from injuries inflicted in the commission of the crime against the victim. Most also pay for loss of earnings when a victim is injured by the crime. Many compensate for replacement services, such as housekeeping and transportation, and most permit recoupment of attorneys fees. Few provide for property recovery. However, for victims of crime to be eligible, they must report the crime promptly and thereafter cooperate with prosecution. The offender need not be convicted of a crime for the victim to be eligible for compensation (National Organization for Victim Assistance, 1987). Crime victim compensation awards are usually grants of "last resort." Thus the crime victim must first look to health and disability insurance for restitution, and funds acquired through litigation may be attached in most jurisdictions for reimbursement of the compensation fund up to the total amount of the award.

Notice of discharge of offender. Homicides committed by incarcerated offenders on furlough from correctional institutions in recent years have stimulated legislative activity to assure that victims of crimes are notified when the criminals involved are no longer in custody. Although definitive research on the rate of violent recidivism by batterers toward partners and family or household members after release from incarceration has not been undertaken, the experience of professionals in the domestic field is that batterers are at high risk of directing postincarceration violence toward partners and children and any persons protecting them (Hart, 1991a). These new statutes require that victims be notified of offenders' discharge from custody at any time, from pretrial release to parole or escape. Few legislatures have adopted this legislation to date.

Law Reform Implementation

The law relating to domestic violence has changed profoundly in the past 15 years. In every state and in the District of Columbia, battered adults can now seek civil protection orders to constrain the violence of abusers. In most states the police may make warrantless arrests for misdemeanor crimes involving domestic violence. Custody statutes have been modified in about half the states to require courts to consider domestic violence in fashioning awards of visitation or custody. Several state codes now exempt the victims of domestic violence and child abuse from compulsory divorce and custody mediation. Many states, whether by case law or by statute, now permit explicit expert and lay testimony on the history of domestic violence and its impact on the battered woman in criminal trials where battered women claim self-defense, duress, or necessity. Governors have begun to address the clemency requests of battered women. In virtually all states, statutes and local rules of court afford victims an array of rights and remedies that enhance victim safety and economic recovery.

Nonetheless, battered women sometimes find that the law may not be an effective tool in the search for safety and independence. The law is an imperfect tool, in part because of the social and cultural context in which it is embedded. It works best when all the other systems are collaborating in a concerted effort to end domestic violence. Legal strategies collapse if the consciousness of the community is not aligned against violence, if emergency services and housing are not available to battered women and children, if human service institutions are not cognizant of domestic violence and are not employing strategies to safeguard victims and hold batterers accountable, and if the family and friends of the battered woman and the batterer do not reject violence as an option in intimate relationships and offer support for safety and change. Legal safeguards work best where society embraces practices compatible with the remedies articulated in the law.

Beyond this, however, the law is imperfect because the application of statutory and case law may be uneven. Courts, prosecutors, police, parole boards, and crime victim compensation boards all exercise a great deal of discretion in implementation of the law. Budgets are tight and priorities are often assigned elsewhere. Prestige is not typically accorded those practicing family law or protecting women and children. Backlash against the legal gains of women and children is now being orchestrated by fathers' rights groups and batterers. As a consequence, battered women in some communities may not find the legal relief and safeguards they need.

To counter any erosion of legal protections for battered women and children, professionals across the country are collaborating to make certain that legal results comport with the safeguards anticipated by law reform efforts. Many communities have developed multidisciplinary task forces to enhance coordinated justice system intervention against domestic violence. Clinicians are active participants in many of these policy-making bodies. Battered women's programs often employ legal advocate specialists who work with the justice system while simultaneously facilitating legal reform.

The law can be a useful tool for battered women and children seeking safety and independence. As statutory law expands and as justice system practices are tailored to afford battered women ready access to the courts, legal possibilities can become realities for battered women and children (Finn & Colson, 1990; Goolkasian, 1986; Herrell & Hofford, 1990).

3

Battered Women: Characteristics and Causes

MICHÈLE HARWAY

Does a woman allow herself to be beaten by her spouse? Are there common explanations about the battered woman who returns again and again to her abuser? These are questions asked frequently by those seeking to understand domestic violence and in particular the battered woman. This chapter describes the violent family, with a focus on the battered woman, based on the work of Lenore Walker and others. After a discussion of the underlying theories, I offer an examination of whether certain women are predisposed to being in abusive situations, debunk some common myths about battered women and their batterers, and describe the relationship issues that characterize a violent couple.

Explanatory Theories About Violent Families

Several psychological and sociological theories have attempted to explain the violent family. Among psychological theories reviewed here are the psychoanalytic, social learning, social psychological, family systems, and feminist theories. Sociological theories to be reviewed include the subcultural and family organization theories.

PSYCHOANALYTIC THEORY

Psychoanalytic theory holds that the individual's personality (developed early in life) predisposes him or her to be violent or to submit to violence. These personality characteristics are often reported as psychiatric diagnoses. In particular, in the Diagnostic and Statistical Manual of Mental Disorders, third edition (DSM-III) the diagnosis of a dependent personality disorder is explained using an example of a woman who tolerates an abusive marriage (cited in Russell, 1988). The DSM-III-R appendix includes a description of self-defeating personality disorder (SDPD) as one of a handful of proposed "new" diagnoses. Some of the diagnostic criteria for SDPD are as follows: a persistent pattern of self-defeating behavior, including choosing people and situations leading to disappointment or failure; rejecting attempts of others to help; inciting angry or rejecting responses from others and then feeling hurt, defeated, or humiliated; failing to accomplish tasks crucial to personal objectives despite the ability to do so; and engaging in self-sacrifice unsolicited by the recipients of the sacrifice (American Psychiatric Association, 1987). The self-defeating personality disorder has been critiqued by Caplan (1991) "as an unwarranted pathologizing of traditional, socialized 'feminine' behavior" (p. 163), by Walker (1991) as describing as maladaptive those behaviors that battered women and other victims of interpersonal violence adopt to keep themselves from serious harm, by Pantony and Caplan (1991) as a diagnostic category with very little empirical evidence to support its existence, and by L. S. Brown (1991) as a label that could lead "to serious harm to women by declaring certain normative, post-traumatic responses to such violence, as indicative of a serious, deeply rooted characterological flaw" (p. 142).

Consistent with the pathological label applied to battered women by the psychoanalytic approach, some writers from this camp describe battered women as having a basic need to provoke violence, as displaying passive hostility that contributes to the violence, and as having a masochistic motivation that promotes continued violence (Blum, 1982; Snell, Rosenwald, & Robey, 1964; Whitehurst, 1974). However, no empirical support for these postulates exists. Hotaling and Sugarman (1986), who reviewed more than 400 studies, found no support for personality traits such as masochism, passivity, and low self-esteem occurring more often in battered women than in any other group. Indeed, some studies suggest that battered women demonstrate particularly ingenious powers of survival (Rounsaville, 1978; Stark, 1981).

More recently, Root (1992) has delivered a stinging critique of approaches to understanding battering (and other situations of trauma) that involve applying diagnostic labels. The conceptualization of posttrauma responding as a personality disorder (based on the DSM-III-R Axis II diagnosis of post-traumatic stress disorder [PTSD] or of borderline personality disorder, commonly given to battered women) comes from a belief that such posttrauma response is an individual's *pathological* reaction to battering, rather than, as Root sees it, behavior designed for survival. When Axis II diagnoses (or the beliefs that underlie them) are used to guide treatment, the therapist deals with the battered woman from the perspective of a "personal deficit model," rather than looking at her behavior as the result of an interaction between the woman and the context within which she is traumatized. Moreover, her functioning is seen as the result of "coping skills deficits or characterological weaknesses." The treatment (which may be seen as blaming the victim) may serve to retraumatize the woman by denying her experience of reality and by failing to shore up her self-confidence during her recovery.

SOCIAL LEARNING THEORY

Gelles (1979) has reported that women who grow up in violent homes learn to accept or tolerate violence and to expect it in their own adult relationships. In fact, findings of extreme violence in the parental homes of battered women are common (Walker, 1984a).

The theory of learned helplessness that has been used to explain battered women's seeming passivity in the face of violence is extracted from the work of Seligman (1975) and replications with other animal species. Seligman trained dogs to expect that any behavior they might use to escape an aversive stimulus would not be predictable in controlling the consequences they experienced. Although the dogs at first appeared to become passive and submissive, a response that Seligman dubbed learned helplessness, in fact they discovered coping strategies to minimize the pain they expected. For example, what originally appeared to be passivity—the dogs lay in their own feces—was in fact an effective coping mechanism—fecal matter is a good insulator from electrical shock. Seligman also reported that the earlier in life learned helplessness was taught to these dogs, the more difficult it was to teach them to respond voluntarily again, even in situations where their behavior was effective. Similarly, the battered woman may early on learn to believe that nothing she can do will permit her to escape or protect her from her husband's violence, and she loses the ability to predict that what she does can affect the outcome. Walker (1984a) theorizes that learned helplessness is one reason the battered woman does not perceive that she is able to escape the violent relationship. As with Seligman's animals, Walker's research shows that battered women lose the ability to predict the outcomes of their behavior.

While the theory of learned helplessness has come under attack by some (Breines & Gordon, 1983; Gelles & Strauss, 1989) and has been modified by others (e.g., Blackman, 1989, describes learned helplessness as not resulting immediately from abuse but as a reaction over time to battered women's realization that their partners' violent behavior cannot be controlled), it remains a leading explanation of the learned behavior of battered women.

SOCIAL PSYCHOLOGICAL THEORY

A social psychological view is taken to explain the strong emotional bond that forms between the battered woman and the batterer, a condition Painter and Dutton (1985) call traumatic bonding. These researchers note the similarity to other conditions in which strong emotional ties are developed under conditions of maltreatment, for instance, when hostages develop positive feelings for their captors or when abused children are strongly bonded to abusive parents. *Traumatic bonding* refers to the "strong emotional ties that develop between two people when one person intermittently harasses, beats, threatens, abuses or intimidates the other" (Painter & Dutton, 1985, p. 364). (Other writers also describe the bond between battered woman and batterer; e.g., Follingstad, Neckerman, & Vormbrock, 1988; Hilberman, 1980; and Symonds, 1979, relate it to the Stockholm syndrome, originally described by Ochberg, 1980, as the emotional bond that develops between captor and hostage.) The two features that battered woman/batterer, hostage/captor, and abused child/perpetrator dyads have in common, Painter and Dutton note, are a power imbalance (so that the mistreated person believes him- or herself to be dominated by the other) and the intermittent nature of the abuse.

Over time, power imbalances tend to increase, leading ultimately to psychopathology in the individuals involved (Bettelheim, 1943; Zimbardo, Haney, & Banks, 1973). Painter and Dutton (1985) describe the person in the lower position as becoming more negative in self-appraisal, less capable of existing independently, and more needy of the higher-position person. Dutton and Painter (1981) also describe the higher-position person as developing a need to maintain the connection with the lower-position person, thus embroiling the two individuals in a mutually interlocking relationship.

The periodicity of abuse has been described by Walker (1984a) as the *cycle of abuse*. She shows that the battered woman is victimized by the repetitive nature of the cycle of violence, which consists of three phases: the tension-building phase, the acute battering phase, and the loving, contrite phase. The loving and kind behavior of the batterer during the third phase appears to provide reinforcement for the cycle, allowing the battered woman to convince herself that her batterer is capable of change. The cycle then begins all over again, with the violence usually escalating in frequency and severity.

Painter and Dutton (1985) explain the powerful reinforcing nature of the alternating aversive and loving aspects of the cycle by noting its similarity to the learning paradigm of intermittent reinforcement: Amsel (1958) and other learning theorists have described the intermittent reinforcement schedule, in which the reinforcer is provided in a random fashion, as one that is highly effective in producing behavior that persists and is difficult to extinguish. Many studies have demonstrated that intermittent patterns of maltreatment create strong emotional bonds in both humans and other animals (see, e.g., Harlow & Harlow, 1971; Scott, 1963). Painter and Dutton conclude that the repetition of the buildup, trauma during the battering, and the reconciliation that follows serve to bond the battered woman to her batterer traumatically and cause her to remain in the relationship. As the cycle occurs repeatedly, the likelihood that the woman will leave the relationship becomes more remote. Painter and Dutton's conclusions are supported by others such as Rounsaville (1978), who speculates that the intermittent nature of the battering followed by a loving reconciliation leads the battered woman to ignore the problem or distort its meaning to that of an aberration in the relationship. Walker (1979) describes the immediate reaction of the woman following the violence as "dissociation coupled with a sense of disbelief that the incident is really happening" (p. 62). The period immediately following the battering is experienced by the woman as one of extreme aversive arousal coupled with feelings of self-blame, depression, and helplessness. These feelings leave the battered woman vulnerable and dependent for some period of time after the incident. During the loving phase, the batterer's contriteness and behavior serve to relieve the woman's fears temporarily and allow her to believe that she is in control, that he will change, that violence will not recur. By behaving as the ideal loving husband during this phase, he reduces the aversive arousal he has created and reinforces the likelihood that she will stay in the relationship.

FAMILY SYSTEMS THEORY

Family systems theorists describe the battered woman and her abuser as "mutually causal elements" (Giles-Sims, 1983, p. 18). The violence is seen as something to which both partners have contributed. Thus Hoffman (1981) describes battering as the way in which "overadequate women" and "underadequate men" relate, with violence used by the husband to reestablish the equilibrium in the relationship. Similarly, Weitzman and Dreen (1982) see the violence as resulting from the partners' complementary needs to maintain homeostatic patterns. Men and women in violent relationships are said by family systems therapists to be experiencing difficulties in separating from their families of origin and to be using violence to regulate the closeness/distance theme in the relationship (Coleman, 1980; Cook & Frantz-Cook, 1984). These theories have been criticized by feminist writers such as Bograd (1984) and Pressman (1989) as leading to a "blame the victim" mentality. (For further review of family systems approaches, see Chapter 6.)

FEMINIST THEORY

Writers such as Bograd (1984) and Gondolf (1985a) take a feminist approach to the understanding of wife battering. Male striving for control and dominance, coupled with a need to demonstrate power, is seen as the root of wife battering. Campbell (1985) has also proposed that in times of social change, when appropriate sex roles are not clear, men are more likely to use violence to keep women in their place. Moreover, attitudes about the legitimacy of male control in a marriage are associated with wife battery rates. Yllö (1984) found that women in husband-dominated couples in states with relatively high women's status were especially at risk for violence; similarly, women who dominated decision making were particularly at risk in states where women's status was low. Coleman and Straus (1986) analyzed a national sample and found that violence rates were highest in male-dominated couples. Egalitarian couples had the lowest rates of conflict and violence. (More detail about feminist theories concerning domestic violence can be found in Chapter 6.)

SOCIOLOGICAL THEORIES

The subcultural theory holds that wife battering occurs because of cultural norms that permit this violent behavior. Because of cultural differences among groups, violence may be especially approved of among certain social classes and ethnic groups. That violence is acceptable among some is evidenced by the results of a survey conducted by Gentemann (1984), who found that 19% of women surveyed agreed that wife assault was sometimes justified. Older, less educated, and lower-income women were particularly likely to agree with this statement.

The family organization theory, described by Straus (1980), indicates that the family is conflict ridden and has a high potential for violence. Increasing isolation of the family also serves to shield from public view any potential abuse. Because stress is likely to affect isolated families disproportionately, and because such families may not have the resources to deal appropriately with stress, violence is more likely to occur (Farrington, 1980). According to this theory, the organization of the traditional family maintains power inequalities that may further increase the likelihood of violence. Finally, traditional sex roles (as taught and modeled in many typical families), which accept boys as aggressive and girls as passive and submissive, set the stage for these same relationships in adulthood.

Characteristics of Battered Women

What are battered women like? Hotaling and Sugarman (1986), who reviewed more than 400 studies, conclude that battered women are different from nonbattered women only in the extent of the violence in their families of origin. No psychological predisposing traits were found: "There is no evidence that the status a woman occupies, the role she performs, the behavior she engages in, her demographic profile or her personality characteristics consistently influence her chances of intimate victimization" (p. 118). Their analysis concludes that risk markers for being battered do not consistently include impaired cognitive functioning, traditional sex role adherence, or lack of assertiveness (although much research, including Walker's, suggests that these factors may be the *result* of battering). Nor do battered women, more often than other women, appear to be diagnosable as having dependent personalities. Hotaling and Sugarman conclude that "these findings do not augur well for theoretical models of victimization that focus on characteristics of victims" (p. 118).

That battered women are not demonstrably different from other women is supported by Walker's (1984a) research. She interviewed 403 self-identified battered women, 17-59 years old, in the Rocky Mountain region. The women were all intelligent, well-educated people holding responsible jobs and quite successful in appearing to be like everyone else. Maintaining appearances of normality in order to cover up the violence often exacted a heavy psychological cost from these women, leaving them isolated from others and often psychologically vulnerable. Walker's research, however, shows no specific personality trait that suggests a victim-prone personality for the battered women. In support of this finding, battered women who left their abusive situations were less likely to go into new relationships, and when they did, they were rarely violent ones.

Walker and Browne (1985) present data demonstrating that although gender has an impact on the experience of being a victim of an intimate's violence, no particular personality pattern leads to a person's becoming a victim. Rather, they suggest that women—who are socialized to adapt and submit and who are likely to become victims of men's sexual violence or physical abuse—may not develop adequate self-protection skills as children, especially if they come from childhood homes in which females are victimized. Walker has described this factor as susceptibility to violence (based on reported events occurring with some regularity in the lives of the subjects). Events suggesting a susceptibility factor include early and repeated sexual molestation and assault, substantial violence by members of the individual's family of origin, perceptions of critical or uncontrollable events in childhood, rigid sex role socialization, and experience of other conditions that put the individual at high risk for depression.

This susceptibility factor could interfere with a woman's ability to become free of violence. The women interviewed for Walker's study believed that their batterers could kill them; however, even though they were cognizant of the danger, they also felt confident that they could help the batterers change. This form of denial and other psychological sequelae that constitute the battered woman syndrome are described by Walker as symptoms adopted as survival techniques in situations that are filled with violence. Findings also support the appropriateness of the terror experienced by the women in the face of the violence and validate the women's fears that separation will make the violence worse.

Characteristics of the Relationship Between Batterer and Battered Woman

Sex role attitudes. The batterers in Walker's (1984a) sample had much more traditional sex role attitudes than did the women, and may have evaluated their wives' feelings for them by how well the women fulfilled their stereotypical sex role functions. When the wife was relatively liberal or assertive, the husband with a violence-prone personality may have been unable to tolerate this conflict and expressed himself through battering. In Walker's sample there were also disparities in education, socioeconomic status, and income between batterer and battered, with the men often faring worse than the women. Men and women also came from different ethnic, racial, and religious backgrounds. Because of the sexist orientation of the men, they may have been unable to tolerate the disparity in status between themselves and their wives, and used violence to lower the perceived status difference.

Jealousy. Uncontrollable jealousy on the part of the batterer was reported by almost all the battered women in Walker's study. This manifested itself early in the relationship as extra attention and flattery that masked extreme insecurity, neediness, and possessiveness of the woman's time and attention. Initially flattered by the attention, most of the women came to resent the intrusiveness and control it eventually became. Later, the men often accused their spouses of having sexual relations with other men and women, and even extended the jealousy to family and friends.

Sexual control. Most women in Walker's sample reported entering into sexual relations with their batterers early on, because of the men's seductive and charming nature and the short-lived promises they made. In one-third of the cases, this early sexual involvement resulted in pregnancy and subsequent marriage. Later in the relationship, sex was used as a power weapon to dominate the women in the same manner as physical violence. Marital rape was commonly reported.

Psychological control. Battered women protect themselves against more beatings by developing heightened sensitivity to the batterers' emotional cues and placating them to forestall more violent episodes (Walker, 1984a). This form of psychological control is of benefit to the batterer, who simultaneously views the woman as being highly suggestible to outside influence. The batterer thus fears any outside person who might minimize the batterer's influence and control over the woman's life. For this reason, he keeps her socially isolated as much as he can. His psychological control over her is powerful.

Battering incidents. Walker reports that the violence used against the women in her sample always escalated in frequency and severity over time. Weapons were more likely to be used as time went on. The need for medical attention also increased over time, but only two-thirds of women who needed medical care sought it. Overall, the probability that women would seek help increased over time from 14% to 50% at the final incident, leaving fully 50% who did not seek help no matter how severe the violence. Violent acts were most likely to occur on weekends, during the warm summer months, and from 6 p.m. to midnight. The battering incidents usually began and ended in the home.

Are Battered Woman Characteristics a Result of Battering?

Although Hotaling and Sugarman (1986) conclude that there is little support for underlying differences between battered women and other women, some studies do describe differences. One explanation for such findings is that the researchers may be focusing on the results of the battery rather than on the predisposing characteristics of the battered woman. Numerous studies examine the coping mechanisms used by these women.

Follingstad et al. (1988) examined existing studies of battered women in order to understand how battered women's reactions could become a life-style. These authors' focus was on the unique coping mechanisms of the battered woman, which in many instances work against her by causing her to become more engaged in the relationship. In reporting on the literature on battering, Follingstad et al. compared battered women to victims in general, victims with rape trauma syndrome, trauma victims, and victims of chronic abuse. Like other types of victims, battered women reported feeling safest from harm in the warmth and comfort of their homes. However, that is exactly where they are in the greatest danger, and this very discrepancy may be, Follingstad et al. argue, at the heart of understanding the reaction of the battered woman: shock, disbelief, and denial, followed by terror, then attempts to reestablish the level of safety previously believed to have existed, followed by depression with intermittent inner-directed rage and outbursts of anger. Hilberman and Munson (1977-1978) report that the reactions of battered women closely approximate those that have been documented for rape victims. These include insomnia, anxiety, depression, terror, and nightmares.

Janoff-Bulman and Frieze (1983) describe the reactions of battered women as most resembling those of post-traumatic stress disorder, which many victims of trauma have. These reactions include reexperiencing the trauma through nightmares, flashbacks, and/or intrusive thoughts of the trauma; numbing to the external world; and a variety of anxiety-related symptoms, such as sleep disturbance, avoidance of stimuli associated with the trauma, and intensification of anxiety when confronted with reminders of the trauma. The diminished decision-making and problem-solving abilities that some describe in battered women could well be the result of repeated exposure to trauma.

Dutton, Chrestman, and Gold (1991) compared PTSD symptoms of women who were battered but not sexually abused as children with those of women who were both battered and sexually abused as children and women who were not battered but sexually victimized as children. While all three groups showed evidence of posttraumatic stress, those who presented for treatment of sexual abuse showed more distress than those who presented for treatment of domestic violence. Dutton et al. speculate that this may be because battered women focus more on the battering situation than on their own internal distress. In another study, Halle, Burghardt, Dutton, and Perrin (1991) found that more than one-third of battered women in their sample had also been sexually abused by their partners. Regardless of whether or not they had been sexually abused by their partners, the battered women experienced similar rates of prior sexual abuse during adulthood and during childhood. Most interesting, however, is the finding that women who experienced multiple forms of abuse had higher scores on measures of psychological distress, suggesting that cumulative effects of multiple abuse may exacerbate the effects of battering alone. Halle et al. suggest that this may explain why some women who do not report severe physical violence have high levels of psychological distress. If this is so, therapists need to assess not only for current battering, but also for concurrent sexual abuse, past adult sexual abuse, and childhood sexual abuse.

Follingstad et al. (1988) describe the variety of coping styles that battered women might adopt in coming to terms with the abuse. These coping mechanisms allow the woman to survive the battering, but most also ensure that she will remain in the abusive relationship. One key coping mechanism involves understanding why the abuse has occurred. Among the rationalizations developed by battered women to understand the context within which the battering has happened are (a) denial of the injury the woman has experienced, (b) attribution of the blame to forces outside the control of both the perpetrator and the recipient, (c) self-blame, (d) denial of emotional or practical options, (e) wanting to save the batterer by helping him overcome his problem while continuing to tolerate the abuse, and (f) the need to endure the violence for the sake of some higher commitment, such as religion or tradition (Ferraro & Johnson, 1983).

Psychotherapists working with battered women are often surprised to see the women blaming themselves for causing the abuse, for not being able to modify the occurrence of the abuse, or for tolerating the abuse. However, as Miller and Porter (1983) note, this coping mechanism allows the woman to maintain the illusion that she is still in control of her life, and to believe that a "just world" exists in which people get what they deserve and bad things do not happen to good people. Unfortunately, her perception of control often serves to keep her in the abusive situation, frustrating the efforts of those who would encourage her to leave. In support of this position, Hendricks-Matthews (1982) reports that therapy is less successful for women who self-blame than for those who blame their batterers.

After the initial battering incident, the woman often sees the violence as an aberration and as something she can control, and she focuses on identifying ways of preventing the abuse from reoccurring. Eventually, she may become discouraged: Some research has shown battered women to have a significantly greater external locus of control than women in normative samples, with battered women in longer relationships having greater external locus of control than battered women in shorter relationships (Cheney & Bleker, 1982). Similarly, Feldman (1983) found that battered women who continued in their relationships had greater external locus of control than did either battered women who left their relationships or control women. This suggests that something about being in or continuing in an abusive relationship erodes a woman's sense of control over her own destiny, ultimately resulting in the passivity or numbness that some have reported in battered women (see Hanks & Rosenbaum, 1977, or Walker's explanations of the battered woman syndrome and learned helplessness).

Depression has also been reported in the literature as a characteristic of battered women (Douglas, 1982; Walker, 1979, 1984a); however, it may be the result of yet another coping mechanism. Expressing anger toward the batterer could well have the effect of increasing the violence. Repressing the intense anger experienced in response to a beating may instead have greater survival value. Carmen, Rieker, and Mills (1984) found that 66% of the battered women they studied reported turning their anger inward, as opposed to 22% who directed their anger outward and 12% who used mixed or other modalities. These same authors and others relate anger turned inward to depression, grossly disturbed self-image, alcoholism, and suicidality (see, e.g., Hilberman, 1980; Pfouts, 1978).

That depression is a result (rather than a causal element) of family violence is supported by Feldman's (1983) findings that battered women still in their abusive relationships were significantly more depressed than were women who had left their relationships. Suicidality is also quite prevalent among women who have been abused (Gayford, 1975; Stark, Flitcraft, & Frazier, 1979). Both depression and suicidal ideation may be erroneously seen as evidence of pathology by many mental health professionals, rather than as the result of a pathological situation.

On the positive side, Mills (1985) describes a schema of coping strategies for ending a violent relationship. The framework for this schema, that victimization is a gradual process resulting from abuse rather than from inherent characteristics of battered women, is supported by the fact that the women in Mills's sample described the beginnings of their relationships as positive, and as becoming violent only subsequent to their entering into a commitment. Mills's qualitative study suggests a five-stage process for ending an abusive relationship:

1. *entering a violent relationship:* a period of vulnerability during which unclear judgment predominates
2. *managing the violence:* attaching meanings to the violence and developing strategies to cope with it
3. *experiencing a loss of self:* a period of loss of identity and isolation, with a focus on placating the batterer
4. *reevaluating the violent relationship:* triggered by specific events, outside validation, and contradictory insights attained along the way

5. *reconstructing the self:* moving away from a self-image of being a battered woman to one of being a survivor rather than a victim

Working With Battered Women

Psychotherapists who work with this population have a choice: They can focus on searching for evidence of pathology in their clients and orient the therapy to remedying this, or they can look for the positive characteristics that battered women as a group possess, which some writers are beginning to describe. For example, Schechter (1982) points to battered women's strength, persistence, and survival skills, in contrast to their widely portrayed weakness and passivity. Root (1992) has developed a multifaceted theory of trauma that explains much of the symptomatology described in battered women. Some of the basic tenets of Root's conceptualization of trauma are as follows:

1. Experiencing trauma makes a permanent change in a person's view of the world, her sense of self, and her feelings of security in the world.
2. Trauma "exceeds the limits of human capacity to process and integrate horrible experiences into a coherent perception of self and self-in-relationship to others and the world" (p. 260).
3. What is experienced as traumatic can be identified as such only by the traumatized individual, and not by any outside observer (even a therapist).
4. Person-perpetrated violence is a particularly powerful traumatogen, as is violence experienced under conditions of isolation (two aspects that characterize the battering relationship).
5. The traumatized individual must find new meaning in her experience in order to reorganize her perception of the world and her sense of self.
6. The behaviors of traumatized individuals that are seen as pathological by mental health professionals are evidence of these persons' very attempts to reorganize their worlds in meaningful ways—they are survival behaviors: "Disorganized and unusual behavior following horrible experiences are normal responses to traumatic events" (p. 237).
7. Because so often traumatized individuals (especially battered women) are blamed or questioned about the accuracy of their reports, the reactions of others also serve to retraumatize the victim.

Psychotherapists need to recognize the resilience of battered women, which not only allows them to survive, but is a core quality that may help them recover. (See Chapter 8 for a discussion of techniques for working with battered women.)

4

Therapist Perceptions of Family Violence

MICHÈLE HARWAY
MARSALI HANSEN

More than a decade ago, Lenore Walker (1979), a pioneer in research and intervention with violent families, presented and then dismantled 21 common myths about domestic violence. Some of these concerned beliefs about characteristics of battered women (e.g., battered women are masochistic; middle-class women do not get battered as often or as violently as poorer women), others had to do with assumptions about batterers (e.g., batterers are violent in all their relationships; batterers are psychopathic), and still others were common suppositions about the efficacy of intervening with violent families (e.g., once a batterer, always a batterer; police can protect the battered woman). These myths are unsupported by research and clinical theories, and yet most are still widely believed today.

Not only is the average American likely to believe many of these myths, but the average mental health professional also is likely to have incorporated some (or all) of these erroneous conceptions into his or her belief system. How do these beliefs affect the type of intervention the mental health professional makes when dealing with a client who has been in a battering relationship? The question is not an unimportant one in view of the rather alarming recent domestic violence statistics in the United States. In Chapter 1, we reviewed prevalence figures that demonstrate variously that violence affects 8.7 million couples (Gelles & Straus, 1989), anywhere from 121 couples per 1,000 to 510 couples per 1,000 (Straus & Gelles, 1988), as many as 25-33% of married couples (Koss, 1990), and that 16% of couples experience violence at home every year (Strauss & Gelles, 1989). The differences in prevalence figures are reported to be due to a variety of factors: the estimate that fewer than 1 out of every 250 spouse assaults is reported (Steinmetz, 1977); the fact that some studies (notably the National Crime Survey) have asked for reports about crime (and most people do not think of family violence as a crime; Gaquin, 1977-1978); the fact that respondents to previous surveys may not have been honest (Gelles & Straus, 1989), and myriad other reasons.

Reports on the seriousness of family violence have also varied. Okun (1986) found that two-thirds of his 300 respondents had been extensively beaten up or worse; 1 in 6 had been threatened with a knife or gun, and 1 in 30 had actually been attacked with a knife or gun. These same women reported that the most recent episode of violence resulted in 28 fractures and 22 serious injuries (such as back injuries, torn ligaments, dislocations, ruptured eardrums, broken teeth, and stab and bullet wounds). Only 24% of these women had ever received medical treatment for injuries received during conjugal assaults, largely because their partners had prevented them from doing so. Other research indicates that in many instances the violence may be so extreme as to result in murder, with lethality in cases of wife battering most likely to occur when the woman tries to leave (Browne, 1987). Moreover, 70-80% of women who are murdered are killed by their husbands, members of their families, or close friends (Dobash & Dobash, 1977-1978).

Regardless of which figures one believes, these data indicate that family violence is widespread and that it can be quite serious. The data also indicate that virtually every psychotherapist (regardless of whether he or she specializes in domestic violence or not) will at some point in his or her professional career treat a violent couple, or someone involved in a violent relationship. Thus it is particularly important that psychotherapists be skilled in recognizing the signs of domestic violence and in intervening appropriately.

Recently, the role that therapists play in the treatment of violent families has come under close scrutiny (see Cervantes, Chapter 12, this volume). Family therapists, in particular, have been criticized because they address family violence within the theoretical context of systemic patterns, thereby obscuring the seriousness of the act (Bograd, 1984; Pressman, 1989; see also Hansen, Chapter 6, and Hansen & Goldenberg, Chapter 7, this volume). If these criticisms of therapeutic intervention are valid, then therapists may in fact be harming the very people they intend to help. Until recently, little research had looked directly at therapists' conceptualizations in cases of abuse; we report on two such recent studies here. The purpose of the first study was to examine how therapists assess and intervene in cases involving domestic violence.

Study 1

METHOD

Subjects

Subjects were 362 members of the American Association for Marriage and Family Therapy (AAMFT) who responded to a mailed questionnaire (a response rate of about 20% from a randomly selected sample of the total AAMFT membership). Respondents were 53% female and 47% male. Most described themselves as marriage and family therapists (66%); only about 14% said they were psychologists. Their education was primarily at the master's level (54% with a master's degree or M.S.W., 32% with a doctorate, the remainder with some other degree). A majority indicated that their primary theoretical orientation is family systems (59%); 11% described themselves as having an existential/humanistic orientation, 10% reported "other," and 8% reported a psychoanalytic orientation.

Procedure

Respondents were presented with one of two actual cases in which family violence was implicated (one of the scenarios was a case in which, unbeknown to study participants, the woman was later killed). Respondents were asked to give a conceptualization of the case and to state what interventions they might make.

RESULTS

When asked to describe what was going on in this case, 40% of practitioners in the sample failed to address the issue of violence. Moreover, among those identifying the conflict the severity was minimized: 91% of those who addressed the conflict considered it mild or moderate.

Recognition of family violence is an important first step, but no less important are the therapists' descriptions of how they would intervene. Given that even those who addressed the violence underplayed its seriousness, the interventions they subsequently recommended were inappropriate. Fully 55% of respondents said they *would not* intervene as if the violence required any immediate action. Only 11% said they would obtain protection for the wife, by helping her develop a safety plan, getting her to a shelter, or helping her get a restraining order. By contrast, 14% would work on the couple's communication style. When asked what type of outcome they would expect from their intervention, 23% responded that they expected some type of pessimistic outcome. Without intervention,

68% indicated that there would be violence or that abuse (to child or spouse) would increase. Only 8 persons out of 362 foresaw the possibility of lethality.

The results were consistent across respondent characteristics (master's or doctoral education, psychologist or other license, and gender). There were few differences by theoretical orientation of the respondent.

DISCUSSION

The results of Study 1 are alarming. They open to question the readiness of therapists to intervene appropriately in cases of domestic violence (Hansen, Harway, & Cervantes, 1991; Harway & Hansen, 1990b). It is unclear from these results whether therapists are missing the indicators for violence and therefore are generating inappropriate interventions or whether they *can* identify violence as a cause for concern but cannot intervene appropriately. Also, as a majority of the sample was made up of marriage and family therapists, we considered the possibility that the results were idiosyncratic to the sample studied and may not be generalizable to all psychotherapists. Consequently, we undertook a second study in order to answer these questions.

Study 2

METHOD

Participants

Participants consisted of 405 members of the American Psychological Association's (APA) Divisions 12 (Clinical Psychology), 29 (Psychotherapy), and 42 (Independent Practice) who responded to a mailed questionnaire (a response rate of about 30% from a randomly selected sample of the total membership of these divisions selected because they were most likely to include psychotherapists). Respondents were 71% male and 29% female, with a mean age of 50. Almost all described themselves as psychologists (99%). Their education was overwhelmingly at the doctoral level (99% Ph.D.s). Most spent a majority of their time doing direct (clinical) service (median of 80% of their time). Primary theoretical orientations reported by respondents included 22% cognitive, 21% psychoanalytic, 12% existential/humanistic, 8% behavioral, and 7% family systems. An additional 30% reported a variety of lesser known and more idiosyncratic orientations. Of particular interest is the majority acknowledgment of the influence of feminism on therapeutic approach (80%

saying they were somewhat or greatly influenced by feminism in their therapeutic approaches). A claim to having been influenced by feminism appears to be the socially acceptable response, at least among our sample.

Procedure

Questionnaires were mailed to a random sample of the memberships of Divisions 12, 29, and 42 of the APA. The therapists were asked to provide background information (demographic data and information about professional affiliation, theoretical orientation, and the impact of feminism on therapeutic approach) and then were presented with a case in which family violence was implicated (an actual case of rather extreme domestic violence was employed; see the appendix to this chapter). Respondents were asked for a DSM-III-R diagnosis based on the case. They subsequently were informed that the case resulted in the husband murdering his wife. Respondents were then asked to describe the following: the interventions they might have made if, prior to the outcome, they had been given the opportunity to provide counseling; the underlying dynamics they saw in the case; their goals for intervention; the expected outcome of the intervention; and the legal/ethical issues raised by the case (all open-ended questions).

RESULTS

General Findings

The single most common diagnosis that therapists made was one focusing on the couple's marital problems (V61.10), made by 23% of respondents. Next most common was a diagnosis indicating that both James (the husband) and Carol (the wife) were suffering from some form of pathology (usually James was found to be suffering from intermittent explosive disorder or a conduct disorder and Carol from a self-defeating or dependent personality). An additional 16% diagnosed only James. More than one-third of the respondents (36%) claimed that they did not have enough information to make a diagnosis.

Supporting evidence was gathered in relation to the therapists' descriptions of the underlying dynamics of the case (supplied by respondents after they were informed that the case had resulted in Carol being killed by James during a violent episode). Almost a third of the sample felt that the dynamics of the case were couple dynamics (31%). Only 19% pointed to James's dynamics, and another 16% were vague about whose dynamics were being implicated; 8% seemed to "blame the victim" and another 3%

referred to the couple's dynamics but focused on James. Another 21% claimed that they did not have enough information to describe the underlying dynamics of the case.

In spite of now knowing about the lethal outcome of the case, only 50% indicated that the intervention of choice (had an opportunity for counseling existed prior to the outcome) would be to seek protection for the wife. Another 27% said that they would want to assess the couple further to ascertain the seriousness of the violence and 11% said they would focus entirely on the problem as a couple's problem, with interventions focused on getting the couple to communicate or vent their feelings. Finally, two respondents blamed the victim, intervening in such a way as to suggest that Carol was responsible for James's violent behavior.

The goals for these therapists' interventions suggest the thinking that underlies the interventions to be applied. Three major response tendencies characterize the respondents' intervention goals; we have named the three response-type groups Contextualists, Communication Interventionists, and Avoiders.

Contextualists (54% of the sample) employed crisis intervention because their focus on the context of the case (rather than simply on the process of counseling) suggested to them that Carol was in grave danger. Thus the goal of their interventions was to remove Carol from the situation of danger through an immediate divorce or the development of a safety plan.

Communication Interventionists (34% of the sample) focused on the dynamics of the case to the exclusion of external cues. This resulted in their applying interventions in therapy without recognizing the practical context of the case (and thereby missing the need to intervene in an immediate and practical way). It seems as if the therapists in this group believe they must do therapy, no matter what is called for.

Those in the third group, the Avoiders (9% of the sample), were hesitant to make any decision without further information. They responded with virtually no formulations of dynamics or descriptions of appropriate interventions.

Finally, when prompted to describe legal/ethical issues raised by the case, 23% of respondents were concerned about a possible duty to warn the intended victim, 19% were concerned about providing protection for Carol, and 17% had a variety of questions about the role of the therapist in a situation that one described as "more legal than therapeutic." Some 10% felt the need to assess the level of danger further, 8% were worried about issues of confidentiality or secrecy between the therapist and the members of the couple (a nonissue in the vignette), 5% were concerned about their duty to report child abuse, and 4% boldfacedly indicated that the case raised *no* legal/ethical issues.

Findings Related to Contextualists, Communication Interventionists, and Avoiders

We next looked at the types of interventions practiced by respondents in each of the three goal groups. Contextualists were substantially more likely to seek protection for Carol and her children (whether or not they also wanted to help James) than to do anything else (84% would so intervene). Communication interventionists also intervened by seeking protection for Carol, but in much smaller proportions (32%). Most therapists in this group would address the couple's problems or advise the woman in a more passive manner (50%). Finally, Avoiders used a variety of interventions, the most common of which were to gather more information (reported by 29%) or to address the couple's problems (21%). Only 20% would seek protection for Carol.

In describing the dynamics of the case, Contextualists most often focused on the couple's problems (50%), but they were also frequently likely to see James's dynamics as the major problem (21%). Similarly, Communication Interventionists were likely to see the couple's problems as the most important dynamic (49%), with James's problems being the next most frequent mention (25%). Avoiders most often avoided specifying the dynamics (50% said they needed more information), although 39% did mention the couple's problems as an underlying dynamic of the case. Among the legal/ethical issues raised by the case, the Contextualists most often mentioned protection for the wife (25%) and their duty to warn (22%), the Communication Interventionists mentioned questions about whether the role of the therapist is legal or therapeutic (21%) and the duty to warn (19%), and the Avoiders had the highest proportion of any group mentioning the duty to warn (42%) and the need to assess further the level of danger (21%).

To summarize, the Contextualists were inclined to intervene through crisis intervention because their focus on the context of the case (rather than simply on the process of counseling) suggested to them that Carol was in grave danger. Thus the goals of their interventions were to remove Carol from the situation of danger through an immediate divorce or the development of a safety plan. In terms of actual intervention, Contextualists were more likely to seek protection for Carol and her children than to do anything else. In fact, seeking protection for Carol was mentioned rather consistently throughout by Contextualists in terms of intervention, goal of the intervention, and ethical/legal issues, and the safety of the client was the outcome on which this group most frequently focused. About half or more of the therapists from the behavioral, family systems, and psychoanalytic theoretical orientations were Contextualists.

Communication Interventionists focused on the dynamics of the case to the exclusion of external cues, which resulted in their applying interventions in therapy without recognizing the practical context of the case (and thereby missing the need to intervene in an immediate and practical way). An underlying assumption appears to be their belief in the omnipotence of their therapeutic intervention. While some therapists in this group said they would seek protection for the wife, most indicated they would address the couple's problems or advise the woman in a more passive manner. Communication Interventionists were likely to see the couple's problems as the most important dynamic. In terms of legal and ethical issues, Communication Interventionists were most often unclear about whether the role of the therapist is legal or therapeutic in such cases and were concerned about their duty to warn. Many cognitive and existential/humanistic therapists in this sample were Communication Interventionists.

The Avoiders avoided. These therapists were hesitant to make any decision without further information. They provided virtually no formulations of dynamics or descriptions of appropriate interventions. Moreover, the most common response given by this group throughout was that they needed more information. In the legal/ethical area, those in this group most often gave responses that were legally self-protective but relatively passive on behalf of the client: They had the largest proportion of all advocating the importance of warning an intended victim. A small number of Avoiders were found in every theoretical orientation group except family systems.

Other Differences by Theoretical Orientation

Were there certain patterns of responding that favored certain theoretical orientations? Seeking protection for the client was related most often to being an eclectic therapist (30% of those advocating protection indicated having an "other" theoretical orientation). However, this group was the single largest group ($n = 70$). By contrast, there were only 14 family systems therapists. Because of the large discrepancies in numbers of therapists in each theoretical orientation group, it made more sense to examine the types of responses given by therapists of different theoretical orientations to each of the questions we posed.

When we examined whether the therapists' theoretical orientations were related to their intervention goals, we found large discrepancies: Although 84% of family systems therapists were Contextualists, only 47% of cognitive and 43% of existential/humanistic therapists were also Contextualists. The existential/humanistic therapists were somewhat more likely to be Communication Interventionists, and 42% of cognitive therapists were also likely to be Communication Interventionists.

Table 4.1 Response Tendency by Therapeutic Orientation (in percentages)

	Contextualist	*Communication Interventionist*	*Avoider*
Behavioral	58	26	16
Cognitive	47	42	12
Existential/humanistic	43	44	13
Family systems	84	15	—
Psychoanalytic	70	23	8

However, in spite of their espoused goals, we found when we examined what therapists said they would actually do that family systems therapists were more likely than any other group actively to seek protection for the wife (65%), followed closely by cognitive therapists (63%). Psychoanalytic therapists were least likely to seek protection (40%). One-fifth of family systems and cognitive therapists would assess the case further prior to intervening. Almost one-quarter of existential/humanistic therapists would focus on the couple's problems as the primary means of intervention.

DISCUSSION

This study was designed to answer some questions that our previous research had left unclear. To recapitulate, we wanted to ascertain (a) whether findings of our previous study were spurious or idiosyncratic to the sample studied, (b) whether therapists are able to identify violence as a cause for concern but are unable to intervene appropriately, and (c) whether therapists are missing indicators of violence and therefore are generating inappropriate interventions.

Results of this study support those of Study 1 in that a substantial proportion of our psychologist respondents did not generate appropriate interventions even when told outright that the case was one of domestic violence with a lethal outcome. This is consistent with the results of our previous research, which indicated that a substantial number of marriage and family therapists presented with a case of domestic violence did not address the violence and suggested inappropriate interventions. Thus the results of both studies taken together suggest that psychotherapists with different professional affiliations seem to respond similarly.

The fact that both studies resulted in relatively consistent findings suggests that many psychotherapists (with a variety of types of training) are unable to formulate appropriate intervention plans even when explicitly told that a case is a violent one. Moreover, it also appears that therapists are unprepared to assess for dangerousness in violent families. In support of this, our findings show that DSM-III-R diagnoses (made prior to learning about the homicide) and assessments of dynamics (made after learning that the case had resulted in a murder) are very similar: A substantial proportion of respondents used a V code for marital problems (V61.10) as a diagnosis and after being told that a murder had occurred still speculated that the underlying dynamics of the case were heavily dependent on the couple's issues. Only a handful of respondents, either before learning of the homicide or after, focused on the pathology of the perpetrator. While few therapists blamed the victim (few gave a diagnosis to Carol or felt the underlying dynamics of the case were related to her), systemic issues were often mentioned.

In addition, it is noteworthy that a number of respondents were unwilling either to make a diagnosis, claiming insufficient information, or to outline the underlying dynamics of the case. Many others felt that they had insufficient information even after they were told that Carol had been murdered. It appears that an important cross section of the therapeutic community was unable to *assess* properly the danger inherent in this case of domestic violence. These findings are cause for concern about the readiness of psychotherapists to identify violence and its cause.

In evaluating whether therapists are insufficiently trained in intervening in cases of family violence, let us consider these findings: Even after being informed that the outcome of the case was that Carol had been killed by James during a violent episode, fully half of our sample, when asked what intervention they could have made prior to the fatal outcome, failed to invoke crisis intervention. An ideal intervention in this case would have been to concentrate on ways to obtain protection for the wife or to ensure her safety (Pressman, 1989). Instead, 27% still wanted to assess further the violence inherent in this family, and another 11% proposed intervening through couples' communication exercises or the venting of feelings. Finally, a few respondents suggested interventions with Carol to tone down her behavior, thereby implying that Carol was responsible for James's behavior. Thus therapists' *knowledge of the appropriate intervention* in a case including homicidal violence, for at least half the respondents, was not focused on ensuring the safety of the victim. These findings indicate that some psychotherapists' interventions have the potential of being dangerous to the client.

Having answered our initial questions by concluding that a large number of therapists are unable to assess properly the danger inherent in cases of domestic violence and that many more are not able to intervene in a timely and appropriate manner, we must emphasize that not all therapists behave in the same way. To reiterate, in our sample we found three major response tendencies, which can be summarized as follows:

- *Contextualists:* These individuals respond through crisis intervention, because their focus is on the context of the case (rather than simply on the process of counseling) and they are aware that the wife is in grave danger. The goal of intervention is to remove the woman from the situation of danger through an immediate divorce or the development of a safety plan.
- *Communication Interventionists:* These therapists focus on the dynamics of the case to the exclusion of external cues (resulting in interventions that do not consider the practical context of the case and therefore miss the need to intervene in an immediate and practical way). Most therapists in this group would address the couple's problems or advise the woman in a more passive manner. Certainly, the couple's problems are seen as the most important dynamic.
- *Avoiders:* These practitioners are hesitant to make decisions without further information. They do not frequently present formulations of dynamics or descriptions of appropriate interventions. Moreover, the most common response given by this group is that they need more information.

Subjects in each of these different groups presented very consistent responses throughout the questionnaire; thus, there is reason to believe that the typology presented here may be applicable to different subgroups of therapist types. However, this notion requires further research. If these subgroups can be substantiated through future research, this would have implications for tailoring additional training for different types of therapists. Family therapy and feminist arguments about the importance of context in working with violent families are supported here in that at least half the sample attended to context with their interventions.

Finally, what do these results have to tell us about the therapist's legal and ethical responsibility regarding protecting the client? Unlike in cases of child and elder abuse, there are currently no reporting laws covering spousal abuse. As Cervantes argues in Chapter 12 of this volume, in the absence of laws regarding spousal abuse reporting requirements, the ethical responsibility of the therapist must revolve around the duty to warn and the responsibility to provide effective treatment. Our data indicate that the provision of effective treatment will be dependent on therapists' obtaining additional training in working with violent families. Therapists will also need to take more active political and legal roles in clarifying the legal aspects of treating violent families.

Summary of Findings

The two studies presented here suggest that some substantial proportion of therapists are unprepared to intervene appropriately in cases of domestic violence. Study 1 indicated that 91% of therapists failed to recognize the seriousness of violence in altercations between couples and that 40% failed to address the issue of violence at all. Because even those who addressed the violence underplayed its seriousness, the interventions they subsequently recommended were inappropriate. In Study 2 we found that a substantial proportion of psychotherapists, from a variety of theoretical orientations, were unable to formulate appropriate intervention plans even when explicitly told that a case was a violent one. Many of these therapists were unprepared to assess dangerousness in violent families and were unable to protect their clients from harm.

Therapists must become sensitized to patterns of violence within families and learn how to intervene appropriately. The provision of effective treatment in these cases in the future depends on many therapists' obtaining additional training.

Appendix: Case for Study 2

Carol and James have been married 10 years. They have two children: Dana, 9, and Tracy, 7. James is employed as a foreman in a concrete manufacturing plant. Carol is also employed. James is upset because on several occasions Carol did not return home from work until two or three in the morning and did not explain her whereabouts to him. He acknowledges privately to the therapist that the afternoon prior to the session, he had seen her in a bar with a man. Carol tells the therapist privately that she has made efforts to dissolve the marriage and to seek a protection order against her husband because he has repeatedly been physically violent with her and the kids and on the day prior, he grabbed her and threw her on the floor in a violent manner and then struck her. The family had made plans to go shopping, roller skating, and out to dinner after the session.

5

Studying Battered Women and Batterers: Feminist Perspectives on Methodology

MAUREEN C. McHUGH

A brief review of the literature on battered women is a difficult thing to provide; there has been an explosion of research on this and other forms of violence against women in the past two decades. To a large extent this proliferation of research can be attributed to the feminist movement. Feminists have called attention to the prevalence of violence against women starting with rape in the 1960s; they have urged societal institutions to address these issues more adequately. Conducting psychological research on the prevalence, causes, and treatment of violence against women has been one contribution that feminist psychologists have attempted to make to the feminist movement.

Most of the researchers and many of the clinicians working in this area consider themselves feminists and perceive their work as directly or indirectly advocating for women. Yet, in a recent review my colleagues and I concluded that the research conducted to date has not been particularly feminist, and may have limited usefulness for women who have been battered (McHugh, Frieze, & Browne, 1992). Similar conclusions have been reached by others, including Yllö and Bograd (1988).

Two major foci of the research on battered women are reviewed here. The review begins with a critique of the research concerning definition, measurement, and incidence of woman battering, and then examines the research on the victims and why they stay in abusive relationships. Possible explanations for why these questions have been the focus of research attention are explored, and some problems and inadequacies of each of these research approaches are identified. More recent research focusing on the batterer is then critically reviewed. The chapter ends with discussion of the questions a feminist perspective would suggest.

Defining, Measuring, and Documenting the Violence

HOW COMMON IS WIFE ABUSE?

A substantial amount of research effort has been focused on this question. One of the earliest issues addressed, the prevalence of woman battering continues to be central and controversial. Early estimates of both incidence and prevalence were based on reports from intact couples and applied only to abuse occurring within current marital relationships. Later, community (urban) samples yielded higher estimates when women respondents were asked if they had ever been assaulted. Incidence rates are further increased if we include women who are battered in the context of nonmarital relationships.

It has been estimated that more than one-fourth of marriages involve at least one incident of physical assault (see McHugh et al., 1992, for a complete discussion of incidence). Straus, Gelles, and Steinmetz (1980) report 28% in their national survey of more than 2,000 homes. Russell (1982) reports 21% for her San Francisco sample of current or previously married women. Frieze, Knoble, Washburn, and Zomnir (1980) found that 34% of a general community group of ever-married women reported being attacked at least once by a male partner.

Why is it important to assess or document the prevalence of assault on women in the context of their intimate relationships? Why was this one of the first questions asked, and why do incidence rates continue to be important today? Incidence rates are important for the individuals who set mental health and family policy, and for those who make decisions about the distribution of resources. By providing statistical evidence of the extent of wife abuse, researchers have played a critical role in making this a social issue (Caplan, 1985). How much abuse occurs is an important piece of information in determining what levels of societal response (e.g., from the legal system, the police, physicians, mental health professionals) are needed. Incidence and prevalence rates have been used as the basis for obtaining resources to cope with the issue on a societal level. Funding for police training, shelters, and additional research is dependent on our ability to demonstrate the extensiveness and severity of the problem.

Incidence rates also have important etiologic and intervention-related implications. The argument that abuse of women by their partners is the result of individual pathology is not very convincing if it can be shown that this is a phenomenon that occurs in 35-50% of relationships. Pathology, by definition, cannot be normative behavior. If physical violence occurs in many or most couples (in the United States), then we should consider structural or cultural factors as causes. High incidence rates are typically interpreted as indicating the existence of structural or societal causes, such as societal support of male aggression, relationship scripts that include woman battering, and institutional support for battering.

It is not clear that the documentation of the high prevalence of wife battering has influenced either researchers' or clinicians' perspectives on the etiology of woman battering. Researchers continue to investigate primarily individual- or dyad-level variables, and clinicians continue to attempt to intervene at the individual behavioral or intrapsychic level or at the dyad or family process level.

One could also challenge the helpfulness of this research for battered women themselves. From the perspective of the woman who is battered, is the most important or interesting question, How many other women were also beaten today? Although incidence rates hypothetically could encourage battered women, along with the rest of us, to view such assault as a societal problem that is culturally produced, other research suggests that this is not a likely outcome. Knowing that others suffer does not reduce a victim's pain or anguish (Fiske & Taylor, 1984), nor does it suggest a solution.

MEASURING THE VIOLENCE

Despite the proliferation of research, much of it interested in the incidence or prevalence of wife battering, insufficient work has been conducted on the design and refinement of measurement instruments. No standardized scale or measure has been developed for clinical use in assessing the presence or degree of relationship violence. Intake interviews and schedules do not typically include questions about interpersonal violence (von Erden & Goodwin, 1992), even though incidence rates suggest that such questions should be routinely asked. As von Erden and Goodwin (1992) note, initial responses to direct questions about violence may not be revealing; battered women may hesitate to reveal the source of their distress to strangers, who may or may not report back to the abusive partner.

In the literature on woman battering, most of the research has relied on the use of the Conflict Tactics Scale (CTS) designed by Straus (1979) and used extensively by Straus, Gelles, and their colleagues (e.g., Straus, 1980; Straus & Gelles, 1986; Straus et al., 1980). Continued use of this scale allows for comparability of results, but it also perpetuates inadequacies in the literature. The CTS has been seriously criticized (e.g., for an extensive critique, see Yllö & Bograd, 1988). Questions on the scale are set in the context of settling disputes in a conflict situation, and may not elicit information about attacks that "come out of the blue." Further, the scale does not differentiate initiated violence from acts of self-defense, nor does it assess the seriousness of the injuries inflicted.

As a direct result of these inadequacies, use of the CTS has led to confusion over the mutuality of domestic violence. Strauss et al. (1980) have concluded that mutual violence is more common than unilateral domestic violence. Others, including Browne (1989; Browne & Dutton, 1990), have challenged this conclusion. Women's violence is typically in self-defense, and is less likely to result in serious injury (see McHugh et al., 1992, for an in-depth discussion). Moreover, the CTS does not include questions about psychological abuse, verbal assaults, or sexual abuse. Partly as a result of reliance on this scale, less research has been conducted on the effects of psychological and sexual abuse within intimate relationships. Researchers have not examined the relationship of nonphysical violence and abuse to physical aggression. The recent development of the sexual experiences survey by Koss to measure sexual abuse in intimate relations (see Koss & Dinero, 1988) and the Psychological Maltreatment of Women Scale (Tolman & Bennett, 1990) to explore psychological abuse indicates that these topics will receive more attention in the future.

ACCURACY OF REPORTS

Researchers have typically been criticized because information on violent acts is gathered from only one member of a couple. A clinician seeing a client individually experiences a similar problem. When corroborating evidence has been available, it has suggested that battered women, especially those who have been battered over a long period of time, tend to underestimate both the frequency and the severity of the violence they have experienced. Kelly (1988) suggests that forgetting and minimizing are two coping strategies used by battered women. Experts working with battered men note that they greatly underreport their violent actions and that they exaggerate the involvement of their female partners in the commission of the violence (Browne & Dutton, 1990; Sonkin & Durphy, 1985).

The problems raised by this evidence of inaccuracy of reporting for both research and clinical practice are clear. In interviewing or treating male perpetrators and women victims, researchers and therapists should seek third-party corroboration and/or seriously question the accuracy of the reports of both partners.

TERMINOLOGY

Researchers and clinicians have not agreed on the terms, labels, or measures to be used in discussing the infliction of intentional physical and psychological injury on women in the context of their intimate relationships. The interchangeable use of terms such as *assaultive, abusive, aggressive,* and *violent* has led to conceptual ambiguity and confusion (Browne, 1989; Brush, 1990). Several critics have objected especially to the terms *domestic violence, family violence,* and *spouse abuse* because they feel that such terminology obscures the dimensions of gender and power that are fundamental to understanding the abuse of women (Breines & Gordon, 1983; Schechter, 1982). These generic terms ignore the context of the violence, its nature and consequences, the role obligations of family members, and the processes that lead to abuse. Such terms can lead to biases in how the causes and solutions of wife abuse are conceptualized and treated (Bograd, 1988a). Further, terms such as *wife abuse* and *wife battering* are not sufficiently inclusive; many women are battered by intimates in nonmarital relationships.

TAKING THE WOMAN'S PERSPECTIVE

Typically, researchers have employed social, legal, conceptual, and methodological perspectives in deciding what constitutes wife abuse. Women's definitions and conceptualizations of violence have been infrequently examined. Feminist research, however, seeks to examine women's experiences from their own perspectives. Thus for research to be feminist it must have as its paramount purpose the exploration of women's own labels, thoughts, and beliefs about the experienced violence. Further, how a woman labels or defines the situation may determine the extent and direction of her help-seeking behavior. When Kelly (1988) examined battered women's own conceptualizations of their experiences, she noted that women changed their labels of their experiences over time; as the episodes increased and escalated, women were likely to relabel earlier incidents as abusive.

Kelly (1988) reports that the terms typically used to label partner violence caused problems for some of the women in her study. The term *wife beating* was seen as applying only in marital situations, and *battering* tended to be understood in terms of severe frequent physical violence.

The emergence of such new terminology as *dating violence* and *lesbian battering* allows more women to speak about their experiences with violence in intimate relationships. Having labels for our experiences helps us to organize and understand the patterns of our daily lives. Yet, giving each form of violence experienced by women in their intimate relationships a different name or term may obscure the persistent and pervasive nature of such violence and may prevent us from examining the violence for underlying causes. Assigning different women different labels for their experienced violence may be a way of dividing and isolating us.

Focus on the Victim

WHO IS THE VICTIM?

Some of the earliest research served to challenge misconceptions about the identity of battered women. Research documented that abuse can occur across regional, occupational, ethnic, racial, and class groups. However, the process of challenging conceptions about the identity of victims of intimate battering continues; "new" victim groups have recently been identified.

An expanding literature on dating violence confirms Makepeace's (1983) contention that dating violence is as extensive as marital violence. For example, Deal and Wampler (1986) report that 47% of their college sample had some experience with violence in dating relationships. Use of the term *wife abuse* and explanations that focused on marital roles and family structures obscured the realities of relationship violence. Makepeace and others have suggested that the "discovery" of dating violence calls into question many of our interpretations and explanations for intimate violence.

Recent research suggests that we have ignored at least one other group of victims of relationship violence: battered lesbians. Documentation that lesbian women are often abused by other women (Bologna, Waterman, & Dawson, 1987; Kelly & Warshafsky, 1987; Myers, 1989; Renzetti, Chapter 15, this volume) raises new questions for researchers. For example, theories that tie wife battering to legal and social codes of marital conduct may not be helpful in explaining either dating violence or lesbian battering, and theories that tie woman battering to male aggression cannot easily explain lesbian battering.

Very little research has been conducted with lesbian or gay male couples, even though such couples seem to be good comparisons for heterosexual couples, given theoretical models of battering that are based on male sex roles or marital roles. This oversight reflects the operation of heterosexism in our selection of research questions and populations. Lesbians have remained invisible in the psychological literature even when we have attempted to study women's experiences. The problems and experiences of lesbians are not seen as informing us about the nature of human relationships.

WHY DOES SHE STAY?

This is probably the most often asked question about woman abuse. In class discussions, in public forums, and in the research literature, people continue to voice this question first and foremost. This question may reveal the most basic ideology about woman battering: If the woman would leave, she wouldn't get beaten. The primary and most popular intervention strategy is focused on the victim; the solution is to relocate the woman, physically and psychologically. This perspective is increasingly seen as both victim blaming and counterproductive.

Early research focused on the logistical reasons some women did not leave abusive husbands. Lack of money, transportation, and a safe place to go were initially emphasized (Bowker, 1983; Browne & Williams, 1989). Other social factors affecting women's decisions to stay were also explored. Loss of social status, disapproval of family and friends, and feelings of failure or guilt for abandoning the relationship have been suggested as factors (Dobash & Dobash, 1979; Frieze, 1979; Walker, 1979). Abused women's perceptions of alternatives may be influenced by societal expectations related to gender and role relationships that encourage women to be self-sacrificing and adaptive and to care for and protect those close to them, regardless of the cost (Browne, 1987; Walker & Browne, 1985).

Subsequently, researchers and clinicians began to emphasize psychological factors underlying women's decisions not to leave. Walker's (1977, 1979, 1983, 1984a) work suggests that battered women have learned helplessness. They allegedly have developed motivational, cognitive, and behavioral deficits as a result of the battering. Woman battering has been compared to being a prisoner of war (Romero, 1985) or a torture victim (Chandler, 1986). Chandler's (1986) phenomenological analysis of battered women's experiences suggests that overriding fear and a loss of a sense of self characterize the severely battered woman. Other current research perspectives emphasize the emotional bonds that battered women form with their abusers (Browne, 1987; Dutton & Painter, 1981; Walker, 1983). Browne (1987) and Walker (1984a) note that abused women report that their partners were extremely attentive and affectionate early in the relationship. They showed great interest in the women's whereabouts, expressed the desire to be with the women all the time, demonstrated intense affection and jealousy, and wanted an early commitment to a long-term relationship. Over time, these behaviors that were initially seen as evidence of love became intrusive, controlling, and triggers to assault. The women became emotionally and geographically isolated, making them vulnerable to abuse. The abusers' concern for their wives' whereabouts became a form of surveillance, and the batterers were often described as evidencing severe and delusional jealousy (Frieze et al., 1980; Hotaling & Sugarman, 1986).

The fact that women stay in relationships because they fear retaliation from violent partners has been obscured by our attention to economic, social, and psychological factors. The battered woman fears that her partner will retaliate against her, her children, or her family if she tries to leave (Ridington, 1978). This fear of her abuser finding her or others he has threatened is a realistic one. Women who have left abusive partners have been followed and harassed for months or even years, and some have been killed (Browne, 1987; Jones, 1981; Pagelow, 1980). Evidence suggests that in many cases the man's violence escalates in response to a separation (Fields, 1978b; Fiora-Gormally, 1978; Pagelow, 1980). Goodwin and McHugh (1990) have labeled the stalking, coercive harassment, and threats of violence that occur in the context of the attempted breakup of a romantic relationship "termination terrorism."

VICTIMS OR SURVIVORS?

Thus even a woman's decision to stay may actually reflect her survival instinct, rather than either masochism or helplessness, as has repeatedly been suggested. An important feminist criticism of the research on woman battering is that it has focused attention on the woman as victim while ignoring her strengths and efforts to leave.

Some researchers have begun to emphasize the help seeking, coping mechanisms, and survival skills of battered women. For example, Gondolf and Fisher (1988) critique the learned helplessness model of wife abuse and examine the ways in which battered women in their Texas sample acted assertively and logically in response to the abuse. The women in their sample, like the women studied by Bowker (1983), persistently sought help from a wide range of sources. The more intense and prolonged the abuse, the greater the variety and the extent of their help seeking. (For a discussion of these issues, see Harway, Chapter 3, this volume.) These studies suggest that there are cognitive, motivational, and behavioral deficits not within the battered woman, but within the individuals and agencies that fail to respond adequately to her requests for help.

IMPLICATIONS OF VICTIM-FOCUSED RESEARCH AND TREATMENT

Most of the research on wife abuse has focused on the supposed inadequacies of the battered woman. Original formulations of the battered woman as masochistic or pathological have been repeatedly challenged (e.g., Caplan, 1985; Gondolf & Fisher, 1988; Yllö & Bograd, 1988), yet this perspective and other newer victim-blaming perspectives continue to influence both the research and the treatment of wife abuse. For example, the "theory" that some women who have experienced abuse seek out abusive situations and partners is a new variation on a worn masochism hypothesis. Further, the formulation that battered women are suffering from helplessness is widely held even though newer evidence indicates that abused female partners actively seek help and demonstrate cognitive and behavioral coping strategies (Bowker, 1983, 1984; Gondolf & Fisher, 1988).

Why has the research focused so heavily on the inadequacies of the battered woman? In earlier work I have outlined some of the explanations for victim blaming that may apply here (McHugh, 1987, 1990). Victim blame is viewed by social psychologists as resulting from the individual's need to believe in a just world (Lerner, 1984) and in her or his own invulnerability. Caplan (1985) has argued that the focus on the female victim as responsible for the violence is the legacy of Freud. Alternatively, it can be argued that the focus on the battered woman, both in the research and in clinical practice, stems from the fact that the victimized woman is the one who most typically has sought professional help (McHugh, 1990). Thus women's help seeking, a positive coping response, might ironically have led to them being labeled inadequate and pathological. Not only does these women's entry into shelters and therapy make them more accessible to researchers, but their presentation as clients makes them available for intervention by professionals. Since the women's behaviors and personalities are the ones we can measure, and possibly change, their behaviors and personalities must therefore be the ones that are viewed as problematic. A feminist analysis suggests that we challenge both the view of women as passive victims and our tendency to focus our research and intervention efforts on them.

Focus on the Batterer

Surprisingly enough, only recently has anyone addressed the more obvious questions: Why does *he* beat her? What is the matter with *him*? In a recent special issue of *Violence and Victims* on wife assaulters, the editors, Sonkin and Dutton (1988), note that research on men who assault their wives is in an infancy stage and suffers from a lack of theoretical organization. Several reasons have been suggested for the lack of research in this area. Batterers have been relatively inaccessible. Until recently, the little research that was conducted was focused on incarcerated batterers. In this same vein, the more recent focus on male batterers may stem from recent court mandates for treatment of batterers (Sonkin & Dutton, 1988). Feminist researchers may ironically have led to the focus on victims because of their preference for working with women victims rather than interviewing or treating male perpetrators.

PREDICTING MALE VIOLENCE

Everyone's interests would be served by research that contributes to our ability to predict violence. Conceptually, the ability to predict behavior is viewed as the best indication of the validity of any particular theory and research. If behavior could be predicted, then secondary and tertiary interventions could be developed to prevent the abuse from developing. Potential victims could use such information to avoid or to extricate themselves from relationships before violence or serious injury occur. The information would be important to therapists who are responsible for protecting their clients from serious injury and legally liable for failure to warn individuals who are potential targets of their clients' aggression.

It is surprising, given these potential benefits, how limited we are in our ability to predict relationship violence and dangerousness. Individuals who are violent in the context of the family have been largely ignored by researchers studying dangerousness (Sonkin, 1986). In one recent study of the dangerousness of abused wives, Browne (1987) compared cases of female-perpetrated homicide with cases in which the woman was abused but did not commit homicide. The two types of cases were distinguished by the frequency of male-perpetrated violence, the severity of the woman's injuries, the man's threats to kill the woman, the woman's suicide attempts, the man's intoxication and drug use, and the man's forcing the woman to engage in sexual acts. Thus the best predictors of an abused woman's dangerousness are all behaviors of the abuser.

Failure to demonstrate empirically that abused women are characterologically different from their nonabused counterparts has helped to shift research focus to the characteristics of abusers (Rosenbaum & O'Leary, 1981). However, a single profile of the woman-abusing male has not developed. Rather, the depictions of wife assaulters in the literature are contradictory. Dutton (1988b) suggests that such contradictions stem from differences in sampling and from the fact that the population of batterers is actually quite heterogeneous. Attempts to differentiate assaultive from nonassaultive husbands on personality and attitude measures have been generally unsuccessful.

There are, however, some *behavioral* risk markers for husband-to-wife violence. In 1986, Hotaling and Sugarman examined case comparison studies from 400 different reports. Only 1 of 42 different victim characteristics met the criteria for inclusion as a consistent risk marker for wife battering: Women who are victimized physically by their husbands are more likely to have witnessed violence between their own parents when they were children. The authors conclude that there is no current evidence to substantiate the position that women with a particular personality characteristic contribute to their own victimization. It is not possible to identify female victims by studying only women's characteristics. Of the 38 characteristics of the abusers studied as potential risk markers for men's use of violence, 9 showed a consistent pattern of findings. These included the husband's use of violence toward the children, sexual aggression, witnessing parental violence as a child, committing violent acts toward non-family members, alcohol use, and drug use. Batterers were also consistently found to be less assertive and to control fewer educational and economic resources than their nonabusive counterparts. Hotaling and Sugarman conclude that the battering of women within intimate relationships would be better understood as the *outcome of male behavior.*

BATTERER AS VICTIM OR PERPETRATOR?

The research conducted to date on batterers depicts them as victims. Violence in the batterer's family of origin is frequently cited as a factor in wife beating; batterers are more likely than comparison subjects to have been abused as children, to have witnessed their fathers beating their mothers, and to have been disciplined with corporal punishment as children (Caesar, 1988; Rosenbaum & O'Leary, 1981; Roy, 1982). Recently, the association between exposure to violence as a child and later marital violence has been challenged as questionable because of reliance on wives as informants and failure to include nonbatterers as comparison groups (Caesar, 1988). Thus the research available to date is riddled with inadequacies.

Batterers are also often described as "out of control" by both clinicians and researchers—for example, as having poor impulse control (Star, 1983) or as being in an uncontrollable rage (Deschner, 1984). Ptacek (1988) points out that the language used by clinicians to describe male violence and male batterers is similar to that used in the accounts given by batterers themselves. In a qualitative analysis of batterers' attributions, Ptacek concludes that their accounts consist of more excuses than explanations; male batterers tend to deny their behaviors, excuse themselves of responsibility, and at the same time offer justifications for their actions. Common excuses include loss of control and victim blaming. Justifications include denial of "real" injury and the wife's failure to fulfill the obligations of a good wife. Ptacek (1988) contends that similar perspectives are often held by clinicians, many of whom view male violence as beyond the batterer's control and as provoked by the wife.

Other evidence, however, contradicts the perspective that the batterer is out of control. The bruises and injuries inflicted by many batterers are not readily visible, suggesting thoughtful and intentional battery. Many abusive husbands systematically eliminate their wives' options by monitoring their money and movements prior to the onset of any physical violence (Frieze & McHugh, in press; Walker, 1983). Some men drink enough alcohol to provide an excuse for battering, but are not drunk when the violence occurs (Frieze & Knoble, 1980).

More research needs to examine systematically what men gain from assaulting their wives. Browne and Dutton (1990) contend that men who assault their wives gain personal feelings of power and feelings of controlling situations that felt unmanageable prior to the violence. Other researchers have emphasized the impact that a single episode of violence has on the power dynamics within the couple (Frieze & McHugh, in press; Goode, 1971; Walker, 1984a). This "functional" perspective emphasizes that men gain something from the battering; they batter to get what they want, or to get their own way.

One excuse offered by batterers, and subscribed to by many clinicians, wives, and researchers, is that the batterer acts under the influence of alcohol. Research indicates that when the husband has been drinking he is held less responsible for his violence, whereas if the wife has been drinking she is held more responsible for his violence (Richardson & Campbell, 1980). Other research documents wives' belief that their husbands' violence is "caused" by the men's alcohol problems (Bowker, 1983; Cooley, Chapter 17, this volume; Frieze & Knoble, 1980; Pagelow, 1981b).

Research does indicate that alcohol and drug abuse is a risk marker for husband-to-wife violence (Hotaling & Sugarman, 1986). Further, the research indicates that abusive men with severe alcohol or drug problems are apt to abuse their partners both when drunk and when sober, are violent more frequently, and inflict more serious injury on their partners than abusive men who do not have a history of alcohol or drug use. They are also more apt to attack their partners sexually, and are more likely to be violent outside the home.

The association between substance abuse and wife abuse is not well understood. Some have suggested that alcohol is a disinhibiting but not a causal factor (Pagelow, 1981b; Sonkin, Martin, & Walker, 1985). Others suggest that abusers drink to excuse their own conduct (Gelles, 1974). Sonkin and Durphy (1985) suggest that aggressive men use substances to dull the guilt and sadness they feel.

Thus the researcher and the clinician as well as the general public have focused on excuses for the abuser's behavior rather than on an analysis of the functional aspects of wife abuse. Batterers have been more often viewed as victims, as out of control, as influenced by drugs, or as provoked by their wives than as criminals engaging in dangerous and offensive behaviors. At the same time, wives who have viewed their husbands' violence in these ways have been blamed for not leaving and for not realizing the potential danger these men pose to their wives and children. Have we as researchers committed these same errors?

INTERVENTIONS

The feminist perspective suggests that interventions aimed at the batterer are more appropriate than those aimed at changing the battered woman. Research indicating that the woman remains at risk for violence and homicide even after terminating the relationship and physically relocating suggests the need to intervene legally and/or therapeutically with the batterer. Other evidence for the importance of effective intervention with the batterer is the finding that violence developed in a first marriage is maintained in subsequent relationships (Kalmuss & Seltzer, 1986).

Treatments for batterers have been developed. Many of the treatment approaches reported in the literature stress the need for the therapist to challenge the abuser's rationalizations and excuses. In addition, most treatment groups attempt to identify and confront ingrained beliefs, such as general attitudes toward women, beliefs about power in intimate relationships, and beliefs about patriarchy.

Individuals working with batterers need to be aware of the potential for substance abuse. Similarly, those individuals working within drug treatment programs need to be able to identify and treat batterers.

Several recent studies have reported successful programs; nonviolence has been reported for 64-85% of men in some programs (Dutton, 1987; Edleson, Syers, & Brygger, 1987; Saunders & Hanusa, 1984). One hazard of male treatment is that if men remain at risk for violence despite treatment, their partners may be imperiled by their false belief that their abusers have been cured (Sonkin, 1986). It is imperative that the facilitators of treatment programs for male abusers make it clear to the batterers and their partners that the risk of violence still exists, provide resources for safety and support for the female partner, and remain in contact with the women victims as a means of knowing if the violence has truly ended.

Conclusion

This review suggests that the research process and the questions researchers ask are strongly influenced by societal assumptions, by the accessibility and accuracy of respondents, by priorities of funding sources, and by personal biases and perspectives. Only a small portion of the research has investigated questions that battered women themselves might ask. Further, much of the research has not been particularly helpful for designing effective interventions.

The research on battered women has not been particularly feminist. Feminist research examines women's experiences from the perspective of the women themselves. The questions and the responses of women are central to the feminist research endeavor. The feminist researcher advocates for women rather than blames them. Feminist research is used to improve the conditions and status of women.

Assumptions about women and gender roles have kept us from "seeing" some women who are battered by their intimates. The "discovery" of dating violence, postmarital violence, and lesbian battering exposes our underlying ideologies and also reiterates the prevalence of battering in close relationships. Despite overwhelming evidence of the widespread nature of woman battering, few researchers have adopted a structural or cultural perspective. Little cross-cultural research has been conducted. Although woman battering has been documented as common across age, class, race, occupation, and now marital status and sexual orientation groups, many clinicians continue to remain oblivious to its prevalence. Clinicians may be treating women victims for the psychological consequences of their beatings without knowing that they are abused. Such treatment appears to be misdirected.

Intervention efforts also continue to be focused on the individual or dyad level. Increasingly, however, interventions are being focused on the male abuser. The outcome of interest in terms of interventions had previously been the battered woman's departure from the domicile, but this focus is now being questioned, because research indicates that the batterer continues his assaults on the same woman or other women after termination of the relationship and the woman's physical relocation. More recent research has focused on the question of whether intervention aimed at the male actually leads to a termination of the violence.

Feminists have challenged researchers to consider seriously the experiences, perspectives, and questions of the battered woman (Kelly, 1988; Yllö & Bograd, 1988). A feminist approach might begin with the description of the experiences of individual women, taking their concerns about their safety and their ability to feed their children seriously (e.g., the study by Kelly, 1988). The feminist perspective encourages us to make visible the experiences of invisible victims such as battered lesbians. Researchers should also focus on questions directed toward the development of effective interventions, including programs for batterers, societal-level transformations, and the evaluation of current interventions, including shelters.

6

Feminism and Family Therapy: A Review of Feminist Critiques of Approaches to Family Violence

MARSALI HANSEN

Many feminist therapists maintain that the field of family therapy is insensitive to women's issues and is sexist in its approach to women in the family (Avis, 1988). These challenges have been launched by specialists in family therapy (Goldner, 1985a, 1985b; James & McIntyre, 1989; Pressman, 1989; Wheeler, 1985) and in the psychology of women (Bograd, 1984; Hare-Mustin, 1978; Yllö, 1988). Feminists argue that family therapy's conceptualization of family functioning and of female development within the family is restrictive and insensitive to the needs of women. Particular criticism has been aimed at family therapy's ignoring, and thereby denying, the significance of the historical, cultural, and social contexts in which families function (James & McIntyre, 1983).

Specific concern focuses on times when societal values have direct impact on the functioning of the family and addressing the greater social problem becomes a primary responsibility of the therapist in order to ensure the safety of members of the family (Margolin, 1982; Willbach, 1989). These times include, but are not limited to, instances of wife abuse, child abuse, and incest. Critics argue that the social and political reality in which the family functions has a direct impact on the process within the family itself and on the approaches available to any therapist attempting to intervene with the family (Wendorf & Wendorf, 1985). For example, legal and ethical considerations would compel the professional to attend to the physical safety of the client as a prerequisite of providing adequate treatment (Sonkin & Ellison, 1986). Thus providing adequate treatment requires attention to the parameters in which the client functions, especially the social, cultural, and political context of the family, which may dictate the physical safety of the client (Margolin, 1982; Wendorf & Wendorf, 1985; Willbach, 1989).

Feminist Theory and Family Therapy

Feminists within the field of family therapy are challenging the field to address the issue of gender more appropriately. Major criticism centers on the failure of family systems theorists to include the importance of gender roles and the development of gender identity in the formulation of family functioning. Critics argue that family theorists have struggled to avoid linear, causal interaction patterns in their depictions of families and have instead presented relationships in the family system neutrally, without addressing the differences in the experiences of men and women. The position of neutrality would be difficult to maintain if issues of gender were addressed directly (Willbach, 1989). Exploring differences commonly experienced by the sexes would clearly highlight the lack of equality experienced by women. Feminist theorists argue, therefore, that the experience dictated by gender is central to individual identity development and cannot be separated from individual functioning or from the individual's functioning within the family (Goldner, 1985b; Pressman, 1989). Second, gender-specific roles are central to the functioning of society, and roles within the family cannot be separated from the social, political, and cultural context systems in which the family functions (Goldner, 1985a; Hare-Mustin, 1978; James & McIntyre, 1983). Thus family systems theorists, in their efforts to avoid linear causality within the family, have failed to attend to the impact of the greater social system on the family (Bograd, 1984; Goldner, 1985a; Pressman, 1989). These two premises are at the center of the controversy raging between feminist and more traditional family therapists (Dell, 1989; Taggart, 1985).

HISTORICAL CONTEXT

Feminist family therapists generally agree with the mainstream of feminist psychotherapy about the interrelationship and direction of the relationship between feminism and therapy. Feminist therapists have maintained that psychotherapy is based on a history of gender insensitivity (Marecek & Hare-Mustin, 1991). Approaches to psychotherapy have operated within the cultural context and subsequently have incorporated gender biases of the times (Weiner & Boss, 1985). Feminist critics argue that most psychodynamically oriented psychotherapy (Freud and beyond) is based on the primacy of the relationship of the child to his mother (*sic*). Subsequently, the relationship with the mother is blamed for impairing the foundation of the child's later emotional development (Caplan & Hall-McCorquodale, 1985). Fathers were mentioned as approaches to therapy expanded, but the major criticism addressing the father's behavior was his absence, rather than his interactions with the child. The implicit assumption was that if the father had been present, the mother's involvement would have been diminished and the father could have provided an adequate role model and appropriate influence for his son. Feminist critics argue that such a position only highlights the low status assigned to the role of women in the household. Such a position also diminishes the power assigned to the role by placing father in the position of mother's supervisor and supporting the assumption that the father could be a better mother than the mother, if only he had the time and inclination (Hare-Mustin, 1978).

Family therapy elaborated and renamed these earlier formulations within this historical context of psychodynamic theory. Mothers continued to be viewed as the primary caregivers and as responsible for the emotional tone of the family. Fathers were recognized as the executives of the family, responsible for providing the "appropriate amount of detachment." The earliest family therapy theorists focused upon concerns about the involvement of mothers with their children. These concerns included the belief that mothers' interaction patterns with their children resulted in childhood schizophrenia (Fromm-Reichman, 1948), psychosomatic illnesses, and many other disastrous outcomes (Caplan & Hall-McCorquodale, 1985).

Among the first theorists of family therapy, Bateson and his colleagues at MRI suggested it was the family's (primarily the mother's) communication patterns that resulted in the development of the schizophrenic symptoms (Bateson, 1972). The conceptualization of an individual experiencing the bombardment of dysfunctional communication is most often characterized by the mother commanding her child to respond when no correct response is possible (Nichols & Schwartz, 1991). Though the early works in this area are under heavy criticism (Jacob, 1975), research continues to examine the maintenance of schizophrenic symptoms through family communication patterns, with the primary focus being mother-child interaction (Mintz, Mintz, & Goldstein, 1987; Roff & Knight, 1981).

Another early family theoretician, Murray Bowen, examined the process of individual differentiation from one's family of origin. Bowen's (1978) theory recognized the ideal individual as detached and objective and the more pathological individual as emotionally reactive to the affect of others. Mothers were consistently identified as having the primary emotional relationship with the child and thus having the primary responsibility for the success of the differentiation process. In addition, the opportunities for separation and identity development outside the primary relationship were clearly greater for male children. Though these opportunities were never specified as "male opportunities," women who sought them were suggested to have other problems, such as role confusion (Bowen, 1966).

Feminist theorists have struggled with the sexist implications of Bowen's early work (Riche, 1984). Some feminist family therapists attempted to restate and rephrase many characteristics of his writing in their efforts to generate a theory that addresses the current social/political focus on the differentiation of self and empowerment among women (Lerner, 1985b; Riche, 1984).

More recently, structural theorists have also failed to challenge the historical roles of women in the family (Minuchin & Fishman, 1981). Rather than reformulate gender-specific roles, they have made efforts to define and perfect the execution of the traditional roles of the family. Fathers are encouraged to be more involved, often to supervise and direct the responsibilities of their wives. The mother's deficiencies and overinvolvement with her children are blamed on the lack of involvement of her spouse ("If he'd been watching, she never would have screwed up") and her own natural inclination (perhaps even genetic predisposition) to nurture her children (Goldner, 1985a).

Feminist theorists espouse the philosophy of feminist therapists and state that these early schools of family therapy developed within the zeitgeist of a time when the mother's role was clearly in the home and with her children (Goldner, 1985a). This zeitgeist, both social and theoretical, dramatically influenced the formulation of theories of family functioning and the interventions that followed.

ROLE OF SOCIETAL CONTEXT

Feminist family therapists argue that subsequent theories of family therapy have been influenced by popular political and cultural orientations as well (James & McIntyre, 1983). In addition, the political orientation of the times influences not only the formulation of the theory but what the therapist is actually capable of seeing when viewing a client (Willbach, 1989). Feminist scholars contend that the "context-free, gender-free" orientation of many current approaches to family therapy promotes inequality among the sexes. Feminist critics argue that there is social, political, and economic inequality between the sexes (Hare-Mustin, 1978), and that this inequality includes (but is not limited to) unequal opportunity for credentials and experience in the workplace, difference in treatment by legal systems, and physical differences in strength, power, and status within and outside the home. In failing to acknowledge these legitimate and documentable differences, and instead focusing on the interchange between family members as if the sexes entered the exchange with equal status, the family therapist is in fact colluding with male clients and promoting their advantages (Taggart, 1985). Noncontextual theorists are therefore abdicating a responsibility to recognize their own political and cultural orientations. By presenting their theories as "culture free," they are, in fact, promoting the status quo—a status quo that heavily favors the majority male culture.

Feminist theorists, feminist family therapists among them, recognize the power and status differentials between the sexes (Bograd, 1984; Goldner, 1985a; Hare-Mustin, 1978; James & McIntyre, 1983; Pressman, 1989). Within this context they promote equality of opportunity and gender-free roles. They recognize that women who work outside the home have, in relation to men, lower-paying jobs, fewer opportunities for advancement, lower status in the workplace, and less access to experience and credentials that would improve the work experience (Hare-Mustin, 1978; Weiner & Boss, 1985). They also acknowledge that, within the home, the roles traditionally assigned to women (e.g., housekeeping and child care) have lower status and less influence (e.g., day-to-day decision making as opposed to making the "major decisions" within the home) (Goldner, 1985a). Men, who are the beneficiaries of the power differential, have the responsibility for assigning any new roles and the status associated with the roles (Goldner, 1985a). Thus powerful roles are perpetuated. Current economic trends are resulting in more women in the work force—in low-paying, low-status jobs—and in the decline of the status of the roles associated with the care of the home (Gillespie, 1971; Goldner, 1985a; Hare-Mustin, 1978). Feminist authors have also raised specific questions regarding the distribution of responsibilities in the home (Wheeler, 1985). Family therapists who promote the involvement of the father in the home are believed to promote inadvertently the reduction of the parameters of the one powerful role women in the home maintain.

ROLE OF GENDER DEVELOPMENT

Feminist family therapists have stressed the importance of the conceptualization of gender role development; gender dictates experience (Goldner, 1985b). Research documents the importance of gender identity at the very earliest stages of development (Maccoby, 1990) and the invariance of the experience. Research clearly indicates that children are the sex they are raised as, regardless of their physiology (Money & Ehrhardt, 1972). Developmental psychologists have long documented the differential treatment of sons and daughters by both mothers and fathers (Maccoby & Jacklin, 1974). Sons receive more positive verbal feedback from their mothers. Girls play more cooperatively with peers at a very early age and have a communication style that emphasizes collaboration and agreement, whereas boys are more hierarchical in their relationships with peers. Boys as young as 33 months old will dominate the interaction when playing in mixed-sex groups (Maccoby, 1990). Feminist family therapists stress the importance of these early gender-based experiences in later interaction patterns between the sexes and subsequent interactions between couples (Goldner, 1985b; Weiner & Boss, 1985). The literature supports the continuation of gender patterns into adulthood (Maccoby, 1990), and developmental differences are likely to play a major role in family interaction patterns (Goldner, 1985b).

Feminist family therapists challenge the more traditional approaches to family therapy to address the developmental gender differences in their conceptualizations and treatments of families (Goldner, 1985b; Weiner & Boss, 1985). By not addressing gender differences, family therapists are likely to continue to assume that developmental patterns for the sexes are the same, and thereby to deny the reality and the experiences of the female members of the families they treat. Feminist theorists maintain that a therapist who does not address these differences will utilize a male model of experience (Wheeler, 1985).

ROLE OF THE THERAPIST

A primary principle of feminist therapy addresses the role of the therapist in the experience. Feminist psychotherapists maintain that the subjective experience of the therapist is an important component of the therapeutic process, both in assessment and in intervention (Willbach, 1989). Self-disclosure on the part of the therapist is therefore encouraged rather than discouraged. Feminist therapists encourage clients to participate in establishing treatment goals. Such therapists make major efforts to avoid placing clients in the one-down position traditionally employed in therapy. The feminist approach recommends that the therapist articulate her own values clearly to the client and present herself as a female role model to her female clients. The goal of the approach is to counteract the impact of the negative social sanctions that women clients have experienced by addressing these directly (Pressman, 1989; Wheeler, 1985).

ROLE OF LANGUAGE

Feminist therapists have long stressed the importance of recognizing gender-biased language. From the choice of pronouns to the descriptions given to battering (the use of active or passive verb tenses), language can create experience (Lamb, 1991). Feminist family therapists recognize this position and stress the importance of the therapist's attention to these details in conceptualization and treatment of families (Bograd, 1984; Lamb, 1991). The therapist who identifies the mother's sensitivity to her children's feelings as "enmeshment" and perceives the "detached, individuated, individual" as ideal is likely to view the family differently and to have different goals for therapy than the therapist who pursues a communication style that focuses on commonality rather than exchange bargaining, and thereby is more consistent with the styles of women and men in well-functioning couples (Maccoby, 1990). In addition, the words the therapist uses with the family will reinforce alliances with the participants and may seek to confirm or deny their personal experiences (Bograd, 1984). Feminists maintain that there is no "gender-free" mode of communication or choice of words, and that to be gender free is to support the dominant culture's view of reality.

SUMMARY

Feminist therapists have been challenged for making a nonpolitical practice of therapy political and for functionally forcing their own polemics on innocent families (Flemons, 1989). Feminist family therapists have responded to these criticisms with the position that all acts are political (James & McIntyre, 1989). So-called nonpolitical action by therapists functionally reinforces the reality of the dominant male culture and denies any alternatives to women. The goal of feminist therapy is to increase the opportunities and choices available to women. In family therapy, this goal is translated into an increase in opportunities for roles, status, and power within and outside the home. The traditional family within the historical, cultural, and political context is not believed to be supportive of women's mental health. Research indicates a greater proportion of married, widowed, and divorced women than single women among the seriously mentally ill (Mowbray, Herman, & Hazel, 1992). Perhaps a therapist who continues to perpetuate this traditional family model without presenting alternatives to the client may be believed to be jeopardizing the well-being of the women in the family (Goldner, 1985b). Therapists who strive for "context-free, nonsexist, non-gender-based" approaches to family therapy may in fact deny the members of the family the opportunity to address very real issues of gender bias and discrimination. The nonpolitical, therefore, is political. Exploring the political context opens the door for alternative experiences, validates the reality experienced by the clients, and promotes the mental health of the female participants in the therapeutic process. Current feminist approaches to male clients indicate that men, too, benefit from this expanded experience (Brooks, 1990; Dienhart & Avis, 1990; Ganley, 1990).

Feminist Critique of Traditional Family Therapy Approaches to Battering

Feminist psychologists and feminist family therapists also criticize family systems approaches to battering (Pressman, Cameron, & Rothery, 1989; Yllö & Bograd, 1988). The emphases of theorists, often psychologists, and therapists differ slightly: Feminist psychologists focus on the issue of battering itself, with the primary focus on stopping the abuse (for additional references on this topic, see McHugh, Chapter 5, this volume), whereas feminist family therapists question the dysfunctional nature of the family and couple, and see the abuse as a symptom of the greater need to improve the status of the woman in the abusive relationship (Goldner, Penn, Sheinberg, & Walker, 1990). Both feminist psychologists and feminist family therapists express concern about the dangers inherent in current family therapy conceptualizations of battering (Bograd, 1988a; Goldner, 1992; Hare-Mustin, 1978; Pressman, 1989). These conceptualizations include formulations that result in therapists blaming the victim, perceiving "coresponsibility" for the battering, and failing to recognize any responsibility for the battering.

VICTIM BLAME

Victim blame is a major concern of both feminist psychologists and feminist family therapists. Extensive research has focused on the characteristics of the victims in abusive relationships (see Harway, Chapter 3, this volume). These women have been characterized as dependent, immature, clinging, hysterical, and masochistic. Many authors have elaborated on the characteristics of participants in abusive relationships and have identified personality variables of the victims that further support the conceptualization of battering as a response provoked by the victim. The victim is, thus, directly or indirectly, blamed for her own abuse. The effort to diagnose this behavior of battered women has led to efforts to include a diagnostic category of sadistic personality disorder and self-defeating personality disorder (Kass, Spitzer, Williams, & Widiger, 1989). Outcry from the professional community was sufficient to prevent the inclusion of this diagnosis in DSM-III-R. However, practicing therapists, including family therapists, do appear to diagnose battering victims on the basis of preexisting psychological characteristics (see Harway, Chapter 3, and Harway & Hansen, Chapter 4, this volume) and to develop their interventions based on these conceptualizations (Hansen, Harway, & Cervantes, 1991; Weitzman & Dreen, 1982). The resulting interventions implicitly blame the victim, as they are based on the assumption that the victim's own dynamics contributed to the events (Bograd, 1984). Women who experience this process in therapy are likely to continue to regard themselves as responsible for the battering. As this perception most often results in the couple entering therapy (Goodstein & Page, 1981), change in the pattern of interaction is unlikely.

CORESPONSIBILITY

Feminist family therapists and feminist psychologists challenge the conceptualization of "coresponsibility" for battering (Bograd, 1984; Pressman, 1989). Family systems theorists often maintain a commitment to the conceptualization of circularity, reciprocal interactions, and nonlinear causality within the system (Magill, 1989). Such theorists have failed to address the behavior of the batterer, instead focusing on the sequence of the interaction. Feminist theorists maintain that the concept of coresponsibility is, in fact, a more subtle version of victim blame (Bograd, 1984; Goldner et al., 1990). Even seeing the couple together in therapy can be challenged as implying that the wife has some responsibility for her husband's abusive actions. The question is raised, If wife battering were perceived as the husband's individual problem (e.g., loss of control of aggression toward others), would the wife be involved in treatment, especially if it were court ordered, or would a nonspouse victim of his aggression go to even the initial treatment setting with him? However, in cases of spouse abuse many therapists initially, and/or throughout treatment, involve the wife in the therapeutic process (Cook & Frantz-Cook, 1984; Goldner, 1992).

A difficulty facing abused wives is getting their spouses into treatment, because most batterers are reluctant to come and do not perceive themselves as having a problem (see Gondolf, Chapter 9, this volume). The wives, however, often believe, at some level, that they themselves may be contributing to the abuse, and are likely to be far more receptive to treatment (Walker, 1991). The therapist, therefore, is likely to find out more about the wife's "contribution" from both of the partners than about the actual seriousness of the battering and the behavior of the batterer.

Feminist therapists have identified the potential harm to individuals that can result from beginning couples therapy and the collateral treatment of coresponsibility. First, diagnostically, the therapist is not likely to obtain a clear picture of the severity and extent of the abuse when the couple is seen together (Cook & Frantz-Cook, 1984). Research shows that abusers are likely to minimize the extent of the aggression and wives are likely to collude with this presentation of events (Goodstein & Page, 1981; Rosenbaum & O'Leary, 1981). Both fear of subsequent abuse and embarrassment add to the obscurity of the presentation to the therapist. For example, the wife may think, "If the therapist really knew how bad it was he'd wonder what I'm still doing here, or focus on my leaving, which I'm not sure I want to do." In addition, the wife may believe the therapist would support her spouse regardless of how much the therapist knew, especially if the therapist is a male (Bograd, 1984; Cook & Frantz-Cook, 1984; Goodstein & Page, 1981).

A third problem arises with the presentation itself. The wife is likely to be more receptive to treatment and the natural inclination of the therapist is to begin work where the system is most flexible. By focusing on the wife, the therapist functionally colludes with the husband in focusing on his spouse's contribution to the couple's problems, thus reinforcing the position that the husband is not solely responsible for his aggressive action. The wife's role of assuming responsibility for the violence yet having no control of the aggression is further perpetuated, now not only by the spouse but by the therapist as well. Coresponsibility has functionally become victim blame, and the system has no need to change.

NO RESPONSIBILITY

Family therapy has also been challenged as advocating "no responsibility," that is, neutrality, when not advocating coresponsibility (Bograd, 1984; Willbach, 1989). Feminists argue that the concept of no responsibility is similar to denying the contextual reality and power differential present in all families (Bograd, 1984). Minuchin (1984) states, "Focusing on the male as monster makes people experience their individual separation, and perpetuates defensive aggression. *The goal should be to explore and improve people's interdependence*" (p. 175). His position has resulted in outrage from members of the feminist community who maintain that no responsibility implies coresponsibility and ultimately, directly or indirectly, results in victim blame.

Other family therapists who have not been so blatant in their presentation of victim blame continue to be challenged for ignoring the social and political context that sustains family violence (Taggart, 1985). The avoidance of reference to social and political factors perpetuates the presentation of no responsibility for the violence. Status and power are real constructs that affect interpersonal interaction within the family (Gelles, 1980; Gelles & Straus, 1989). The literature on battering clearly identifies the impact and interaction of these constructs in abusive relationships (Gelles & Straus, 1989; Teichman & Teichman, 1989). Men who have lower-paying jobs than their wives are more likely to be abusive (Hornung, McCullough, & Sugimoto, 1981). Physical differences in strength exist between men and women, and the concept of a fair physical fight among equals is an impossibility in a marriage (Gillespie, 1989), yet the physical dominance of men makes the physical fight a possible option for them in their efforts to modify the status difference.

Cultural and social sanctions affect the existence of wife abuse (Mugford, Mugford, & Easteal, 1989). Society's responses to woman battering have ranged from seeing it as justifiable (a man has a right to beat his wife) to seeing it as a privacy issue (what occurs between a husband and wife is a private matter) to blaming the victim (e.g., "the-bitch-deserves-it" defense for homicide) (Mugford et al., 1989). These social pressures functionally remove the legal consequences imposed for other forms of violence and may even provide implicit social reinforcement for violence (Mugford et al., 1989). Thus battering occurs within the larger social context, and the concept of no responsibility views the family in isolation while leaving the greater social condoning of violence toward women unchallenged (Bograd, 1984).

Family formulations and treatment plans that ignore the greater social system have been challenged as not being systemic in their approach, but instead utilizing an individual, pathological model that has been expanded to include the couple. In efforts to remain true to systemic thinking, these approaches have viewed the family in isolation from society as a whole. Therapists have examined reciprocal sequences and circular interaction patterns between the couple but failed to address the impact of external circumstances and values that might affect these behaviors. Such systemic approaches are open to the same criticism launched by the original family theorists regarding models of individual psychotherapy: The client, in this case the family, is being treated outside the social context (James & McIntyre, 1983; MacKinnon & Miller, 1987; Taggart, 1985). As the original family theorists pointed out, context, be it the individual within the family or the family within society, has a major impact. Unless therapy addresses the greater social systemic maintenance of battering behavior, that behavior is likely to continue and may become a dangerous, potentially life-threatening symptom (Willbach, 1989).

The no responsibility approach within family therapies further endangers the victim by functionally obscuring the seriousness of battering.

Theorists who conceptualize couples as experiencing problems with the "symmetry-complementarity ratio" (Weitzman & Dreen, 1982) or with "individuation, sex role polarization, and use of violence as a distance regulator" (Bograd, 1984) may direct the focus away from the violence and fail to address the need for protection. Therapists who conceptually focus on reciprocal interaction patterns, impaired relationship structures, and "repetitive sequences of dysfunctional behavior" may functionally create distance for themselves from a very difficult problem, that of stopping the behavior of a man who does not see himself as responsible for his own actions.

The therapist's own detachment allows greater comfort and serves to create the myth that the therapeutic intervention has greater potential impact on the system than it actually does. If one does not recognize the violence itself as a problem, one can believe that change will occur without one's needing to address the violence or the man's perception of responsibility. The myth of the batterer's "innocence" is further maintained by the myth of no responsibility. Thus the therapist has overcontextualized the problem as one of many problems within the marital dyad, has obscured the physical and emotional experience of the violence, and has functionally eliminated the man's responsibility for his own actions.

The question arises, Do family therapists apply the technique of "reframing" or rephrasing the problem in abusive marriages to create a problem they feel more capable of addressing? The danger in such reframing seems obvious. Both members of the couple will recognize the therapist's discomfort and attempt to present instead material that the therapist is comfortable addressing. Data indicate that most abused women have seen more than one therapist, usually only once, and that most therapists fail to address the violence (Goodstein & Page, 1981). When therapists fail to address the violence, clients are less likely to return to therapy, and instead may return to their abusive relationships.

Another concern follows from inattention to the specific content of the violence in the relationship. Most forms of therapy work best when the client perceives a problem and desires to change, or when circumstances are such that change is inevitable. As noted above, the male batterer is not likely to perceive his problem. In addition, the greatest predictors of change in family therapy involve the woman and her options. Women involved in battering relationships are likely to have few options available to them. Factors that affect the availability of alternatives for a woman include her education level, the existence of alternative housing, and restrictions in mobility imposed by the ages of her children (Silverstein & Taffel, 1991). The perception of a need for change or the circumstances that promote change are not likely to be experienced by abusive men, or by women who perceive few alternatives available to them. Therefore, change is even less likely to occur when the therapist functionally distances the problem by not addressing it directly or by reframing the symptom into nonexistence.

Summary

Family therapy has been criticized for perpetuating the victimization of women, both directly and indirectly. Therapists who attribute marital violence to the woman's prior personality style and provocative behavior engage in maintaining the perpetrator's view of the interaction and are likely to support the continuation of violence. Therapists who address the violence as a problem shared by the members of the dyad deny the perpetrator's responsibility for his own actions. Family therapists who continue to conceptualize battering within systemic, non-gender-based, context-free frameworks frequently engage in obscuring the seriousness of the acts and allow for the perpetuation of a potentially lethal reality (Dell, 1989). Feminist theorists and feminist family therapists warn of the dangers inherent in conceptualizing battering as the woman's problem, the couple's problem, or no one's problem (Bograd, 1984; Pressman, 1989). Only when we recognize that battering is "solely the responsibility of the man," that "no woman deserves to be beaten," and that the social/political context has a direct impact on the maintenance of the behavior, is the family system likely to change (Bograd, 1984; Goldner, 1985a; James & McIntyre, 1983, 1989).

7

Conjoint Therapy With Violent Couples: Some Valid Considerations

MARSALI HANSEN
IRENE GOLDENBERG

Family therapy has been widely criticized as a treatment approach for domestic violence cases (Bograd, 1984; Goldner, 1985b; Pressman, 1989; for a complete review, see Hansen, Chapter 6, this volume). Critics express particular concern that therapists inadvertently promote the wife's coresponsibility for her husband's behavior when they treat the wife and the husband together in couples therapy (Bograd, 1984). Feminist therapists focus on individual interventions that include empowering the wife and helping her to leave the dangerous situation (see Register, Chapter 8, this volume) along with the treatment of the man in a batterers' group (see Gondolf, Chapter 9, this volume).

In this chapter, we discuss the limitations of individual treatment approaches. Therapists are becoming increasingly concerned that many women remain in violent relationships in spite of therapist recommendations to leave (Goldner, 1992). Indeed, even when women leave these relationships they often return to them. In fact, therapists may increase the danger to these women when their recommendations to leave do not include specific attention to safety factors. Often, when women attempt to leave, the risk of serious harm from their spouses increases (Walker, 1981). Moreover, given that batterers rarely perceive themselves as having a "psychological problem," most batterers are not responsive to individual psychological interventions, and many batterers have chronic histories of spouse abuse (Walker, 1981). However, they may be encouraged by their wives to attend conjoint sessions. Thus a discussion of conjoint therapy is critical for a full consideration of therapeutic interventions.

Gaps appear in our understanding of abusive relationships. Research has focused on factors that predict abuse in relationships (see McHugh, Chapter 5, this volume). Evaluation research has focused on treatment programs for abusers (see Gondolf, Chapter 9, this volume) and the effectiveness of individual programs for the recipients of abuse (see Register, Chapter 8, this volume). However, little has been written on couples who successfully retain their relationships and successfully terminate the violence (Goldner, 1992). Few studies have been undertaken to examine therapeutic approaches that address the expressed needs of women to retain their relationships or therapeutic efforts that focus on recognizing the qualities of the relationships that may have attracted these women originally.

Several theorists have addressed the issue of why women remain in abusive relationships or return after brief absences. Walker (1991) presents a conceptualization that suggests women remain because of legitimate fear of reprisal if they leave. Her data, in fact, support the perception that women who leave violent relationships risk serious harm and even death. Elaboration of this theory also suggests that women in violent relationships are often caught up in the "cycle of violence" (Walker, 1991) and may be "seduced" by the promises to change made by their spouses following violent episodes. Graham, Rawlings, and Rimini (1988) propose that women experience an emotional need for nurturance and support following violent episodes and may experience the apologizing, emotionally attentive spouse as filling this need. These authors describe this phenomenon as similar to the Stockholm syndrome, which is often experienced by hostages. The victim identifies with the captor and focuses on the captor's momentary kindnesses to the exclusion of the captor's other behaviors. However, Graham et al. acknowledge the differences between hostages and battered women, especially the salient characteristic of the wife's original choice to be in the relationship. Theorists have also postulated that the woman experiences the development of learned helplessness and becomes so depressed she cannot foresee an alternative to her current circumstances (Walker, 1984a).

Further research, however, has attempted to understand the women in battering relationships, particularly those women who remain (for greater detail, see Harway, Chapter 3, this volume). The literature indicates that battered women often do utilize social services, and that more seriously abused women are likely to utilize these services to a greater extent than are less seriously abused women (Walker, 1979). In addition, studies indicate that battered women's responses on standardized measures of intellectual performance are more similar to individuals who have experienced trauma than to individuals who are experiencing depression (Ferrant, 1992). Further elaboration on the conceptualization of battering victims as trauma victims suggests, as Seagull and Seagull (1991) put it, that these women "may believe they have no right to be angry or upset unless they continue to suffer" (p. 16). These authors suggest that the women may perceive a need to remain in their relationships to document and provide a living testament of their horrendous experience. Seagull and Seagull label this experience "accusatory suffering," and they point out that this need to keep an open wound may seriously jeopardize treatment unless it is addressed by the therapist. Other researchers have proposed that women in violent relationships come from homes where violence was experienced and may have a view of violence as an unavoidable, expected occurrence (Hanks & Rosenbaum, 1977; Hotaling & Sugarman, 1986). However, pertinent literature suggests that women in abusive relationships have a wide range of family experiences, and the family of origin hypothesis for victims has yet to be supported (Harway, Chapter 3, this volume; Pagelow, 1981a). Therapists currently struggle with the problem of women who may not want to leave their violent spouses (Goldner, 1992; Goldner, Penn, Sheinberg, & Walker, 1990).

Certainly each of the hypotheses suggested here is true for some women, but none explains the entire population. Several authors have diagrammed alternatives to the belief that all couples who are violent should be separated (Rosenbaum & O'Leary, 1986; Saunders, 1977). These diagrams have provided therapists with decision trees to direct clients toward appropriate treatment. If the couple responds affirmatively to questions such as, "Are guns in the home?" or negatively to questions such as, "Is the wife safe?" the therapist intervenes to protect the safety of the wife. If the abuser answers yes to specific questions about his behavior, the therapist is directed to intervene at a behavioral level. If the couple responds affirmatively to questions regarding wishes to remain together, this leads toward structured couples counseling. Walker (1991) also strongly advocates the evaluation of conditions in the home, including an assessment of the potential for severe violence, weapons in the home, and so on, although she provides a less detailed map for therapists to follow.

We concur with the belief that violence occurs in a wide variety of couples (varying by age, ethnicity, education level, marital status, sexual orientation, and other presenting problems, such as alcohol abuse). Within this perspective, a variety of approaches to treatment are worthy of consideration, including conjoint therapy, individual therapy, and group intervention. However, as with all therapy, the question of safety must be addressed first. If the therapist cannot feel confident of the safety of the client, or fears for her own safety, alternative interventions must be considered (whether safety issues concern suicide, homicide, or battering). Not all individuals are likely to respond to couples therapy. When psychosis or major personality disorders are evident, couples therapy alone is less likely to be effective, regardless of the presence of violence in the relationship. However, the frequency of battering in relationships (28-33%; Koss, 1990) would suggest that male batterers are not *all,* necessarily, psychotic or character disordered, because the frequency of abuse in relationships is much greater than the documented occurrence of these forms of psychopathology. Couples free of psychosis or major personality disorders may present relationships likely to be receptive to conjoint intervention.

Feminists have criticized family therapists for blaming the victim through focus on the couple. Family therapists respond with the concept that "blame" has no place in therapy, be it of the recipient or of the perpetrator of the violence. The purpose of therapy is to change the transaction in the relationship, not to affix blame to one person or another. Research shows that helping the perpetrator to develop insight into responsibility for the violence fails to reduce the violence or to modify his behavior (see Gondolf, Chapter 9, this volume), and, in fact, attributing blame for the violence to the perpetrator may perpetuate the woman's perception of her own ineffectiveness and victimization. Assigning blame (real guilt) to one or another or both individuals fails to focus on the issue of both people having inadequate skills to solve the original problem.

We present below some suggestions for the appropriate use of conjoint therapy. We have made an effort to clarify conditions and goals for the effective application of this modality. Conjoint therapy using systemic approaches may be pursued with some couples while addressing the concerns expressed by feminist family therapists. Change is possible while still retaining the integrity of the couple and family therapy as the therapeutic modality *when the couples are not currently engaged in a violent transaction.* However, attention to characteristics of the social context and the safety of the clients is critical. Change in the couple's relationship through the use of this modality might be most effective, as multiple characteristics of the relationship and the interrelated needs of the individuals in the relationship are addressed as they occur.

Other authors have noted that the frequency of violence in couples indicates an immediate need for marriage and family therapists to develop a clear approach (Cook & Frantz-Cook, 1984; Hansen, Harway, & Cervantes, 1991). (For a more in-depth critique of family therapy approaches, see Hansen, Chapter 6, this volume.) Models have been proposed that address battering within couples therapy. For example, Cook and Frantz-Cook (1984) propose an approach to couples that incorporates many systemic concepts. They specifically address the need for protection and cessation of the violence prior to involving the couple in treatment and provide therapists with a specific treatment plan for addressing and establishing safety. The remainder of their treatment focuses upon "systemic formulations" of family characteristics that could sabotage the goal of stopping the violence. Indeed, cessation of the violence appears to be the major objective. Moreover, there is an implicit assumption that if the violence were to cease, the relationship would be fine. Within this conceptualization, the legitimate needs of the couple are formulated only in relationship to the aberrant behavior. However, unless other legitimate problems evident in the relationship are addressed in therapy, some form of nonsupportive interaction between members of the couple will continue. Cook and Frantz-Cook describe the violence as the major focus of the treatment process, and their approach to violence is a direct one that addresses the husband's responsibility for his behavior. They appear less clear in their examination of other components of the relationship that may result in increased tolerance of this deviant behavior, such as reasons the wife may give for staying in the relationship. In addition, although they recommend the violence be addressed directly in the initial phase of treatment, their subsequent recommendations may be difficult for therapists to implement, because the range of interpretations possible from their conceptualizations is so great it is not clear from their descriptions what interventions need to be made (for further elaboration, see Hansen, Chapter 6, this volume).

Weitzman and Dreen (1982) have proposed another systemic view of wife abuse. Their approach conceptualizes wife abuse as largely a couple's problem and "blame" appears to be affixed to the marital dyad rather than to any one individual. Although the violence is addressed in this approach, the approach can been criticized as implying coresponsibility for the violence (see Hansen, Chapter 6, this volume) and thus as implying some pathological functioning on the part of the victim. Weitzman and Dreen's approach does require the assessment of the "couple's overall psychosocial functioning, particularly whether they demonstrate sufficient self control as to preclude further violence" (p. 265) before proceeding with the conjoint intervention. Other systemic formulations of the violence include the perceptions that violence is a battle for control that involves a shift from a complementary to a symmetrical relationship, and that violent couples struggle with themes of distance versus intimacy, jealousy versus loyalty, dependence versus independence, rejection versus unconditional acceptance, adequacy versus inadequacy, and power versus powerlessness. Violent couples are believed to maintain more rigid rules than do nonviolent couples and to utilize violence as a means to reduce the stress in the relationship. Violence is recognized as a learned response, but it is believed to be learned by both members of the couple. As we have noted, this approach has received wide-ranging criticism from feminist family therapists (Hansen, Chapter 6, this volume).

Violence is regarded as dangerous and often within the control of the individual. Violence is also regarded as regulated, both condoned and admonished, by the larger social context in which it occurs. From our perspective, neither the perpetrator nor the recipient of the violence is regarded as a "hopeless victim," but as an active individual; she can develop the ability to protect herself, he has the ability to prevent his own destructive behavior. Most important, the couple's relationship is believed to be characterized by more than just the violence, and these additional characteristics are important focuses of treatment. As with the treatment of a family when alcohol abuse is present, the abuse must be stopped. Only after the abuse stops can the characteristics of the relationship be examined. However, an important focus of treatment begins when the violence has stopped, one that is often ignored by feminist therapists. Therapists must examine naive assumptions that all abusive relationships automatically must end in separation, and that when the abuse stops the therapy has been successful and termination of treatment is imminent. Instead, termination of violence is the beginning of a critical phase in the therapeutic process. In the section that follows, we describe the rationale for working with violent couples in conjoint therapy.

Purpose of Conjoint Therapy

After the violence has stopped, interventions are focused on helping the abuser recognize that he has some control, and power over, his own actions while at the same time *empowering both members of the couple.* The woman may experience impaired self-esteem and a chronic view of herself as a victim because of her experience of long-term battering (Walker, 1981). In the empowerment process, the initial phase can focus on removing the role of victim from the repertoire of the woman. Violence in relationships maintains the double bind of the woman being seen by the batterer as having the "power to provoke the violence," but not as having the power to stop it. Empowerment and the beginning of healing can result from helping battered women to choose to leave or to remain in the relationship *when the threat of violence has been removed* (Magill, 1989).

Working with couples conjointly also serves to empower the therapist. Separating a couple for the purpose of treating the battering behavior often projects the implicit message that the batterer is stronger than the therapist or that the therapist is afraid of the batterer. Such an intervention may suggest that the therapist cannot prevent the batterer from acting in a threatening manner and cannot effectively protect the client. When the therapist is also female, the message to both the batterer and the spouse is magnified. The style of provoking violence and yet being unable to prevent it may be perceived by both members of the couple as characteristic of the woman and may subsequently be generalized to all women. This phenomenon further compounds the perception of the batterer that women are responsible for his behavior and the perception of the spouse that women are victims and powerless.

At some point in the therapeutic process, the recipient of spouse abuse needs to regain some sense of her own power and to acquire the skills of self-protection. What better place to acquire these skills than in the relationship that provoked her sense of victimization? In addition, the wife needs to learn to recognize potentially dangerous situations and to take appropriate measures. Many women who leave abusive relationships have lost the skills to assess interpersonal interactions accurately (Walker, 1989a). The ability to recognize the precipitant of violence without accepting responsibility for the actions is a critical skill, and the therapist can help in this process of acquisition. The therapist can effectively teach this skill by highlighting cues for both members of the couple and then acting to prevent the sequence of violence from being carried out, if necessary. The therapist attends to the angry communication of the woman, which, by virtue of her experience, may be distorted and indirect. The therapist validates the woman's anger, clarifies her communication, and insists that the man respond *verbally.* The therapist works to clarify the communication of the man as well, while validating any sensitivity and gentleness in his response. The evasive quality of communication must be addressed early through the therapist's observation of the transaction, before too much rage becomes a part of the couple's communication breakdown.

Goals of Treatment

The primary goal of conjoint therapy with couples when violence is present is to eliminate the violence and retain the qualities of the relationship that brought the couple together *if they were together for adaptive reasons.* Alternatively, a goal may be to help the couple recognize the maladaptive reasons that brought them together and help them to separate comfortably. As noted, the couple are likely to sabotage any intervention if the therapist focuses entirely on the problematic components rather than on the positive qualities recognized by the couple. Specifically, the members of the couple may question the accuracy of all the therapist's observations if the positive qualities in both the husband and wife are not recognized along with the negative qualities.

An accurate assessment by the therapist is critical. Clients who are psychotic or experiencing other forms of serious psychopathology such as schizophrenia should be exempted from this therapeutic approach. In addition, therapy should be terminated when drug or alcohol abuse is ongoing in either spouse, and should resume only when abstinence has been attained.

If there is a real threat of violence in the session, *in any therapy situation,* the therapist must terminate therapy or the session. Therapy works only when people can talk and act out their feelings in a reasonably controlled way. Therapists are responsible for the assessment of the potential for people to work with each other and for keeping the tension at a level where people can continue to work.

A second goal of this type of therapy is to reduce the "flood" of emotion in the relationship. With violent couples both parties are likely to be overwhelmed by their emotional experiences; the abuser is likely to be overwhelmed by his own rage and the victim is likely to be overwhelmed by her fear. The couple's accurate perceptions of emotions and interactions are likely to be impaired unless the overwhelming emotional climate can be reduced. A therapist can decrease the intensity of the emotional interaction and increase the accuracy of the perceptions of the participants. The therapist should begin sessions by addressing the successes the couple has experienced and their moments of successful communication. Setting the stage for success and taking control of the session from the beginning will help the therapist. The counselor must establish clear ground rules for communication before the session moves toward focusing on areas of conflict. It is important that the therapist recognize that intensity and the expression of intense affect are not necessarily good. It is up to the therapist to prevent the session from being swamped by the expression of anger and hostility (Bagarozzi & Giddings, 1983). If the intensity becomes too great, the therapist should refocus the session by changing the subject to a more constructive, less affectively flooded topic. However, he or she must take care to continue to address the areas of conflict and to avoid minimizing the feelings of the participants.

A skilled therapist is able to regulate the tension in a room by using techniques that are part of the family therapy armamentarium. For instance, the therapist may (a) change the subject, (b) ask the clients to speak to the therapist and not to each other, or (c) reframe the client's stated wants in a less inflammatory way. An inexperienced therapist might allow "old fights," "sore issues," and "recycled conflicts" to reemerge in the therapy setting without some specific purpose. Likewise, the inexperienced therapist might perceive that something good is automatically occurring if people are expressing their feelings (no matter how ragefully or how unsuccessfully). Such venting is counterproductive with couples who have violent histories (Bagarozzi & Giddings, 1983).

The batterer is likely to need the help of the therapist to increase his sense of responsibility for both what he says and what he does (Walker, 1981). A goal of therapy, therefore, is for the therapist to intervene as the couple communicates in the therapeutic session. The therapist can help the battered woman accurately identify precursors to emotional outbursts from the batterer. This intervention can be done without the therapist deflecting the responsibility for the outbursts and without heightening the emotion in the room. Intervention can be much more effective when the specifics of the communication patterns are observed and addressed as they occur between the couple rather than as described by either the batterer or the victim.

A third goal of treatment is to increase the perception of choices for both clients. The husband needs to increase his perception of alternatives to abusive behavior and the wife needs to increase her perception of alternatives to participating in the abusive sequence as well as her perception of alternatives to the roles of provocateur and helpless victim.

A fourth goal of therapy is to provide corrective emotional experiences. A powerful positive, corrective emotional experience is very different from an emotionally explosive one. Exposing the tender, frightened, and powerless feelings behind the rage, whether it is of a battering parent or a physically abusive husband, can be an extremely powerful intervention in a conjoint session. When a woman experiences the strength in a transaction, she sees herself differently. A man experiencing himself as gentle can help to expand the range of expressions available to him.

A fifth goal of therapy is for the therapist to ally with the societal expectations and to engage that part of both clients that agrees that physical abuse is unacceptable. The therapist can initiate this process by highlighting the social, moral, and ethical constraints that underlie the therapeutic process (Margolin, 1982; Wendorf & Wendorf, 1985; Willbach, 1989; Sonkin & Ellison, 1986). For example, a therapist cannot permit someone to steal from a purse in the session any more than he or she can allow a client to be threatened by or to threaten physical violence. People can get hurt emotionally during therapy, but such trauma does not occur with the therapist's covert or overt agreement. In the unspoken contract between therapist and client are the moral issues present in society. The therapist has the responsibility to verbalize that abuse is an inadequate and inappropriate attempt to solve a real problem. Whether the abuse is physical or verbal, both people are attempting to solve the problem.

Additional issues interfering with the functioning of the relationship are likely to surface as alternative modes of communication are acquired by the couple. Physical violence and emotional abuse are likely to obscure topics that members of the couple wish to avoid. Specifically, problems such as alcoholism, unemployment, sexual dysfunction, and incest can be avoided when violence, fear, and blame dominate a relationship. Violence serves to obscure such issues and to prevent their being addressed in the relationship and in therapy. These problems need to be attended to as therapy progresses and as the couple acquire the skills to communicate.

Case Example

Mark (32) and Anna (30) have been married for six years. They have a 9-month-old son. They are recent immigrants from Canada who started a plumbing fixture business three years ago. They work together in business and share an office at the store. They presented in therapy a year and a half ago. Mark had lost his temper in "the worst fight of their relationship" and had hit Anna so hard in the face that she developed severe bruising. The couple had been involved in other fights prior to this episode, and Anna had been physically hurt on each occasion. The relationship has always been a rocky one, with conflict being an element from the beginning. There was no physical abuse for the first few years, but there was some intense verbal abuse. Mark discloses prior abusive relationships during an individual interview. He loves Anna very much but considers her responsible for the violence: "She provokes me by refusing to run the business in the way it should be run." When she is interviewed separately, Anna discloses that the violence has been more extreme than was indicated in the initial conjoint session. She states that she was frightened to tell the therapist the details while Mark was in the room. Mark is subsequently referred to a batterer group and Anna begins individual therapy. Six months later, after being violence free, Mark and Anna return for couples therapy.

A therapist who treats this couple could begin by addressing the violence and by exploring the skills Mark and Anna have acquired in their individual work. The perception of physical and emotional abuse should be combined into a recognition that a destructive pattern of interaction had existed in the relationship. Alternatives to this destructive, degrading style of interaction will be the focus of future sessions. The therapist discusses the abuse beginning with the initial session and sets the stage for open communication. The therapist then moves to a discussion of the early relationship, when feelings of tenderness and caring dominated. Subsequent interventions by the therapist will tie this prior time of gentle feelings to the current efforts to improve the relationship. This gentleness will help to integrate emotionally, into the foundation and current functioning of the relationship, the skills Mark and Anna have acquired through their independent work. The focus of the therapy will continue to be on efforts to enact positive transactions and conflict resolution in the therapy sessions. Any unspoken problems will be addressed as trust increases between the partners and between the therapist and the couple.

Summary

In conjoint therapy the therapist is aware of the positive qualities of both partners. She or he addresses the qualities in the man that are positive and rewarding and directs these back into the transaction of the couple. Thus the woman feels understood and not stupid in her choice of spouse. Likewise, the abuser's self-esteem is raised, as is his perception of his ability to employ alternative strategies to meet his needs. The recipient of violence becomes empowered in the relationship as she acquires the skills to address her victimization, while both members of the couple learn more effective and adaptive strategies for resolving conflict.

Sometimes the outcome of therapy will be the therapist's agreement that she or he, as a competent, strong individual, cannot effect change in the abusing spouse; this at least gives the abused woman a sense that she is not alone in her inability to make things work. The recipient of the violence then may recognize that her separation from her spouse comes only after a concerted effort, both by herself and by others, and that all possible avenues to salvage the "good qualities" of the relationship have been explored. At this point in therapy the woman may need to grieve the demise of the relationship and her dreams of a future with her spouse. The therapeutic process of grief will continue with this focus of nonjudgmental recognition that battering is individually controlled behavior that occurs within the context of a relationship but is not viable within a relationship.

8

Feminism and Recovering From Battering: Working With the Individual Woman

ELIZABETH REGISTER

Wife battering is now recognized as a significant social problem. Sociologists (e.g., Schechter, 1982; Straus & Steinmetz, 1974) and feminists have challenged the psychopathological model of woman abuse by arguing that the private troubles of violent families are in reality public issues (Bernard, 1982; Pagelow, 1981b; Straus, Gelles, & Steinmetz, 1980) and that battering is not a personal issue but a political and social one (Rubin, 1979, 1983). Feminists view woman abuse as a gender issue (Bograd, 1984; Goldner, Penn, Sheinberg, & Walker, 1990; Pizzey, 1974; Smith, 1984) consisting of an abuse of power situated in and supported by the institutionalized patriarchy (Dobash & Dobash, 1977-1978, 1979; Luepnitz, 1988). Feminist scholars began reporting results of their research and recommended treatment of battered women almost 20 years ago (Dobash & Dobash, 1977-1978, 1979; Fleming, 1979; Martin, 1976; Pizzey, 1974; Walker, 1979). From this work, recommendations for the treatment of the victim have emerged. This chapter focuses on individual psychotherapy approaches with the battered woman.

Defining Battering

Battering itself is variously defined. For instance, Gayford (1978), Moore (1979), and Deschner (1984) define battering as "a series of physically injurious attacks on an intimate or family member that form part of a repeated, habitual pattern." Walker (1979) includes emotional abuse in the repeated, habitual cyclic pattern. Deschner (1984) indicates that if a woman does not reward the act of violence by changing her behavior as a consequence of the violence, even many repetitions will not lead to a firm habit acquisition. Ganley (1981) defines three different kinds of battering behavior, which may overlap. All are means of intimidation intended to control the victim and to impose the batterer's will upon his mate:

1. *Sexual battering:* This includes physical attacks on the woman's breasts/genitals or forced sexual activity, accompanied by either physical violence or the threat of physical violence.
2. *Psychological battering:* This includes threats of suicide, violence against the woman or her family, punching holes in walls, threatening to take the children away, threatening deportation of foreign-born wives, threatening to kidnap children and take them to a foreign country, and forcing the victim to do degrading things (e.g., to eat cigarette butts left in an ashtray or to lick the kitchen floor). It also may include controlling the victim's activities, such as sleeping and eating habits, social relationships, and access to money, and constant attacks on the woman's self-esteem through verbal abuse or total denial of her ideas and feelings and doing things intentionally to frighten her into submission, such as speeding in traffic or playing with weapons. Psychological battering is reported by some women as their most painful battering experience.
3. *Premeditated and intentional destruction of property and pets* (usually the victim's favorites): For example, take the man who said, "I got so angry, I got my rifle and was going to kill her and then I decided, 'I'm not going to prison for killing her,' so I started taking aim on all her favorite knick-knacks and shot each one of them off the wall. Some of them were worth a lot of money too" (Ganley, 1981; Ptacek, 1984).

All of these definitions of battering emphasize the abuse as a repeated, habitual behavioral activity that occurs more than twice.

Not all battered women are married to their batterers. In recognition of this fact, Moore (1979) suggests that the terms *battered woman, battered wife, battered spouse,* and *battered partner* be used interchangeably. The term *consort battering* is neutral in reference to gender or legal status and can include a variety of relationships, such as boyfriend, live-in, significant other, or partners in a gay or lesbian relationship (Deschner, 1984; Loulan, 1988). Stark and Flitcraft (1988a) suggest simply *woman battering.* These terms have evolved in response to widespread recognition that we are discussing physical violence against women by men, predominantly (Moore, 1979).

Assessment: Deciding What and How to Treat

Guidelines are needed to help therapists determine appropriate approaches to treatment. First, the therapist needs to assess the level of violence on a continuum from mild or moderate to severe. Using this framework, mild abuse might include yelling (if it leads to violence), pushing, slapping, shoving, holding, verbal abuse, and name calling (the most common forms of violence; Straus et al., 1980). Moderate abuse might include punching with fists, hitting in the face or head, pulling and dragging by the hair, and kicking. Severe violence often includes the use of weapons (such as guns or knives), clubbing, choking, or running down with a car (Moore, 1979). In assessing the extent of abuse and injuries, the counselor can ask very specific questions in order to assess the degree of danger to the woman (Pizzey, 1974; Pressman, 1989; Walker, 1979). The battered woman tends to minimize the severity of her abuse as a major means of coping with an intolerable situation.

The assessment process begins with the initial phone call, usually made by the wife. During that call, the therapist must pay particular attention to the clues provided by the woman's description of the situation. If a woman makes a statement such as, "My husband and I are fighting a lot," this should lead the therapist to focus on the word "fight" and to ask the woman to detail what happens when they "fight." Direct questions are often helpful, such as, "Is there any physical violence involved?" If the client answers in the affirmative, the therapist should explore the kinds of violence, remaining aware of the above-described tendency for minimization and denial within these relationships.

It is important that the therapist be aware of the availability of battered women's shelters. When the client is in crisis and at risk of severe violence, it is appropriate for the therapist to refer her to such a specialized facility, thereby ensuring her safety and that of her children. While at a shelter, a woman will receive multidimensional services, such as individual counseling, emotional support, education, legal assistance, and advocacy.

In less severe cases, the therapist may see the woman alone for further assessment, as she is likely to have difficulty speaking freely in the presence of the batterer for fear that another battering episode will follow any public acknowledgment of the extent and severity of the violence (Giles-Sims, 1983; Pressman, 1989; Walker, 1984b). In the first session, it is important for the therapist to elicit descriptions of the three most recent episodes of battering and of the worst episode. In determining the appropriate treatment, it is also useful for the therapist to find out what was occurring prior to the battering, what happened afterward, how the battering stopped, who else got involved, and what impact the battering had on the woman (Fleming, 1979; Giles-Sims, 1983; NiCarthy, 1982; Walker, 1977, 1979). Subsequently, the therapist will need to assess the tactics used to resolve conflicts between the woman and her batterer. The Conflict Tactics Scale may be useful for this purpose (see Straus, 1979, specifically the section devoted to assessment of the husband-wife violent behavior; see also Coleman, 1980; Giles-Sims, 1983; Walker, 1979). Focusing on the specifics of the battering behavior reinforces for the woman that the therapist is taking her life situation seriously and encourages her to do so also. Further, such focus demonstrates that the therapist is concerned for her safety and cares what is happening to her. For some women, their therapists may be the first people who have ever listened to them so attentively. When the assessment is complete, treatment can begin.

Treatment for the Individual Woman: The Feminist Perspective

Feminists maintain that the problem with violent relationships is not the violence per se, but that the batterer (usually male) uses the violent behavior to control his partner (Pressman, 1989; Stark & Flitcraft, 1988a; Walker, 1984b). If one accepts that the politics of gender inequity is the major issue, intervention should target situational factors (Stark & Flitcraft, 1988a).

Psychotherapists who fail to deal specifically with the acute battering incident (either directly or indirectly) and choose instead to focus on the psychological consequences of the incident are less likely to be helpful to their clients (Brodsky & Hare-Mustin, 1980). From the feminist perspective, a short-term goal of individual work with a battered woman is to ensure her safety and to eliminate all battering behaviors. From this perspective, constant attention to ending the violence is necessarily prerequisite to any other individual therapy goal (Ganley, 1981; Pizzey, 1975; Walker, 1984b). Ensuring the woman's safety may require her to use social control (such as calling the police or obtaining a restraining order). This action is usually most effective following the battering incident-explosive phase of the cycle of abuse (Walker, 1984b). The long-term counseling goal is one of empowerment and the development of emotional and material resources so that the woman may remove herself from the victimizing situation (Fleming, 1979; Walker, 1984b). The focus of therapy ought not be on either saving or ending the relationship directly. Assisting and supporting the woman while she finds her own way of protecting herself is an empowering intervention in individual therapy whether the woman decides to stay in or leave the relationship. A recent exchange illustrates the point: A client stated, "Someday I am going to leave this man," and the therapist replied, "Okay. In the meantime, how are you going to keep yourself safe until you decide to leave?" Encouraging the battered woman to leave her partner before she is ready, by contrast, may be a form of disempowerment (Ball & Wyman, 1977-1978).

Empowerment may consist of helping the woman strategize and plan what she can do to protect herself the next time an attack happens. Focusing on her own safety when she is not in physical danger may seem strange to her, but it is important for the therapist to underline that this is the time when she can think with a clear head. During a period of calm, for instance, the client might select a room in the house that can be locked from the inside and where she might be able to get away from an attack. Or when the victim senses an attack coming, she might move closer to the door to avoid getting cornered and to enable her to get out of the house quickly. The therapist can also encourage the client to consider some articles she can hide to help her during a crisis, such as extra money, a spare set of car keys to get her to safety, extra clothing, extra glasses, medication, identification cards, medical insurance or welfare cards, and other important legal papers. It is helpful if the client thinks of putting these items in some easily accessible place or giving them to a friend in case she has to escape quickly. Escape plans should also be rehearsed. Not only does the development of such plans help the client protect herself from the next episode of violence, they encourage her to tap into her cognitive abilities on her own behalf—a step toward self-empowerment and independence (Fleming, 1979; Ganley, 1981; NiCarthy, 1982).

Overcoming the woman's helplessness is more difficult when the victim chooses to remain with her battering partner. Trying to change the relationship to a nonbattering one may be a slow and unrewarding process. The focus of therapy is to treat the battered woman as an individual, strengthening her independence and teaching her new skills in order to reverse the learned helplessness brought on by the battering (Pressman, 1989; Walker, 1979). The client is likely to need help in two major areas: The first is practical information regarding resources available to her, and the second is empowerment. Enabling the client's empowerment includes providing her help with whatever confusion or difficulties interfere with her goal achievement, such as lack of assertion, fear of authority figures, fear of failure, and ambivalence. The client needs to hear that she does not "make" the perpetrator hit her or cause the perpetrator to lose control (Adams, 1988). The frequent conception that "if I got it right my husband would be a loving partner" needs to be addressed. The therapist needs to educate the victim to the need for her spouse to receive help or, unless she leaves, the violence will not end (Pressman, 1989). Because the abuser chooses to use violence to control his mate, it is his responsibility to focus on self-control to counteract his poor impulse control (Sternbach, 1990). Her focus must be on deciding how to protect and empower herself. Holding the woman responsible for protecting herself is essential (Goldner et al., 1990).

Principles in Working With Battered Women

The following principles can be applied when working with battered women. The concepts are abstracted from the writings of feminist psychology.

1. Feminists maintain that violence and abuse are never appropriate in an intimate relationship and that a woman should not have to bargain for her safety—it is her right (Ball & Wyman, 1977-1978; Fleming, 1979; Ganley, 1981; Neidig & Friedman, 1984).
2. Battering is recognized to be a social and political problem (Straus & Steinmetz, 1974). Gender inequality is perceived to be a social reality, and battering is an abuse of power within a social context. The battered woman is not perceived to be crazy or "sick" (Fleming, 1979; Goldner et al., 1990; Walker, 1979). In order to provide effective treatment, the therapist needs to assume that the battered woman is potentially healthy and able to take care of herself and her children. The battered woman's life situation may have created a sense of "learned helplessness" (Walker, 1977) that undermines her self-confidence. Ball and Wyman (1977-1978) state that "one of the major goals should be to increase the woman's feeling of being in control of her life."
3. Feminist therapists recommend that the therapist know his or her own limits in regard to the outcome of therapy. Any message sent by a therapist that he or she is invested in the woman's ending her relationship is likely to contribute to feelings of guilt and unworthiness, and to undermine empowerment of individual choice. Support and information are useful to the battered woman while she makes her own choices (Fleming, 1979; Ganley, 1981; Phillips, 1974).
4. Abusiveness tends to escalate in severity and frequency if not treated (Ganley, 1981; Neidig & Friedman, 1984; Walker, 1979). However, clinical evidence suggests that abusive men are not motivated to seek treatment unless there are strong external pressures to do so (Fleming, 1979; Ganley, 1981; Walker, 1979). The most effective pressure is for the woman to threaten to leave or actually to separate from the man (Adams, 1988; Roberts, 1984; Saunders, 1984). However, when such threats are undertaken, the potential lethality of the interaction increases.

Steps in Intervening With the Battered Woman

Ensuring the client's safety. The first step in treatment is to ensure the safety of the battered woman, either by finding a way to stop the violence or by helping her find a safe haven away from the batterer. A therapist can help the woman find a shelter or safety with a friend or family (Fleming, 1979; Pizzey, 1975; Walker, 1979). Battered women may need help in identifying their fears, such as fear of the abuser finding them (it may be helpful for the therapist to remind the client that the client-therapist relationship is a confidential one). Fears of reprisal are valid; statistics support the reality of death for some battered women who try to escape their abusers. It may be useful for therapist and client to explore backup safety plans. Behavior rehearsal of safety plans is a recommended strategy (Ganley, 1981; Neidig & Friedman, 1984; NiCarthy, 1982).

Listening to and believing the client. When a battering crisis occurs, the victim may need someone to listen to her and believe her. The reported violence must always be taken seriously. Battered women are more likely to minimize or deny the extent of the violence than they are to exaggerate it (Fleming, 1979; Martin, 1976; Walker, 1979). Denial or minimization are particularly pronounced in longer-term or more violent relationships (Walker, 1979). The victim needs to tell her story in her own way, without being interrupted or pressured to begin problem solving. The history of the relationship contains valuable information, and, in order to make changes, the battered woman often needs to understand herself and her situation. The victim will need to recall, in detail, the extent of the violence and how she feels about it physically and emotionally (Walker, 1979). How others, including the therapist, react to the knowledge of the battering is important to recovery (Ganley, 1981; Neidig & Friedman, 1984; NiCarthy, 1982). Shame, guilt, and feeling that she alone has this problem can contribute to the isolation and lack of trust of the battered woman (Fleming, 1979).

Identifying the client's feelings. Numbness or helplessness may camouflage the anger the battered woman repressed while she lived in fear during the tension-building phase of the abuse cycle (Walker, 1979). It may be helpful for the therapist to label the victim's feelings with words she understands. Victims are likely to need help in distinguishing between ventilating feelings for emotional release and taking impulsive action based on feelings alone. The therapist needs to be careful not to condone violent acts, and yet support the victim's right to feel angry (Ganley, 1981; Neidig & Friedman, 1984; NiCarthy, 1982).

Identifying the impact of the violence on the client's behavior. The victim may need help acknowledging the ways in which she has adapted to the violence in order to protect herself or "prevent" the violence. She may need help in recognizing that while she may have contributed to her partner's stress, she did not cause or "provoke" his behavior. The victim is likely to benefit from understanding that the abuser is capable of expressing anger in other ways besides violence (Adams, 1988; Ganley, 1981; Neidig & Friedman, 1984; NiCarthy, 1982).

Self-empowerment. The victim is likely to have many skills that she has used to survive in her situation and may need help in identifying them. Self-esteem, self-care, and self-nurturance are identified as necessary for the woman to reach an empowered position. This process requires a drastic change in attitude that includes a shift from the victim's focusing on her partner to focusing on her own needs (S. L. Brown, 1991; Fleming, 1979; Walker, 1979), and she may be slow in developing this attitude. A battered woman may believe that the relationship with her partner is necessary for her survival, and therefore may give her own needs very low priority. The therapist may point out to the battered woman that the tolerance, patience, loyalty, and commitment she has contributed to maintaining her relationship are the very elements that have allowed the abuse to continue (Goodrich, Rampage, Ellman, & Halstead, 1985).

Problem solving. Instruction in problem-solving skills often begins after safety is assured. A therapist can help the woman acquire skills and tools to identify and solve problems, especially focusing on how to get help from various social agencies. Developing lists of problems and then establishing small steps to be taken to reinforce success and achievement may be particularly fruitful, especially in identifying the outcomes, rewards, or natural consequences of each step's achievement. Victims need to learn to perform these steps for themselves so that they may begin to feel empowered and in control of their own lives (Fleming, 1979; Ganley, 1981; Neidig & Friedman, 1984; NiCarthy, 1982).

Dealing with social agencies. The battered woman may need someone to be her advocate in systems such as welfare, law enforcement, courts, schools, and medical agencies (Fleming, 1979; Walker, 1979). A therapist can teach her methods for getting help by giving her information about how to find resources. Many victims become isolated from the external world and develop learned helplessness as a survival mechanism; they will require some time to unlearn old behaviors and to learn new ones (Walker, 1979). Anyone who has ever moved from one region of the country to another has had some small experience of the kind of disorientation experienced by the battered woman who is on her own for the first time. Such disorientation is occasioned by the need to establish new roots in a foreign environment, including finding new housing, schools, doctors, grocery stores, and banks. The sense of disorientation and fear experienced by the battered woman as she goes about reestablishing herself and her children in a new community may be great and may require a great deal of courage and support.

Support groups. In the second phase of therapy, getting the battered woman into an ongoing support group is adjunctive to individual therapy. Such group participation has been identified as essential for understanding and growth for empowerment (Brodsky & Hare-Mustin, 1980; Fleming, 1979; Ganley, 1981). The connections from support groups can enable victims to move beyond isolation and guilt about "their" problems. A group can provide victims the support and freedom to explore their options.

Ongoing therapeutic support. A battered woman may remain in therapy until she perceives that the violence has stopped and then may return to the relationship. The therapist needs to keep her or his door open to the victim in this transitional time, letting the client know the therapist is available if the woman's situation worsens.

Therapeutic Blind Spots

Therapists may have difficulty attending to important characteristics of the battering couple. Some have been criticized for efforts to save the battered woman even if she does not want to be saved (Pizzey, 1974). Such a direction on the part of the therapist may indicate to the client that she is not being heard or accepted by the therapist. Such focus may place the therapist in the untenable position of validating the societal bias that tells the woman that she is not competent to make her own decisions or form her own judgments. Therapists have been cautioned not to make their clients feel like failures (Fleming, 1979; Ganley, 1981; Walker, 1979). Stark and Flitcraft (1988a) report that some therapists may behave like rejected lovers and identify with the assailants' anger when their battered clients reject their benign paternalism and return repeatedly to their abusers.

Another important characteristic to which a therapist should attend is the magnitude of the power inequity found in violent relationships. In our culture, women are often taught not to be powerful or to use their strengths and influence in their own behalf (Bepko & Krestan, 1990; Gilligan, 1982;

Goodrich, 1991; Lerner, 1985a; Schaef, 1986). This is one of the cultural factors that limits women's repertoire of available responses to abuse from significant partners. Therapists, especially family therapists, need to monitor their systemic circular causality thinking and look at the perceived power differential internalized within the individual woman that facilitates the loss of power to act in her own behalf (see Hansen, Chapter 6, this volume). All persons do not have equal power in a relationship, and power inequities, especially economic inequities, do limit one's options (Carter, 1989; Dobash & Dobash, 1979). The status of "wife" is less powerful than the status of "husband" in the hierarchy of our culture (Bograd, 1986; Heilbrun, 1988; see also Hansen, Chapter 6, this volume).

Feminist therapists have been criticized for possible inclinations to use the individual woman as an opportunity to "reform the patriarchal system." If the therapist succumbs to this temptation, the woman is again likely to be disempowered and her experience devalued, which is itself antithetical to feminist thinking (Fleming, 1979; Goodrich et al., 1985; Walker, 1979).

Therapists have been cautioned to monitor the pacing of the intervention. The therapist's own yearning to see the client be less dependent, to value herself more, and to demand more for herself can result in the therapist pushing too hard and moving too fast. When these efforts inevitably fail, frustration and anger are in store for the therapist, and the client will be left in confusion and despair (Fleming, 1979; Ganley, 1981; Goodrich et al., 1985).

For the female therapist, the fact that the battered woman must choose between being compliant and loved and being independent (Walker, 1979) may converge with the therapist's conflict between beneficent caretaking and support for female autonomy. Unfortunately, many therapists may still identify more readily with vulnerability, depression, and low self-esteem than with appropriate aggressive action, particularly among women (Stark & Flitcraft, 1988a).

The therapist must deal with both an internalized fear of strong women and a corresponding tendency to project a male stereotype of how women should be (dependent, helpless, submissive) through exaggerated emphasis on the therapist's professional role as helper. Lerner (1984) cautions the therapist against seeing the projected stereotype as a way to devalue the omnipotent maternal figure by inverting the therapist's relationship to her and treating the patient or client like a little girl. The result is that the woman is put in the same double bind during treatment that she experiences at home. She will get approval only if she behaves in a relatively dysfunctional and ultimately unsatisfying way (Stark & Flitcraft, 1988a).

The therapist must examine his or her own attitudes about, experiences with, and reactions to violence. It is imperative that therapists working with battered women recognize the role and effects of violence in their own lives. Therapists must be willing to speak openly about violence—physical, sexual, emotional, and social (Fleming, 1979; Ganley, 1981; Martin, 1976; Walker, 1979). At the same time, the therapist must be careful not to impose his or her own values on the battered woman. The therapist's reactions to the woman's responses will communicate strongly and may be seen as a bossy imposition of the therapist's values onto the woman's experiences (Fleming, 1979; NiCarthy, 1982; Walker, 1979). This does not mean that the therapist cannot disagree with the woman's behavior or methods of dealing with problems (Ganley, 1981). It does mean that a good therapist tries to understand the woman's feelings of frustration, lack of education, previous life-style, and so on. A proper empathic relationship with the woman will help the therapist separate anger from a wish to influence new behaviors. This is especially crucial when working with women of different ethnic backgrounds (Billings-Beck, 1991).

The Therapist and the Battered Women's Shelter

While the private practitioner can provide support and encouragement as the woman moves toward autonomy, one of the most successful forms of treatment seems to be the woman-dominated system of shelters for battered women (Brodsky & Hare-Mustin, 1980). These shelters provide crisis intervention techniques after acute battering incidents as well as social support to change the context of unequal power in which battering develops. Victims may regain much of their strength and confidence within a supportive community away from their batterers. The convergence of mutual support and caretaking with individual autonomy may result in empowerment. Social connectedness and advocacy provided by shelters may enable victims to consider options available to them within a safe, nonpressured environment. Many shelters provide short-term residential counseling. If a battered woman decides to separate from or divorce her abuser, the private practitioner may be of great support to her in ongoing therapy as she strengthens her sense of self (Stark & Flitcraft, 1988a).

A description of the multidimensional program at Haven Hills Shelter in California is provided below as a prototype of services available to the battered woman for temporary respite from abuse and as a useful referral source for psychotherapists. The battered woman may use the shelter as a refuge while she breaks the cycle of abuse (Giles-Sims, 1983). Staff members at Haven Hills work with the individual woman who seeks shelter by utilizing the following processes:

1. empowering the woman to recognize and respect her feelings and thoughts enough to make healthy choices
2. raising the woman's awareness and insight into her background
3. exploring with the woman her sense of identity learned in her family of origin and in her current social sphere
4. helping the woman to recognize the messages and beliefs she was carefully taught and how they affect her now
5. helping the woman to recognize how she sees the world and her place in it
6. helping the woman to confront early childhood trauma and her feelings, then and now, toward the perpetrator(s) and the protector(s)
7. helping the woman to relinquish faulty defenses so that she can develop coping mechanisms to tolerate profoundly painful feelings
8. helping the woman to work through abandonment and separation issues in depth in order to help bring about a person who is able to maintain her boundaries under stress and anxiety

The work is done through psychodynamic, social learning, cognitive, and behavioral approaches along with supportive therapy. Support groups, offered in four-week segments, supplement individual therapy at the shelter. Support groups focus on domestic violence education, communication skills, parenting/reparenting skills, education regarding dysfunctional systems, and education regarding relationships and addiction (Billings-Beck, 1991).

9

Treating the Batterer

EDWARD W. GONDOLF

But what is being done with the men who abuse and batter women? This has been a rising question over the past decade. It initially came in response to the battered women's movement. Battered women's advocates joined with men's consciousness-raising groups to counsel men in an effort to help battered women. With 30-50% of women in shelters returning, at least for a time, to their batterers, and the majority of separated batterers moving on to batter or abuse another woman (Gondolf, 1988a), it made sense to attempt to change batterers' behavior as well as interrupt it. The founding batterer programs, emerging in the late 1970s, relied primarily on consciousness-raising techniques that attempted to resocialize men into alternative ways of thinking about and acting toward women.

Since that time, three major developments have helped to expand and diversify efforts to deal with batterers. One is the movement led by shelter advocates and victims' rights proponents to criminalize wife battering. Its primary objective has been to bring sanctions against perpetrators that would help deter battering and motivate men to change (Ganley, 1987). As a result, numerous court-mandated counseling programs for batterers have emerged over the past five years (see Gondolf, 1991, for a review).

A second development is the advent of social workers, psychotherapists, and even family counselors in batterer counseling. Battering is generally conceived by these professionals as a manifestation of underlying psychopathology, dysfunctional communication patterns, or childhood trauma that needs therapy (e.g., Deschner, 1984). Conventional family systems, cognitive-behavior treatments, and Gestalt techniques have been adapted to deal with battering men individually, in groups, and with their partners.

While the predominant form of batterer counseling remains a psychoeducational modality with groups of batterers, many batterer group programs have accommodated cognitive-behavioral techniques, and a few psychoeducational couples programs persist.

The turn toward "helping" the batterer—that is, focusing treatment on the individual man rather than specifically confronting his behavior—has been boosted by the rise of the mythic-poetic men's movement with Jungian roots. This popularized stream of thought, epitomized in such recent best-sellers as *Iron John* (Bly, 1990), *King, Warrior, Magician, Lover* (Moore & Gillette, 1990), and *Fire in the Belly* (Keen, 1991), attributes abuse and battering to childhood trauma, absent fathers, and emasculation experienced in the modern work world. In this vein, men are victims, too. Psychodynamic approaches that incorporate myth, storytelling, and rituals are seen as the means to recapture a mature sense of manhood for batterers as well as men in general (see Waldo, 1987).

This chapter attempts to offer some guideposts to the diversity of batterer programs that proliferate before us in the 1990s. It draws on the founding concerns of shelter advocates who have experienced and led much of the thinking in the field of domestic violence. The feminist principles underlying much of the battered women's movement speak to safety and justice for women (Bograd, 1988). The main objective of batterer counseling, in this light, is to serve the woman by decreasing the physical harm, mental abuse, and terror she experiences, but also by increasing her self-determination, control, and empowerment. Feminists tend to view men's abuse of women as a means toward power and control over women and as an expression of inherent fear of and contempt for the feminine (Taubman, 1986).

With this framework understandably comes controversy and even objection to the efforts to "treat" batterers. If battering is fundamentally a crime—an act that violates individual human rights—then it warrants some sort of punishment that might restrain and deter such behavior. Batterer counseling can appear, according to some critics, as "coddling" batterers. At the same time, some form of counseling or treatment may further deterrence or act as an effective substitute. Fortunately, research and experience increasingly point to what we can and cannot expect from batterer counseling, and how it might be shaped to support women in their "recovery" from battering.

This chapter begins with a discussion of the efforts to establish a batterer profile and the implications of this inconclusive effort for program development. More needs to be done to sort out antisocial and sociopathic batterers who are at higher risk of reoffending and the least responsive to conventional batterer counseling. A review of the different types of batterer programs is offered, and a trend toward the features promoted by profeminist programs and away from individual and couples counseling is highlighted. An examination of program outcomes or "success rates" follows. The many limitations of the prevailing outcome studies may make it difficult to assert some conclusive success for batterer programs themselves. However, there is at least some evidence that batterer programs play a part in a wider constellation of informal and formal interventions.

This overview of the field suggests that batterer counseling is, first of all, not a unified venture. It is far from a "cure-all" and sometimes it is even a disservice to battered women. But with appropriate cautions and collaborations, batterer programs offer additional support to the efforts to stop wife battering. Besides reinforcing the individual efforts of some men to change their behavior, batterer programs present a visible symbol to the community that men can and should change. They also provide a laboratory for improving and shaping the direction of things to come.

Defining Batterers

One of the more elusive questions in the field is, Just "who are those guys" we call batterers? Who and what are we attempting to "treat"? A substantial portion of the recent research has attempted to profile batterers (see Dutton, 1988b). This line of research—comparable to psychological studies in the related fields of criminology, alcohol and drug abuse, and child abuse—seeks to establish characteristics that may be used to identify potential batterers and aspects that warrant treatment. In the process, contradictions and inconclusiveness in the profile research have also prompted a turn toward a more diverse representation of men who batter women.

BATTERER CHARACTERISTICS AND TYPOLOGIES

Clinical observations and preliminary studies have surfaced a profile of the batterer as an inexpressive, impulse-driven, traditional, and rigid personality with low self-esteem and frequent drug and alcohol problems (Dutton, 1988b). Much like the ongoing debate over the presence of an "addictive personality" in the alcohol field, there is increasing speculation that no conclusive "batterer profile" exists (Edleson, Eisikovitz, & Guttman, 1985; Hotaling & Sugarman, 1986). Most of the profile research is based on limited clinical samples or contradicts itself. The few studies with control groups, in fact, suggest that, although batterers in treatment have more personality and alcohol problems than do "nonbatterers," batterers

as a group do not differ substantially from the general population of men (e.g., Hamberger & Hastings, 1991).

The research on batterer characteristics has recently moved to the formulation of a typology of batterers. One conception, based on batterers' behavior, suggests a continuum of sporadic, chronic, antisocial, and sociopathic batterers (Gondolf, 1988c). The severity and kinds of wife abuse are greatest with those who are violent outside the home: the antisocial and sociopathic batterers, who also tend to have more criminal arrests and drug and alcohol problems. While this range of batterers may still hold a similar predisposition toward woman abuse, additional factors such as alcohol and drug abuse, psychopathology, and violent subculture appear to exacerbate and complicate the battering—and the men's response to treatment. Several studies indicate, in fact, that men with alcohol and drug problems, criminal histories, and antisocial personalities are more likely to drop out of programs and to reoffend (Grusznski & Carrillo, 1988; Hamberger & Hastings, 1989).

IMPLICATIONS FOR PROGRAM DEVELOPMENT

The findings regarding batterer characteristics have important implications for program development, especially in light of feminist concerns. First, the lack of a substantiated profile should help diffuse the tendency, particularly in the media, to promote some deviant stereotype of batterers. Such a stereotype too easily reinforces the tendency of men to dismiss their abuse by insisting, "But I'm not one of *them*!" Similarly, women who encounter men who do not fit the profile are more likely to have a false sense of safety or assurance. Second, the preoccupation with a profile may divert programs from treating the real issues and sufficiently accounting for the compounding problems of some individuals.

Third, the notion of a unified batterer profile furthers the pell-mell expansion of batterer counseling. As a result of greater public awareness and court-mandated counseling, a wider range of batterers are coming to batterer programs. However, many simply do not belong there; the chances of antisocial and especially sociopathic batterers responding to counseling are low (Gondolf, 1988c). In fact, some of these men are "system failures" who have been in and out of law enforcement programs, drug and alcohol treatment, and psychiatric care. Moreover, if these men do remain in programs, they are so resistant or deceptive that they often undermine the progress of those who have the potential to change.

Batterer programs need, therefore, to evaluate mental health, criminality, and alcohol and drug problems of batterers in order to assess sufficiently the men's suitability for batterer counseling (see Sonkin, 1987). This task carries some awkward compromises, however. To invest too much in batterer assessment may again divert the program emphasis on accountability for the woman abuse and open the door to psychiatric diagnoses that lead a program back to mainstream mental health treatment. An effective social history may be sufficient to surface troublesome and intransigent cases without undoing a program's objectives. Another alternative is to use orientation sessions to assess further the men's motivation and their suitability for further counseling (Tolman & Bhosley, 1989).

BATTERER PROGRAM LIMITATIONS

Batterer programs must increasingly identify their limits for a number of reasons. There are some men being "dumped" on batterer programs who would be better served by incarceration, psychiatric hospitalization, or residential alcohol and drug treatment—or some combination of these. Batterer counseling might be established as an adjunct to these facilities (indeed, this is yet another trend in the making). Moreover, refusing to treat some men may, paradoxically, help women. One of the strongest predictors of a women returning to her batterer is the batterer's being in counseling (Gondolf, 1988a). Counseling too easily is taken as potential "cure" in our society, and women understandably tend to hold great hopes for it. Moreover, their batterers tend to expect congratulations and reconciliation for having submitted to counseling: "I've gone to counseling, now you should take me back." Women are less likely to let down their guard or return to a dangerous man if he is refused counseling.

In the midst of this attention to the effects of counseling on battered women, one caveat of controversy remains: batterer program contact with the battered woman. Should a program obtain the woman's assessment of the abuse in order to offset denial and monitor the man's progress? Should a program contact the woman to assess her sense of safety and independence in order to evaluate "success"? While some programs with feminist sympathies actively use the woman's input and evaluation in the course of treatment, others strongly oppose it. "Partner contact," as it is frequently called, can too easily become surrogate couples counseling. Program staff are inadvertently put in the middle of the couple and react to expectations of the two individuals. Furthermore, there is concern, as with couples counseling in general, that the woman may be placed at risk when she shares information about the batterer. The partner contact, according to some shelter advocates, may also divert the battered woman's attention from her own recovery toward the man's. In partner contact, she is essentially being asked to "take care" of her man, rather than herself.

The answer may lie in using women's shelter staff or battered women's advocates, rather than immediate victims, to offer guiding input and focus.

Specific details about a particular batterer may not be that necessary. Staff can generally assume that he has been abusive by his mere referral to the program. There are means to confront his denial and elaborate his abuse, as discussed below, other than involving the woman (see Hutchinson, 1987). Additionally, there is nothing much that programs can do about the woman's report anyhow. Carefully monitoring the man through partner contact may, in fact, create an illusion of safety. The best position for the woman may again be paradoxical: If she is advised forthrightly that the program cannot assure her safety, she may be prompted to seek more substantial help and thus keep additional pressure on the man to change.

Program Structure

"Counseling is not *counseling,* is not *counseling*!" The approaches, formats, and structures of batterer programs vary considerably nationwide, as program surveys (Feazell, Mayers, & Deschner, 1984; Pirog-Good & Stets, 1985) and program descriptions (Caesar & Hamberger, 1989) indicate. The curricula of batterer programs might be loosely categorized as anger management, skill building, and resocialization (see Adams, 1988, for further discussion). Programs sympathetic to feminist concerns tend to employ a composite of cognitive-behavioral techniques adapted to address the underlying belief system that sustains and justifies abuse of women—the "cognitive set" of men (for published treatment manuals, see Gondolf, 1985b; Sonkin, Martin, & Walker, 1985; Stordeur & Stille, 1989).

ANGER MANAGEMENT

Anger management programs, as the description suggests, focus on identifying the "provocations" that contribute to anger, "cues" that precede angry outbursts, and strategies, such as "time-outs," to interrupt the escalation toward battering (see Sonkin et al., 1985). Anger management is a principal component of the majority of programs, even when accompanied by components that deal with sex roles and nonviolence education.

The underlying assumption in this approach is that battering is anger driven rather than an outgrowth of a sense of male privilege and control. Intentionally or not, many batterers may, as a result, project their battering and avoid confronting its roots by thinking, "My anger made me do it!" Furthermore, men with a penchant for control see themselves as controlling one more thing, their anger, rather than letting go of some responsibility and entitlement. Anger management too easily becomes a "quick fix" in some men's minds, as well. With a few convenient gimmicks, they assert that they are "cured" while not having to change substantially the underlying dynamics of their relationships (Gondolf & Russell, 1986).

SKILL BUILDING

The skill-building programs offer a sequence of psychoeducational sessions that attempt to address the psychological deficits associated with batterers: They rely on instruction, exercises, and discussion to improve communication patterns, stress reduction, and sex role images, with better conflict management, assertiveness training, and cognitive restructuring (Hamberger & Hastings, 1988; Stordeur & Stille, 1989). This curriculum usually includes components that teach the kinds, cycle, and consequences of abuse, as well. Again, there may be a secondary effect to this "treatment" that feminists would oppose. Batterers might easily construe their violence as some sort of psychological problem that they need to "fix," like a mechanic tinkering with a car. In some cases, programs inadvertently create nonviolent terrorists who simply learn new methods for getting their way as part of their "skills" acquisition.

PROFEMINIST RESOCIALIZATION

The programs that align themselves most expressly with battered women's concerns focus on what might be termed "accountability" education, which attempts to confront men's tendency toward power and control (Adams, 1989; Pence, 1989). A substantial portion of these programs is used to expose the range of abusive behaviors: put-downs, ridicule, withholding money, social isolation, intimidation, threatening children, and sexual abuse. Also, cost-benefit analysis, safety plans, and control logs are frequently employed to focus on the behavior in question and point to safer alternatives. *Cost-benefit analysis* refers to a group exercise in identifying the gains and consequences of violent behavior and of nonviolent behavior. *Safety plans* are outlines of strategies and procedures to be used to avoid being abusive and violent. In *control logs,* batterers record instances in which they attempted to control their partners or spouses during the previous week. They identify as well the circumstances of those instances and how they might have handled them differently.

These "profeminist" programs attend to group dynamics as well as to individual denial and rationalization. One concern of feminists is that an inadvertent tolerance of abusive thinking is often present in batterer groups. The male bonding that emerges in intense group sessions too easily becomes collusion. Two things, therefore, become essential in profeminist programs. One is confrontation, much as is done in many drug programs, to challenge the deep-seated tendencies in our society to justify and excuse abuse of women and violence in general. Another essential is to provide for monitoring by battered women's advocates (Hart, 1988b). Having the advocates observe and evaluate group sessions, contribute to curriculum development, and colead or speak at group sessions helps keep women's concerns at the center of batterer treatment.

There are, of course, some criticisms and reservations about this approach (see Gondolf, 1988b). Some see the profeminist programs as too "ideological," as attempting to impose a worldview on a captive audience. Others contend that these programs smack of male bashing and push many already defensive men away. Still another group of critics suggest this approach is naive to the complex interactive dynamics of abuse and battering. From the feminist viewpoint, what is important is the outcome in terms of achieving safety and justice for women. (Program outcomes are weighed in the subsequent section.) What emerge across respected and prominent programs are some commonalities that are especially associated with profeminist programs but also may be incorporated in other program types.

PROGRAM TRENDS

The trends among programs include an increased effort to confront the denial, self-pity, and rationalization associated with abuse and its continuance. This is in part accomplished by dissecting weekly behaviors and group participation in terms of their potential abusiveness—their control, manipulation, disregard, or subjection of another person. It is also furthered by elaborate behavioral inventories or checklists that identify the full continuum of abusive behaviors. Another trend is to identify the aspects of male socialization or "the male experience" that reinforce the abusiveness. This is done through exercises dealing with men's use of language, relationships with their fathers, and misuses of peer support.

Finally, many programs attempt to foster commitment to long-term change, as opposed to quick-fix therapy. Men are encouraged to develop alternative support groups and to participate in follow-up or complementary treatment and active self-monitoring. Batterer programs are increasingly using a phased approach to treatment that corresponds with a developmental course of change (Fagan, 1989; Gondolf, 1987a): (a) an orientation or didactic phase that teaches men about the dynamics and extent of their abuse, (b) an issues phase that discusses the obstacles to change and how to deal with them, and (c) a support phase that attempts to reinforce and extend alternative behaviors (e.g., Stordeur & Stille, 1989). Admittedly, few men complete what is conceived as an 8- to 12-month program, but the phased approach conveys the message that treatment is a long-term process. Men are therefore less likely to assume they are "cured" through brief attendance or piecemeal accomplishments.

REMAINING PROGRAM ISSUES

Even with the increased number of batterer programs, the number of batterers who actually attend any program is still dismally low, considering the number of battered women in shelters and the estimates of abuse in the community as a whole. Men who batter women are much more likely to present their problems as related to alcohol, stress, unemployment, or marital conflicts, given the ambiguous sanction for battering. Consequently, there is a heightened effort to train human service professionals to recognize and address battering more efficiently. In fact, a variety of studies have shown that so-called generalists (Gondolf & Foster, 1990), medical practitioners (Kurz, 1987), psychiatric staff (Gondolf, 1990b), drug and alcohol counselors (Gondolf & Foster, 1991), family counselors (Hansen, Harway, & Cervantes, 1991), and social workers (Borkowski, Murch, & Walker, 1983) have systematically neglected domestic violence in clinical assessments and treatment. All of these studies recommend clinical protocols and specialized treatments to counter the shortcomings they substantiate.

Individual and couples counselors, therefore, are advised to use abuse inventories or screening tests, investigation of control and anger cues, and victim reports to help expose abusive behavior. Referral to established domestic violence programs that assure that the abusive behavior will be confronted and monitored is urged as well. If such a program is not available for batterers, a counselor might consider establishing at least a batterer group, drawing on the number of training conferences and program manuals now available (e.g., Gondolf, 1985b; Sonkin et al., 1985; Stordeur & Stille, 1989).

Perhaps the most intense controversy concerns the appropriateness of couples counseling for domestic violence cases (see Hansen, Chapter 6, this volume). As suggested above, the vast majority of programs employ a psychoeducational, perpetrator group, as opposed to couples counseling, and a movement toward establishing nationwide standards for court-mandated counseling currently opposes couples counseling. There are, of course, some obvious practical reasons for this. Many battered women are reluctant to confront their batterers or to be in counseling with them for fear of reprisals, and many batterers are openly opposed to couples counseling because of their denial and projection of the blame. There are, however, criminological (Fagan, 1989) and therapeutic (Bograd, 1984) objections as well. From a criminological perspective, laws regarding assault, inside or outside the home, specify a perpetrator and a victim for one illegal act—or "count." A sentence is given, at least in principle, in an effort to punish, restrain, and/or rehabilitate the perpetrator. Increasingly, victim assistance or compensation is offered to the victim to facilitate psychological and financial recovery from the criminal act. Therapeutically, one of the fundamental principles in "cessation treatments," in general, is that the individual perpetrator take responsibility for his behavior in order to change it (Fagan, 1989). This process takes a very concentrated effort with court-mandated batterers, who are shown to have heightened levels of denial and minimization. If couples counseling is to be introduced, it is therefore generally recommended that it be after successful completion of a batterer program and after at least six months of nonviolence. As suggested previously, couples counseling may be ineffective and even dangerous with a substantial portion of batterers considered to be antisocial or sociopathic (see Chapter 7).

Program Outcomes

Without a doubt, the most asked question of batterer programs is, What is your success rate? The implication often is that the program outcome can be compressed into some "bottom line" intelligible to consumers—and investors. The reality is that it is not that easy, and skepticism about the contribution of batterer counseling to women's safety may be warranted, despite some simplistic interpretations of outcome that would support budding optimism. The outcomes of batterer programs remain somewhat elusive because of the difficulty in measuring "success," numerous methodological shortcomings, and high subject attrition in follow-up studies (Gondolf, 1987b, 1987c). Nevertheless, two recent reviews of single-site outcome studies point to a few tendencies worth noting (Eisikovits & Edleson, 1989; Tolman & Bennett, 1990).

SUCCESS RATES

The batterer program evaluations suggest that approximately 60% of program completers are not physically assaultive at a 6-month follow-up, according to victim reports (Tolman & Bennett, 1990). There is some indication, however, that most batterers (60%) are verbally threatening and abusive during this period (Edleson & Syers, 1990; Tolman & Bhosley, 1990). Also, those who are arrested and mandated by the court to enter counseling are less likely to reoffend than those who are only arrested, according to a quasi-experimental study of a 16-week anger control program (Dutton, 1986).

Unfortunately, there have been no controlled studies that effectively compare different curriculum approaches and conclusively indicate which approach is generally most effective in reducing battering and with what type of batterers. Analysis of controlled comparison studies in the mental health field suggests that program curricula or approaches do not substantially differ in short-term outcomes (e.g., Wilner, Freeman, Surber, & Goldstein, 1985). These studies suggest that the significant factors influencing outcome may be in the process of treatment rather than in the content. For instance, a coherent message of change, alternative role models, and social support are shown to be related to a positive outcome irrespective of treatment modality. A controlled comparison study has, however, demonstrated that a didactic format is more effective in reducing recidivism than self-help or guided discussion, at least in the short term (Edleson & Syers, 1990). All of these factors tend to be more in line with the resocialization efforts of the profeminist programs than with the other approaches in the field.

SHORTCOMINGS OF OUTCOME STUDIES

There are several considerations that need to be weighed in interpreting the outcomes of batterer programs. The most important one perhaps is the tremendous dropout rate that programs experience. Most "success" rates are calculated on the basis of those who complete a three- to six-month program. Dropout rates vary considerably with the length, type, and screening of the program (Demaris, 1989; Gondolf, 1990a; Pirog-Good & Stets, 1986), but one recent dropout study revealed a typical pattern in one program (Gondolf & Foster, 1991; see also Demaris & Jackson, 1987). Out of 200 men who contacted the program by phone, approximately 50 appeared for an intake interview, 25 participated in more than one counseling session, 12 completed three months, and 7 completed six months. Only 2 of the original 200 callers completed the entire eight-month program. Success rates would no doubt be radically reduced if program dropouts were considered, and would be dismal if the "no-show" callers (or preprogram dropouts) were used as the basis of calculation.

A second consideration in weighing program "success" is the context of the program. Most program evaluations do not weigh the contribution of a variety of social factors that may be in operation. Additional police action, an impending divorce, and participation in Alcoholics Anonymous are just a few of the factors that may account for the "success" programs claim (Cocozzelli & Hudson, 1989). A noted study of formerly battered women, moreover, demonstrates that a constellation of formal and informal interventions are associated with the cessation of violence (Bowker, 1983).

Third, most of the "success" studies do not account for the nature and extent of the failures. Are there situations in which a woman returned to a man in response to counseling and was killed as a result? How do we know whether the program "benefits" outweigh the "costs"? Some women advocates would argue that definitions of success are too narrow to begin with. Rather than simply looking at the reduction in assaults, the improvement in a woman's "quality of life" should be assessed. How has the batterer dealt with child custody? Does he continue to pursue, coax, or harass the woman? Does the woman have a greater sense of independence and self-worth? Also, the impact of the program on the battering incidence in the community at large might offer a more meaningful indication of "progress."

IMPLICATIONS OF OUTCOME STUDIES

The uncertain "success" of batterer programs does not necessarily discredit their potential contribution to stopping wife abuse. Rather, it points to some additional program goals. For instance, batterer programs might do more to reduce "false hopes" and to alert women and men to the tendency toward dropping out of programs. More needs to be done actively to prevent dropout, through group pressure, follow-up calls, safety plans, and preprogram orientation. The evidence as to whether court mandate reduces dropout is as yet inconclusive (e.g., Saunders & Parker, 1989). Of course, all of this is difficult when funders press for a return on their dollar registered in high "success" rates.

Further, the risks to women from batterer counseling might be eased by more effective screening. As previously discussed, antisocial and sociopathic batterers, who are increasingly being sent to batterer programs by the courts, may be referred elsewhere or even refused treatment outright. Also, programs need to assess lethality explicitly throughout a man's treatment. While violence remains difficult to predict, even for experts, imminent danger is often very obvious. Serious depression, drug and alcohol use, threats, and available firearms, for instance, usually warrant additional warnings and intervention (Hart, 1988a).

Finally, these considerations point to the need for greater coordination among community services (e.g., Brygger & Edleson, 1985, 1987). Batterer programs cannot and do not stop battering by themselves. There needs to be collaboration with the courts that assures the programs' right to refuse certain court referrals and decisive action for delinquent court-mandated batterers (e.g., Soler, 1987). Compatible mental health and alcohol and drug facilities also need to be identified. Unfortunately, research indicates that staff at these facilities tend to underidentify woman battering and do not specifically address battering in treatment (Gondolf, 1990b; Gondolf & Foster, 1991). For instance, we found that approximately 40% of alcohol inpatients ($n = 218$) indicated assaulting their partners in the previous year, and 80% of their partners reported being assaulted by their husbands. Yet only 5% of the clinical records indicated any woman battering (Gondolf & Foster, 1991).

Cooperation with shelter and victim services can additionally help in giving women the opportunities they need to empower themselves: Transitional housing, available transportation, child care, job training, and legal council contribute to a woman's leaving a dangerous batterer and also to a batterer's behavior change (Gondolf & Fisher, 1988). In addition, batterer programs might do more case management and "aftercare" planning in order to promote men's participation in a variety of social supports that maintain and further their change. In sum, batterer programs need to be more conscious of and attentive to the community and social contexts in a way that incorporates and activates a diversity of community sanctions, resources, and services. As feminists, who tend to see battering as primarily a sociological problem, have long argued, reorganization and restructuring of the social context are the changes that are ultimately needed.

Conclusion

As mentioned at the outset, this discussion of batterer programs attempts to identify the issues involved in batterer treatment, rather than to teach one ideal model or approach. It is hoped that family counselors, psychotherapists, and social workers, in particular, might find this a useful guide when referring men to batterer programs or receiving referrals from such programs, as well as in attempting to treat batterers within their respective services.

Feminist concerns indicate that some sorting with regard to batterer programs is in order. Increased precautions need to be taken with the increasing numbers of antisocial and sociopathic men being sent to batterer programs. These men may need more restrictive and comprehensive interventions to assure the safety of the victims and to increase the likelihood of some degree of rehabilitation. Also, all batterer programs are not the same, and some may have less acceptable secondary impacts than others. The limitations of anger management and skill-building programs, for instance, may make them less desirable than long-term phased programs that offer a progression of approaches. Batterer programs need, moreover, to address more systematically the problem of dropout and lethality, and to collaborate with additional services to intensify, extend, and maintain treatment effects.

To this end there is a rising movement toward establishing nationwide standards for batterer programs—ones that assure some "quality control" and proper representation of victim concerns. These standards take various forms in a handful of states: as legislated standards for court referrals, policy guidelines for state funding, or program requirements for shelter referrals. The standards usually prescribe assumptions that the perpetrator is accountable for his violence, checks on victim blaming and projection, curriculum components for stopping the violent behavior and promoting safety, and a didactic group format for the perpetrators (see Gondolf, 1991). The potential regulation, of course, has its critics, but regulation of related fields such as mental health treatment and drug and alcohol treatment—and even dieting programs—suggests that some standards for batterer programs may be a matter of "catching up" to the demand for quality control.

In sum, batterer programs do have a contribution to make as one facet of an ever-widening campaign against woman battering. They are far from a single solution, however, and must not detract from battered women's efforts to receive the help they so desperately need and deserve.

10

Psychotherapy Supervision: Training Therapists to Recognize Family Violence

BEVERLY J. GOODWIN

As other authors in this book have noted, the literature published over the past few years on the subject of family violence has expanded exponentially. The thrust of much of that body of literature has addressed one of three areas: (a) speaking to the prevalence and pervasiveness of domestic violence within society by collecting demographic and epidemiological data (e.g., Koss, 1990; Straus, 1977-1978; Walker, 1979), (b) identifying the nature of the problem by investigating the dynamics of marital and family relationships (e.g., Bograd, 1984; Kalmuss, 1984; Margolin, 1988; Pagelow, 1981b; Straus, Gelles, & Steinmetz, 1980), or (c) offering clinical techniques or treatment programs for victims and/or perpetrators (e.g., Geller & Wasserstrom, 1984; Gondolf, 1987a; Hendricks-Matthews, 1982; Lynch & Norris, 1977-1978; Sonkin, Martin, & Walker, 1985; Walker, 1984a). Even though there has been a multifold expansion in our knowledge base on family violence over the past few decades, there are other topic areas related to family violence that have been overlooked or have received minimal attention. The topic of psychotherapy supervision is one such subject area that has received marginal attention in the literature (Goodwin, 1990; Goodwin & McHugh, 1991).

Although it is a professional assumption and expectation that every clinician *will* receive ongoing supervision, it is difficult to find in the family violence literature a discussion of how supervision prepares supervisors or therapists to recognize and provide clinical services to victims and/or perpetrators of domestic violence. Clearly, considering the role of supervision in the preparation of supervisors and clinicians is an especially timely, yet neglected, topic area.

This chapter narrows the discourse on family violence to focus on the subject of supervision and to explore the possible role that supervision might have in training supervisors and therapists who handle cases of domestic violence. This objective will be accomplished through (a) discussion of the nature and purpose of supervision; (b) description of traditional (psychoanalytic) and nontraditional (feminist) forms of supervision and consideration of the contributions of each to the issue of family violence, and in particular the effect on supervisor-trainee and trainee-client dyads; and (c) conclusions and recommendations offered to aid future effort in this area.

The Nature and Purpose of Psychotherapy Supervision

Although supervision is a value-laden process (Duran, 1990), it has been an undervalued enterprise. Supervision has been called the "quiet profession" by Alonso (1985), for seldom is much consideration given to the goals and objectives of the act. Bent, Schindler, and Dobbins (1992) remark that "the most neglected area of a psychologist's education and training is learning how to be supervised and how to supervise others" (p. 124). Few supervisors receive formal training in the role of supervisor, even though supervision is a competency area with an established body of knowledge, skills, and attitudes.

There is no agreed-upon type of supervision shown to prepare psychotherapists better than any other. Different types of supervision have been developed within a given theoretical perspective; consequently, a single theory has generated both a form of psychotherapy and a type of supervision.

The impact of supervision on the client and treatment outcome is a factor that has specific professional and ethical implications. This problem is compounded when we consider special populations, such as those who experience domestic violence. Statistics on domestic violence present an alarming portrait of family life. Koss (1990), in a recent article summarizing data on the prevalence of family violence, notes that anywhere from 25% to 33% of married couples experience some type of violence within the home. Relationship violence is a widespread and serious problem in this country if the statistics on courtship violence (Makepeace, 1983; Stets & Pirog-Good, 1989) are considered within the same domain as domestic violence. Those in this special population are probably overlooked when supervision occurs, given that the wealth of information on domestic violence is routinely not included in academic or training experiences.

It is safe to say that there is a dearth of information related to domestic violence included in the core curriculum and training experiences of trainees, unless family violence is a specialty area or an interest of a faculty member. With a few exceptions, a naive view is perpetuated that relationship violence is not commonplace. Moreover, when domestic violence is a presenting complaint in therapy, often the solution to this problem is to encourage the termination of the relationship (e.g., Walker, 1989a), to label the victim (e.g., Rosewater, 1987; Walker, 1987), or to work toward changing the behavior of the wife, who is the perceived instigator or is at least seen as coresponsible for the violence (Hansen, Harway, & Cervantes, 1991). Since parsimonious attention usually is given to this area, we have not begun to wrestle with how best to incorporate this knowledge base into effectual models of training. As has been noted:

> Formal, systematic training for psychotherapy supervisors can have substantial and wide-reaching effects. It can advance the training of psychotherapists; it can provide improved treatment for their patients. Reciprocally, it can benefit the quality of the patients' lives, the lives of their families and society at large. (Hoffman, 1990, p. iii)

A systematic approach is necessary to incorporate into the core curriculum, electives, training, and supervisory experiences the knowledge we have accumulated on relationship violence. This dominion should no longer be partitioned into a specialty area. It is also necessary to acknowledge that relationship violence knows no confines and can touch the personal lives of professionals and professionals in training, too. We should not overlook the possible victimization experiences of those who are our supervisors and/or trainees, just as we can expect that many of our clients have experienced domestic violence. If we fail to notice such concerns, blind spots occur and ineffective treatment is delivered. In all, the profession has not responded to this legitimate and well-established need; a population has been underserved and has not received adequate attention and clinical services. Through supervision we may better be able to attend to the pressing problems identified above. Because supervision approaches most often follow the therapeutic orientation of the supervisor, additional factors may have some impact on the supervision of trainees working with violent families.

The following section contrasts two forms of psychotherapy supervision. Particular attention is paid to a traditional and a nontraditional form of supervision, and to the relationships between supervisors and trainees and trainees and clients when working with cases in which domestic violence is an issue.

Theories of Supervision

Although there are myriad issues involved in the training of practitioners, it is assumed and often required that anyone matriculating through an accredited training program will receive a specific amount of supervision. The type and goal of supervision provided depend on the theory of supervision embraced. There are several traditional theories of supervision, each based on a particular therapeutic orientation. The four major traditional theoretical perspectives are the psychoanalytic, humanistic, behavioral, and developmental orientations. Feminist approaches to supervision have also developed. Regardless of the theoretical perspective, supervision serves two main functions, more or less: to teach clinical skills and techniques to the trainee and to facilitate the trainee's understanding of the interpersonal process of therapy (Porter, 1985).

This section focuses on psychoanalytic and feminist approaches to supervision, with particular attention paid to (a) a general description of each theory of supervision and (b) a description of the supervisor-trainee and trainee-client dyads as they relate to the issue of family violence.

A TRADITIONAL TYPE OF PSYCHOTHERAPY SUPERVISION: PSYCHOANALYSIS

How supervision is conducted is dependent on the supervisor's therapeutic orientation. The psychoanalytic approach to supervision is widely known and will be explored below. Although it may seem unnecessary to discuss such a familiar theory, with the recognition that domestic violence is a normative experience it is timely to consider whether psychoanalytic supervision is sensitive to the needs of therapists, trainees, and clients.

The Theory Underlying the Type of Supervision

Psychoanalysis was introduced by Sigmund Freud in 1895 and evolved over a 45-year period (Carver & Scheier, 1992). Psychoanalysis was launched with the publication of *Studies in Hysteria* (Breuer & Freud, 1895/1964) and ended with *An Outline of Psychoanalysis* (Freud, 1940/1964), which was published posthumously (Hjelle & Ziegler, 1992). Psychoanalytic theory has the longest history of any modern theory, and all other theories accept, reject, or revise psychoanalytic constructs.

Psychoanalysis has multiple meanings. To quote Hjelle and Ziegler (1992), "The term 'psychoanalysis' has three meanings: (1) a theory of personality and psychopathology, (2) a method of therapy for personality disturbances, and (3) a technique for investigating an individual's unconscious thoughts and feelings" (p. 86). Simply put, with its multiple meanings, psychoanalysis has multiple purposes: Psychoanalysis, as a theory, is designed to describe the dynamics of personality functioning and the etiology of behavior disorders; psychoanalysis, as a method of therapy, is designed to make conscious to the patient that which is unconscious and to restructure the patient's personality, which has been fixated (damaged) by childhood traumas, crises, and conflicts; psychoanalysis, as a technique, is designed to aid in clinical intervention and in structuring supervisory experiences.

Psychoanalytic supervision mirrors the process of psychoanalytic psychotherapy, which includes four major phases: "(1) the opening phase, (2) the development of transference, (3) the working-through of transference, and (4) the resolution of transference" (Okun, 1992, p. 110). These phases are also expected to occur during psychoanalytically informed supervision, with transference to the supervisor being a major focus of the supervision.

An expectation is that the therapist and supervisor have received extensive training, including personal therapy that is lengthy and rigorous and designed to uncover the supervisor's and clinician's unconscious motivations and needs and to restructure the personality that has been fixated (damaged) by childhood traumas, crises, and conflicts.

Those who contributed to the development of psychoanalysis seldom concerned themselves with the issues of the acculturation of family roles, sexual politics, or the gender bias inherent in the theory (Luepnitz, 1988)—all issues that must be considered by those working with battering. In psychoanalysis, instead, the focus is on power of the libido and the innateness of behavior, role confusion of women and mothers, childhood pathology, penis envy, and castrating women, to name a few.

In some circles psychoanalysis and sexism are considered compatible because of the way psychoanalysis addresses the role of females within the family and in society. If violence is occurring in a relationship, the therapist trained in psychoanalysis might ignore or downplay the importance of the violence, blame the victim for the violence, or suggest some inappropriate intervention (Hansen et al., 1991), and the psychoanalytically trained supervisor will then fail to train supervisees appropriately in how to deal with such cases.

Since classical psychoanalytic approaches to supervision devote much interest to the interaction between supervisor and trainee, the focus in this chapter will move to a discussion of the relationship issues.

The Supervisor-Trainee Dyad

Okun (1992) describes the supervisor-supervisee relationship in psychoanalysis as "a directive, authoritarian relationship" (p. 111). She continues by stating that "the relationship is not reciprocal; the helper is an expert authority figure and remains detached, objective, and completely neutral, so that transference will develop without contamination by the therapist's personhood" (p. 111). Moreover, the psychoanalytically informed supervisor is often described as anonymous, sharing few experiences or opinions and not openly sharing of him- or herself. This approach seems to go against what Porter (1985) stresses as critical to the development of clinical skills for the trainee, which leads to improvement of clients: a quality relationship between supervisor and trainee, which cannot occur in the distanced manner of the supervisor described by Okun (1992).

Porter (1985) discusses several areas of conflict between the supervisor and trainee occurring in traditional supervision, including (a) issues of differential power and authority, and (b) the evaluative nature of the relationship, similar to a therapy session in which the psychopathology of the trainee is explored. Porter states that sometimes "supervisors are exploiting their power and status, inhibiting the trainees' learning, and modeling a destructive therapeutic style" (p. 334). Such a supervisory relationship might contribute to negative experiences for both the trainee and the client. The focus of the therapy may then be on the psychopathology of the battered woman and may ignore the power differential between batterer and battered, especially when trainees then use what they learn in supervision with battered clients.

Another conflict that might occur is a theoretical one. An assumption inherent in many traditional models of supervision is that congruence exists between the theoretical views of the supervisor and those of the trainee. With a match in theoretical viewpoints, the trainee will probably welcome and experience some ease in the behaviors modeled by the supervisor. Dissimilarity between the theoretical viewpoints of the supervisor and the trainee makes for a disastrous situation for all parties involved, including the client, especially in cases of violence, because the therapist will then approach the case from a pathology perspective. As mentioned above, there is probably some connection between theoretical similarities and treatment outcome, too.

In a traditional supervisory relationship, the trainee is expected to be open enough to self-disclose "secrets" and intimacies; to be nondefensive when criticized concerning knowledge base, skill expertise, and personality characteristics; and to perform skills and techniques that may not be appropriate, comfortable, or fitting for the personality of the trainee. Can complete openness on the part of the trainee be expected, especially considering the evaluative nature of the relationship with the supervisor? With attention focused on the supervisor-trainee interaction, the trainee learns (a) skills that perpetuate authority, not egalitarian interactions (Okun, 1992; Warburton, Newberry, & Alexander, 1989); (b) assessment techniques that might ignore gender and emphasize psychopathology (Brown, 1990; Rosewater, 1985); and (c) defensive and nonintrospective behaviors that might lead to insensitivity and negative treatment outcomes (Hoffman, 1990). These could all have negative impact on the treatment of clients dealing with family violence.

Clearly there are major shortcomings in the traditional psychoanalytic approach to supervision. Such an approach ignores or downplays the unequal distribution of power in the patriarchy and in therapy (Goodrich, 1991). The gendered aspects of the behavior of females as supervisors, trainees, and clients are considered defective when compared with those of males. Pathology and negativism are explored, but health and positivism are not considered. The differences are exploited, with the male being the victor.

In all, the trainee who receives this type of training may, among other effects, (a) provide a less than adequate intervention that is theoretically sound but practically biased and abusive, (b) side with the authority figure without understanding the implications of this act, (c) reinforce hierarchical behaviors that do not perpetuate growth or health, and (d) fail to recognize the impact of gendered behaviors on the dynamics of relationships. The trainee may then unknowingly relate to violent clients or battered women from this perspective, and thereby intervene in contraindicated ways.

The Trainee-Client Dyad

The number of females in the mental health profession has increased, and gender now is considered by some to be extremely salient and important in understanding the functioning of any dyad, whether it be supervisor-trainee or therapist-client. Gender is considered to be especially important for the cross-gender dyad. In traditional approaches to supervision, little attention is paid to issues that arise with same-gender dyads.

Warburton et al. (1989) see some gender-role behaviors of females as facilitating the therapeutic process, and others as less useful. The female trainee/therapist may need to establish her authority and credibility early on in therapy in order to be effective. An overlooked problem is that the trainee may come to use behaviors modeled by the supervisor that might not necessarily contribute to a positive therapeutic relationship. More specifically, Warburton et al. mention empathy and the focus on relationships as benefiting female trainees, and passivity and the overuse of qualifiers as interfering with the therapeutic process, especially with the male members of a family. These behaviors might not be modeled by the supervisor, but they may be important nonetheless.

If the supervisor models authoritarian and unfeeling behavior, the trainee might adopt those styles; if the supervisor is a victim, those behaviors might be reinforced in the trainee; if the supervisor is a perpetrator, the trainee might take on those behaviors. What is the impact of all this on the client? It might be assumed that family violence is an issue only for the client, and not for the supervisor or the trainee. Situations in which direct services are being provided to those experiencing family violence or supervision is being given to trainees when family violence is the identified problem may trigger memories for the supervisor/survivor or perpetrator and lead to the provision of less than competent services. It appears that the supervisor and the trainee might benefit from intervention that addresses issues related to their own victimization, if that is the case. But if an authoritarian stance and objectivity are undertaken, will this ever happen?

It is my assertion that some of those trained in psychoanalysis take on a worldview that is structured to acknowledge some, but not all, aspects of behavior. The language is imprecise, the theory is "culture bound," and a hierarchy is perpetuated in social roles and relationships. The functioning of those who have been victimized is seldom acknowledged other than to describe it in terms of pathological behaviors.

The subsection below explores a nontraditional theory of supervision. This model, a feminist one, is considered by some to be the antithesis of psychoanalysis (Chesler, 1972/1989) and instead is "culture sensitive," not "culture bound," meaning that feminist approaches have evolved over several generations to consider the complexities of human behavior.

A NONTRADITIONAL TYPE OF PSYCHOTHERAPY SUPERVISION: FEMINISM

Just as there are several traditional types of supervision, there are also several nontraditional types of supervision in use. Feminism is one such nontraditional approach. Often, feminist therapy is associated with the behaviors of females, although it is not assumed that only women can provide feminist therapy or supervision, that all females are inherently supportive of the feminist perspective, or that all males are in disagreement with the feminist philosophy. The feminist model evolved out of discontent—discontent with traditional models such as psychoanalysis that focus on anatomical and innate differences, and discontent with sexism and the role of females in the family and in society. Supervision based on feminism is similar to that based on psychoanalysis in that it is designed to teach clinical skills and techniques and to facilitate the trainee in understanding the interpersonal process of therapy (Porter, 1985); however, it also has many differences that can affect therapists working with violent families.

The Theory Underlying the Type of Supervision

Feminist supervision evolved out of an ideology that has been around for many decades. There have been different waves of feminism, with the most recent beginning in the late 1960s, when feminist therapy and supervision were advanced (Rosewater & Walker, 1985). There is no single person associated with feminist therapy; rather, it is a "value system around which new conceptualizations about therapy with women have been developed" (Faunce, 1985, p. 1).

> Feminist therapists focus on understanding gender as both a cause and a consequence of women's experiences in a male-dominated culture. They expose the limitations and constraints of the traditional normative value bases of existing psychological theories. Thus, their reason for being is to challenge and question the attitudes toward women of the prevalent psychological theories, which have been largely developed and practiced by male theorists and therapists. Feminist therapists believe that those theories advocate the maintenance of the status quo of a male-dominated, hierarchical society. (Okun, 1992, p. 126)

Feminist therapy does not include a lengthy or elaborate vernacular. The theory is not as intricate as psychoanalysis, but, just like psychoanalysis, it has become a part of our culture. It is not designed only for treating women, but rather focuses on women as forming a distinct cultural group.

The feminist model of supervision initially emphasized the socialization of gender roles and behaviors. However, this model has broadened in emphasis to include more than gender differences as its focus. With women being culturally different from men, feminist therapy acknowledges the sociocultural and sociopolitical factors that affect the lives of women (Goodwin, 1990). Feminist therapy also acknowledges cultural differences among people.

> The term *culturally different* is often used for people who may be identified as different on the basis of overt physical characteristics, such as skin color or facial

> features; social and economic status; or ethnic heritage. It is more accurate to think of culture as consisting mostly of *internalized* values and beliefs, or emotional and mental qualities. Culturally different individuals do not necessarily have overt physical characteristics or identifiable ethnic heritages that distinguish them from the dominant cultural group. The culturally different individual is defined as one who has internalized values and beliefs about the world that are different from those of the dominant culture. (VandeCreek & Merrill, 1990, p. 196)

Feminist therapy and supervision incorporate notions of cultural sensitivity and multiculturalism. Because those who experience family violence represent heterogeneous and culturally diverse groups, theories, intervention techniques, and supervision approaches to this problem must be culture sensitive rather than culture bound (Boyd-Franklin, 1989; Goodwin, 1990, 1991; McGoldrick, Pearce, & Giordano, 1982). Feminist approaches to supervision, therefore, seem to be ideal for trainees who deal with violent families.

Exactly how feminist supervision and cultural sensitivity work together is elucidated by Sue and Sue (1990) and Sue and Zane (1987) in their discussions of how knowledge of a culture can relate to therapeutic success. Sue and Zane feel that while general knowledge about a culture is only remotely related to any goal of therapy, there is much variability of views within all cultures. A more proximal factor to successful therapeutic outcome is the therapist's credibility. The therapist's knowledge of the specific culture of the client can greatly increase the therapist's credibility (although many factors relate to that credibility, some of which may not be under the control of the therapist, such as sex, race, and age). This knowledge can have an impact on the conceptualization of the problem, goals of treatment, and the methods of intervention.

Mio (1989) believes that knowledge is not enough to increase cultural sensitivity, and that structured, one-on-one contact with someone of a different cultural group has more impact. Supervision can be useful in developing culturally sensitive practitioners.

Lopez et al. (1989) present a four-stage model of supervision for the development of culturally sensitive mental health professionals. The therapist moves through the following stages:

- Stage 1: unawareness of cultural issues
- Stage 2: heightened awareness of culture
- Stage 3: burden of considering culture
- Stage 4: movement toward cultural sensitivity

In Stage 1 of this model the therapist/trainee does not think in terms of culture and sees no relationship between cultural background and psychological functioning. Therapist/trainees in Stage 2 realize that culture is important in understanding clients and their functioning and are hesitant in working with culturally different clients. Stage 3 therapists/trainees are in a state of confusion. They are overwhelmed by the notion of culture and feel that it might distract from clinical effectiveness. Therapists/trainees in the last stage have reached cultural sensitivity. They are able to test out cultural hypotheses and are able to understand the role of culture in the psychological functioning of clients.

Following this model, feminist therapy also attempts to be culture sensitive. Feminist therapy promotes understanding of the myriad systems that affect both females and males. This knowledge of systems is carried into the relationships feminists have with each other, their trainees, and their clients. The relationships between the supervisor and the trainee and between the trainee and the client are explored in more detail below in light of the foregoing discussion of feminist therapy and cultural sensitivity.

The Supervisor-Trainee Dyad

In a feminist model of supervision, the relationship between the supervisor and the trainee is unlike the one described above for more traditional approaches. The relationship is not authoritarian, but reciprocal. The supervisor shares his or her personhood with the trainee. The supervisor is not detached, objective, or neutral. The relationship is not designed to be structured around skill level or educational attainment. Much emphasis is placed on the nature and functioning of the supervisory relationship, not on the psychopathology of the trainee.

In Porter's (1985) discussion of the philosophy behind feminist therapy and supervision, she delineates feminist supervision in terms of a four-stage model that is developmental in nature. Movement occurs back and forth among the following stages at any given period of time:

- Stage 1: introducing a feminist perspective
- Stage 2: exploring sexism and socialization in society
- Stage 3: exploring the trainee's attitudes
- Stage 4: taking a collective perspective

Here the focus is on acquainting the trainee with the feminist perspective by discussing the impact of culture on gendered behaviors. Attention is paid to the oppressive nature of the patriarchy, sexism, and the socialization of power and authority. The trainee is asked to introspect by considering personal values, beliefs, and attitudes. The trainee also is asked to consider the connectedness of behavior by moving from an individual to a group perspective in the hope of making relations less hierarchical. Egalitarianism, an important objective in the feminist model, is stressed.

Like traditional approaches, feminist supervision considers the impact of the supervisor-trainee relationship on effectiveness and treatment outcome, but not the conflicts inherent in the roles and the relationship. Instead, behavioral change and abilities are explored, especially the ability for empowerment—a key notion for the therapist to impart to a battered woman in treatment.

Wheeler, Avis, Miller, and Chaney (1989) present another feminist approach to supervision that is related to family therapy training. They, too, write about the supervisor-trainee relationship, saying that the primary characteristics of this interaction involve "the minimization of hierarchy and the use of social analysis" (p. 148). They posit that the power differential in the roles of supervisor and trainee can be minimized by the supervisor's encouraging shared responsibilities for contracting for specific learning and change; the evaluation of self and other, with feedback to the other party; and the avoidance of jargon and sexist language, so that intent is less likely to be misunderstood. The supervisor and trainee can perform social analysis to explore issues of gender; by sharing didactic materials, they can examine the position of women in society and in the family.

The feminist approach to supervision speaks to many issues raised in discussions of relationship violence. Feminist therapy acknowledges that our society is based on a division of power that many times occurs along lines of gender. Feminists understand that the system of patriarchy has had an enormous impact on our understanding and discussion of family violence in that it depreciates the criminality of the perpetrators by fostering the notion of coresponsibility, with therapists blaming the victim for instigating the violence received (Hansen et al., 1991). Because of patriarchal notions, the victim is socialized into believing that it is her fault her partner is angry and violent. Feminist therapy and supervision also consider the socialization of violence through the media and interpersonal relations, with females often being objectified, silenced, subjugated, beaten, and killed. A trainee supervised by a feminist supervisor would be exposed to the role of society in promulgating and maintaining the violence experienced by the individual woman.

Feminist supervision does not overly concern itself with the dynamics of same-sex or cross-sex dyads, but some attention has been given to the discussion of power, both personal and interpersonal (e.g., Douglas, 1985; Smith & Siegel, 1985). There is some question whether male supervisors/therapists can empower female trainees, and whether males are capable of providing feminist supervision or therapy. Feminist therapy is considered to be flexible enough to accommodate diverse dyads, for it is a tenet of feminist therapy and feminist supervision that the supervisor does not exploit his or her status and power, will not inhibit the trainee's psychological growth and learning, and will model a therapeutic style that is empowering to the trainee. In turn, this modeling of egalitarianism can empower the battered client by acknowledging that, in contrast to the battering relationship, there are ways of relating that do not require one person to have power and control over the other (Porter, 1985).

The Trainee-Client Dyad

As in traditional approaches to supervision, in feminist approaches the quality of the trainee-client dyad is integral to the functioning of the supervisor-trainee relationship. However, in a nonhierarchical relationship (supervision informed by feminism), what is expected of the supervisor is expected of the trainee. The trainee and the supervisor behave in a similar fashion. The trainee might discuss how patriarchy, sexism, and the socialization of power and authority have affected the psychological functioning of the client. He or she might also explore how media messages reinforce or extinguish particular behaviors.

How the supervisor behaves vis-à-vis the trainee is a model for how the trainee will behave with the client. Just as the supervisor might share skills with the trainee, the trainee might share skills with the client. Just as the supervisor might share reading materials with the trainee, the trainee might share information with the client. Taking the client through the four stages developed by Porter (1985) furthers the spirit of egalitarianism that is prevalent in feminist therapy. Feminist therapy stresses flexibility, positivism, and change in regard to the client, the trainee, and the supervisor. Feminist therapy offers hope. In particular, the battered client gains hope for healthier relationships when she experiences mutual respect, positivism, and flexibility—relational characteristics she may never before have known.

Although psychotherapists have been slow to recognize relationship violence as a societal problem, feminists have long been in the forefront of this discussion. Feminists realize that the probability is great that, regardless of clinical specialty area, therapists will frequently encounter clients involved in violent relationships, either as perpetrators or as victims.

From the overview presented above, it appears that feminist therapy and supervision come out of a vastly different philosophical background from that of psychoanalysis and other traditional modalities, and thereby produce vastly different outcomes for supervisors, trainees, and clients. As a "culture-sensitive" approach feminist therapy is able to address the complexities of behavior. It seldom deals with absolutes; rather, its focus is on change.

Conclusion

The literature on family violence has demonstrated the severity and enormity of this societal problem that has become almost a normative experience. The mental health profession has been challenged to develop a response to this concern, yet a response has been slow in coming. The intent of this chapter has been to direct attention to one clinical competency area—psychotherapy supervision—that could have the potential for training vast numbers of mental health professionals to recognize and intervene in therapy cases where relationship violence is evident.

This chapter has explored the nature and purpose of supervision, with particular attention given to psychoanalytic and feminist approaches. The dynamics of supervisor-trainee and trainee-client dyads have been examined as they affect the process and outcome of therapy in general and the therapeutic relationship in particular, where domestic violence is a concern.

This review of approaches to supervision concludes that psychoanalytic supervision, as a traditional and culture-bound approach, might lead to disastrous results for those who are in violent families, because the focus in supervision will not be on the severity of the violent behavior but on the innateness of behavior, unconscious motivations, and the gendered nature of pathology. Feminist supervision, a nontraditional and culture-sensitive approach, might be more attuned to the needs of those in violent families by virtue of its being better able to understand the subtleties of intra- and interpersonal relations, gender-typed behaviors, and the effects of systems such as the patriarchy.

The following systemic/institutional changes, which follow from the preceding analyses, are recommended for the profession if it is to change the status of family violence from that of a specialty area, of interest to a few, to a competency area required of all supervisors and trainees within the limitations of their theoretical orientations:

- A systematic evaluation should be undertaken for each type of supervision to assess whether its philosophical assumptions are congruent with the goals of feminism and whether it is a culture-sensitive approach. The impact each kind of supervision may have on the socialization of professional behavior, on the supervisor-trainee dyad, on the trainee-client dyad, and on the treatment outcome of the battered client should also be assessed.

- Classes that teach the knowledge, skills, and attitudes involved in supervision should be required of all students. Training programs that teach the knowledge, skills, and attitudes involved in supervision should be required as continuing education experiences.
- The core curriculum and the intervention core should be broadened so that the topic of relationship violence is integrated throughout a program. This will require a commitment of resources and a redesign of all courses and field experiences.
- All models of supervision should be examined for their cultural sensitivity to the issues that a battered client presents in therapy.

11

Impact of Abusive Marital Relationships on Children

PEARL S. BERMAN

Witnessing abusive marital relationships has such a profound and complex impact on children that an entire book has been written on the topic (Jaffe, Wolfe, & Wilson, 1990). This chapter is limited to a brief overview of the scope and nature of the problem and a discussion that highlights, from a feminist family therapy perspective, the impact of male-initiated spousal violence on the immediate, short-term, and long-term development of children. Issues in treatment and professional ethics are also raised.

Straus and his associates, in two national surveys of family violence, estimated that 11-12% of females reported incidents of spousal abuse within the home during the past year, and 28% reported a violent incident over the course of their marriage (see Straus & Gelles, 1986; Straus, Gelles, & Steinmetz, 1980). Interspousal physical aggression has been found at higher levels within the early stages of couples' relationships (O'Leary et al., 1989) and young, low-income families with young children have higher levels of physical aggression (Straus et al., 1980). Abused women have reported that children were usually present during acts of verbal and physical aggression with their mates (Hinchey & Gavalek, 1982). In addition, 30-60% of families with interspousal violence may include child physical or sexual abuse (Hughes, 1982; Straus et al., 1980). Carlson (1984) has estimated that at least 3.3 million children between the ages of 3 and 17 are witnessing, if not directly experiencing, violence.

The research on the effects of children's witnessing abuse has been confusing, with some studies appearing to contradict others. Fantuzzo and

Lindquist (1989) and Fantuzzo et al. (1991) have cited many methodological explanations for these contradictions, including the following: Studies have often confounded the effects of experiencing child abuse with witnessing spousal abuse; studies have treated children of diverse ages, such as 4-16 years old, as homogeneous groups; nonviolent comparison groups have not been matched on socioeconomic, family composition, ethnic, and level of family discord variables; nearly all children studied have been from battered women's shelters and thus may not be representative of the population of children experiencing spousal violence; studies have depended on parental (usually mother's) reports of children's behavior; and many studies have employed retrospective designs.

Keeping these methodological issues in mind, we can still draw some generalizations from the research conducted thus far. For instance, studies have suggested that the greater the number of stressors on the child, the more severe the effects. Children who witness violence and are directly victimized have shown more severe effects than those who only witness the violence (Hughes, Parkinson, & Vargo, 1989; Straus et al., 1980). Children from homes with verbal abuse show less severe effects than do children from homes with verbal and physical abuse, and children experiencing both of these types of abuse and moving to battered women's shelters show the most severe effects (Fantuzzo et al., 1991). Shelter groups have shown the greatest levels of externalizing and internalizing problems as well as the lowest levels of social competency in comparison to other abused children (Fantuzzo et al., 1991; Jaffe et al., 1990). Longitudinal studies investigating the cause of this greater negative outcome for shelter children and demonstrating whether it is short or long term have yet to be done.

Studies have also suggested heightened sensitivity of younger children to the negative effects of interspousal violence in comparison to older children. For example, Hughes (1988) found that preschool children exhibited more behavior problems and lower levels of self-esteem than did school-age children. However, while older children have shown greater capacities to cope with anger, they have also shown heightened sensitivity and involvement in the conflicts of others as well as less frequent displays of affect in response to parental fighting (Cummings, Vogel, Cummings, & El-Sheikh, 1989; Cummings, Zahn-Waxler, & Radke-Yarrow, 1984). Thus the influence of spousal violence may be more subtle for older children. For example, adolescent girls may have negative attitudes toward marriage or a distrust of men, or they may become victims of their boyfriends' violence (Jaffe et al., 1990).

Immediate Effects of Children's Witnessing Parental Violence

As the child is witnessing and/or being a victim of parental violence, what immediate effects may result? Whatever was happening immediately prior to the violent event—eating, sleeping, socializing, or whatever—may stop. Physically, the child may be intentionally or unintentionally injured and his or her basic needs for food and warm clothing may not be met during violent episodes (Jaffe et al., 1990). The child focuses on the violence, thus necessarily ignoring other stimuli in the environment. Thus the cues that become salient for learning cause-effect relationships are related to violence. Cummings and associates have demonstrated that young children are affected by the background climate of aggression, not just anger and aggression directed at them (Cummings, Pellegrini, Notarius, & Cummings, 1989; E. M. Cummings et al., 1989). Children's responses to background aggression may include increased emotional arousal, distress, and increased aggressiveness. Repeated exposure to anger may increase sensitivity to expressions of anger and lead to greater distress and intervention responses (Cummings, Zahn-Waxler, & Radke-Yarrow, 1981; J. S. Cummings et al., 1989), and repeated exposure to aggression may lead to heightened sensitivity and greater likelihood of interpreting cues as aggressive (Eron, 1987). Young children are at home most of the time, which makes them more vulnerable to declines in quality care and background aggression than older children, who have more opportunities to be at school or other locations of safety (Masten, Best, & Garmezy, 1990).

At school, children exposed to violence can appear distracted or inattentive; they may be thinking about the abuse or they may be tired from being awake during fights or being hypervigilant at night for recurrences of the violence (Jaffe et al., 1990). Children in shelters have been found to lose interest in their peer group (Jaffe et al., 1990). Fantuzzo et al. (1991) hypothesize that placing children in shelters separates them from their natural support systems, such as peers, neighbors, relatives, and familiar toys, thus leaving them more defenseless in the face of family stress. Ironically, the immediate effect of ensuring the children's physical safety—through removal to a shelter—may also serve to decrease their ability to cope psychologically with the violence.

Short-Term Effects of Children's Witnessing Parental Violence

The longer a child is exposed to violence, the more likely it is that the violence will have short-term, in addition to immediate and possibly transitory, influences on the child. Cummings et al. (1981) found that frequent fighting between parents was associated with children's making repeated attempts at intervening within the conflict. The most common reactions of children were distress and withdrawal, however, some children responded with anger and others with affectionate/prosocial behavior. Children's differential responses to observing violence may mirror differences in their personality development. Three early patterns of reactions to family violence can be conceptualized: the child behaving as a victimizer of others (externalizing reaction), as a victim (internalizing reaction), or resiliently.

THE VICTIMIZER

The research of Gruszynski, Brink, and Edleson (1988) and Straus et al. (1980) indicates that many child witnesses of parental violence become aggressive and engage in delinquent acts. Sonkin, Martin, and Walker (1985) found that 24% of adult batterers had, as children, attacked one of their parents. Boys from violent homes have been found to be highly aggressive with peers and with other adults. Although sons may initially hate the spousal violence, many come to direct violence at their mothers, sisters, or girlfriends (Barnett, Pittman, Ragan, & Salus, 1980). At school they may be unwilling to do schoolwork, rebel against authority, and fight constantly with peers (Barnett et al., 1980; McKay, as cited in Jaffe et al., 1990).

How might this victimizing behavior begin? Children learn the roles and behaviors of their own sex by observing and interacting with their parents (Bandura, 1973; Straus et al., 1980). Within the violent home, children learn that violence is the basis for power and control (Jaffe et al., 1990; Straus et al., 1980) and that inequality of power, with men being more powerful, is acceptable (Wilson, Cameron, Jaffe, & Wolfe, 1989). Children in these violent homes learn that women nurture but are weak and victimized (Carlson, 1984) because they are insignificant, incompetent, or less important than men (Frieze, 1987; Walker & Browne, 1985). Lessons on intimacy within the violent family may teach that it is acceptable to hurt physically those you love (Carlson, 1984; Straus et al., 1980). Violent parents teach children communication and problem-solving skills that highlight violence as an appropriate and effective method for conflict resolution (Carlson, 1984; Walker & Browne, 1985; Wilson et al., 1989) and as the primary mode for demonstrating dissatisfaction and desire for change (Straus et al., 1980). The greater community teaches children that it supports violence by doing little or nothing about it when family violence is reported to community services (Wilson et al., 1989) and through tacit social support for males' expressions of dominance and control (Walker & Browne, 1985).

Dodge, Bates, and Pettit (1990) have found children from violent households to exhibit cognitive deficits in the processing of social information, including failure to attend to relevant cues, bias in attributing hostile intentions to others, and lack of competent behavioral strategies to solve interpersonal problems. This and other research suggests that the experience of physical harm can lead the child to conceptualize the world in deviant ways and thus to develop a victimizer identity (Eron, 1987; Garbarino, 1990).

While both boys and girls may begin developing victimizing identities, there may be a higher prevalence among boys. Within the United States, sex role socialization encourages the development of different behaviors for males and females, with males encouraged to be less verbally expressive and more physically aggressive (Hartnett & Bradley, 1987). In a cross-cultural study, Zammuner (1987) found that males were more likely than females to become angry in response to provocation and more likely to engage in physical aggression when aggressive behavior was viewed as socially acceptable. In addition, boys are more likely than girls to show angry responses to witnessing interpersonal aggression (E. M. Cummings et al., 1989). In terms of response styles, Achenbach and Edelbrock (1981) have found boys to present more externalizing problems (impulsivity, aggression) and girls to present more internalizing problems (anxiety, depression, fear). Similarly, approximately 9% of boys are diagnosed with conduct disorders, in comparison to 2% of girls (American Psychiatric Association, 1980).

THE VICTIM

Rather than becoming victimizers, some children may come to see themselves as powerless and valueless and thus assume a victim role (Barnett et al., 1980). In response to violence, some children become withdrawn, clingy, dependent, and socially isolated (Alessi & Hearn, 1984; Dodge et al., 1990; Hughes, 1988). How might this begin? A basic role of the family is to provide safety and security (Minuchin & Fishman, 1981). Within the violent home, children learn that to survive physically, women must focus on how to avoid being punished, rejected, or physically abused (Berman, 1989). Abused women become hypervigilant of their male partners in attempts to avoid violence (Berman, 1989; Walker, 1984a; Walker & Browne, 1985). In terms of interpersonal relationships, these children might conclude that women are powerless and that it is not safe for them to be independent (Straus et al., 1980) or for children to be independent either. As children become older and strive for independence, the batterer may respond with attempts to control them as he has controlled his wife (Walker, 1984a). When children turn to their mother for nurturance and safety from a violent father, she may be unable to offer it (Van der Kolk, 1987)—proving that she is as incompetent as her partner has indicated she is (Frieze, 1987). In such families, women's personal needs are considered unimportant, and the needs of others must always come first (Berman, 1989; Frieze, 1987). Problem-solving and communication strategies in these families suggest that violence is inevitable and/or an indicator of love (Carlson, 1984; Walker & Browne, 1985) and that victims are responsible for the violence or must at least tolerate it (Wilson et al., 1989).

Dodge et al. (1990) hypothesize that internalizing outcomes may be mediated by attributions of self-blame and expectations that aggression would not succeed in eliminating negative outcomes. This belief on the part of the children that aggression will not help protect them may be supported by their witnessing of their mother fighting back but not succeeding in protecting herself (Straus & Gelles, 1986). Walker (1984a) stresses that while men use violent acts for power and control, women use them in self-defense—to stay alive or to minimize their own injuries. Finally, over time, abused women begin to deny and minimize the extent of the violence, underestimate the lethality of the situation (Browne, 1987; Walker & Browne, 1985), and display signs of learned helplessness (Walker, 1984a). These maternal tendencies might prevent their children from establishing a meaningful context for understanding the abuse (Garbarino, 1990) and may provide, especially for their daughters, a model of passive and ineffectual problem solving. These passive tendencies can be reflected in school by low academic achievement, school phobia, difficulties in concentration, and social isolation (Hughes, 1986).

Compounding these factors, sex role socialization encourages girls to be insecure and dependent and boys to be independent and self-confident (Hartnett & Bradley, 1987). It also encourages them to model the same-sex parent (Barnett et al., 1980), for girls to respond to provocation by becoming anxious and boys by becoming angry (Zammuner, 1987), for females to respond with passivity and acceptance to aggression and domination by males (Walker & Browne, 1985), and for the former to view their self-esteem in terms of their relationships and their ability to maintain these relationships (Walker & Browne, 1985). Thus sex role socialization increases the likelihood that more girls than boys will respond to the violent family situation by beginning to assume a victim role.

THE RESILIENT CHILD

Resilience is the most positive route for the child's identity. While *resilience* has been defined in many ways, within the context of family violence it might best be defined as effective coping, where the child makes efforts to restore or maintain internal or external equilibrium under threatening circumstances (Masten et al., 1990). What lessons might children learn from their parents' abusive relationship that could encourage the development of a resilient identity? Some abused women continue to be nurturing parents (Jaffe et al., 1990), and researchers have underscored the potency of strong emotional support from a nonabusive adult in aiding resilience (Egeland, Jacobvitz, & Sroufe, 1988; Kalmuss, 1984; Kaufman & Zigler, 1987; Masten et al., 1990). Garbarino (1990) hypothesizes that the ability of the mother to provide a strong, nurturing adult role model who can give meaning to the violent events (for example, that violence is a result of alcohol abuse, chronic unemployment, or lack of education) might provide a positive cognitive accommodation to the violent events, thus generating resilience in the child. Alternatively, while parents involved in marital conflicts may have decreased parenting skills (Emery, 1982), children with natural competencies and feelings of self-worth can fill in the parenting gaps. Jaffe and associates (1990) report that older girls may be especially likely to try to protect their younger siblings during episodes of violence and to offer nurturance at the end of these episodes. From these supportive, nurturing relationships the child can learn that respect and love from mothers and younger siblings can be gained through nurturance rather than violence.

Children may see their parents' problem-solving and communication patterns as ineffectual: Their fathers explode and their mothers focus on survival of, rather than escape from, the violence (Walker, 1984a). Through relationships with supportive adults and peers outside the family, school-age children receive concrete evidence that rewarding relationships exist and that people can be available to them in time of need (Egeland et al., 1988). For teenagers, who have the capacity for abstract reasoning, these experiences allow them to imagine and try out relationship patterns that are different from those used by their parents. Finally, through seeing the negative effects of violence on family members, children can make conscious decisions that their own future family lives will be different (Egeland et al., 1988).

Being resilient is not equivalent to being happy and secure. Resilient children, in their desire to offer protection and nurturance to their mothers and younger siblings (Jaffe et al., 1990), may stay at home with the violence when they could leave. By trying to protect their mothers and younger siblings and to calm their fathers' anger, they generate cross-generational coalitions that violate the integrity of both the spouse and child systems. The resilient child is put in the position of having to grow up too quickly and take on more responsibility within the family than is developmentally appropriate (Barnett et al., 1980). It is the role of the parents to protect children, not the reverse (Minuchin & Fishman, 1981). However, despite these difficulties, some children show resilience in terms of functioning well academically and with peers (Jaffe et al., 1990). Turning to schoolwork and peers provides an avenue for day-to-day escape and can lay the groundwork for future life success.

PREVALENCE RATES

Although the descriptive and empirical research literature on child witnesses indicates the existence of victimizing, victimlike, and resilient reactions to family violence, there are no prevalence rates for these reactions based on epidemiological studies. Most existing studies compare group scores on mothers' reports of child behavior. The presence of children with elevated scores on internalizing and externalizing behavior is almost universally reported. There are usually no direct discussions of resilient reactions to family violence. Rather, resilience is implied by the fact that some child witnesses do not show elevations on either internalizing or externalizing scales.

Long-Term Effects of Children's Witnessing Parental Violence

The greater the extent and duration of the abusive situation, the more likely that short-term effects of abuse will become long-term effects. What factors might lead to remediation rather than hardening of the immediate effects so that long-term adjustment becomes more positive? Some research suggests that nurturance and aggression, both the amount experienced from the parents and the levels developed within the child, may hold the key.

Eron (1987), in a 30-year longitudinal study of children from a general population, found that low levels of nurturance, high levels of discipline, strong family and extended family support for violence, and low identification with the parents at age 8 were predictive of aggression both 10 and 20 years later. Straus et al. (1980) found that boys and girls are most likely to be abusive parents when their same-sex parent was abusive. They also found a stronger relationship between being physically punished by a father and later being violent toward a spouse. In addition, abused school children and children exposed to conjugal violence have been shown to display limited empathy and to respond inappropriately to the distress of others (Hinchey & Gavalek, 1982; Main & George, 1985). In contrast, Koestner, Weinberger, and Franz (1990), in a 26-year longitudinal study of empathy, found children were most likely to become empathic adults when both of their parents enjoyed being involved with them, inhibited aggressive behavior, and permitted and encouraged affiliative needs. Thus family violence may disrupt the development of empathic and prosocial competencies in young children. These disruptions may be especially potent for boys, as they are socialized to be more aggressive and less nurturant (Hartnett & Bradley, 1987). The consequences of watching violent television (Eron, 1987) or being exposed to an unresponsive legal or social system (Wilson et al., 1989) may serve to send the child a community message that violence and unequal power between males and females is acceptable, thus increasing the potential for a negative long-term impact on the child's development.

A major task of adolescence is the development of a stable sense of personal identity. If long-term negative consequences prevail, how might male and female teenagers behave? Teenage girls who have witnessed their fathers' abuse of their mothers have been shown to distrust men and marriage or to begin to experience their own personal victimization within dating relationships (Jaffe et al., 1990). They may also come to the attention of the court system by running way, by becoming involved in prostitution, or by engaging in unruly behavior (Rutter & Giller, 1983). Teen boys may be more likely to become engaged with the court system through assaultive behavior (Grusznski et al., 1988; Rutter & Giller, 1983). Being a victim of physical abuse as well as a witness of it increases the probability of violent behavior from males, with the most violent delinquents coming from the most violent homes (Lewis, Shanok, Pincus, & Glaser, 1979; Straus et al., 1980).

In terms of developing negative adult identities, batterers, as children and adolescents, were often witnesses to violence within their families (Finkelhor, Hotaling, & Yllö, 1988). Sonkin et al. (1985) found that 45% of male batterers saw their mothers being abused by their fathers, and 50% either saw their mothers abused or were themselves abused. They also found that 68% of individuals who witnessed violence as children say their children have viewed their own violence, and 57% say they use physical punishment on their children. Walker (1984a) reports that 66% of battered women were themselves victims or witnesses of violence as children.

While negative outcomes occur, these data also clearly indicate that many children from violent homes become nonabusive mates and parents. In Kalmuss's (1984) sample, 94% of the adults who had witnessed spousal violence as children were not involved in severe spousal violence within their present families, and 88% of the adults who had both witnessed and experienced physical abuse as children were not involved in severe spousal violence within their present families. Kaufman and Zigler (1987) report that two-thirds of the abused and neglected children they studied became adequate parents. Factors found related to resilience in adulthood include having had a supportive relationship with a nonabusive parent as a child, participating in therapy, having nurturant adult relationships outside of the family, having a personal commitment to nonperpetuation of the cycle of violence, and having a supportive, nonviolent spouse (Egeland et al., 1988; Kalmuss, 1984; Kaufman & Zigler, 1987).

Treatment

The modes and lengths of treatment most appropriate for children and their parents will vary by the immediacy of the violent episodes, the age and sex of the child, the child's short-term response to the violence (victimizer, victim, resilient), and the stage of recovery of the parents.

From a feminist family therapy perspective, female values of nurturance and male values of independence and competence within family relationships must receive equal respect throughout treatment. The goal of egalitarian relationships between spouses must be underscored (Straus et al., 1980). In addition, the roles of parents and children must be clarified and allocation of family responsibilities must be negotiated. Specifically, parents need education about the effects of their behavior in general, and violence in particular, on their children; education about their role in the nurturing, protecting, and socializing of their children; and training to build the skills they need to parent children of different ages effectively. Children need help with identity development (e.g., Am I separate? What is a girl? What is a boy?), their view of family life (e.g., parental versus child responsibilities), and interpersonal relationships (e.g., how to get needs met and conflicts resolved without violence). Skill building in the areas of positive peer relationships and academics may also be needed.

Ending violent interactions is a key step in family recovery. Abused women often view the end of violence as being in the hands of the batterer (Walker, 1984a) or appear unmotivated to take action (Frieze, 1987). They may maintain ties with an abusive partner because of a desire for intimacy for themselves and/or their children (Walker, 1984a). Women have also stayed with batterers because they felt a male-dominated household provided stability for their children (Davidson, 1978). Thus treatment focused on parent-child relationships in which the mother is educated about the negative impact on children of witnessing violence might increase women's motivation to end the violence. Similarly, the negative effects of insufficient nurturance should be conveyed. Capitalizing on women's motivation to protect their children over themselves can be helpful: Basta (1990) found that mothers whose children had also been victimized had less contact with their batterers after leaving a shelter than did other abused mothers. Since abusive men expect all of their needs to be met by their mates (Walker, 1984a), education about the negative effects of violence and the attracting power of nurturance in developing deeper relationships with children, spouses, and peers might provide motivation for change.

Existing research on the effectiveness of treatment and types of treatment most appropriate for children is equivocal because of its sparseness as well as its problems concerning small sample sizes and lack of control groups. Children who have witnessed spousal violence have primarily received group therapy located within battered women's shelters (Alessi & Hearn, 1984; Grusznski et al., 1988; Hughes, 1982; Jaffe et al., 1990; Wilson et al., 1989). While many groups have covered issues of family relationships and male-female relationships, the model developed by Grusznski et al. (1988) has most directly confronted issues of gender stereotypes as well as issues of appropriate family responsibilities and boundaries.

Developmental Issues in Treatment Planning

While feminist family therapy provides valuable guidelines for the treatment of family violence, developmental issues must be considered if interventions are to be effective with children. Children's thinking in the preschool years is egocentric. They have an exaggerated view of their impact on the world, and they understand the world in terms of immediate, concrete events (Berger, 1991). As a result, children often view themselves as responsible for the violence (Straus et al., 1980); for example, "Dad beat my mother because I left my clothes on the floor today." This tendency for self-blame will be accentuated if children observe parents fighting about their upbringing or if children are told that the violence is their fault and that it will stop if they behave (Grusznski et al., 1988). To be effective, explanations of family violence for this age group need to be simple and concrete.

While school-age children are still egocentric, they are developing the capacity to be logical. Thus they can understand more complex explanations of violence and how it is influencing their families as long as these explanations are tied to concrete reality. Thus present-oriented explanations of family violence made in terms of their specific family situation will be more effective than abstract, general discussions of violence within American society.

Children progressing from elementary school into high school develop the capacity for more advanced reasoning. However, teens use advanced reasoning only in realms where they have received encouragement and intensive experience. Many adolescents who can think abstractly about academics are egocentric about topics personally relevant to themselves; for instance, feelings of invincibility or uniqueness may cause them to underestimate life risks (Berger, 1991). Thus teens have the capacity to think abstractly and to envision lives for themselves that are different from those of their parents, in which they take into account the needs and values of others. However, they need support from significant others (parents, therapists) to do so and to see the parallels between their own victimization or victimization of others and the behavior of their parents.

The larger the age range of children within a family, the more complex family treatment becomes. Treatment themes need to be addressed repeatedly, varying the level of the discussion to suit the cognitive ability of each family member. Parents can be empowered by being taught how to use developmentally appropriate language to help their children profit from treatment.

Ethical Issues in the Treatment of Children

Research to date suggests that most victims return to their batterers, bringing along their children. Thus children continue to be exposed to an environment that can perpetuate the intergenerational transmission of violence (Gentry & Eaddy, 1982). Children will not be able to change their attitudes or behavioral reactions to violence if violence is continuing at home (Jaffe et al., 1990). Ensuring the physical safety of the child is critical if treatment interventions are to increase the likelihood of resilience in the child and to decrease the possibility of the child's adopting victimizing or victimlike behavior. If parents refuse treatment or profit minimally from it and the child remains with them, therapists face limited options. They can clearly spell out for parents that the violent experiences at home will have an ever increasing negative influence on their children, and they can help children develop age-appropriate protection plans. Children may be at greater risk if they are the only ones receiving comprehensive treatment. A violent parent may not appreciate a child's attempts to communicate openly. Finally, the male perpetrator should be involved in family treatment sessions only when other family members want his presence and it is emotionally and physically safe for him to be there (Grusznski et al., 1988).

Summary

Every year, millions of children witness and are influenced by family violence. Research suggests that the effects of these experiences vary according to the age, sex, number of additional life stressors, and level of social and emotional support available to the children involved. In summarizing across studies diverse in terms of age range and overall methodology, victimizing, victimlike, and resilient reactions to violence have been noted. Almost universally, these studies have examined the behavior of children at one point in time. Whether, for example, the aggressive male preschooler becomes the teen batterer and finally the violent spouse needs to be examined prospectively through longitudinal research. Feminist family therapy offers valuable insights into the dynamics of family members and provides guidelines for the comprehensive treatment of violent families. These insights and guidelines need to be validated empirically.

12

Therapist Duty in Domestic Violence Cases: Ethical Considerations

NANCYANN N. CERVANTES

Recent statistics suggest that as many as 31% of couples engage in violence toward each other (Koss, 1990), indicating that most mental health professionals will work with violent families at some point in their careers. Therapist response to family violence has been explored from the perspective of what constitutes the most effective treatment modality (Madanes, 1990; Pittman, 1987; Thaxton, 1985; Walker, 1991). Therapist responsibility for effective treatment of these clients is particularly important, given that 50% of murder victims are murdered by their spouses (Stump, 1985).

Therapist interest in spousal abuse is closely related to the rise of the feminist movement in this country. Since the mid-1970s, legal reforms have been instituted in almost every state in an effort to provide greater protection for victims of domestic violence (Caringella-MacDonald, 1988). These include mandatory arrest laws, restraining orders that can be obtained *ex parte* (based on the request of one spouse), and civil suits that can be brought against the abusing party. Prior to these legal reforms, spouse abuse was viewed as a private matter under the husband's control. Currently, victims have greater access than before to more effective protection and treatment (Caringella-MacDonald, 1988). However, even these legal advancements still do not dispel the myth that domestic violence is in a different, and less serious, category from violence between strangers.

The focus of this chapter is the ethical responsibility and/or duty that therapists have when confronted with spousal violence cases. This responsibility is different from that which applies in cases of child abuse or elder abuse. Violence against children has been addressed through child abuse reporting laws in all states. Some states have also adopted elder abuse reporting laws in an effort to begin to address the protection needs of the elderly and other adults who are incapacitated. In both of these examples, the laws are intended to protect individuals who are unable to care for themselves because of their age or disability. Both kinds of laws also impose legal requirements on therapists, specifying that therapists are mandated reporters. Spousal abuse has not, to date, been covered by mandatory reporting requirements.

In the absence of legal mandates regarding reporting, the ethical and legal issues can be divided into two categories: responsibility to provide effective treatment and duty to warn/protect. The term *ethical responsibility* will be used in this chapter to describe obligations and duties arising from ethical mandates; the term *duty* will be reserved for legal mandates.

Effective Treatment

As therapists have become more sensitized to the presence of violence in the family, they have increased their awareness of the need to address safety issues. In cases involving a clear statement by the client that she is being physically abused, therapists have usually interpreted their responsibility to promote the welfare of the client (APA Code of Ethics, 1992) as advising the woman to remove herself from the dangerous situation. Pittman (1987) details a treatment approach that advises the woman of the necessity to remove herself physically from the violent situation. Rosenbaum and O'Leary (1986) provide an assessment decision tree that clearly outlines the therapist's responsibility to provide information and advice to the woman in a violent marital relationship in order to facilitate her leaving the situation. Both of these approaches take a "problem-solving" stance, with the problem of the violence needing to be eliminated before the productive work of therapy can begin. In actuality, the responsibility of the therapist is to achieve the cessation of the violence.

The therapist who accurately assesses the problem and develops an appropriate treatment plan for the remediation of the problem is acting ethically to provide effective treatment. To date, the treatment of women victims of spousal abuse has focused upon victims who are clearly identified (women in domestic violence shelters, couples referred by the courts for treatment for domestic violence). Therapists, unless they are actively involved in treating spousal abuse cases, have not assumed a proactive role in identifying victims of spousal abuse among their therapy clients. The recognized theories of psychotherapy do not specifically address the implications of domestic violence for mental illness except to focus on the historical significance of growing up in a violent home. Violence during childhood is viewed by all major theoretical orientations as contributing significantly to later mental health problems as well as to violent tendencies in adulthood. However, mental health professionals are struggling with understanding how family violence contributes to the current emotional and behavioral functioning of clients.

ASSESSMENT

Rosenbaum and O'Leary (1986) advocate a proactive responsibility to assess for violence even when it is not the primary presenting complaint. Abused wives frequently present with problems of anxiety, depression, and somatic complaints (Gayford, 1975). Since the majority of women seeking treatment have these complaints, it would be prudent for therapists to inquire about current and past abusive relationships in all cases. In addition, surveys of police reports have found that 65% of abused women have received psychiatric care. The majority of these women have reported that prior therapists failed to inquire about abuse (Goldstein & Page, 1981). In a recent survey, Hansen, Harway, and Cervantes (1990) found that therapists working with families ignored or minimized the existence of violence when it was present in the family. Since the battered woman herself tends to minimize the presence and importance of the violence, the tendency is for the therapist and the client to formulate a treatment plan that does not address the issue of the violence, but rather attempts to treat the symptoms of anxiety, depression, and somatic complaints.

Pittman (1987) advises therapists working from a family systems orientation to inquire about spousal abuse within the relationship. His formulation of domestic violence as an exaggerated courtship ritual between two individuals who are incapable of expressing love and affection for each other without the violence is typical of the school of thought that the responsibility for the domestic violence is shared between the couple.

To date, the shared responsibility formulation has been addressed as a treatment issue in the literature. Therapists who identify with a feminist perspective have criticized the shared responsibility model as providing ineffective treatment (Walker, 1991) because the responsibility for the violence still falls on the woman. The shared responsibility model emphasizes the woman's role as provocateur. Effective treatment is defined by Walker (1991) as the cessation of the violence and the prevention of future violence, which is accomplished by having the man take full responsibility for the physical violence. In order to bring the ethical issue into focus, the therapist must view the woman as a victim of the abuse regardless of her apparent participation in the violence cycle. When the woman is viewed as the victim of the violence, the ethical responsibility of the therapist becomes clearer: The cessation of the violence, as an ethical rather than solely as a treatment issue, then transcends theoretical orientations. The logic utilized is similar to the arguments justifying interventions to stop child abuse. The child is the victim of the abuse regardless of whether the abuser attempts to justify his or her behavior as provoked by the child. While some readers will object to this apparent characterization of the woman as "childlike," it is important to understand that, similar to a child who is being abused, the woman actually has no ability to stop the violence. For ethical considerations, I do advocate that the woman is the victim; however, I would be hesitant to advocate for a similar characterization in the legal system. At this juncture, I reiterate: I use *ethical responsibility* here to describe obligations and duties arising from ethical mandates and reserve the term *duty* for legal mandates.

There is little debate that therapists have an ethical obligation to their clients if the clients are "victims," because by definition victims are individuals who are unable to prevent the action against them. The assessment for the presence of spousal violence is a positive ethical responsibility directly related to the acceptance of the premise that the woman is a victim of the violence.

TREATMENT

Delineation of treatment responsibilities deriving from ethical responsibilities requires more complex analysis. As with all ethical responsibilities, a standard of care must be articulated. Minimally, discharge of the ethical responsibility to the client as victim would require knowledge about state laws pertaining to domestic violence and awareness of the local resources available to assist the client and her family (Madanes, 1990; Pittman, 1987; Walker, 1991). The domestic violence laws in some states provide for treatment of the victims as well as the perpetrators under court diversion programs. Shelters for battered women usually have some short-term therapy available in addition to other services designed to assist women to become self-supporting. Thus there are two distinct ways in which domestic violence victims may come to therapy: The first is with domestic violence as the primary presenting problem, as a referral either from a criminal justice system diversion program or from a shelter or other agency with a specific mission to assist battered women; the second is with presenting problems of somatic complaints, depressive symptomatology, or anxiety. The first may be referred to as *overt* domestic violence victims and the second as *covert* domestic violence victims.

Treating Overt Victims

Therapists treating overt victims are assumed to be knowledgeable about domestic violence and, thus, committed to the cessation of the violence. Their ethical responsibility is to provide effective treatment. However, even among these therapists there is disagreement over the criteria of successful outcome. If successful treatment is defined as the woman leaving the abusive situation, the success rate is usually 50% (Goodman, 1990). However, as therapists have become more sophisticated in their work with victims of abuse, they have found that many times the woman does not want to leave the relationship because of emotional issues (fear, shame, love) and/or financial/security issues (children, lack of employment skills, unwillingness to give up a particular standard of living). The ethical issue that then arises is the basis for helping the woman achieve her goals of remaining in the relationship and of being free from abuse.

The clinical literature has attempted to prescribe appropriate treatment for victims (Goodman, 1990; Walker, 1991; see also Hansen, Chapter 6, and Hansen & Goldenberg, Chapter 7, this volume) and families (Willbach, 1989). These writers view the ethical responsibility of the therapist as twofold: first, to accomplish the cessation of the violence, and second, to provide therapy to prevent future violent interactions.

Treating Covert Victims

Therapists treating covert victims of spousal abuse represent the class of therapists most directly confronted with potential ethical and liability issues. As with other clients, the ethical responsibility to provide effective treatment consists of three phases. The initial phase is the accurate assessment of the problem, the second is the development of the treatment plan to address the identified problem, and the third and most crucial phase is the execution of the treatment plan. The second and third phases are critical to therapists working with overt victims, because the assessment phase has been handled by the criminal justice system or the victims themselves are able to state that the violence is the primary problem. The first phase, however, is particularly critical for therapists treating covert victims.

Malpractice Liability

Would the therapist be liable if he or she did not provide an initial assessment for violence and, if violence is present, formulate a treatment plan for the cessation of the violence? Currently, there is no case law answering this question. The assessment phase for spousal abuse cases is deceptively simple. The therapist need only inquire about the presence of violence in the home. However, the consequences of implementing routine inquiries regarding violence are worrisome to therapists. One immediate consequence is that the therapist becomes aware of an abusive relationship and is then ethically obligated to provide treatment or to refer the client to a therapist who can.

Because abused spouses also tend to minimize the presence of violence and the severity of the abuse, therapists must guard against a tendency to accept abused spouses' disclaimers of danger too readily as releasing them from the ethical responsibility to provide treatment to stop the violence. The result of the minimization of danger by both the therapist and the client is a treatment plan that does not address the core problem of violence, but instead focuses on the symptoms of anxiety, depression, and somatization. Such treatment does not address the root cause of the symptoms, and thus the symptoms are unresponsive to treatment, which can be ethically construed as a failure to provide effective treatment.

Of more concern perhaps is case law that comes out of a related field. Woody (1988) found that nonmedical therapists had been held legally liable for not referring clients to physicians for assessment of potential medical problems that ultimately proved fatal. The therapists had not asked the appropriate questions and were held liable for their omission. Extrapolating from this case, a therapist who does not ask the appropriate questions to assess abuse may still be held liable if such abuse occurs and the client is found injured or dead. Under the law there is no excuse for a mental health professional's lack of appropriate assessment.

The second phase of the ethical responsibility to provide effective treatment concerns the development of the treatment plan. Therapists, regardless of how they learn of domestic violence in their clients' lives, have an ethical responsibility to formulate appropriate treatment plans. Pope and Vasquez (1991) reviewed closed cases of malpractice against psychologists occurring from 1976 to 1988. They found that incorrect treatment (incompetence in the choice or implementation of the treatment plan) accounted for 8.4% of the total costs and 13.2% of the total claims. These cases do not address the specific issue of liability raised in this chapter, but as abuse victims become more aware of their right to be free from physical violence in the home, therapist exposure to liability increases, especially as violence eventuates in injury or death.

The third phase of the ethical responsibility to provide effective treatment is the implementation of the treatment plan. The clinical literature contains many examples of attempts to define appropriate, effective treatment for domestic violence victims (Goodman, 1990; Walker, 1991) and their families (Willbach, 1989). These writers view the ethical responsibility of the therapist as twofold: first, to accomplish the cessation of the violence, and second, to provide therapy. Therapy has become the crucial element in breaking the violent pattern within families. The debate about what constitutes effective treatment for spousal abuse will and should continue.

The following guidelines are offered to stimulate discussion concerning the need for therapists to discharge their ethical responsibilities when treating violence in the home:

- thorough assessment for violence
- development of a safety plan with clients
- therapist knowledge of legal protections
- therapist knowledge of community resources (shelters, support groups, legal resources, and so on)
- assessment for and reporting of child abuse (if children are present in the home)
- continuing education for therapists working with clients from violent homes
- treatment plans that address (a) potential for continued violence, (b) individual versus couples therapy (safety issues addressed and documented), (c) treatment for the perpetrator, and (d) monitoring and documentation of safety issues

Duty to Warn/Protect

Returning to the original question, Should a therapist be held liable for not making an initial assessment for domestic violence? Ramifications of holding a therapist liable for this initial assessment would include the necessity of providing a course of action once the domestic violence was uncovered. Currently, all states have laws that theoretically provide protection from abuse, including mandatory arrest laws, restraining orders that can be obtained *ex parte,* and civil suits that can be brought against the abusing party. However, none of these measures has been sufficient to stop the cycle of violence. One of the real frustrations for law enforcement agencies is the deadly violence that can occur even when an individual has taken all the necessary legal steps to prevent the violence. U.S. Surgeon

General Antonia Novello views domestic violence, primarily against women, as an important issue of public health. "Every five years, domestic violence claims as many lives as were lost in the Vietnam War—about 58,000," she says (quoted in Klein, 1992).

With regard to therapist duty, there are no legal mandates requiring the reporting of spousal abuse to the criminal justice system. As mentioned earlier, mandatory reporting laws have been implemented in all states to address violence against children. These laws impose a legal duty and an ethical responsibility upon therapists. Some states have adopted elder abuse reporting laws to address the protection of the elderly and other adults who are incapacitated. The intent of both elder abuse and child abuse reporting laws is to protect individuals who are unable to care for themselves because of their age or incapacitation.

Therapists' reactions to these laws have ranged from favorable to tolerant to opposed. Therapists may be opposed to abuse reporting laws because compliance results in the violation of confidentiality, which is the cardinal ethical responsibility of therapists. Victims of spouse abuse have not, to date, been protected by mandatory reporting requirements, perhaps because adult women are not perceived as individuals in need of special protection. Some therapists argue that because women are adults with no discernible impairment that requires special protection, the ethic of confidentiality should not be violated.

Despite the absence of legal reporting mandates, therapists have an ethical responsibility to protect victims of potential violence from harm. This ethical responsibility became explicit with the landmark decision of *Tarasoff v. Regents of the University of California* (1976). Subsequent case law has attempted to define the boundaries of therapists' duty to protect potential victims of violence (Leslie, 1990; Mills, Sullivan, & Eth, 1987; Sonkin, 1986). Sonkin and Ellison (1986), in their review of these case decisions, found that the research on the prediction of violence rather than the research on domestic violence had been utilized to shape public policy. The distinction is crucial in a consideration of the ethical responsibilities of therapists because the literature on the prediction of violence is more encompassing than the literature on domestic violence; prediction literature extends to unprovoked violence between acquaintances and even strangers.

California, in an attempt to clarify the question of therapist liability, drafted a law in 1985 that resulted in limiting therapists' liability for failure to warn of danger. The therapist has a duty to warn when the client makes a serious threat of physical harm to an identifiable victim. If an abusive spouse is the client, then the therapist has a duty to warn the victimized spouse of potential physical harm. Anecdotal information gathered from therapists suggests that therapists find the execution of this duty frustrating because the victimized spouse already "knows" of the danger and because the alternatives available to the therapist for preventing the harm are not clearly defined. The 1985 California law is not intended to protect abused spouses; rather, it is intended to protect therapists from liability, especially breach of confidentiality.

Therapists who treat solely the victims of spousal abuse are not mandated by current laws to warn their clients of danger from abusing spouses. Theoretically, a therapist would not be liable for failure to warn even if the client is eventually killed by her spouse because the first criterion of the California law requires the therapist to respond only to threats from clients. Ironically, however, the therapist treating the victimized spouse would be required to warn the abusive spouse if the victimized spouse (client) made a threat of serious physical harm.

The California law emphasizes the duty to warn of danger, not the protection from danger. A duty imposed upon a therapist should always imply a course of action the therapist can follow to discharge the duty. In this case, the therapist discharges the duty by warning the potential victim and by notifying the police. The underlying assumption seems to be that once the police are notified, the laws designed to protect the victim will be enforced. The duty to protect the victim thus shifts from the therapist to the criminal justice system and the victim herself.

In states that have not followed California's lead and clarified the issue of therapist liability with regard to duty to warn or protect, the therapist must be familiar with state laws pertaining to these issues.

Summary

In the near future, treatment of spousal abuse cases is likely to become one of the major ethical issues facing therapists. Geffner (1990) predicts that the interpretations from *Tarasoff* of a duty properly to assess, treat, and warn of potential danger will be extended beyond the mental health professions to include shelter workers, advocates, and others working with abuse victims and perpetrators. In order to avoid the imposition of mandates from the legal system and to minimize therapist liability, mental health professionals need to take part in continued discussion of ethical responsibilities and the development of standards of care that will appropriately discharge these ethical obligations. Guidelines have been provided in this chapter to serve as a basis for the formulation of standards of care. Treatment for the cessation of violence is clearly the responsibility of the therapist; therefore, therapists must assume an active role in assessing for violence, even when violence is not the presenting problem.

13

A Multicultural Perspective in the Treatment of Domestic Violence

NANCYANN N. CERVANTES
JOSEPH M. CERVANTES

Within the past decade in the United States, interethnic/interracial tensions, the flooding of schools and business environments with people of varied ethnic and cultural backgrounds, and the questioning of long-held beliefs about health and well-being have forced us to examine seriously the impact of cultural diversity in our population (Schlesinger, 1992). More specifically, increases in urban violence, overcrowded and tense school environments, and reports of domestic violence have moved government and social agencies to examine the impact that different ethnic/cultural peoples have had in the escalation of violent situations. Violence also has cultural significance within the family. Sex roles within the family are defined by cultural parameters, and it is these parameters that influence the theories and techniques used in treating domestic violence. What, then, are the cultural or multicultural issues that need to be addressed in our understanding of domestic violence?

It is the primary premise of this chapter that meaningful and trusting contact between human beings from different cultures, whether at the level of home, school, or business, requires willingness (a) to go outside one's own cultural reference and learn another's point of view, (b) to become aware of one's own ethnic/racial bias, and (c) to learn to appreciate similarities in our interactions as humans. It is a further premise of this chapter that cultural diversity has become a complex and emotion-laden issue. Racial overtones or undertones, the need for "politically correct" postures, and the fear of our own neighbors have significantly heightened and confused our reactions to those from cultures other than our own. The recent onslaught of immigrants from all cultures, with their distinct languages and traditions, has resulted in significant misunderstandings and, at times, violent interactions. This chapter focuses particularly on the application of a multicultural perspective to the issue of domestic violence.

Multicultural Perspective

The terms *culturally diverse* and *multicultural* are used interchangeably in this chapter. Both of these concepts have been used by the mental health community without consistent understanding. Recent attempts in the psychological literature to address cultural themes in the counseling process have helped to provide a finer conceptual base (American Psychological Association, 1990; Comas-Diaz & Griffith, 1988; Ramirez, 1983, 1991; Sue, 1990).

A *multicultural perspective* is defined as a philosophy that affords the development of flexibility and diversity in orientations to life and for the development of pluralistic identities (Ramirez, 1983). The key concepts in this definition are ease of adjustment, adaptability, flexibility of coping ability, and the ability to relate interpersonally across ethnic/cultural/racial lines. Thus all cultures and religions represent important sources of knowledge about life that can be helpful to one's own development.

There are several premises to the assumption of the ability to take a multicultural perspective. The first is that while one is anchored within a particular cultural mind-set, one does not rigidly hold to stereotypical patterns or assumptions of behavior about individuals from other cultures. For example, an African American teenager's use of "ghetto speech" patterns does not mean that he or she has poor or inferior communication ability for English. A second premise is that intelligence, problem-solving skills, and coping abilities are equally distributed within all cultural groups. This means that factors other than culture explain the presence of poverty and gang violence in the barrio, ghetto, and other minority neighborhoods characterized by poverty.

A third premise is that psychological reality is not fixed in time and space. Culture is a dynamic, continuous movement, particularly as one considers socioeconomic, political, and acculturative dimensions. The fact that an American Indian couple from Navajo and Sioux tribal heritages are having marital difficulties does not necessarily reflect the individuals' cultural attitudes; it may be indicative of socioeconomic, community, or other realities. A fourth premise is the creation of a process of synthesis and synergism. People from ethnic minority communities must create innovative, life-enhancing coping styles and strategies in order to maintain a viable identity. To what degree is the "pachuco," the "cholo," or the "gangbanger" a reflection of this synergistic process?

The fifth premise is that it is wholly appropriate to be bicultural/multicultural. Problem-solving skills, personal/familial identities, and general psychological adaptation must come from one's own struggles to live in a multiracial society. Thus seeing all solutions or all useful ways of thinking and feeling as coming from a "white mainstream" point of view is insufficient and inappropriate. In brief, it is quite appropriate to be bicultural/multicultural, because the coming together of two or more cultures creates more flexible attitudes and orientations to life.

A final premise of a multicultural perspective is that cultural diversity is seen as exactly that—*diversity*. To respond to issues of culture as if all people are the same is to engage in cultural racism (Jones, 1988). We are not a color-blind society; there are very real ethnic, sociohistorical, and cultural differences both between and within groups.

When one thinks about cultural differences in this country, the assumption is that one is referring to minority groups and their differences from the majority culture. This assumption is legitimate, although not entirely accurate, because cultural differences exist also between members of the majority culture based on ethnic background and area of the country where these individuals reside. American mainstream culture is not monolithic, despite the majority's adherence to certain values used to define mainstream culture. While recognizing this, for the purposes of this chapter we focus on the interaction between minority cultural values and mainstream culture as this interaction affects domestic violence theory and treatment.

Multiculturalism as a legitimate perspective in mental health care was recently recognized by the American Psychological Association when it sponsored a multicultural task force to promulgate guidelines for working with culturally diverse populations. The task force, of which this chapter's second author was a member, was successful in its endeavor (American Psychological Association, 1990). The guidelines outline the necessary sensitivity psychologists must exercise in order to work effectively with diverse cultural and linguistic populations.

Following are brief descriptions of prominent minority cultures in the United States. It is our experience that significant stereotypical thinking and many myths persist about people of color's inabilities or poor cultural frameworks to deal effectively with mainstream culture. Consequently, domestic violence tends to be understood from a unidimensional view of culture. For brevity's sake, we limit our discussion to African American, Asian American, Native American, and Latino American families. We recognize that every human being has a cultural context, and that members of white Anglo-Saxon Protestant families are no different in this respect; for an extended discussion of this group, we refer the reader to McGoldrick, Pearce, and Giordano (1982).

AFRICAN AMERICAN FAMILIES

African Americans have been very visible with respect to their experience as a people. Jones (1988) and Pinderhughes (1989) have outlined variables that help to define African American psychological responses. The first variable is the influence of racial oppression and discrimination. African Americans are not the only minority group that has suffered from discrimination and oppression, but they are the only group who experienced slavery for much of their existence in this hemisphere. As a result, virtually every African American person must develop a coping strategy for dealing with racial discrimination and oppression (Jones, 1988). Pinderhughes (1989) describes the "victim system" as a circular feedback process that, like other systems, leads to predictability, stability, and identity. Thus the victim system has led to the community becoming an active disorganizing factor that adversely affects the individuals. As a value system, the victim system stresses cooperation to combat powerlessness, strict obedience to authority, strength, toughness of character, and present time orientation. Because the expression of emotions, particularly anger, can lead to trouble with the majority culture, these emotions are often channeled to artistic and creative endeavors. Often, angry emotions are expressed within the community and within the family, resulting in a high incidence of violence (Bell, 1991; Garbarino, Dubrow, Kostelny, & Pardo, 1992).

The second source of values for the African American is American mainstream culture, which emphasizes individuality, independence, future time orientation, success, and achievement. The final value system is African culture, which Nobles (1980) has elucidated as a source for positive adaptation. This value system stresses "we-ness," by which the individual gains identity from the group, spirituality, a flexible concept of time, sensitivity to others, and well developed use of affect. African Americans are thus influenced by three value systems that have distinct and often competing elements. An individual's or a family's decision to seek therapy is usually not related to that person's or family's identity as African American. However, the therapist has the responsibility to understand the client's/family's cultural identity even when it is not the "presenting problem."

The history of African American families is one in which slavery, forced separation of whole family units, and genocide have been significant elements. Garbarino et al. (1992) and Bell and Chance-Hill (1991) have recently begun articulating the idea of dangerous environments and their developmental impact on children. Some of the effects they have noted include the development of posttraumatic stress symptomatology and hyperalertness to the environment but hypoalertness to danger. Out of these effects can develop very defensive styles of coping and relating and, potentially, an aggressive posture that tends to permeate all areas of functioning. The black experience, as noted by renowned poet Langston Hughes, is one of survival in dealing with the white man.

The role of women within African American families is influenced by the cultural values outlined above and the socioeconomic level of the family. The cultural traditions value the role of motherhood and child rearing. While the role of wife is also highly valued, the role of mother takes precedence (Staples, 1990). According to traditional values, the stability of the family is based on the willingness and ability of African American women and men to marry, raise children, and fulfill prescribed family roles. For women, these roles are defined traditionally as the carrying out of domestic functions, the raising and socializing of children, and the provision of sexual gratification, companionship, and emotional support for husbands (Staples, 1990). The husband's role is to provide economic support and family leadership. As many writers and researchers have reported, opportunities to fulfill these roles are often simply not available to African Americans (Hines, 1989; Pinderhughes, 1989; Staples, 1990; Wyatt, 1992).

Conflict between African American spouses that can escalate to violence has been attributed to the stresses resulting from poverty and racism (Hines, 1989). One hypothesis proposed to explain the apparent willingness of the African American woman to remain within a violent relationship is the disparity in the numbers between men and women of African American heritage (Hines, 1989; Staples, 1990). Staples (1990) outlines the reasons for the lack of marriageable African American men, which include higher infant mortality rates, higher mortality rates as young men, greater likelihood of being confined to mental or correctional institutions, and greater likelihood of marriage outside of their race than African American women.

ASIAN AMERICAN FAMILIES

With the end of the Vietnam War and the influx of Southeast Asian immigrants, there is a greater appreciation for the diversity of culture among Asian populations. Kim (1985) discusses the importance of family therapists' understanding the power structure and power distribution within the Asian American family, because Asian cultural values related to family are quite different from Western values. Generally, Asian American families exhibit vertical relationships instead of the horizontal relationships that are more characteristic of Western families. Most Asian cultures place high value on respecting authority figures. Roles and relationships are clearly defined, with corresponding rules for interpersonal behavior.

Using the example of the role of the wife, Kim (1985) also points out that power within the family flows through a dynamic process. Although the wife is generally acknowledged to be subordinate to her husband in most Asian cultures, this subordination is a reality mostly from the public's viewpoint. Within the family, the wife is in charge of everything that happens, including education of the children and handling of financial matters. The husband is responsible for everything that happens outside the home. Thus the therapist working with Asian American families must be aware of this clear distribution of power within the family. In addition, the Asian American will have clear, although unspoken, expectations of the therapist, who occupies a position of authority, with its concomitant rules for interpersonal behavior. The Asian American will assume that the therapist is aware of the power distribution within the family and will work to achieve harmony within the family while maintaining the appropriate hierarchical family structure.

Asians in the United States come from varied cultural, linguistic, and sociopolitical contexts. For the clinician to understand the different power relationships and acculturative patterns of Asian Americans, he or she must establish rapport with the family based on trust within the identified familial context. Women in most Asian cultures are valued for their ability to fulfill domestic responsibilities. They are not as highly valued as men by their families of origin because, in most Asian cultures, women become part of their husbands' families when they marry, and men are expected to support their parents and to bring their wives into the family system. Violence is condoned as necessary discipline by families that utilize physical discipline.

NATIVE AMERICAN FAMILIES

Within the past 25 years, the psychological literature has reflected increased sensitivity to the mental health needs of Native Americans. Everett, Proctor, and Cartmell (1983) and Yates (1987) discuss several service delivery issues and cultural arenas of practice with Native Americans. Attneave (1982) found three significant differences between traditional Native American values and mainstream culture values. The first two concern relationships with others and with nature. Traditional Native

American values emphasize cooperation and harmony among the group as well as with nature in order to ensure the survival of the group. The third difference is found in time orientation, with the Native American placing more importance on the present and the past than on the future. These are generalizations, of course; specific Native American individuals adhere to these values or not depending upon their own acculturation.

Within traditional Native American culture, sex roles were quite specific. The same-sex parental figure had the responsibility to teach appropriate skills, self-discipline, and behavior (Attneave, 1982). Traditionally, both sexes were appreciated, and both made equally valued contributions to the welfare of the group. Native Americans today are confronted with a breakdown in the means of conveying traditional values to boys, because the men have had a more difficult time transforming traditional activities into marketable skills valued by mainstream culture (Berlin, 1987).

Researchers have noted the complexity of the group we call Native Americans. There are more than 400 different tribes, or nations, in the United States, each with its own language base, history, and experiences on the reservation. Further, high rates of alcohol abuse, unemployment, and suicide contribute to domestic violence among Native peoples. Physical discipline (in its extreme, child abuse) traditionally was not utilized by Native Americans as a child-rearing practice, but with the increase in depressive disorders and alcohol consumption, as well as the breakdown of traditional family units as the result of children being sent to boarding schools, physical discipline and its offshoots of child and spouse abuse have increased (Berlin, 1987).

LATINO AMERICAN FAMILIES

Like the other populations discussed above, this group does not constitute a monolith; rather, it consists of many diverse cultural groups who share some similarities, with the most obvious being language. For the most part, individuals are defined as Latino American if they are native Spanish speakers or come from a Spanish-speaking heritage (Spanish surname). Much has been written about Latino families, although primarily the literature has concentrated on Mexican/Mexican American groups (Cervantes & Ramirez, 1992; Falicov, 1982; Murillo, 1971; Ramirez, 1989; Trankina, 1983). *Spanish speaking* encompasses a wide range of ethnic/cultural groups with varying sociopolitical, historical, and acculturative bases. The values outlined below are those that are generally shared by Latino Americans, but the therapist is reminded that individuals adhere to these values, or do not, based on acculturation and group identity.

Latinos value family (*la familia*) highly, and the individual's needs are considered secondary to those of the family as a whole. The family is the primary social unit, and is characterized by a bond of loyalty that includes the immediate family and the extended family as well as a network of friends and neighbors in the community. Respect for self and others is an essential value. The respect derives from the individual's ability to perform his or her designated roles appropriately. Many Latino cultures have clear class systems that allow for little mobility; however, focusing on inner qualities allows the individual to achieve a sense of self-worth that is independent of socioeconomic status.

Spirituality is an important value in most Latino cultures. Religious rituals and celebrations are an integral part of the community and the individual's life. Belief in a spirit world that is invisible and influential in daily life is not uncommon. The relationship between spirituality and therapy for minority populations has been explored in depth by Cervantes and Ramirez (1992).

Sex roles are clearly defined among Latinos. Women are usually expected to fulfill the traditional roles of wife and mother, even if employed outside the home. Men have the responsibility of providing for and protecting the family. *Machismo* is the term used to define the male role of responsibility and toughness. Aggression is often associated with this concept. Latino women also adhere to the traditional values of motherhood and loyalty to the husband. They will often endure physical abuse within the home because of their adherence to the values of *la familia* (Ramirez, 1991).

The acculturation factor as well as the uncomfortable predominance of significant immigration from Mexico and Central and South America has led to intense rivalry, tension, and envy among ethnic groups within the Latino population in their efforts to establish themselves in this country.

The preceding overviews of minority cultures provide an introduction to some of the cultural issues and values that influence therapeutic work with these populations. As has been noted, predominant in all of the described groups are sociopolitical reactions: feelings of disenfranchisement that arise from racism and discrimination. These factors are significant contributors to the phenomenon of domestic violence among people of color.

Multiculturalism and Feminism

A basic function of culture is the definition of appropriate sex role behavior. Feminism originated as a political movement to gain the right to vote for women in the United States in the nineteenth century (Carlson, 1990). In the 1960s, feminism became more than a political movement, although political activism is still evident among some individuals who identify themselves as feminists. Academic disciplines have accepted feminism as the equivalent of a theoretical orientation. Feminism, both as a political movement and as a theoretical orientation, has advocated for the equality of the sexes, which is often in direct conflict with cultural values.

Feminists view the inherent inequality between the roles assigned to the sexes as the cause of injustice and, therefore, violence against women. Feminists argue persuasively that cultural values that result in the devaluation of women contribute to violence against women. Three cultural attitudes reported in the literature that support violence against women are sex role stereotyping (gender role), adversarial sexual beliefs, and the acceptance of interpersonal violence (Burt, 1980). *Sex role stereotyping* refers to acceptance, by both men and women, of assigned roles for each sex. The failure of an individual to fulfill an accepted stereotype can lead to disappointment and rage. *Adversarial sexual beliefs* refers to the assumption that men and women have different interpersonal agendas that result in unavoidable conflict and tension between the sexes. Finally, the cultural *acceptance of interpersonal violence* as a legitimate conflict resolution technique allows spouses to justify to themselves and others the use of violence within the home. This belief reinforces the attitude that violence is an appropriate means for interacting with others (Donat & D'Emilio, 1992).

According to feminists, the presence within a cultural milieu of sex role stereotyping, adversarial sexual beliefs, and acceptance of interpersonal violence results in the condoning of violence against women. Minority cultures that incorporate these attitudes can be viewed as potentially violent toward women.

The adoption of a multicultural perspective does not allow for a simplistic analysis of culture in order to assess for violence. Specifically, do the traditional values of minority cultures lead to violence against women? The feminist argument that particular cultural values (e.g., that women are responsible for domestic and family care and men are responsible for family leadership and economic security) automatically lead to a devaluing of women within the culture would support a belief that minority cultures are more likely to condone violence against women when violence in present in the family. Research does not support such a simplistic explanation, however. Empirical studies have shown that when socioeconomic factors are controlled for, no cultural differences are found in the incidence of domestic violence. Gondolf, Fisher, and McFerron (1988) studied black, Hispanic, and Anglo residents at a women's shelter in order to determine the most influential factors. The groups were differentiated most by economic variables and least by abuse factors. There was no significant difference among groups in the incidence or severity of the abuse. In a review of the empirical literature on African American victims of abuse, Coley and Beckett (1988) found a psychological profile similar for both minority and mainstream culture women. They conclude that the data do not support the myth that minority women are more likely to be victims of abuse.

Viewed as a societal (cross-cultural) problem, domestic violence must be explained as a breakdown of cultural norms that value the sex roles, resulting in the stereotyping of sex roles. When sex roles become stereotyped, there is an inflexibility in their implementation within the family that does not allow for individual expression. Where domestic violence is present, both men and women are found to adhere to stereotyped sex roles. Factors that are consistently found to be related to domestic violence are economic variables and power relationships. The economic variables are more complex than simple socioeconomic level, because abuse has been found on all socioeconomic levels (although abuse among lower socioeconomic groups is more likely to come to the attention of authorities). Even at higher socioeconomic levels, abused women perceive their own economic independence to be precarious.

Power in relationships is the most cogent variable. Feminists have long argued, correctly, that the power differential in society between men and women results in violence against women. Indeed, therapists who work with batterers are frequently confronted with the batterers' need to control and to have power over their spouses.

Feminism encompasses political, legal, sociological, and psychological views of women and their roles as individuals and as members of families and society. Since the reactivation of the women's movement in the 1960s, the proper role for women, both inside and outside the family, has been hotly debated (Ware, 1989). Because the women's movement has challenged very basic cultural values related to power distribution within society, its critics have blamed feminism for the breakup of the family and the apparent demise of familial values cherished by mainstream culture. What the women's movement has challenged in actuality are the expectations for behaviors within the family that have resulted from the culture of industrialized Western society (Luepnitz, 1988).

As the feminist movement has achieved more dignity and autonomy for mainstream (Western industrialized) women, these women are eager to spread the doctrine of liberation to other cultures. "However, it is not sufficient to seize upon a few superficial likenesses which reassure us and confirm our own view of the problems we have, and assume that their own problems are precisely the same as ours" (Armstrong, 1986, p. xiii). African American and Native American writers have attempted to explain the meaningful differences in the definitions of equality (feminism) for mainstream culture women and minority culture women. The African American woman's experience has been described as one of having to overcome sexism, racism, and classism, because the white woman, in her efforts to leave the home and seek equality with men, wanted someone at home with the children. White feminists have tended to see minority culture men as more sensitive and less likely to be violent toward women in their interactions, an experience inconsistent with that of minority women (Combahee River Collective, 1989).

African American women have experienced both racism and sexism, but have not as a group been willing to take on both; they have, for the most part, not joined with white mainstream feminists. Native American women have a similar view toward mainstream feminism. Native American women seek equality in two ways that do not directly affect mainstream women. First, they struggle to promote the survival of a social structure whose notions of family differ from those of mainstream culture. Second, they struggle on a societal level to preserve a connectedness with the land, legally and spiritually, in order for the People to survive (Shanley, 1989).

Culturally and historically, religion has been a powerful force in defining the relationships between men and women. Most religions are male dominated, with women having subordinate positions. Interestingly, Christianity has the potential to produce an ideal of liberated and autonomous women who are equal to men, but, unfortunately, this ideal has not become an actuality (Armstrong, 1986). Feminism has attempted to confront the long-held contempt for women that arose from religious interpretations of the doctrine of Original Sin (Armstrong, 1986). Religious scholars could conceive of only one purpose for women, which was to bear children. This basic contempt for women as individuals directly contributed to the antagonism that condones violence between the sexes in mainstream culture as well as many minority cultures.

Historically, as Western society granted more dignity and autonomy to women and rejected, at least in part, the contempt for women grounded in religious teachings, love as a vital source of satisfaction and personal fulfillment gained prominence. Love has become such a sacred feeling that contemporary society holds the strong belief that if one truly loves another, one can forgive that person almost anything (Kagan, 1989). With the advent of romantic love, men and women hold the expectation that they will find happiness, fulfillment, and a quasi-therapeutic relationship in marriage (Luepnitz, 1988). Because contemporary spouses have such high expectations for marriage, their disappointment when these expectations are not met can be devastating. This is reflected in high divorce rates (sometimes as high as 50%) and in continued high expectations—the rate of remarriage is estimated to be 70-80% (Weitzman, 1985). More important, disappointment in romantic love is reflected in the phenomenon of domestic violence when the blame is placed, by both spouses, upon the woman for the failure of fulfillment. It is a well-documented phenomenon that abused women often take responsibility for their abuse and, even with legal and therapeutic intervention, return to their batterers (Schutte, Bouleige, Fix, Malouff, 1986; Schutte, Malouff, & Doyle, 1988).

A tension exists between culture and feminism that goes beyond male domination of women. Women are influenced by their ethnicity and cultural heritage, and they bring this perspective to their understanding of women's rights within their own cultural boundaries. However, despite differences in their interpretations of feminism, all agree that violence against women, especially domestic violence, is a grievous violation.

Cultural assimilation presents interesting conflicts for minority individuals. The general premise is that violence is not tolerated, but violence may be socially acceptable under certain circumstances (e.g., self-defense or revenge for a serious wrong). For women experiencing domestic violence, these contradictory maxims have led to the guilt and feelings of responsibility for the violence that have been identified as part of the basic psychological profiles of battered women regardless of racial/ethnic origins. An interesting line of anecdotal research has shown that as violent minority families are exposed to their traditional cultural value systems, the abuse cycle can be broken (FireThunder, 1991).

While tension appears to exist between cultural values and the goals of feminism, it is an illusion that results from the differing vantage points assumed by the multiculturalists and the feminists. Both adhere to a belief in a basic equality between the sexes that should result in a mutual respect. The cultural perspective can lead to an assumption that adherence to traditional values will result in harmony between the sexes. Feminists argue that adherence to "traditional values" (women responsible for the functioning of the family and men responsible for the functioning of the community) can result in an unequal distribution of power, with the man's role being more highly valued. Both of these perspectives have merit, and it is the responsibility of the therapist who assumes a multicultural/feminist perspective to achieve a balance between the points of contention in order to allow the minority couple to integrate successfully the mutual respect necessary to avoid violence in the relationship.

A final issue that both affects and defines the relationship between multiculturalism and feminist orientation is the societal observation of cultural diversity itself. People of color no longer fit into nicely defined ethnic/racial categories; perhaps they never have. The increased amalgamation of various cultural groups interacting together at all levels of society has resulted in multiethnic marital couples. Three distinct levels can be identified: majority-minority culture relationships (e.g., Anglo-African American), minority-minority culture relationships (e.g., Native American-Asian), and mixed minority-minority/majority culture relationships (e.g., Latino/Japanese-Vietnamese/African American and Latino/Anglo-Asian/African American). The potential variety in relationships and subsequent families is endless. The implied issue in these various scenarios is the increased complication of trying to understand "cultural expectations" from a unidimensional viewpoint. A more productive approach is to acknowledge the realities of diversity, the relative weakness of therapeutic assumptions that can be made, and the need to be willing to be educated by the client system as to the relational tenets that it holds. For instance, How are decisions made? How is conflict handled? What cultural expectations have been learned? How is power balanced or not?

Multiculturalism advocates respect for patterns of behavior and consciousness within cultural diversity. Feminism honors the integrity and freedom of the woman regarding free choice, equal opportunity, and equal distribution of power in relationships. The essence of preventing domestic violence must involve both perspectives in the assessment, treating, and healing processes.

Case Presentation

CASE A

Jorge and Maria, a couple in their mid-40s, have been together for approximately 11 years. They were married by the civil court 4 years ago, and they have five children, of whom the oldest (adolescent male, age 16) is from Maria's prior relationship. Both are originally from Central Mexico. Jorge came to the United States 20 years ago as a penniless immigrant with less than a fourth-grade education. He managed to secure both fluency in the English language and significant experience in the business world. During this period, Jorge acquired five grocery markets and a liquor store. Although he was financially successful as a businessman, his family involvement suffered critically. The combination of long work hours, a history of poor emotional contact with his family, and a tendency to be distrustful of others made for low frustration tolerance and past instances of physical/emotional abuse of Maria. Jorge reported having been physically battered as a child by his own father.

Maria met Jorge when she became his employee; she was a 21-year-old single parent at the time. Maria also came from an emotionally abusive household. As Jorge and Maria's marriage developed, the anger and animosity between them increased: Jorge suffered from a basic mistrust of people and the financial pressure of sustaining his businesses; Maria wanted more family time from Jorge and more money to support their family adequately. The couple presented for therapy after several physical confrontations had occurred between them and they realized that the state of the marriage was clearly having a negative impact on the emotional health of the children.

Initial interventions included separate interviews to assess family history, abuse patterns, and expectations of the marriage. The acculturative aspects of their respective social histories in the United States were evaluated: levels of familial support, coping styles, experience with discrimination, facility with the English language, and expectations of self and children. Second, the couple entered into a verbal contract for no physical/emotional abuse. Third, as a means of assisting each to maintain a feeling of "centeredness," they were guided to discuss any cultural strengths they individually/collectively found useful. Finally, their problem-solving skills were focused upon in order to build a basis of trust, particularly for Jorge, to facilitate discussion of their long-standing resentments toward each other in the therapeutic setting.

Significant understanding developed between Maria and Jorge, especially in becoming identified with previously unspoken cultural strengths. Jorge's level of distrust continued to be paramount, although the couple's problem-solving abilities improved. Maria and Jorge were discharged from therapy when they felt they had accomplished as much as they could for the present. There were no reported instances of physical abuse throughout the five months of treatment. The spouses' respective abilities to handle difficulties more effectively and to feel more closeness as a couple also improved. At the time of the final visit, strong interpersonal tensions were still evident.

CASE B

Kieu and James, a multiethnic couple, were seen for therapy over a period of six months. Kieu is Chinese American, originally from China. James is Japanese American; he was born in the United States and his parents are from Japan. Kieu and James grew up in different areas of the country: Kieu on the East Coast and James in a small farming community in Central California. Both reported coming from uninvolved and punitive backgrounds. Kieu indicated that her father was very distant and emotionally abusive. Her first marriage, which lasted 10 years, was emotionally abusive also. James reported growing up in a household where the mother was quite passive and unwilling to protect herself or her children from the abuse of her husband. James reported that his father was prone to discipline him and rebuke him harshly and was aggressively authoritarian with everyone.

The couple entered therapy after three months of courtship and five months of marriage, the second for both. Primary complaints centered on communication problems, physically threatening posturing toward each other, and significant frustrations over adapting to each other's relational styles. Discussion of stereotypes that the two had learned about their own and each other's cultures helped to open lines of communication that had not been evident before. An increased level of trust was derived from a therapeutic discussion of the connection between their own perceived helplessness as children and the need to cope with life under the label of "minority group member." These discussions were interwoven with the therapist's own shared experiences as a Latino, which added to the credibility of the therapeutic process. Predominant in the treatment were the couple's extreme expectations of each other as well as strong feelings from Kieu, who had internalized an attitude about Japanese men, whom she perceived as noninsightful and motivated solely by financial gain.

At the end of therapy, communication between Kieu and James had improved greatly. They were subsequently more willing to share unrealistic expectations and stereotypes in a healthier manner.

These two cases help to illustrate significant principles in treatment from a multicultural approach. In Case A, the therapist conducted a review of personal backgrounds in order to assess the degree of familial trauma experienced in the couple's own histories. From this discussion, the clients were able to identify the interplay between their cultural affirmations (Mexican men are protectors of family; women are respected and loved for their devotion to child rearing) and the need for problem-solving abilities. It quickly became evident that their family histories gave them very few emotional resources that would allow consistent trust to be part of their relationship. Thus the therapy held a tense partnership between what they wanted to be true culturally and what they pessimistically expected from each other. They had a very difficult time believing that they could genuinely trust each other's intentions. The combination of having each take responsibility for his or her own anger, distrusting intentions, and internalized ideals of what a "true Mexican family" was supposed to be helped to stabilize the couple through the termination phase of treatment.

Case B presents more directly the need for close examination of cultural histories, which in large part were interfering with effective relational compatibility. In addition to the couple's own childhood memories, Kieu had learned from her extended family of origin an animosity toward people of Japanese descent. At a more general level she also had internalized distrust and anger toward the Japanese for their invasion of China during War World II. The anger, distrust, and long-held stereotypes of Japanese men were affecting Kieu's relationship with James on both conscious and unconscious levels. From this discussion emerged significant cultural stereotypes each held about the other that helped to defuse the anger and permit problem solving to occur spontaneously. Further, treatment allowed Kieu and James to join as members of oppressed minority groups, thus facilitating a partnership with historical connection and cultural unity.

It is significant to note that both cases above also point to the use of the therapist's own cultural background as a medium to facilitate trust and prompt discussion relevant to multicultural agendas. Cervantes and Romero (1983) examined several therapist issues that affect therapeutic process and interventions. Within that context, therapist responsibility and countertransference become especially poignant for the professional dealing with different cultural groups. This discussion is taken up more directly in the next section.

Therapist Responsibility

As in all clinical work, the beginning place for all therapists in the conduct of psychotherapy is with the self. The therapist must be sensitive to his or her own family history and cultural reference point. While this is not a novel idea, it is underscored as a major criterion in the development of the multicultural therapist. Some common problems that stem from a therapist's failure to understand his or her own personal concerns are described below.

Illusion of color blindness. This is the tendency of the mainstream culture therapist to ignore the impact of his or her own "whiteness" on the culturally different client. In brief, such a therapeutic posture removes the client from his or her own social/ethnic/racial environment, which leads to identifying deviations from majority norms as pathological. Equally relevant along this line is the therapist's need to question his or her own professional education, as generally it has included little multicultural training or experience (Cervantes & Romero, 1983).

Assumptions of societal unfairness. This is the therapist's tendency to believe that all problems of the client revolve around the condition of the client's being a member of an "ethnic minority" in an oppressive environment. While it is significant to note the impact of racism and discrimination in the treatment of cases, it is by no means the only dimension to consider in understanding the dynamics of behavior. Generational states, acculturation effects, and multiracial and idiosyncratic familial patterns are all major exceptions to this assumption.

"Great White Father syndrome." This is the tendency for the therapist to communicate a sense of omnipotence and a feeling that he or she wants nothing but "good" for the client. What this stance communicates, although the therapist may have professionally appropriate intentions, is that the client is powerless and needs the therapist to "save" him or her.

Implied in the discussion thus far is the expectation that therapists must see themselves within their own familial-cultural milieus and then recognize culture as a significant parameter in human functioning. A related issue is the development on the part of the therapist of an awareness of community standards and ethnic/cultural makeup that will assist him or her in orienting to an appropriate appraisal of how to progress therapeutically. For example:

- High gang concentration in an area can mean potential school achievement problems, drug/alcohol abuse, and angry, hostile teenagers and young adults.
- Generational stability of the community can help to identify services for immigrants in contrast to those for families that have been in the community for several years. Issues of domestic violence differ when couples and families are battling over basic survival needs as opposed to racism and discrimination experiences.
- Knowledge of the sociopolitical history of the targeted group is again useful for understanding some of the psychological rationale for movement to the United States. For example, comparisons among different ethnic groups, such as Cuban, Salvadoran, Haitian, Southeast Asian, and Chinese, yield very different historical roots and responses to the pressures of assimilation.
- Tribal background of Native Americans is significant, particularly if an individual has moved out of the tribe. For instance, there are important differences between the person from the Sioux tribe who is coupled with a member of the Navajo tribe with regard to familial and cultural expectations.

Finally, the therapeutic agenda for the therapist becomes more concrete as he or she begins to examine some of the relevant counseling issues surrounding domestic violence. The following are some issues to consider:

1. *Assessment for dangerousness:* The necessity to assess for dangerousness is discussed by Harway and Hansen in Chapter 4 of this volume. Suffice it to say that the therapist must determine the importance of this dimension.
2. *Distinctions among individual pathology, relational conflict, and strained cultural expectations:* Training programs have historically weighted assessment in favor of individual functioning. What have not been well integrated

have been consideration of relationship variables and acculturative stress. Relational conflict occurs as a function of the particular developmental stage of the family (Carter & McGoldrick, 1989). In brief, types of relational/family conflict vary depending upon the presence of children, their ages, available familial support, and so on. Recent research suggests that developmental and safety processes are drastically altered when families grow up in what have come to be see as "war zone" communities (Garbarino et al., 1992; Hines, 1989). Thus the acceptance of violence as a way of life desensitizes family members to violence within the family itself.

3. *Evaluation of familial resources:* Resources must be examined in light of the extended family networks of many people of color.
4. *Inclusion of a respected family member in the therapy context:* For some clients from some cultural groups, a family member can be helpful as a negotiator and as a stabilizing element in therapy.
5. *Establishment of a level of belief in the culture of origin:* Through affirmation of the family's cultural background, the therapist can enhance members' sense of connection and history.
6. *Teaching of cultural skills that may impede domestic violence:* The therapist can emphasize the inherent respect within the cultural framework for the individual members of the family.
7. *Development of safety contracts:* The therapist can introduce contracts as needed to emphasize that violence within the family is not a culturally acceptable mode of interaction.
8. *Requiring the potential perpetrator to leave the volatile environment:* This step should be taken to prevent further familial decompensation.

Recommendations

The understanding of a multicultural perspective, especially when viewed within the potential or realized escalation of anger resulting in violence, can be a very complex and often confusing clinical event. Many issues need to be addressed at several levels, and these must incorporate cultural linkages between therapist and client systems. Several recommendations and conclusions follow:

- The multicultural perspective is defined as the ability to relate, assess, and evaluate the presentation of clinical symptoms from a framework that views the client system within a cultural context.
- The therapist may engage in the storytelling presentation of complaints often utilized by clients to facilitate her or his ability to discriminate between healthy and unhealthy elements of the system. In order to accomplish this goal, the therapist must be aware of her or his own cultural background and resulting values and expectations.

- The therapist must acknowledge the strong socioeconomic and discriminatory parameters in many cases of domestic violence with people of color. Societal factors (alcohol and drug abuse, poverty, and community violence) contributing to domestic violence should not be confused with cultural expectations and values.
- A close conceptual relationship exists between multicultural and feminist perspectives. Both emphasize relational trust, equality in the distribution of [illegible] paradigm of respect across the client system.
- [illegible] influence the treatment outcome when there is a [illegible] of women and a lack of respect for cultural [illegible] viewed as potentially overwhelming [illegible] viewed as a distinct [illegible]
- [illegible] the emergence of [illegible] ists to continue to [illegible] cultural orientation.

14

Domestic Violence and Child Custody

MARSHA B. LISS
GERALDINE BUTTS STAHLY

The impact of domestic violence on women's lives has been the focus of most of this volume. However, in addition to women, there are others who are affected by domestic violence—children. When children are exposed to domestic violence, their lives are also damaged and disrupted. When the woman makes the decision to leave the batterer, her decision changes the children's environment as well as their relationships with both parents. Although it may seem that the mother's decision to leave will protect her children from further exposure to battering and its effects, the continuing involvement of the batterer in the lives of both the children and their mother may create new problems, exacerbate old problems, and prevent healing of the damage that has already occurred (Bessenyey, 1989; Stahly, 1991). Given that the man's need for power and control is an important component of domestic violence, divorce may actually exacerbate his need to control, as evidenced in bitter and never-ending custody disputes (Chesler, 1986; Stahly, 1991). In this chapter we examine what is known about domestic violence as an issue in custody decisions, outline ongoing research in this timely field, and review the types of cases and decisions judges have dealt with so far.

History of the Treatment of Domestic Violence in Custody Cases

Historically, under common law, children were considered the father's property, and upon divorce custody of the children was awarded to him.

Evidence of the father's beating of the mother or the children had no place in any court of law in any jurisdiction and was acknowledged in some circles as a matter of privacy and due course. The home was the man's castle, and abuse of either children or spouse was no one else's business (Aries, 1970). It was only in the late nineteenth century that child abuse was addressed by any modern court. In the twentieth century, industrialized countries developed new philosophies, such as the tender years doctrine, espousing that, all other things being equal (religion, sexual morality, psychological disturbance), custody should be awarded to mothers during the early childhood development period. This philosophy continued until almost the present day. During the 1970s the tender years doctrine began to be questioned, and in 1981 the Supreme Court of Alabama struck down the presumption of the tender years doctrine based on failure to provide equal rights to fathers (*Devine v. Devine,* 1981).

In place of the tender years doctrine and presumption of maternal care, the standard adopted in most states became the "best interests of the child." This standard, criticized by many as vague and lacking in guidance, definition, and parameters, does not require that any special weight be given to the sex of the parent (Chambers, 1984). Either mother or father might be awarded custody.

In recent years, attention has focused on "joint custody," another index of the changing view of the needs of children. In this model, parents share child custody responsibilities after dissolution of the marriage. The literature on joint custody indicates that when it works, it may be the ideal (Kelly & Wallerstein, 1982). In theory, joint custody is designed to afford the child access to continuing involvement by both parents. In California, the increasing number of parents awarded joint custody by the courts shows that it is almost routinely granted in disputed custody cases, generally without consideration of the special circumstances created by domestic violence (Judicial Council Advisory Committee, 1990). A growing body of literature in psychology urges parents to develop joint parenting arrangements following divorce (Hetherington, 1979; Teyber & Hoffman, 1989). However, recent data show that although joint custody works well with cooperative, dissolution-resolved parents with flexible schedules, these success stories may highlight the unusual rather than the normative family. In families that fall short of these characteristics, joint custody seems to foster continuing conflict for parents and children (Wallerstein & Blakeslee, 1989). It is within this framework of the "best interests of the child" and the tensions regarding custody and decision making post-dissolution that we will discuss child custody and domestic violence.

The role of domestic violence within the home has only recently been addressed by litigation and court decision as well as legislation. In the past, many courts would have found such allegations irrelevant to children's custody determinations; if found relevant at all, they would often be discounted as mere artifacts of the custody dispute process and not as substantial events in themselves. It was not until 1980 that the *Index to Legal Periodicals* even included a listing for "domestic violence."

As of this writing, at least 30 states have enacted domestic violence legislation, which may be the basis for women's turning to the courts for sole custody awards. States are being encouraged to enact more specific links between domestic violence and custody awards. For instance, effective January 1, 1991, judges in California (Civil Code Sections 4600, 4608) must consider allegations and evidence of a history of domestic violence in cases of child custody. However, no directives on how or to what extent they must consider it are provided; each judge must use her or his own discretion in evaluating, or even considering, the evidence. It should also be noted that it took California legislators five attempts over a course of several years to agree on the legislation, in spite of gender-neutral language. The legislation was supported in part by advocates for battered women and abused children; its strongest opponents were fathers' rights groups. This step, not the first of its kind in the nation, incorporates the consideration of family violence as part of the definition of "in the best interests of the child." Discussions of the best interests of the child and the negative effects of family violence on children's growth and development can be found elsewhere in this volume.

Some of the changes in custody determinations are not due solely to the efforts of advocates in the field of domestic violence. Rather, a combination of interests and forces—including the fathers' rights movement, the emergence of changes in women's life-styles and economics, the breakdown of rigid sex roles, and the custody issues related to them all—led to the courts' consideration of other custody patterns. One result has been the opening of judicial minds to aspects of domestic life not previously considered, including allegations of violence. Before this time, allegations of domestic violence or child abuse would not have been raised by attorneys, who were reluctant to bring up what were thought to be irrelevant issues. Paradoxically, the move toward greater sex role equality and equality of treatment by the courts and legislatures has also resulted in a loss of power by women in their traditional domain: At one time, nothing was as certain as the role of the mother in the upbringing of her child.

The Issue of Control and Custody

Many writers cite issues of control as part of the continuing battle between parents, both before and after marital dissolution, and mothers are often blamed for not cooperating and for creating difficulties (Hetherington, 1979;

Kelly & Wallerstein, 1982; Teyber & Hoffman, 1989). Some psychiatrists and, to a lesser extent, psychologists have even taken the position that women who allege abuse ought not to be given custody, because they are actually manipulating the system and are using the allegations because they are "vindictive or delusional" (Gardner, 1989; Green, 1986). Gardner (1989), in fact, goes so far as to recommend that a mother who reports child abuse and believes in her child's report should lose custody and have limited visitation, to be withdrawn if she continues to support the child's unfounded report. These views are alarming, especially at a time when the extent of the epidemic of child abuse is beginning to be acknowledged by our judicial branches, children are finally being listened to and believed, and research is upholding the credibility and validity of children's testimony (Goodman, Bottoms, Herscovici, & Shaver, 1989). Many true reports may be classified as unfounded because of the difficulties inherent in meeting standards of proof when a crime is committed against a child in the family. In the first study to include a large nonclinical sample of parents engaged in custody disputes, the rate of false and unfounded reports was not significantly higher than that found when custody was not an issue (Thoennes & Tjaden, 1990).

Whereas most mothers may be at a disadvantage in custody situations, financially and emotionally, battered women are in an even more disadvantaged position (Chesler, 1986). For the mother, the concern is how to report or handle abuse that occurs during custody. According to Gardner and his followers, if she supports her child's allegations she should be denied custody. If she fails to act, she betrays her child's trust and allows the abuse to continue. Further, this quandary applies not only to abuse of the child but to her own abuse as well. The battered woman may not be treated as powerful and effectual compared with the aggressive, more controlling abuser. Walker (1989a) suggests that the woman's fear of and/or anger with her partner may work against her own advocacy in the courtroom. Neither the passive, ineffectual demeanor common to a woman during abuse nor her emerging empowering anger is helpful to her when she presents her case to the court. The controller, who can remain calm yet assertive, unfortunately may be perceived by the court to be a more viable parent.

Often, the court will not consider past domestic violence in a family custody dispute. In addition, if the battering per se is not considered, but the woman's history of attempting to cope with the violence is introduced (e.g., psychological counseling, use of tranquilizers, leaving the home and returning), the batterer may actually appear to be more stable even though in fact he created the destructive environment. Some mothers who are victims may be concerned that if they remove themselves from the abusing situation the father may retaliate by hurting the children, and therefore the mother again fails to protect her children. If the mother has been the victim of the father's abuse herself, she must now consider the problem in dealing with him on support and visitation issues until her children reach the age of majority and move from the home (Stahly, 1990, 1991).

The custody decision itself does not cut the mother off from involvement with the abusing father. She will continue to find him abusive and intimidating, as has been described elsewhere in this volume. If control is the major point of the domestic violence, separation may actually increase the man's need to regain or reassert his authority position and control his "property." The children and visitation become central control issues. The woman may find herself in a relationship with the battering man in which control of the children rather than physical violence becomes the basis of terrorization. Threats and/or occasions of violence may also continue. In fact, statistics from the National Crime Victims Survey show that the amount of abuse after marital dissolution is even greater than predissolution, with nearly 70% of violence reported postseparation (U.S. Department of Justice, 1986). These statistics are especially noteworthy because they focus on the full range of crimes citizens experience, both reported and unreported. The woman who has been abused and who does not perceive that law enforcement or the courts can help her without her needing to fear the loss of her children may not report the violence, and thus it does not show up on any traditional measure of crime.

The woman who has been continually abused may be so terrorized that she is intimidated into making custody arrangements contrary to her wishes and may be unable to assert her legitimate claims for fear of later retaliation. She may feel it is better to give up some support or property or visitation than to assert herself and her children's best economic interests if she feels this action will increase their physical and psychological danger. The fear of losing custody of her children, legally or through later kidnapping by the abuser, may leave the woman no choice but to stay in the abusing relationship (Stahly, Oursler, & Takano, 1988). Chesler (1986) cites a substantial number of cases in which violent, misogynist men have sought and won custody of their children. Further, some women allow their ex-mates to take custody of their sons in the hope that in this way they might shield their daughters (San Francisco Domestic Violence Project and Neighborhood Law Centers, personal communication). One avenue a mother may pursue is to obtain protective orders restraining the father from contact with her and her home. Usually, however, these orders are for limited periods of time, such as from six months to a maximum of three years. Two issues then emerge: What happens at the end of that period, legally and in daily life? And if the father disregards the order, will law enforcement really be there to help her eject him from her home and vicinity? Additionally, when the mother tries to protect herself her actions may be construed as interference with the father's visitation rights.

The battered woman is faced with a double bind in her initial decision to leave the situation or stay. If she is the primary target of the man's violence and has no safe shelter for herself and her children, she may perceive only two options: Stay in the violent home or relinquish control of the children to the batterer. The decision she makes initially may eventually lead to her losing her children. She may be perceived by the children as the parent least willing to fight for them; the batterer may suggest to them that she is not interested in their welfare. Children in custody disputes often want to place blame; with the batterer's encouragement, they may blame their mother. When a mother has been terrorized into submission, she may be perceived as the less influential and powerful parent; she may be seen as ineffectual, despite her interests in protecting the children and herself. Ironically, her children, especially her sons, may identify and align themselves with the powerful and aggressive father model. The result of this pattern may be aggression and abuse by sons toward the mother and ultimately other women as well. In a study of the effects of family violence on college students' attitudes toward women, Stahly (1983) found that male students who had observed their fathers battering their mothers held significantly more negative attitudes toward women than other males, including those who had been abused by their own mothers. These misogynist attitudes may ultimately result in failure to establish intimate relationships, thereby perpetuating male dominance and violence.

A contrary pattern may also emerge, in which the children align with the mother for protection from the aggressive father. Following divorce these children may fear visitation as a time when they are unprotected. In this pattern, the mother's actions to protect the children may be counterproductive if the court places credence in the Gardner (1989) "parental alienation" theory and theories that trivialize the father's violence and blame mothers for children's reasonable fears. Even children who do not get caught in the middle of the destructive alliance with either parent may be in a bind. If the father uses visitation as an occasion to abuse the mother further, the children may be put in the untenable position of feeling some responsibility for the continuing abuse and yet wanting some relationship with the father. Does the child now have to give up visitation with dad to protect mom? In a system of supervised and monitored visitation this theoretically would not happen. Unfortunately, many courts trivialize the violence and view supervision as an infringement of a father's rights. Even when courts are persuaded to require supervision, given the dearth of facilities and monitors and the lack of funds available from courts and institutions to support visitation plans, too often the parents must fend for themselves. The end result is that too often the violence continues, either against the woman or transferred to the child directly.

Challenging Custody Decisions

There are virtually no published studies dealing specifically with divorce, custody, and domestic violence. However, there are anecdotal and case histories and many articles, including those discussed above, with conjectures about the issue. Chesler (1986), while presenting primarily case history data, suggests that in a sample of several hundred cases of custodial challenges, "good enough" mothers lost these challenges about 70% of the time, often to men who were abusive of the women and the children. She further hypothesizes that it is abusive, misogynist fathers who are most likely to institute custodial challenges in attempts to punish the errant mother and retain sole control over their offspring.

There are no published data comparing the rates of custodial disputes by characteristics of the marital relationship. However, a recent exploratory study examined 150 randomly selected files of marital dissolution from a Southern California district courthouse between January 1983 and December 1988 (Suchanek & Stahly, 1991). Characteristics predicting custodial challenge and outcome were coded, and findings supported the previous case history data, including the possible role of control and misogyny in custodial challenges by battering men. Dissolution cases in which violence toward the woman had been asserted (usually in support of a restraining order) were significantly more likely to include custody disputes. These allegedly violent fathers were also more likely to fight for custody of sons than of daughters, and were more likely to be in arrears in child and/or spousal support. The notion that violent fathers are more likely to win a custodial challenge was not supported, but the violence was apparently not a factor considered by the court, given that they were no less likely to win than were fathers with no allegations of violence. One limitation of this small exploratory study is the lack of a measure of persistence. A number of anecdotal cases cite the long-term persistence of the battering man in pursuing and harassing the woman (Stahly, 1991), using legal as well as extralegal means. If such persistence is common among battering men, they might win custody ultimately.

Threats of kidnapping and/or custody battles and the continuation of violence may be significant factors in keeping women in violent relationships (Stahly et al., 1988). In a pilot study of battered women's experiences with child custody, in which 94 women participated, batterers' threats to

Table 14.1 Frequency of Custody Problems Reported by Shelters

Problem	*Number*	*%*
Batterer threatens child kidnapping	33,852	34
Batterer kidnaps child	10,687	11
Batterer threatens custody action	22,813	23
Batterer files custody action	7,168	7
Batterer wins full custody in spite of evidence of physical abuse of child	2,997	3
Batterer wins full custody in spite of evidence of sexual abuse of child	2,262	2
Batterer wins full custody/no child abuse	1,844	2
Batterer wins joint custody	19,850	20
Batterer wins joint custody in spite of evidence of physical abuse of child	7,881	8
Batterer wins joint custody in spite of evidence of sexual abuse of child	3,682	4
Batterer receives unsupervised visitation in spite of evidence of physical abuse	12,401	12
Batterer receives unsupervised visitation in spite of evidence of sexual abuse	6,970	7
Batterer uses visitation as occasion for verbal abuse of woman	24,719	25
Batterer uses visitation as occasion for physical abuse of woman	9,512	10
Batterer uses threat of kidnapping to force woman to return	21,121	21
Batterer uses threat of custody action to force woman to return	19,236	19
Woman goes into hiding because of court order that fails to protect child	3,881	4
Shelter staff testifies for mother	2,004	2
Shelter staff cites evidence of physical abuse of children by mother	5,833	6
Shelter staff subpoenaed by father	1,143	1
Shelter staff cites evidence of sexual abuse of children by mother	915	1
Shelter staff believes both mother and father are unfit custodial parents	2,655	3

keep the women from leaving included hurting the children (25%), kidnapping the children (25%), and taking the children through a custody action (35%). In discussions in the literature of the reasons women stay in and/or return to violent relationships, the women's fears for their children's safety and well-being have been consistently overlooked. In this sample, 20% of the women reported returning to the batterer at least once because of his threats to hurt or take the children.

Although substantial anecdotal and clinical data are available on the problems battered women are having with child custody, no published survey data have measured the extent of the problem. Stahly (1990) recently conducted a survey of the experiences of shelter staff in order to get a first view of the extent of custodial problems encountered by women seeking shelter services (see Table 14.1). Of the 105 questionnaires distributed to shelters in California, 39 were returned and 37 provided usable data. The shelters reported serving 6,034 women and 8,550 children as residents and 14,637 women and 4,204 children as nonresident clients; they provided telephone hot line counseling to an additional 87,378 women during the one-year period beginning January 1, 1989.

Shelter staff were asked to reconstruct from their case files and staff logs information regarding the extent of problems with custody and visitation experienced by their clients. According to the data reported as well as additional comments added by respondents, it is apparent that continued violence and harassment around issues of custody and visitation are problems of a significant number of battered women. Of the more than 100,000 women reported on by the shelter staff, 34% had children threatened with kidnapping and 11% of the batterers had actually kidnapped a child. In 23% of cases, batterers threatened legal custody action; in 7% of the cases known to the shelter staff, such actions had been filed; and in 7% of the cases the battered women won full custody. Considering both disputed and undisputed cases, 20% were granted joint custody. Disturbingly, shelter staff reported that batterers who had not directly abused their children actually won full custody less often (1,844) than fathers who were physically (2,997) or sexually abusive (2,262). Under these circumstances, a woman may feel her only alternative is to flee the jurisdiction of the court, and shelter staff reported knowing 3,881 battered women forced into hiding by court orders they felt endangered their children's (and often their own) safety. Since most custody actions and outcomes are likely to occur after the woman has left the shelter and is often no longer in contact, these figures are likely to underestimate the true occurrence of problems in the population. One limitation of these findings is that there may be a tendency for shelter staff to recall the most difficult cases, or for such cases to come to shelter staff's attention.

Also disturbing in magnitude is the tendency of the courts apparently to ignore violence and abuse in orders regarding visitation. In 24% of the cases, the battering man used court-ordered visitation as an occasion to continue verbal and emotional abuse of the woman, and in 10% of the cases, physical violence continued. The best interests of the child seem also to have been overlooked in the courts' granting of unsupervised visitation in spite of evidence of physical abuse of the child (12,401 reported cases) and sexual abuse (6,970), and joint custody in cases of physical abuse (7,881) and sexual abuse (3,682). Shelter staff may find themselves embroiled in custody proceedings; they reported that on 2,004 occasions staff had testified in support of the mother's petition, and an additional 1,143 received subpoenas from the father to testify against the mother. Staff did report that some mothers were physically abusive (5,833) and a small proportion sexually abusive (915) of their children (this contrasts with the beliefs regarding fathers that 21,587 were physically abusive and 9,557 sexually abusive of their children); in 2,655 cases, the staff expressed the belief that neither parent was fit.

Shelter staff expressed a wide range of frustrations. Supervised visitation, even when granted, proved less than satisfactory. A number of specific problems were cited, including difficulty in finding a trustworthy monitor of visits; the placement of financial responsibility for monitors on mothers; the practice of ordering the mother to monitor visits, thus placing her in physical danger; and the practice of allowing fathers to "veto" monitors suggested by the mother, thus sabotaging the arrangement. In this last situation the judge may order unsupervised visitation because "the parties cannot agree." Even when supervised visitation is satisfactory, few courts continue it beyond a few months, with the father's "good behavior" under supervision taken as evidence that he can now be trusted alone with the children in spite of credible evidence of past physical and/or sexual abuse.

The shelter staff cited other problems as well, such as the economic inequities that allow the father to make a better "self-presentation" in court, the refusal of court personnel and evaluators to take domestic violence seriously, the appointment of psychologists or psychiatrists to evaluate the family who have no understanding of domestic violence and tend to blame the woman, and the refusal of child protective services agencies to respond when allegations of abuse occur within the context of a custody dispute. The criminal and family courts also seem to work at odds with each other. As one shelter worker summed it up:

> No cooperation between criminal court and family law—criminal stay-away order overridden by visitation orders. Judges do not have knowledge of domestic violence, its effects on kids, or typical behavior of batterers, restraining order violations not acted upon, lawyers have not a clue as to how to protect women and kids, court psychiatrists continue to treat these cases the same as any other and make orders and recommendations that assure the batterer that he can continue to harass, punish, control and abuse his ex-wife and their kids. Battered women are not believed despite criminal convictions [of the batterers]. Kids are not listened to. Professional experts on domestic violence are blocked from testifying, examining or recommending in court.

Responses by the Courts

Although public and professional reactions to the statistics on domestic violence have focused attention on custody decisions, and legislators have responded with changes in statutes to allow for the admissibility of evidence of domestic violence in custody matters, there is scant mention of domestic violence in published court opinions. The reason for the lack of cases may at first appear perplexing, but it may be related to the fact that fewer cases are being appealed and settlements being reached, so that judicial decisions are not available for discussion. Traditionally, judges have been extremely reluctant to terminate a parent's rights and to prohibit visitation totally. A review of a few recent cases is illustrative of some changes in attitudes of court officers.

In 1980, the Pennsylvania courts refused to limit visitation unless the *child* was in direct harm. For example, in *Dena Lynn F. v. Harvey H. F.* (1980), not only was there no restriction placed on interaction between the parties in the presence of the child, but the court refused to place a restriction requiring the presence of another adult when the parents met at the time the child was picked up for visitation. However, by 1983 the same courts had changed their attitudes and decisions. In that year, the Pennsylvania courts denied a father visitation in *Hughes v. Hughes* (1983) in a postdissolution visitation case. In this case, the mother's attorney was able to cite a long pattern of physical abuse against the mother. However, mere abuse of the mother was not the only aspect cited by the court. In this case, the father had entered the mother's apartment postseparation and held her and the child hostage for more than eight hours. All that time, he was in violation of a protective order granted the mother. On another occasion he shot the mother *while she was holding the child.* He claimed that he was intoxicated and therefore since he had not harmed the child directly, his intoxication and his behavior should not be held against him. The court strongly disagreed, stating that "his reckless and wanton disregard . . . [and] his constant course of abuse directed at the child's mother confirms his moral deficiency."

In Alabama, in *Sanders v. Sanders* (1982), two children were in the home when the father beat their mother to death. The mother had previously sought help from a shelter based on the father's long history of abuse. The court terminated the father's parental rights upon his release from prison.

In some states in which domestic violence legislation has been enacted, courts have removed children from abusive environments to safeguard their best interests. Two cases from Minnesota are illustrative. In *Kimmel v. Kimmel* (1986), the mother's failure to protect herself and her child from an abusive stepfather was grounds for removing the child from her custody and placing him with his natural father, who had not sought custody. The mother had left the stepfather and secured a protective order for herself and the boy against the abuse. Contrary to the provisions of the order, the mother allowed the stepfather to return to the home, where he resumed his abusive behaviors. The court found that the child required immediate and emergency attention in order to secure his safety.

However, sometimes the courts do not adhere to the spirit of new domestic violence legislation, as in *Bates v. Bates* (1990). Here, the court found no reason to invoke provisions of the Arkansas Domestic Abuse Act if the mother had not first exhausted all remedies available at law. The court found that the mother should have sought protection against the father's actual as well as threatened physical abuse and harassment through the prosecuting attorney or on her own by obtaining a peace bond. The court further noted that she should have had the father arrested if his violence was so great. The court concluded that if the mother was too afraid to ask for assistance at law, the Domestic Abuse Act could be of no assistance to her (this attitude is addressed in many chapters in this volume). This court was clearly adopting the very attitudes that the act had been designed to eliminate, and had not yet been educated about the current state of knowledge about domestic violence.

The 1980s saw the beginnings of change in court attitudes and actions in domestic violence in custody cases. Today, visitation may still be seen as a right of both parents and of the child, so that he or she can have a relationship with each of the parents, but this might yield to the welfare or best interests of the child. For many years, the courts evaded the issue of which standard of proof was required to terminate or restrict visitation rights. In *Barron v. Barron* (1982), the New Jersey court articulated the standard as "clear and convincing" evidence. The use of this high-level standard showed the importance of parental relationships, which should be terminated only with "extraordinary proscription." What remains unclear from the cases and statutes cited above is the type of evidence that can be considered sufficient to establish a clear and convincing set of facts. How much abuse, noted by which witnesses, with what type of psychological profiles and effects on children, are all questions yet to be answered by the courts or legislatures. Indeed, the courts appear ready to act *only* when there has been a very long history of abuse that has been documented by medical and shelter staff, and where the child has already been damaged by the abuse between the adult parents. Preventive mental health issues and the impact of development within a violent home are not yet part of these cases. "It seems evident from these few cases that only in the most serious situations will a court completely deny a parent visitation" (Bessenyey, 1989).

Conclusions

Until recently it was assumed that the problems of battered women were primarily problems of empowerment and leaving. Most of the efforts were directed toward these goals. What we have highlighted in this chapter is that in custody decisions the battered woman's vulnerability to the batterer's aggression will continue until the woman's children reach majority. The implications for the woman's physical well-being and care for the children are substantial, with the threat of violence and intimidation constantly in the background. The number of cases of postseparation violence is evidence of the magnitude and validity of these concerns (U.S. Department of Justice, 1986).

Some battered women have taken recourse in dramatic means, such as fleeing and becoming part of underground networks. The courts then are caught with contradictory evidence and exceedingly difficult decisions. Is it better to force a woman to deal with a batterer even though her safety is jeopardized than to terminate the batterer's parental rights? Some women's actions to protect themselves and their children have resulted in their violating court orders. Such cases prompt courts to focus punitive actions on the mothers; judges then can deal only with disobeyed orders and do not have to focus on the violence and the entire picture. A common result is that these women are cited for contempt and "punished" for their protective actions, which focuses attention on the women and not the best interests of the children.

Although there are growing bodies of research literature detailing the effects of domestic violence and the effects of divorce on children, these two areas remain almost entirely separate. Further research is needed to address the special circumstances of domestic violence in child custody disputes. The concept of "the best interests of the child" must include the right to live in a violence-free environment without continuing threat of harassment from the father. The courts and the array of professionals who deal with the divorcing family must stop trivializing violence against the mother and the effects of such violence on children. The most pressing needs are for effective interventions and alternative custody and visitation strategies that protect both children and parents and preserve all parties' rights to the degree it is safe and reasonable for the mothers and children.

15

Violence in Lesbian Relationships

CLAIRE M. RENZETTI

Lesbian battering has been defined as a "pattern of violent [or] coercive behavior whereby a lesbian seeks to control the thoughts, beliefs, or conduct of her intimate partner or to punish the intimate for resisting the perpetrator's control" (Hart, 1986a, p. 173). As in heterosexual relationships, the abuse may be physical and/or psychological. It is important to note, however, that although published anecdotal accounts of abuse by lesbian victims indicate the problem is a serious one, lesbian battering has been given little attention by family violence researchers. Therapists and other social service providers report seeing an increasing number of lesbian clients who have been abused by their intimate partners, but the lack of evaluative studies leaves them with few guidelines for developing effective strategies to use in responding to these clients (see, e.g., Hammond, 1989; Kanuha, 1990; Leeder, 1988; Morrow & Hawxhurst, 1989). Moreover, as Hammond (1989) points out, "most mental health professionals receive little or no training in either lesbian issues or domestic violence. As a result, the caregiver's own prejudices, stereotypes, or incorrect assumptions are likely to have gone unchallenged and uncorrected, once again putting the lesbian at risk for further victimization" (p. 98).

This chapter discusses some of the critical issues that frequently are raised by victims of lesbian battering, particularly when they seek help to deal with the problem. In addition, it suggests a number of strategies that help providers may implement to increase their effectiveness in responding to lesbian victims. First, however, it would be useful to examine what little empirical research there is on the incidence and forms of lesbian battering.

The Incidence of Lesbian Battering

One of the first published studies of intimate violence that included lesbian subjects was conducted by Brand and Kidd (1986), who compared the reported frequencies of physical aggression (i.e., pain inflicted beyond consent when practicing sadomasochism, physical abuse, attempted rape, and completed rape) experienced by 75 self-identified heterosexual women and 55 self-identified lesbians. They found that male partners in heterosexual relationships committed a greater overall number of aggressive acts than did female partners in lesbian relationships (57 and 28, respectively). Nevertheless, with respect to some forms of aggression, the differences in frequency reported by female heterosexual victims and lesbian victims were negligible. A total of 25% of the lesbian respondents reported that they had been physically abused by their female partners in committed relationships, compared with 27% of the heterosexual respondents in committed relationships with men. Similarly, 7% of lesbian respondents reported having been raped by female dates, compared with 9% of heterosexual respondents who reported completed rapes by male dates.

Several recent studies, rather than comparing heterosexual and homosexual couples, have focused solely on violence in same-sex relationships. Kelly and Warshafsky (1987), for example, studied partner abuse among both lesbian and gay male couples, using a self-selected sample of 48 women and 50 men. Subjects completed a 17-item version of the Conflict Tactics Scale (Straus, 1979), which subsequently was divided into four subscales: assertive tactics of conflict resolution, verbal abuse tactics, physical aggression tactics, and violent tactics. The researchers found that 100% of their sample had used assertive tactics at some point in their relationships, 95% had used verbal abuse tactics, 47% had used physical aggression, and 3% had used violent tactics. Only one significant sex difference was found when the experiences of male and female subjects were compared: Lesbians tended to have less physically aggressive partners than did gay men.

Bologna, Waterman, and Dawson (1987) also have studied violence in same-sex relationships. In a survey of 174 lesbians, 26.4% reported that they had been subjected to at least one act of sexual violence, 59.8% had been victims of physical violence, and 81% had experienced verbal or emotional abuse. At the same time, 68% of the women in the study stated that they had both used violence against their current or most recent intimate partners and been victimized by a partner. Similarly, in a survey of 1,099 lesbians, Lie and Gentlewarrior (1991) found that 52% of their respondents reported having been abused by female lovers or partners, and 30% admitted to having abused female lovers or partners. Of those who had been victims of abuse, more than half (51.5%) reported that they also had been abusive toward their partners.

With the exception of Brand and Kidd's (1986) study, it may appear that the incidence of partner abuse in homosexual relationships is unusually high. Prevalence studies of partner abuse in heterosexual relationships estimate that about one-third of heterosexual couples experience violence (Koss, 1990). Straus and Gelles (1989) report that about 16% of heterosexual couples experience partner abuse *each year.* It must be kept in mind, however, that studies of the incidence of homosexual partner abuse have, by necessity, utilized nonrandom, self-selected samples. There are likely to be significant differences between individuals who volunteer for a study of homosexual partner abuse and individuals who are randomly selected for such a study. Yet it is doubtful that a truly random sample could be drawn for such research, given the stigma attached to homosexuality as well as to domestic violence. How, for instance, would one obtain a comprehensive sampling frame? Consequently, it is unlikely that researchers will ever be able to measure accurately the incidence of lesbian battering. Nevertheless, the studies cited here remain valuable because they clearly demonstrate that lesbians (as well as gay men) not infrequently utilize conflict resolution tactics with their intimate partners that can be characterized as physically or emotionally abusive and sometimes violent.

Forms of Battering

Leeder (1988) has distinguished three types of abusive lesbian relationships: situational battering, chronic battering, and emotional or psychological battering. Leeder defines the situational battering relationship as one in which abuse occurs once or twice as a result of some situational event that throws the couple into crisis. Once the crisis is resolved, the abuse never recurs. My own research with lesbian victims indicates that this type of relationship is relatively rare; only 8 of the 100 participants in my study had been involved in abusive relationships that could be considered situational. More common were chronic battering and emotional battering relationships (Renzetti, 1992).

Leeder (1988) describes the chronic battering relationship as one in which physical abuse occurs "two or more times, demonstrating increasingly destructive behavior. The violence escalates over time and, in many cases, actually leads to life-threatening situations" (p. 87). The emotional battering relationship is more difficult to define precisely, but Leeder argues that it shares the same characteristics as the chronic battering relationship except the abuse is verbal or psychological rather than physical. In my study, 54% of the respondents said they had experienced 10 or more abusive incidents in the relationships about which they were reporting, and 74% experienced at least 6 or more abusive incidents; 60% reported that there was a pattern to the abuse, and 71% indicated that the abuse grew worse over time (Renzetti, 1992). It is important to note, however, that the respondents in my study could not be easily separated into two distinct groups—that is, those in chronic battering relationships versus those in emotional battering relationships. Although the respondents reported a greater overall frequency of psychological abuse, only 11% of the sample indicated that they had experienced psychological abuse only; 87% reported being subjected to both physical and psychological abuse.

The most common forms of physical abuse reported by respondents in my research were pushing and shoving; being hit with fists or open hands; being scratched or hit in the face, breasts, or genitals; and being the target of thrown objects. The most common forms of psychological abuse reported were verbal threats; being demeaned in front of relatives, friends, or strangers; having one's eating or sleeping habits interrupted; or having one's property damaged or destroyed. It also was not uncommon for batterers to abuse others in the household besides their intimate partners. At least 35 of the respondents in the study lived with children (either their own and/or their partners'); in almost one-third of the cases, these children were abused by the violent partners. In addition, 38% of the respondents who had pets in their households reported that their partners had abused the pets as well.

Correlates of Lesbian Battering

The literature on conflict in lesbian relationships provides several clues about the factors that may contribute to partner abuse among lesbian couples. Recent research on two issues in particular—the relative dependency of lesbian partners on one another and the balance of power in lesbian relationships—suggests that abusers may be excessively dependent on their partners for emotional and/or financial support and that abuse is likely to occur in relationships in which one partner has greater resources than the other.

Research indicates that in response to the negativism and hostility of the dominant community toward lesbianism, lesbian couples often nurture their relationships as relatively "closed systems" (Krestan & Bepko, 1980). On the one hand, this fosters emotional intensity and closeness in the relationship, but on the other, it may also generate insecurity by disallowing separateness or autonomy for the partners (Lindenbaum, 1985). Dependency on one's partner, however, is a trait associated with a destructive, culturally prescribed female role. According to Burch (1987), some lesbians develop a fear or hatred of dependency "because it represents identification with the old sense of heterosexual 'femininity.' . . . A woman who fears or even hates her own woman-ness will project this gynephobia onto her lover and feel further devalued herself by dependency on her" (p. 130). Nicoloff and Stiglitz (1987) hypothesize that one consequence of this fear or hatred of dependency is self-destructive behavior, such as alcohol abuse. Another may be violence against one's partner. In my own research, I found significant correlations between partners' relative dependency on one another and violence in lesbian relationships (Renzetti, 1992). The greater a batterer's dependency on her partner and the greater a victim's desire to be independent, the more likely the batterer was to inflict more types of abuse with greater frequency. This finding is consistent with results shown in research on other forms of intimate violence (e.g., Pillemer, 1985).

Conflicts surrounding dependency are related to the balance of power in lesbian relationships. Studies of heterosexual domestic violence have shown that an imbalance of power between partners is a significant contributing factor to abuse. According to Straus, Gelles, and Steinmetz (1980), violence is least likely to occur in egalitarian households in which the relative power of partners is balanced. However, it is unclear in abusive heterosexual relationships whether it is the batterer or the victim who is the less powerful partner. Some researchers have found that violence is especially likely among heterosexual couples when the male partner perceives that his power in the relationship is diminishing (see, e.g., Finkelhor, Gelles, Hotaling, & Straus, 1983); the violence becomes a means for him to assert dominance and control in the relationship. However, others argue that the batterer in an abusive relationship is the partner with the most power (see, e.g., Straus, 1974). In other words, violence is just one of many ways in which the partner's greater power is expressed.

Among lesbian couples, the findings with regard to power differences are also inconclusive. For example, Bologna et al. (1987) report that for some of their respondents, a perceived lack of power was related to being the perpetrator of violence, but among other couples it was related to victimization. Kelly and Warshafsky (1987) found no significant correlations between specific status differentials (income, education, race, religion, and age) and the incidence of partner abuse, although respondents in their study who reported having primary responsibility for major and minor expenses as well as cooking were more likely to be abused by their partners. In my own work, I found significant correlations between some indicators of power imbalance in lesbian relationships and violence in these relationships (Renzetti, 1988). For instance, social class differences between partners were associated with an increase in the overall number of abusive incidents. However, more detailed analysis revealed that the relationship between power imbalance and abuse is a highly complex one, and dependency has greater explanatory power than power differences (Renzetti, 1992).

Clearly, the relationship between power and partner abuse requires more attention if it is to be fully understood. In light of the available evidence regarding the incidence and severity of partner abuse in lesbian relationships, however, it is not surprising that many victims seek help from friends, relatives, and social service providers, thus alerting others to the problem. The sections that follow discuss some of the critical issues raised by lesbian victims who seek help as well as various responses by different types of help providers. The potential consequences that particular responses may have for lesbian victims are explored and strategies for improving the effectiveness of help provision to lesbian victims are suggested.

Victims' Help Seeking and Help Providers' Responses

The sociologist Edwin Schur (1984) has argued that women have difficulty establishing their legitimacy or "worthiness" as victims because they are a devalued group in our society. It may also be argued that the legitimacy problem is exacerbated when the devalued trait of femaleness is combined with other devalued characteristics or statuses, such as being a member of a racial minority group, being poor, being a substance abuser, and/or being a lesbian. Research that draws on the accounts of victims of lesbian battering illuminates how these women in particular must struggle to be deemed "worthy" or "true" victims as they seek help from both official and informal help providers.

In my research, for instance, I found that lesbian victims rarely perceived the sources of official help typically utilized by heterosexual victims as sources of help for lesbians (Renzetti, 1992). Therefore, few sought help from police, attorneys, physicians, hot lines, and battered women's shelters. Those who did seek help from these sources reported that responses usually were negative. Those who went to women's shelters, for example, stated that frequently they were made to feel unwelcome or unsafe; sometimes they simply were turned away. As Hammond (1989) points out, such services were developed to meet the needs of women abused by men: "When shelter workers or advocates meet a situation that appears to defy their own understanding and analysis, the battered lesbian herself is seen as the problem" (p. 95). At the same time, shelter staffers and heterosexual residents may be homophobic, or staff may fear that admitting lesbian victims may jeopardize their funding from individuals or agencies, given the widespread acceptance of homophobic stereotypes among the general public. If the victims are lesbians of color, they may also confront racist stereotypes (Kanuha, 1990). Finally, shelter workers are confronted with a unique problem in offering services to lesbian victims of partner abuse. In heterosexual relationships, they can easily discern who is being battered and who is doing the battering. However, as Hammond (1989, p. 96) maintains—and my own research supports this (see Renzetti, 1992)—sometimes lesbian batterers will identify themselves as victims and seek admission to shelters, especially if their partners have defended themselves from abuse. Accusations of mutual abuse are common in violent lesbian relationships. Consequently, shelter staff may be forced to decide which partner should be provided shelter, and their assessments may sometimes be wrong.

The few respondents in my study who contacted the police, attorneys, or physicians indicated that the responses also were mostly negative. For instance, some respondents stated that the police insulted them or imputed victim complicity in the incident. Studies of heterosexual domestic violence have demonstrated the low priority that police and other service providers (e.g., emergency room personnel) give to domestic violence cases, as well as their tendency to blame the victim (Bowker, 1986; Kurz, 1987; Saunders & Size, 1986; Skolnick & Bayley, 1986). This research shows that sexist stereotypes are still prevalent within these groups, and there remains a tendency for them not to consider most domestic assaults as "real" emergencies.

Kurz (1987), in particular, reports that an active, supportive response to a battered woman appears to be forthcoming only when service providers judge the woman to be a "true victim" on the basis of several factors: (a) if it is obvious that the woman is in immediate physical danger, (b) if the woman has a pleasant personality, (c) if the woman is not under the influence of alcohol or drugs and does not appear to be "crazy," and (d) if the woman is assertively taking steps to end the relationship. In short, help providers appear more likely to respond positively to a battered woman the more she conforms to the traditional stereotype of "respectable femininity" and the more she is perceived to be helping herself. Of course, few battered women, lesbian or heterosexual, are in a position to conform to this stereotype.

The one official help source that the respondents in my study found most helpful was counselors (Renzetti, 1989). For this group, counselors were the second most frequently sought out help source, and 65% of those who went to counselors said they were somewhat or very helpful. In elaborating on their positive ratings of counselors, most respondents noted that these professionals challenged the legitimacy of their partners' actions and offered concrete advice about dealing with the problem. Still, few counselors suggested that victims end the abusive relationship. Instead, most attempted to preserve the relationship and keep the couples together. Often, counselors initiated "couples counseling" despite victims' strong reluctance to participate in counseling with their batterers. Research by Hansen, Harway, and Cervantes (1991) shows that therapists frequently fail to address the issue of violence between the couples they counsel, or they downplay the seriousness of the abuse. Instead, they tend to focus on the dynamics of the couple, such as their communication patterns and ability to express anger or vent feelings. Indeed, Hansen et al. discovered that the failure of therapists to invoke crisis intervention in such cases is often potentially dangerous to their clients.

It is the case that lesbian victims of domestic violence, like heterosexual victims (see, for example, Loseke & Cahill, 1984), do initially wish to save their relationships. The most frequent reasons women in my study gave for remaining in the abusive relationship was that they loved their partners and they thought their partners would change (Renzetti, 1992). At this point, however, enough research is available for counselors to recognize this as a normative response of abused clients and to advise them with respect to more realistic alternatives, such as ending the relationship. Trying to keep the relationship intact may leave the victim open to further abuse, and couples counseling usually is unsuccessful because it overlooks the power differential between the partners, in particular the power of the psychological as well as physical intimidation of the victim by the abusive partner.

Underlying couples counseling is the recognition that batterers as well as victims need help in addressing their individual and interpersonal problems. Two difficulties may emerge from this, however.

First, although Leeder (1988) maintains that chronic batterers have poorly developed communication skills and are unable to express their wishes, my own research (Renzetti, 1992) and that of others (e.g., Morrow & Hawxhurst, 1989) indicates the opposite. Batterers have been found to be charming, articulate, and, perhaps most important, manipulative. As a result, in some couples counseling sessions, the tables are turned; it is the batterer who is cared for, and the batterer and the therapist work together to determine what is "wrong" with the victim. This not only leaves the batterer unaccountable for the abusive behavior, it also shows disregard for the victim's physical and emotional well-being. Indeed, the victim may be placed in further jeopardy because her isolation is increased; now even the counselor from whom she sought help is implicating her in her own victimization, either implicitly or explicitly.

This last point is closely related to a second difficulty. Specifically, many therapists and counselors have adopted a systems model or an addictions model as a framework for their treatment programs, and both of these assume that the victim shares some responsibility for her abuse. Thus the therapist may focus on how the victim may have "provoked" the abuse or may view a victim's alcohol or drug problem as a cause rather than an outcome of abuse; or the therapist may see the victim's decision to remain in the relationship as evidence of her "codependence." In any event, treatment is subsequently centered on changing the victim, without any recognition of the victim blaming inherent in this approach. As Hammond (1980) points out, "Such labeling ignores a premise that is fundamental to the foundation of the battered women's movement: no one deserves to be battered." Furthermore, "by labeling the battered lesbian as 'co-dependent,' or as 'such a victim,' the fact that the batterer alone makes the choice to behave abusively is overlooked" (p. 99).

The issue of "coresponsibility" is especially salient when the victim also used violence against her partner. Such cases usually are considered "mutual battery" by counselors and others. The issue is clouded further by the fact that victims typically express intense guilt if they have been violent toward their partners and sometimes see their behavior as justification for their partners' abusiveness toward them. However, counselors must be careful not to assume that all violence is of the same character when, in fact, there are important differences among battering, self-defense, and retaliation. The nature of the victim's behavior must be clarified before any label is attached to it or any blame affixed. For example, in my study of lesbian victims, 78% of the respondents indicated they had fought back or retaliated against their batterers (Renzetti, 1992), yet when they were asked to elaborate on what they did, most described clearly self-defensive behavior, such as pushing their partners away to avoid being hit.

It must be emphasized that many lesbian victims seek assistance from counselors and therapists because they, unlike heterosexual battered women, cannot go to relatives or friends for help, or because their relatives and friends responded to them negatively. For instance, in my study many victims said they could not ask their relatives for help because their relatives did not know they are lesbians (Renzetti, 1989). Several said that even though relatives knew about their lesbianism, they did not ask them for help because these relatives disapproved of their lesbian relationships and they feared that disclosing the battering would only reinforce negative views. Of those who sought help from friends (57%), the most frequent problems encountered were denial, victim blaming, and cooperation with the batterer. For example, one respondent said, "My friends brushed it off, didn't believe [my partner] was abusive, said it was a two-way street." Another woman reported that her friends did not believe her and, although they would sometimes let her stay with them, they also would call her batterer to tell her where the woman was.

There are some compelling reasons for the lesbian community to overlook or deny battering among its members. For instance, there is the possibility that recognition of the problem will fuel homophobia, especially dangerous during this period of increasing intolerance and antihomosexual sentiment in the United States (Hart, 1986b). Further, abuse of women by women contradicts the widely held belief that physical violence is a "male" or "patriarchal" problem (McAndrew, 1985), and "discussing the issue also threatens the ideals of the lesbian community and our vision of egalitarianism in lesbian relationships" (Hornstein, 1985, p. 3). Nevertheless, a reluctance on the part of the community to take a strong and open stand against violence in lesbian relationships serves to protect batterers by leaving them unaccountable and, in this way, permits the battering to occur. It also increases the isolation, confusion, and pain experienced by victims. Therapists and counselors must be particularly careful not to make the same mistakes as friends, relatives, and other help providers in responding to lesbian victims of partner abuse, because they often are these victims' last or only perceived source of support and assistance.

Strategies for Improving Responses to Lesbian Victims

In sum, although the majority of lesbian victims seek help from third parties to cope with or end partner abuse, they report receiving little useful assistance. They frequently perceive the responses of official or formal help providers, such as the police or shelter staff, as homophobic, sexist, and racist. Relatives', friends', and counselors' responses, although typically rated more highly, also often are negative rather than supportive of the victim or challenging to the batterer.

How, then, can third-party responses, particularly those of therapists, counselors, and other professional help providers, be improved? Lenore Walker's (1979) suggestions with respect to counseling battered heterosexual women are applicable here. She points out that help providers often are called upon immediately following an acute battering incident. At this point, crisis intervention techniques are appropriate. During crisis therapy, Walker emphasizes, it is important to label the victim's experience as battering, especially if she presents herself with her partner, since denial is a common coping mechanism and batterers typically try to justify their actions by focusing on what they feel their partners did to provoke them. Help providers must emphasize the unjustifiable nature of abuse to batterers and provide support to victims. Like battered heterosexual women, battered lesbians need to be encouraged to tell their stories and they deserve to be believed by those from whom they seek help. Indeed, for the battered lesbians who participated in my study, being believed was a top priority (Renzetti, 1989).

Battered lesbians may also seek therapy to cope with the consequences of being abused, but not identify themselves as battering victims. Hammond (1989, pp. 101-103) advises help providers to ask lesbian clients about relationship abuse at intake, using questions such as, "Have you ever been afraid of any of your lovers?" More direct questions (e.g., "Has a lover ever abused you?") might quickly be answered negatively by those who do not or cannot think of themselves as battering victims. In addition, help providers must learn to distinguish between self-defense and battering and to teach their clients to know the difference as well. Hammond also advises help providers to "affirm the message that the victim is not to blame for the abuse and that the batterer acts out of her own choice." The point bears reiterating: The therapist must believe the victim and assume a nonjudgmental attitude toward her.

Walker (1979) points out that individual therapy with battered women should be more action oriented than analytic: "The realities of present alternatives and future goal planning are explored in individual therapy. The battered woman needs to recognize concrete steps she can take to improve her situation. . . . Intervention and collaboration with other helpers are important corollaries of individual psychotherapy" (p. 239). In addition, the counselor should focus on rebuilding the client's self-esteem and helping her to recognize and constructively experience her feelings of anger.

Battered lesbians, like battered heterosexual women, may also benefit from group therapy and support groups (Leventhal, 1990; Porat, 1986; Walker, 1979). However, counselors should be cautious in offering couples counseling in these cases. This is not to say that treatment for batterers should be ignored. On the contrary, a focus of future research should be on identifying the unique needs of lesbian batterers and developing treatment programs specifically for them. But if a lesbian victim presents herself for treatment, the counselor must keep in mind that she alone—not her partner, and not she and her partner as a couple—is the client. Couples counseling should be provided only at the request of the victim. The model offered by Walker (1979, pp. 245-248) may be applicable to lesbian couples if both therapists involved are lesbians. In any event, if couples counseling is attempted, the victim's safety must be ensured, and she should be apprised of the low probability of success in abusive relationships.

Finally, although a number of similarities can be seen between battered lesbians and battered heterosexual women, help providers' responses to them cannot be identical. As Pharr (1986) points out:

> There is an important difference between the battered lesbian and the battered non-lesbian: the battered non-lesbian experiences violence within the context of a misogynist world; the lesbian experiences violence within the context of a world that is not only woman-hating, but is also homophobic. And that is a great difference. (p. 204)

Therefore, an essential step in improving responses to battered lesbians is for heterosexual help providers to confront and overcome their homophobia. As Elliott (1990) notes, "Before you . . . can acknowledge lesbian battering, you must first acknowledge lesbian relationships." At the same time, homosexual help providers must recognize that battering does occur in lesbian relationships, and it should not be minimized. Ultimately, the major goal should be to transform all help providers—be they professionals, friends, or relatives—into advocates, "providing positive emotional support and material assistance for the [victim] while posing a direct challenge to [the batterer] and violence" (Dobash, Dobash, & Cavanaugh, 1985, pp. 162-163).

16

Legal Self-Defense for Battered Women

LENORE E. A. WALKER

For the past 15 years, some battered women who have killed or attempted to kill their abusive partners have been provided a legal defense that rests on the justification of the act they have committed as necessary to protect themselves or someone else (usually their children) from further harm or death. Often called *battered woman self-defense,* the defense has been introduced by attorneys on behalf of their clients to demonstrate to judges and juries that living in domestic violence has such a major impact on a woman's state of mind that it could make an act of homicide justifiable even when at first the facts do not appear to support traditional confrontational self-defense (such as when the man is resting, sleeping, or otherwise not directly engaged in beating the woman at the moment she kills him).

Prior to the introduction of this new view on an old defense, most women who admitted the acts that resulted in their abusers' deaths were told by their attorneys that they had no defense and were encouraged to plead guilty to murder. In a small number of cases, when a battered woman was given any defense at all, it was usually some form of insanity defense (see Jones, 1981). Occasionally, a battered woman who killed a man who also had a long history of violence against others in the community was not charged with a crime, especially if her behavior fit the stereotype of what is often called the "good battered woman victim." This usually means a woman who is poor, passive, easy to get along with, and has no history of other confrontational or violent behavior. Naturally, most battered women cannot meet this mythical standard because they usually have taken some steps to defend themselves and their children, they may have difficulty in getting along with people as a result of the battering, or they are better able to cope with other parts of their lives than they are in their relationships with men.

To get to this point, there has been a relatively new acceptance of expert witness testimony in the trial courts, usually by psychologists trained in the understanding of the psychology of battered women and the effects of being an abuse victim on an individual's state of mind (Bochnak, 1981; Ewing, 1987; Schneider, 1986; Walker, 1984a, 1984c, 1984d, 1989a, 1989b). These psychological explanations of the dynamics of a battering relationship coupled with testimony about the presence of battered woman syndrome have helped meet the legal standard of self-defense, resulting in many not guilty jury verdicts or convictions for lesser crimes than first-degree murder. Further, in recent years battered women's advocates have been encouraging state governors to grant clemency to women who are serving long sentences in prison for killing their abusive partners, recognizing that if these same women went to trial today, they might not be convicted or at least might not receive such long sentences.

In the late 1970s and early 1980s, what became known as the *battered woman self-defense* achieved acceptance within the case law of numerous states. As this defense gained in popularity, attorneys and mental health professionals became more familiar with the dynamics of battering and its psychological impact on victims. Use of this defense broadened to include battered children who killed abusive parents, battered men who killed their abusive partners (usually male), women who have killed abusive female partners, rape victims who killed their attackers, and even battered roommates. It also has been used to explain a woman's participation with a codefendant in criminal acts that also result in harm to a stranger or when children are abused or killed. Soon, expert testimony was applied to cases where other criminal acts were committed by victims of abuse under duress from their abusive partners. Crimes involving money and property, such as embezzlement, forgery, burglary, and robbery and those that are drug related, are sometimes committed by women at the demands of their batterers. The common thread among these seemingly disparate cases is that they use psychological knowledge about the dynamics of an abusive relationship and its specific impact on a particular battered person to meet the legal standard of self-defense or duress, which might not be otherwise met if the history of abuse were not known.

Battered Woman Syndrome

In a legal defense, psychological testimony is used to assist the triers of fact, the judges and jurors, in understanding several important factors about battered women. First, it is important to help determine through psychological analysis whether or not a particular woman is a battered woman by analyzing the history of battering reported, comparing it with reports of other battered women, and reviewing witness statements, medical and mental health records, and other relevant legal documents that are available. Second, it is important to explain whether or not there are measurable psychological effects from the battering and, in particular, if battered woman syndrome symptoms are currently present.

Third, and perhaps most critical, is the analysis of how being a battered woman who demonstrates symptoms of battered woman syndrome affects this particular woman's state of mind at the time of the incident that resulted in another person's death or whatever other criminal behavior must be understood. Obviously, if the woman is found to have battered woman syndrome, the meaning of her behavior at the critical time will be understood through the knowledge about battering and its effects on women in general as well as its unique impact on this particular woman's state of mind. As is described further below, battered woman syndrome is not usually considered a mental illness; rather, it is an expected reaction that occurs in even the most normal people who are repeatedly exposed to abnormal trauma. Thus the defense used in these cases is one of justification of the woman's actions rather than insanity or mental impairment defenses, which would excuse her behavior because of mental illness of some type.

WHAT IS BATTERED WOMAN SYNDROME?

Within the past 10 years, research on battered women has indicated that many of them respond to repeated abuse in a manner similar to others who have been repeatedly exposed to different kinds of trauma. *Battered woman syndrome* is the name given to the psychological changes that may occur after the exposure to abuse. The use of trauma theory together with the psychological understanding of feminist psychology (Dutton-Douglas & Walker, 1988; Rosewater & Walker, 1985; Walker, 1979, 1984a, 1989b), oppression (Brown & Ballou, 1992; Brown & Root, 1990), powerlessness (Blackman, 1986; Browne, 1987), and intermittent reinforcement theories such as learned helplessness (Dutton, in press; Dutton-Douglas & Walker, 1988; Walker, 1977, 1979, 1984a, 1989b) all help us to understand the psychological impact of physical, sexual, and serious psychological abuse on the battered woman.

Battered woman syndrome is considered a subcategory of the generic category of post-traumatic stress disorder (PTSD), which is the official diagnosis that is listed in the *Diagnostic and Statistical Manual of Mental*

Disorders, third edition, revised (DSM-III-R; American Psychiatric Association, 1987).

Assessment of Post-Traumatic Stress Disorder

CLINICAL INTERVIEW

The standard clinical interview is the most often used technique for collecting information about someone who claims to have been battered. Structured interviews with some open-ended and some forced-choice questions seem to be the best way to get the necessary relevant data. Although there has been some attempt to collect the interview data using already published interview formats, it appears that the most reliable and valid data come from a combination of structured and unstructured formats. Obviously, a mental status examination is also necessary in order to know if the data given by the woman are based on reality perceptions. At our offices we use an assessment device that was first developed during a National Institute of Mental Health-funded research project to collect the information in a systematic manner (Walker, 1984a). This interview frequently lasts between 6 and 12 hours. Others, such as Sonkin (1987) and Dutton (in press), have recommended a shorter format. It is important to cover important milestones that are usually obtained in a social history, including childhood information, religious and spiritual data, attitudes toward the roles of women, health patterns, schooling, career patterns, interpersonal relationships, children, substance use, and other relevant factors, including the woman's perception of control over her life.

BATTERING HISTORY

A critical part of the assessment is the collection of a good battering history that includes childhood abuse, such as witnessing or experiencing abuse in the childhood home; sexual abuse or molestation as a child; and adolescent dating history of violence. It is sometimes difficult to get information about incest, especially when the memories are buried. However, certain patterns that are typical for incest victims, such as dissociation, self-mutilation, and eating disorders, may be sufficient to raise the issue, although they are not enough to confirm it. Some women begin to remember their own incest experiences when they witness their abusive partners beginning to sexually abuse their children. Here the flood of memories must be carefully dealt with in order to keep clear the boundaries between the woman's and the child's experiences. It is not unusual for a woman to kill her abuser at the point of finding out about his sexual abuse of her children. Sometimes, the defense of a child may push the woman to take action she might not have taken otherwise.

Also important is a history of adult relationships, including data about significant partners, whether married or not. A complete history of the battering that occurred between the woman and the particular man for whom she is on trial is also important. Any changes in the woman's functioning, relationships with people, and personality should be documented. It is possible to plot the pattern of violence, which includes both the steady escalation of abuse and the three-phase cycle of violence, by taking careful details of four specific battering incidents: the first incident the woman can remember: a typical or several typical incidents, if it is a long-term relationship with different patterns; the worst or one of the worst incidents; and the last incident or the one that resulted in the woman's acting in self-defense. Careful attention to details—such as whether slaps were openhanded or backhanded, whether one or more punches were thrown, whether kicks were delivered with shoes on or off, and the number of times she was thrown against objects—is important in developing an accurate picture of the violence and its repetitive patterns. Sensitive inquiries into sexual abuse within the relationship are also important. For example, many women do not define giving in to sexual demands as rape or forced sex if no physical coercion is used, although intimidation or using sex to calm the man down may indeed be considered abusive within the overall context of the relationship.

It is also important to gather data about the memory changes that usually occur with those who experience PTSD and battered woman syndrome. Intrusive memories of the trauma that spontaneously appear, are aroused by events that remind the woman of the violence, or occur during dreams must be assessed, as well as memories that occur with flashbacks and dissociative experiences. It is common for women facing new battering incidents to experience higher levels of perception of danger because of these intrusive memories, which result in her perception of a need to defend herself even when the objective evidence does not suggest danger. This is critical to the presentation of a self-defense case because it goes to the heart of why the battered woman's perception of danger has an impact on her state of mind at the time of the homicide or other incident that is being evaluated. Psychogenic amnesia, or forgetting important parts of incidents, must also be assessed. Sometimes the partial amnesia that occurs at the time of the actual homicide is a result of intense fear of death or imminent danger; such repression is the unconscious mental defense used by the battered woman to protect herself against the psychic pain and terror.

CORROBORATION WITH STANDARDIZED PSYCHOLOGICAL TESTS

Certain patterns consistent with battered woman syndrome (and rape trauma syndrome, which has a similar constellation of symptoms) can now be discerned on standardized psychological tests to support the credibility of the abuse history given by the woman and its probable impact on her state of mind at the time of the incident for which testimony is offered. Standardized psychological testing that compares an individual to the norms developed for large group data also provides additional samples of how the woman thinks, feels, and acts, which make prediction of her state of mind at the time of the homicide incident more reliable and valid.

The most widely used test is the Minnesota Multiphasic Personality Inventory (MMPI). Rosewater (1985), Dutton (in press), and Sonkin (1987), among others, have found patterns on clinical scales for the MMPI-1 that support the presence of battered woman syndrome and rape trauma syndrome, although there may be many factors that can explain why such patterns are not found in individual women. Those women who have killed and are incarcerated, awaiting trial, often have an elevation on the F scale, which measures how bad a person is feeling, as well as low Ego-Strength in addition to high scores on clinical scales measuring depression (Scale 2), anger (4), paranoia and suspiciousness (6), and confusion (8). The Harris-Lingoes subscale analysis finds that there are often elevations on the Family Discord subscale that elevates Scale 4. Those women who have also been sexually abused show high scores on somatic symptoms (1), hysteria (3), and rumination and obsessive-compulsive behaviors (7). Thus it would not be unusual for a woman who has a history of sexual and physical abuse to have a significantly elevated profile. Different elevations may signify different levels of violence and their impact on the woman.

Other projective tests, such as the Rorschach and the Thematic Apperception Test and figure drawing tests, also can pick up themes that are helpful in validating the woman's story of abuse. For example, scary and violent themes, difficulty in organizing highly emotionally charged information, and themes of powerlessness can often be seen in projective testing without the usual defenses present. These tests are particularly useful for measuring the impact of abuse on battered women who are used to presenting a good outside appearance to the world while feeling as though they are falling apart inside. Although there are fewer empirical data to support the presence of PTSD using projective tests, some work in relation to combat veterans can be useful.

Cognitive testing using the Weschler Adult Intelligence Scale (WAIS-R) may be very helpful in a legal situation to understand how the person makes judgments under stress. Cognitive confusion and judgment that is unduly influenced by abuse can often be ascertained from a careful analysis of performance on the WAIS-R. It is also important to use this test and other cognitive tests to look for possible neuropsychological damage that can result from repeated shaking and head banging or actual beating about the facial and head area. More specific neuropsychological testing may be needed to make a proper assessment.

ORGANIZATION OF THE ASSESSMENT DATA

In organizing the data to determine if PTSD or battered woman syndrome is present, it is appropriate to use the PTSD criteria chart in the DSM-III-R (American Psychiatric Association, 1987, pp. 250-251). Most battered women easily meet these criteria, usually with more symptoms observed than are needed for the diagnosis (Walker, 1991). The diagnostic criteria currently pay inadequate attention to the measurement of disturbances in interpersonal relationships that are caused by the isolation and other psychological intimidation in battering relationships. Sexual dysfunction is also poorly measured using the PTSD criteria currently available. However, it is the only diagnostic category that permits the understanding that any normal person exposed to the abnormal traumatic incidents that affect battering victims can be expected to develop psychological symptoms that can clear up spontaneously, with peer support, or with special trauma therapy, once the person is safe from the trauma.

Some battered women's advocates have objected to the use of the battered woman syndrome diagnostic category in legal situations for fear that women who are responding naturally to potential or actual abuse will be misclassified as mentally ill (Blackman, 1986; Schneider, 1986). Many battered women fear that no one will believe them because they are crazy and that their batterers' taunts will come true. Thus cautions about misdiagnosis and overclinicalizing of the victims of abuse should be given serious attention. The debate around the addition of several new personality disorders to the DSM-III-R proved the lack of sensitivity to women's experiences held by many mental health professionals in positions of power and influence (Brown, 1992; Caplan, 1991; Rosewater, 1987; Walker, 1987).

Root (1992) suggests that all PTSD subcategories need also to be assessed for the additional stressors caused by multiple forms of indirect trauma, such as those from cultural oppression, racism, religious discrimination, gender bias, and other insidious forms of daily harassment. She notes that the impact of battered woman syndrome—or any of the other subcategories, such as rape trauma syndrome, battered child syndrome, child sexual abuse accommodation syndrome, and post-sexual abuse syndrome—can be variable, depending upon the other types of stressors to which the individual is exposed. It is important to note that in my own work with battered women who kill in self-defense, African American women who killed their same-race partners still were twice as likely to be convicted of murder and sentenced to longer periods in prison than those who were Caucasian or from other minority groups. Women who were poor and less educated also appeared to have similar biases against them in the courts (Walker, 1989b). This is not surprising, considering the rise of an underclass in the prisons, particularly with those men and women from low-income and minority-status backgrounds (Walker, 1989b).

Battered Women Who Kill

TERMINATION OF THE BATTERING RELATIONSHIP

Perhaps the most often asked question about battered women in general, as well as those who kill in self-defense, is, Why didn't she leave? Asking this question implies an assumption that leaving will stop the violence. However, more than a decade of working with battered women and their children has taught us that termination of a violent relationship simply does not stop the violence. The point of separation is the most dangerous period in a battering relationship, and the elevated level of danger lasts for at least two years after termination. Browne and Williams (1989) found that there has been an increase in the number of women killed by former partners in 35 states, while there has been a decrease in the number of women who kill their partners in self-defense. This decrease is accounted for mostly in areas where women are offered the most resources to assist them in leaving their batterers.

The research is clear that the point of separation is the time when the violence is most likely to escalate to the point when a homicide, suicide, or more serious assault takes place (Blackman, 1986; Browne, 1987; Dutton, in press; Ewing, 1987; Sonkin, 1987; Walker, 1989b). It is common for an abusive man to tell his partner that if he can't have her, no one can, and that he will kill her rather than let her leave him. Obviously, killing is the ultimate control over the victim. It is not unusual for the man to kill the woman, sometimes the children, and himself rather than face his own distress around abandonment issues. Sometimes the man who wants to die rather than be alone may be unable to commit suicide himself, and thus sets up a situation in which he attempts to manipulate the woman into killing him while trying to defend herself from the danger of his escalating abuse. It is not uncommon for a battered woman who has killed her abuser to report that he placed the gun in her hand and goaded her into using it, threatening to take it and use it on her if she failed to obey his instructions.

Measuring Self-Defense in Battered Women Who Kill

Self-defense is defined in most states as the use of equal force or the least amount of force necessary to repel danger when the person reasonably perceives that she or he is in imminent danger of serious bodily damage or death. The legal definition of some of these terms is critical, because if the legal standards are not met, then psychological expert witness testimony may not be admissible (Ewing, 1987; Walker, 1989b). The key terms here are *reasonable perception, imminent danger,* and *equal or reasonable force to repel serious bodily damage or death.*

FROM REASONABLE PERSON TO REASONABLE BATTERED WOMAN

Most states impose a definition of what a reasonable person would perceive as danger when trying to evaluate whether or not the woman had a *reasonable perception* (Bochnak, 1981; Schneider, 1986). If the standard is an objective one, then it is more difficult to meet, as the average person under the law is generally expected to be a man, not a woman, and certainly not a woman who has experienced a history of abuse. Even when there is a more subjective definition, meaning anyone who knows everything the defendant knew at the moment the decision to take a defensive action was made, it is still difficult for a battered woman's perceptions to be understood as reasonable without expert testimony to explain the typical way any woman, particularly this battered woman, would have perceived the same situation. Sometimes the testimony is offered just to explain the typical way a battered woman would perceive danger. This is less successful, probably because of the difficulty jurors have in applying general information to the specific battered woman's case. Battered women come from a heterogeneous population, so that there really is no one way a battered woman could be expected to think, feel, or act. Rather, it is important to explain each battered woman's thinking, feelings, and actions before the jury so that jurors can understand the impact of the abuse as it affects her particular state of mind.

In some states a distinction is made between *honest and reasonable* and *honest but unreasonable* perception of imminent danger. The latter is often used as a mitigating factor to lower the criminal responsibility to involuntary manslaughter, because the woman honestly believed what she perceived to be danger but it was unreasonable from the facts of the situation (see Ewing, 1987; Schneider, 1986). Here a careful analysis of what is dangerous from a battered woman's point of view is also important. Psychology, which has always tried to measure and understand people's perceptions, has added the research data to help understand the commonalities that would be expected to influence a battered woman's perceptions so that the individual battered woman's perceptions can be measured against a more equitable standard.

IMMINENT DANGER

Imminent danger is the next standard that psychology can help define as it is experienced by a battered woman. Most state legislatures define *imminent* as being on the brink of or about to happen, rather than immediate, which is the colloquial use of the term. This difference is critical in battered woman self-defense cases because frequently the women are hypervigilant to cues of impending danger and accurately perceive the seriousness of the situation before a person who has not been repeatedly abused might recognize the danger. A battered woman may make a preemptive strike, before the abuser has actually inflicted much physical damage, anticipating his next moves from what she knows from previous experience. Or she might wait until the man has stopped for a while, knowing that he will begin his assault again. Ewing (1987) suggests that some women and children who are abused may kill at the point they feel they are in danger of losing their minds from the psychological torture. Although such psychological self-defense is consistent with an abuse victim's perception of danger, it is frequently not a legal defense for murder, although such evidence may reduce the guilt to a lesser level of responsibility.

The data indicate that most battered women fight back at some time (Walker, 1984a); however, the stereotype of the typical or "good" battered woman victim has remained as one who is passive and never tries to defend herself. Most battered women who fight back quickly learn that they may be more seriously hurt, but they sometimes take that risk anyhow, often to bolster their faltering self-esteem. Others may have been trained to fight back no matter how scared they are, often having learned to turn pain into anger and aggressive behavior, as the men who abuse them do.

Many women know that their abusive partners are still dangerous even when asleep; many abusers frequently force their partners to meet their sexual demands upon waking and immediately begin another attack. Often these men do not sleep for long periods at a time, waking easily, especially if their partners are not right by their sides, as they frequently order. Most important is the understanding that a typical batterer stalks and finds his woman when she tries to leave, making escape almost impossible for some battered women. In cases that escalate to homicidal proportions, it is not unusual for the man to have threatened the woman with constant fear of death, often using some version of "If I can't have you, then no one can!" Imminent danger takes on new and ominous meanings in domestic violence situations (Sonkin, 1987; Sonkin, Martin, & Walker, 1985). Here, too, psychology can help the court by offering the known research data about the dynamics of battering relationships and the reasonableness of battered women's perception of imminent danger in general as a way to assess the particular battered woman's level of fear.

REASONABLE AMOUNT OF FORCE TO REPEL DANGER

The third definition, concerning what constitutes reasonable or equal force used to repel feared physical harm or death, is also important in meeting the self-defense standards. A Dr. Jekyll-Mr. Hyde quality, as most battered women have described their batterers' behavior, is frequently seen in the rapid escalation from what might be considered a minor annoyance in a nonabusive home to a battering incident of lethal proportions. As described above, it is difficult to understand how a sleeping man could be perceived as dangerous. It is also difficult for those who have not witnessed or experienced domestic violence to understand how a woman can be so afraid of an unarmed man that she needs a weapon in order to feel equal. Of course, men who batter women are trained to use their bodies as weapons, making it necessary for the average untrained woman to believe she must be armed in self-defense. This factor was cited by the Washington State Supreme Court in its decision in the *Wanrow* case upholding the need for gender-appropriate jury instructions to underscore the difference between men's and women's definitions of self-defense. Most women grab for a gun or knife as a way to make their abusers stop the violence toward them; rarely do these women decide in advance to kill the men. The abused woman knows from previous battering incidents that a certain look in the batterer's eyes, a certain litany of words, a certain pattern of pushes, shoves, and slaps means that worse is yet to come. Sometimes the initiating incident precipitates a flood of memories of previous battering incidents that makes the woman's perception of further physical harm or death even more terrifying and real.

The rules of evidence at a trial do not permit regular witnesses to testify to anything other than facts about which they have direct knowledge.

Those who created these rules of evidence believed that admission of just such facts would make testimony more reliable and valid. However, this has not been true in explaining women's behavior, which is frequently motivated by a combination of discrete facts and the context in which they occur. Opinion about why these factual experiences occurred, or testimony about even the context in which they happened, is rarely permitted, even though excluding it skews the evidence the judge or jury gets to hear (Blackman, 1986; Bochnak, 1981). However, a mental health expert can testify to her or his opinion and can add context to the explanations, provided this testimony is used as part of what the expert opinion is based upon. Expert witness testimony to explain the woman's state of mind at the time of an incident, then, may be the only opportunity for the judge or jury to hear a lot of evidence that is relevant to their understanding.

Therapeutic Errors That May Contribute to a Homicide

ISSUES OF NEUTRALITY AND OBJECTIVITY OF THE THERAPIST

It is important to understand the ineffectiveness and danger of a professional's taking an objective and neutral stance with a battered woman who comes for help, because it is not unusual for the abuse to escalate to homicidal proportions after separation and during the divorcing period. One of the areas of damage frequently caused by repeated trauma is the victim's inability to perceive neutrality. Battered women evaluate everyone with whom they have significant interaction as being either with them or against them. This means that professionals who attempt to behave in a neutral and objective manner will be misperceived by the woman as being against her, which she then translates into being likely to cause her danger or further harm. Those who attempt to treat battered women and their batterers together are subject to the same evaluation by the woman.

THERAPISTS' DENIAL AND MINIMIZATION OF THE VIOLENCE

It is not unusual for therapists to fail to hear battered women's descriptions of the violence or to disbelieve the dangerousness of particular situations. Hansen, Harway, and Cervantes (1991) used analog stories of cases that actually resulted in homicide to assess therapists' abilities to perceive danger. Not surprisingly, they found that therapists with little training in domestic violence were less likely to identify the true dangerousness of these situations. Minimization and denial are techniques that therapists use, particularly when their own emotional levels are raised. Sometimes this happens because the information reminds them of their own lives, and other times it happens because the therapists feel powerless to help these women. Most battered women state that they want a therapist to listen to them in a nonjudgmental way. The validation of the battered woman's perceptions may be the most important therapeutic interaction that she experiences. It is not always important that the therapist know what is best for the client to do; just listening with empathy and compassion can help reverse the psychological trauma and empower the victim. Once the level of violence is ascertained, the woman and the therapist together can plan actions to help stop the violence.

THERAPISTS TRYING TO DO TOO MUCH

At the other extreme, doing too much can also get in the way of the goal of the woman's reempowerment. It is important for the therapist to be there for the client, to listen to and validate her experiences, to help clarify what she is thinking, and to provide a safe place for her to reexperience highly intense emotions as she relates the violence done to her.

ABUSIVE RELATIONSHIPS OR ABUSIVE MEN?

It is popular in systems theory to hold the relationship responsible for the abuse rather than the individual who acts violently. Research data overwhelmingly support the feminist perspective that most of the serious violence in families is committed by men, although women certainly do use violence, often in self-defense, as detailed in this chapter. The typical relationship analysis and sharing of blame that occurs in systems orientations has been found to be detrimental to helping battered women gain safety and become violence free (Bograd, 1988b). It also takes away the responsibility of the man to stop his violence. Some family therapists believe that teaching better conflict resolution skills will stop the violence. This assumes that either the woman or the man does not have appropriate conflict resolution skills; it does not recognize that the dynamics of the violent relationship may make it too dangerous for the woman even to attempt to use such skills, and that lack of consequences lessens the man's motivation to stop his abuse.

In my own research I attempted to compare battered women's behavior in relation to both batterers and nonbatterers. More than half of the 400 women who participated in the study had both types of relationships.

These women reported using appropriate conflict resolution techniques in their nonbattering relationships, but not in their abusive ones. This supports the claim that it is at best unnecessary and at worst dangerous to teach battered women skills so that they can better avoid being abused. The subjects in this study also reported major differences in power and control factors for battering relationships compared with nonabusive ones, and there were also differences in sexual and emotional intimacy in the two types of relationships. Also important was the finding that the women themselves were more likely to use violent responses when they were in abusive relationships than when they were in nonbattering ones (further details about these findings can be found in Walker, 1984a). In all, this study supports the feminist political position that the cessation of violence must be totally the man's responsibility, and that the woman must not be placed in the dangerous position of having to control his behavior.

FAMILY THERAPY AND SUBSEQUENT HOMICIDE

It is not unusual for those who experience family therapy to be propelled closer to homicide, even when the family therapy is performed according to appropriate family systems standards. Sometimes this occurs because the couple comes to the family therapist in a last desperate attempt to save the relationship, and the potential for escalation of the violence as the inevitable changes in the system occur is not clearly understood by the therapist. The following case is a dramatic illustration of some of these problems, which even the best family therapist can experience.

> PL was a 35-year-old battered woman who shot and killed her abusive husband, with whom she had been in family therapy. The therapy notes tracked the effects of the treatment. As the therapist tried to shift the balance of power, using standard family therapy techniques based on family systems theory, the other family members became angry with PL, as she was encouraged to do less to make their lives comfortable and to spend more time on her own needs. The husband became more of a bully by grabbing more of the power, particularly by taking over the management of the wife's business, which had previously been her exclusive function. He quickly stopped "helping out" and refused to allow PL to enter the business without his permission. No longer able to feel needed through her cooking, laundry, and other housekeeping services to the family (chores given up at the suggestion of the therapist in trying to get other family members to assume more of an equitable share of responsibility) and isolated from her business, given up at her husband's demands, PL felt displaced and without value to her family.
>
> As PL became more depressed, she acted out in aggressive ways, including taking a loaded gun and threatening to kill herself with it. She later said she wanted both the therapist and her husband to watch her die. When the therapist

called the police, fearing PL was a danger to herself and others, PL ran out of the office and successfully eluded them. The shift in power in this family came too soon, before the violence was under control. Controlling violence may take a long time or may never occur at all during family therapy.

PL became so scared by the escalation of her feelings of fear and anger that she voluntarily entered a mental health facility, but left after 24 hours when they would not deal with the family violence issues. She then went to a local battered women's shelter, but they refused her admission because she now had a mental health hospitalization record. She went back home. Following the next battering incident, which included her husband's humiliating her by seriously beating and threatening to kill her with a loaded gun in front of others, PL did not commit suicide as threatened but took the gun and shot and killed her husband instead.

PL probably would not have killed her husband even after that particular abusive incident had her perception of the violence not been altered by the family therapy. In a nonviolent family, the power shifts that therapy helped initiate probably would have occurred, but even if the techniques had not worked, the result would not have been lethal. In this case, the therapist kept detailed notes of PL's steady deterioration and her own frustration at not being able to intervene effectively. A battered woman such as PL cannot perceive a therapist's neutrality toward both the abusive partner and herself; she believes that the therapist is either totally on her side or doesn't like her and will directly or indirectly cause her harm. At the same time, therapists with little knowledge of the dynamics of battering relationships or advocates who are not well trained in therapeutic techniques can be expected to set up, unwittingly, similar types of situations that can push the family violence dynamics further toward a homicide.

CUSTODY AND VISITATION ISSUES

The escalation of violence most frequently occurs around issues of visitation and custody of children. All too often, the batterer holds on to his children in the same possessive and psychologically abusive manner that he uses to try to control his wife. Long, drawn-out custody proceedings intensify the battles, as do continued harassment and danger around visitation exchange. Both threats of physical harm and continued legal harassment characterize these disputes, which are harmful for the children and place the mother in continued danger. Often the man is able to charm the evaluators during the brief time he is seen, and the children, delighted to have some limitations placed on their father's behavior during the observation session, give no clues as to the fear they often feel when placed in the middle of his continued harassment. The women, however, are frequently at their angriest point if they are dealing with the emotional effects of the abuse, and let the evaluators know as many of the man's abusive behaviors as possible, unless they are made to feel that this is unwanted information. Then they shut down, thinking they will not be believed. Or they become hostile, thinking it will make no difference anyway, because they already feel invalidated.

When describing their reactions to custody and visitation evaluations, battered women sound like they are describing the helpless and powerless feelings they have concerning the battering incidents themselves. There has been an increase in recent years of women ignoring court orders to permit their children to visit men whom the children claim are abusing them. Some of these women go underground—they move without leaving forwarding addresses, change their names and Social Security numbers, and begin new and, they hope, nonviolent lives. Some of these cases have received a great deal of publicity, but no one really knows how many others go on unknown.

Liss and Stahly (Chapter 14, this volume) and Deed (1991) describe some of the difficulties faced by battered women and their children, and Walker and Edwall (1987) describe custody and visitation evaluation techniques designed to collect the information needed for the implementation of plans that will help keep women and children safe. In earlier work, I have described several homicide cases that reached lethal proportions after the batterer continued his harassment by using the legal system, which failed to protect the children, leaving the women and children vulnerable to continued violence (Walker, 1989a).

Conclusions

In summary, battered women who kill are not different from those who do not kill. All of the differences have been found in the frequency and severity of violence committed by the batterers (Browne, 1987; Walker, 1989a). More than 50% of all women who are killed in the United States are murdered by previously violent husbands, usually when they attempt to terminate the relationship. It is important for mental health professionals to understand the dynamics of violent relationships so that they can avoid inadvertently escalating their already high lethality potential. Properly documented records may be useful should a case end up in court.

Since the introduction of the defense often called the "battered woman self-defense" on behalf of those women who do kill in self-defense, many more women are receiving fair trials. Often they are found not guilty by juries who listen to what the women and other witnesses have to say, and to the testimony of psychologists who help put the information into the context of what we know about the psychological effects of battering on a woman's state of mind. Expert witness testimony about the impact of abuse on women who commit other kinds of criminal acts at the demand of their batterers, in criminal as well as civil cases to measure personal injury, has helped women in their attempts to get justice in the courts. Newer applications of such testimony, in cases such as those of battered children who kill parents in self-defense, demonstrate the usefulness of psychological theory in helping judges and juries to understand victims' states of mind in a variety of situations.

17

Establishing Feminist Systemic Criteria for Viewing Violence and Alcoholism

CYNTHIA S. COOLEY
with KATHLEEN SEVERSON

Alcoholism and battering are forms of violence to the body and the soul. They arise out of conditions of betrayal that are transmitted from generation to generation. They both represent the politics of domination. Each requires a treatment response that will foster empathy and growing responsibility for self and community.

Victim blaming and the pathologizing of women's experience continue to pervade many areas of psychology and family therapy, especially in the fields of alcoholism and violence. It is the aim of this chapter to present feminist systemic criteria for viewing violence and alcoholism by exploring the techniques of clearly naming violence, highlighting linguistic dilemmas facing the alcoholism field, and challenging clients to leave the source of violence. It is hoped that the use of these techniques will lead to fewer women being injured or killed at the hands of others or through their own prolonged alcohol and drug abuse.

> Systems theory is a powerful conceptual tool, but it has its limitations. (Dell, 1989, p. 2)

Alcoholism and violence within the family are two issues that challenge family systems theoreticians and clinicians. For family therapists who treat alcoholic families, specialized training has been widely available since the early 1980s. Yet, although they are very aware that many of their clients have histories of family violence and abuse, few clinicians working in the alcohol treatment field have received adequate training with regard to wife or child assault. In fact, because of the prevalence of violence in alcoholic families, many professionals have come to view violence as a part of the total picture of the "alcoholic family" profile. This has led to the adoption of the false premise that when abstinence is achieved, all other family problems will abate—including the violence. There is, in fact, little if any research to back up this conclusion.

Because of a lack of cross-training, family violence is often overlooked by family alcohol specialists; likewise, alcoholism and drug abuse often are not diagnosed or dealt with by family violence professionals. This lack of awareness is evident in the alcohol and family therapy literature, which contains surprisingly few articles criticizing systems approaches to alcoholism from feminist and other views.

Feminists themselves have focused much of their attention on wife abuse, but very little attention on alcoholic family issues or alcoholic violent families. Feminist critiques of the alcohol field have been focused primarily on treatment issues (e.g., lack of services and funding for female alcoholics, lack of services for women with children, and, more recently, criminalization of addicted mothers giving birth to addicted babies) rather than on theoretical ones. The field is further muddied by the fact that the feminist critique of systems applications to the problem of violence in the family has been hotly contested.

What, then, are the issues when alcoholism and family violence occur within the same family? The aim of this chapter is to present basic criteria for a feminist systemic view of alcoholism and violence. Some of the questions that will be raised are as follows: What is the relationship between alcoholism and violence, and how can clinicians prioritize treatment issues? What do feminists think about the term *codependency*? Finally, how can one simultaneously utilize systems understandings with regard to alcoholism and incorporate a feminist-informed view of violence?

> Determining whether there is a relationship between acute alcohol consumption and family violence is perhaps one of the most difficult tasks in the family violence literature. (Leonard & Jacob, 1988, p. 389)

Few theorists propose a direct causal relationship between alcohol use and wife assault, although research shows the two are often present in tandem. Abusive men who have severe alcohol or drug problems are apt to abuse their partners both when drunk and when sober, are violent more frequently, and inflict more serious injuries on their partners than do abusive men who do not have a history of alcohol or drug problems (Browne, 1987; Frieze & Knoble, 1980; Roy, 1977; Walker, 1984a). Gelles (1974, p. 111) found that drinking accompanied violence against spouses or children in 48% of the 44 violent families in his study. Still, the main supporters for the view that alcohol consumption has a direct causal relationship with violence directed against wives have been shown to be battered women and public opinion (Freize & Knoble, 1980).

Although the relationship between drinking and violence is unclear (estimates of the proportion of batterers who assault their partners while intoxicated range from 48% to 87%), research suggests that both perpetrators and victims tend to blame the alcohol for the violence. As other researchers have noted, Gelles (1974) found that the battered wives he interviewed tended to see alcohol as the cause of the violence (see, e.g., Bowker, 1983; Frieze & Knoble, 1980; Pagelow, 1981b; Roy, 1977); he also speculates that perpetrators of violence may drink to excuse their own conduct.

The disinhibition theory proposes a direct-cause explanation for this phenomenon: Alcohol consumption paralyzes the higher cortical control centers in the brain, with the effect of loosening the restraints that normally contain more primitive behaviors and emotions. Therefore, intoxicated individuals engage in behavior they would not normally engage in while sober. Research indicates, however, that violent men are apt to be violent both when intoxicated and when sober (Browne, 1987; Gelles & Straus, 1989; Roy, 1977; Straus, Gelles, & Steinmetz, 1980; Walker, 1983). Corenblum (1983) asked members of Alcoholics Anonymous about their hitting their spouses while sober and while drinking. Of those who admitted to hitting their spouses while sober, 84% also hit them while intoxicated.

Alcoholism does not cause violence. When a violent alcoholic gets sober, the violent behavior does not necessarily stop. Women and children living in violent alcohol-free families are as much at risk as those living in alcoholic families. Rather than alcoholism causing the violence, it has been suggested that alcohol is used by those prone to violence as societal permission to behave violently (the "disavowing theory," which allows both the batterer and the victim to focus on the intoxication as the problem and to see the alcoholism as the cause of the violence).

Other research in the field of chemical dependency and domestic violence has noted the multigenerational nature of alcoholism and violence (Brown, 1985; Gelles & Straus, 1989; Steinglass, Bennett, Wolin, & Reiss, 1987). Research has demonstrated that men who have witnessed violence between their own parents are three times more likely than those who did not witness such violence to hit their partners (Hotaling & Sugarman, 1986).

Issues of coresponsibility (redefined as codependency, or "no responsibility") that view violence as a symptom of the disease of alcoholism are forms of victim blaming and must be addressed as such. When reviewing the literature on violence and/or alcohol, professionals whose work is informed by feminism will want to keep the following guidelines in mind. Based on Gilian Walker's "A Conceptual Framework for Wife-Beating" (1990), these represent a feminist interpretation of guidelines set up by the Toronto Services Support Group for Assaulted Women. Walker's interpretation is directed at dealing with family violence. A feminist view of alcoholism as it relates to family violence is added here to Walker's original view.

1. *Wife beating is assault, not interaction gone wrong.*
2. *Wife beating is violence against women, not family violence.* A "family violence" orientation leads to a focus on interaction, which leads, in turn, to blaming the victim.
3. *Wife beating is not a sickness, it is a crime.* With the widespread acceptance of alcoholism and codependency as disease, it is important to point out that violence is a crime, and the label of alcoholic or codependent does not change that fact. Any other focus leads to the allegation of coresponsibility, which leads to victim blaming.
4. *Freedom from assault is every person's basic right.* A woman should not have to earn the right to freedom from assault by being submissive, going to counseling, or admitting she is alcoholic, coalcoholic, or whatever.
5. *Men beat their wives because they are permitted to.* The social permission given a husband to batter (either by allowing him to "exercise authority" over his wife or by letting him use alcohol as an excuse) has led to a lack of protection for assaulted women.
6. *Wife beating should no longer be defined as a woman's private dilemma or a dilemma of "codependent women" or "alcoholic women."* It should be seen as a public and community issue.

Linguistic Criteria

LANGUAGE AS A TOOL OF OPPRESSION: THE PROBLEM WITH LABELING

Language is a powerful tool in treating addiction. The taking on of the identity or label of *alcoholic* or *coalcoholic/codependent* has been pointed out as the first step in recovery from alcohol-related problems for many women. Taking on the identity of *alcoholic* assists the individual in confronting the denial that is such a pervasive aspect of alcoholism (Brown, 1985). Similarly, feminists prefer the term *wife abuse* to describe men's violent behavior, arguing that calling violence against women *family violence* obscures the issues (Bograd, 1988).

Turning to the issue of alcoholism as it interacts with violence, language and definition again become important themes. As pointed out earlier, many battered women blame their spouses' drinking for the violence. As Gelles (1974) points out, this may serve the function of providing some kind of hope (i.e., "If he just could stop drinking, things would get better"). He also suggests that blaming the drinking may assist in denial of the realities of the violence, which is less socially acceptable without the excuse of alcohol. Chemical dependency treatment professionals have been trained to focus on addiction and to view all behavior as an aspect of addiction, so although violence against women may not be directly addressed by these professionals, by omission it falls into the category of part of the "disease" of alcoholism and/or "codependency."

Feminist linguists offer us a useful illustration of how the issues can be obscured by language. Sarah Lucia Hoagland (1988) presents the work of Muriel Schultz and Julia Penelope (Stanley), describing how—through mere stylistic choices—something someone does to a woman becomes something that happens to her. What happens to her is then developed into a temporary or accidental characteristic of that woman and, from there, becomes an essential part of her state of character (alcoholic, codependent). The example Hoagland uses to illustrate Schultz's and Stanley's work is as follows:

John beat Mary.

Here we have an agent, *John*; an action, *beating*; and a recipient of that agent's action, *Mary*. *John* is the main topic of the sentence. Generally, if we were to ask questions, we would want information about the situation. Our focus, however, would be on *John,* because the speaker has directed our attention to him by placing *John* first in the sentence.

Mary was beaten by John.

The speaker directs our attention to Mary.

Mary was beaten.

The speaker has focused our attention even more directly on *Mary,* and it becomes difficult to ask questions about John. Losing awareness of John, we lose awareness of John as significant, for we cease thinking of how he is related to *Mary*; indeed, we lose awareness of the idea of a relationship altogether. Instead, we are led to ask of Mary: How? When? Where? Why? Is she all right? We likely will also ask, assuming we would want to hear anything (more) about it: Who did it? But our focus is still on *Mary* and why and how this happened, rather than on *John* and why he did it.

Finally, once we have enough Marys, we have a number of *women beaten* or *battered women* (thereby placing the responsibility squarely on the women).

One can apply Hoagland's example to the language issues regarding alcoholism and codependency. Turning to the issue of alcoholism as it interacts with violence, let us run through the exercise again.

Alcoholic John beat Mary.

The speaker draws our attention first to the issue of alcohol and second to the action, *beat.*

Codependent Mary was beaten by *alcoholic* John.

The issue of violence becomes obscured by the alcohol issues. John and Mary become "alcoholic" and "codependent."

Codependent Mary was beaten.
Codependent battered women
or
codependent women.

Again, the victim becomes responsible.

If Mary were alcoholic, the progression would be as follows:

John beat alcoholic Mary.
Alcoholic Mary was beaten by John.
Alcoholic Mary was beaten.
Alcoholic battered women.

Chemical dependency experts emphasize that alcohol abuse must be treated as the primary issue regardless of family, relationship, or work issues—the logic being that without sobriety, change will not take place. Violence, however, should be the exception. Although alcoholism is considered to be life threatening, violence should always take priority, as it is a more immediate threat.

The issue of labels has been a central aspect of recovery from alcoholism. As one member of Alcoholics Anonymous (AA) states, "My recovery from alcoholism started when I admitted I was an alcoholic. I had to say the words. My recovery from violence started when I admitted I was a batterer. I had to accept that under no circumstances is it okay to hit another human being, especially my wife." This individual provides a model for recovery from both alcoholism and abuse. Both issues need to be addressed and can be addressed within similar frameworks without either issue losing focus. Feminist clinicians may find it useful to collapse the distinction between alcoholism and battering—naming both as violence, either self-directed or other directed (this issue is addressed further in the last section of this chapter).

Treatment: The Narrative of Leaving

The question becomes what to treat first, alcoholism or violence? How can we view both issues, incorporating a feminist-informed critique of systems and violence with a systemic understanding of alcoholism? In 1974, the National Institute on Alcohol Abuse and Alcoholism recognized family therapy as the "most notable current advance in the area of psychotherapy" for alcoholism (Keller, 1974). That same year, Murray Bowen published "Alcoholism as Viewed Through Family Systems Theory and Family Psychotherapy." A number of researchers and clinicians have contributed to the family systems literature (e.g., Kaufman & Kaufman, 1979; Steinglass, 1979; Treadway, 1989) and a feminist-informed systemic approach with specific interventions has been outlined by Bepko and Krestan (1985).

As stated earlier, the literature on systemic views of alcoholism offers little in the way of feminist analysis. Recently, in a chapter titled "The Baby and the Bathwater," JoAnn Krestan (1991) defended the usefulness and importance of the concept of powerlessness. She addressed feminist criticism of the concept of codependency and the issue of powerlessness that is basic to all 12-step programs. Krestan argues that the issue of powerlessness is very specific within AA (i.e., powerlessness over the chemical or another's use of a chemical, not powerlessness over one's life) (p. 231).

Krestan and others have relied on Bateson's view of incorrect epistemology—the belief that one is God. Despite major disagreements with systems theory, Dell (1989) points out that the conviction that power (that is, the attempt to control) can be enormously pathogenic is a major point of agreement between Bateson and those who have criticized the systemic view. As both Krestan and Dell point out, the agreement about the pathogenicity of power seems to get lost amid the debate and rhetoric.

Individual responsibility for sobriety and violence is the basis of any view of alcoholism and violence. Alcoholism is not a symptom any more than violence is a symptom of a "family system"; however, both alcoholism and violence influence how family members exist in any given family.

Given the above criteria, how, then, can treatment issues be addressed? As noted previously, it may be useful to collapse the distinction between alcoholism and battering, naming both as violence—either self-directed or other-directed. Alcoholism and battering are both forms of violence to the body and soul. They arise out of the conditions of betrayal that are transmitted from generation to generation. They both represent the politics of domination. Each requires a treatment response that will foster empathy and growing responsibility for self and community.

Criteria that should guide practice are as follows:

1. Violence arises out of existing power structures within society.
2. Alcoholism and other drug abuse are forms of violence against self.
3. Alcoholism is not a causal factor for violence against others.
4. Personal and collective responsibility is a primary goal of treatment, and "leaving" is the vehicle for change.
5. Individual psychopathology is culturally transmitted and maintained.

In dealing with the issue of violence and/or alcoholism, a useful treatment embodies a narrative of leaving. That is, leaving the source of maltreatment is the underlying theme of the work. This may mean actually leaving a relationship, or it may mean together leaving behind destructive behaviors. It may mean leaving the source of violence against self—alcoholism, for example.

Assessment requires skills that include an understanding of alcoholism and violence with an emphasis on safety for all. Both alcoholism and violence are considered life threatening. Many alcoholics are in need of medical treatment, and often family members living with an abuser are in need of shelter and/or immediate protection. Clinicians should be prepared to offer community resources in response to these issues.

It is beyond the scope of this chapter to discuss the various approaches to assessing violence or alcoholism; however, a few basic guidelines can provide a starting point. The Michigan Alcoholism Screening Test (Selzer, 1971) outlines three basic questions that provide a highly reliable index of the presence of alcoholism (Woodruff, Gruze, Clayton, & Carr, 1973):

1. Has your family ever objected to your drinking?
2. Did you ever think you drank too much in general?

3. Have others (friends, physicians, clergy) ever said you drink too much for your own good?

One can include violence with the questions that Bepko and Krestan (1985) suggest asking:

1. Is there any history of alcoholic drinking (violence) in your family?
2. Is drinking (violence) a problem for anybody in this family right now?
3. Does anyone worry about anyone's drinking (violence)?

The first phase of the treatment involves helping the individuals in the family to name what is happening. Denial is a dissociated state that serves to protect people from the effects of violent behavior and alcoholism. Gathering information by taking a thorough chemical use and violence history will help break this denial.

Once the violence has been named, treatment with the individual or family can proceed. It is in this first stage that the criteria regarding linguistics are fundamental to avoiding the trap of obscuring the violence by focusing on alcoholism. As the member of AA quoted above put it, his recovery from alcoholism started when he admitted he was alcoholic, and his recovery from violence started when he admitted he was a batterer. Both issues, if present, must be named, and safety issues must be addressed before proceeding further.

The second stage of therapy involves securing a commitment to treatment from each of the individuals involved. Here the challenge exists in asking that certain behaviors be terminated in order that the healing can begin. Of primary importance is the commitment to stop hitting, beating, and threatening. The focus on abstinence from alcohol often must be dealt with for the alcoholic batterer to be in a position to terminate abusive violent behavior. Bepko and Krestan (1985) note that during periods of presobriety it is useful if the focus on achieving abstinence involves AA and/or Al-Anon. They also suggest addressing individual issues, rather than interactional ones, in early sobriety, stressing self-focus for all family members. At this time, the therapist may begin to teach new behavioral skills for coping with stress and conflict.

When violence is an issue, the self-focus treatment plan for the batterer can include an anger management program in conjunction with AA or involvement in an alcohol treatment program. As Stephanie Brown (1985) emphasizes, the clinician needs to learn to take a backseat to the interventions that directly focus on sobriety. This is also true of anger management. As clients begin to identify with other recovering individuals in groups, the shame issues attached to alcoholism and violence seem to lessen. It is at this time, however, that the therapist can educate and remind clients that alcoholism and codependency can be viewed as a disease, but that violence has a recovery process that must be addressed with equal focus.

Once alcoholism and violence have been named and reorganized, systems work—including multigenerational grief issues—may begin. As each party to the relationship is encouraged to differentiate and focus on self, the narrative of leaving takes a poignant turn. It is here that clients may begin to have the strength literally to leave, or—at the very least—to begin to grieve the losses of their life together. The alcoholic and/or violent individual is challenged to participate in therapy and support groups specifically for his own survival. The assaulted and/or alcoholic woman is encouraged to do the same.

The task of the therapist is multilayered. To encourage change, the clinician must simultaneously accommodate and challenge the system at this point. Fostering empathy between partners is a powerful tool for healing and continued progress. Clinically, it is helpful at this point to communicate to clients that recovery is a process that takes time and has somewhat predictable stages. This will help clients to bring compassion to their own limitations and frustrations. It takes time to reclaim a sense of self, to learn to live from that sense of self, and to be close to other people without resorting to violence or alcohol abuse. Many recovering individuals find that they cannot continue in their current relationships and remain sober or free of violence. Contrary to the family therapy tradition that focuses on couples staying together, the narrative of leaving focuses on sobriety and violence-free living regardless of the living arrangements.

The closing phases of therapy involve strengthening clients' capacities for inner direction, reinforcing changes that have occurred, and continuing to empower clients toward positive and life-affirming choices—including relationships. The therapist should remain an ongoing resource for the individual, couple, or family as their development through the family life cycle continues. The narrative of leaving starts when the client seeks help, and it continues as violence against self or others is no longer an option. The choice for sobriety and nonviolence is always present and emphasized.

18

Intervening With Violent Families: Directions for Future Generations of Therapists

MARSALI HANSEN
MICHÈLE HARWAY

Evidence that battering is receiving increased national attention comes from a variety of sources. Most significant changes have occurred in the courts and legislatures, where state laws affecting victims and batterers are being modified, sentences for women who have killed their spouses after years of battering are being commuted, and violence against women is becoming headline news at last. In fact, recently the Pulitzer Prize was awarded to a journalist for a series on battered women. At the same time, therapists in increasing numbers are being called upon to provide expert testimony in cases of battering and to provide services to both batterers and victims. Therapists are also beginning to acknowledge that a feminist perspective is influencing their own approaches to treatment (Harway, Hansen, & Cervantes, 1991). The "feminization" of treatment is at the forefront of trends in family therapy, and the application of this perspective to the treatment of battering is recognized as one of the major contributions of the past decade to the field of family therapy ("The Way We Were," 1992). It is time now to take stock of where we are, summarize the gains that have been made, and formulate directions for the future.

Current Status of the Law

LAWS REGARDING BATTERED WOMEN

Many of the legal defenses that directly affect victims of battering have been derived from the work of psychologists within the past decade. For example, the diagnosis of battered woman syndrome is often used as a legal defense by women who kill their abusers. Walker and her colleagues have been active in validating this diagnosis and in explaining how it results from continuous battering. Psychologists and psychiatrists are being called to testify on behalf of battered women who kill and to present testimony concerning currently accepted theories about battering and victimization. As a result, a number of states are reexamining the convictions of these women, at times even commuting their sentences.

Court proceedings in the cases of battered women include examination of the applicability of three long-standing legal precepts. First, courts are addressing the question of *reasonable perception.* The defense is required to explain that it is *reasonable* for the battered woman to perceive that she in imminent danger when she has experienced years of abuse. Psychological formulations may be introduced by both the defense and the prosecution to establish a psychological pattern of perception, and the research literature can be used to describe the impact of abuse on the accuracy of perceptions of women who are repeatedly beaten. Second, the defense is required to establish the *imminent danger* of the circumstances in establishing a necessity for self-defense. For example, a woman who kills under these circumstances may believe that her abuser is still dangerous even when he is asleep. Relevant conditions may be whether she perceives the abuser's behavior to be unpredictable, whether he is a light sleeper, or whether he is someone who does not sleep long and can arise at any moment to continue the abuse. Third, the defense is required to establish that *reasonable force* was used to repel danger. This question has become a point of debate, as some courts have only recently begun to recognize that the reasonable force statutes are based on male standards of strength and that women are not as strong as men. Therefore, self-defense between men may be perceived as combat between equals, without the benefit of weapons. However, a fight between a man and a woman is not a "fair" fight, and a woman may need a weapon to defend herself from harm in contrast to a man in a similar circumstance. Laws that have been in existence since the 1800s assume that both parties are of equal strength and consequently indicate that self-defense cannot be invoked when only the defender has used a weapon. Now courts are beginning to recognize that the use of a weapon by a woman may be equivalent to the batterer's use of fists or hands.

The legal protection of battering victims is changing in many states, as described in Chapter 2 of this volume by Hart. Protective orders and arrest statutes are two specific areas of change. The types of victims who are eligible for protection under protection orders is broadening beyond the strict definition of a marital relationship. Most jurisdictions currently offer protective orders for any adult partner who has been abused, some including same-sex and cohabiting or dating couples. However, the conditions under which these orders can be obtained vary from state to state: Half the states issue protective orders 24 hours a day, half the states have no filing fees for protection orders, and all states allow for the waiving of filing fees if the victim is indigent.

Victims' rights statutes have also been expanded. For example, one-third of all states protect the right to confidentiality of the victim when she is seeing a therapist or being treated in a domestic violence program. This legal protection is in addition to the ethical standards to which helping professions hold their licentiates. Moreover, law enforcement is increasingly required to take a more proactive role in protecting the victim. Enforcement agencies are more often required to inform the battered adult about current options for protective orders and victim compensation in cases of domestic violence. Victims are now permitted to submit impact statements when sentence is being passed on the batterer, and parole boards are discussing the future of the batterer with the victim if the batterer is being considered for discharge from jail. Many states are adopting victim intimidation laws to protect the victim while the perpetrator is under investigation. In 1988, the 1984 Victims of Crime Act was amended to require victim compensation programs to make awards to victims of domestic violence, including medical costs, loss of earnings, attorneys' fees, and other expenses incurred in replacing property or transportation. Recently, there has been legislative activity concerning notification of victims of crime when the criminals are discharged from custody. With the advent of elder abuse reporting laws, battered women over the age of 65 are afforded another avenue to ensure their safety. These women are considered to be victims of elder abuse, and battering is reportable under elder abuse statutes. This additional protection is an important advance, as a substantial proportion of cases of elder abuse are in fact cases of spousal violence.

LAWS REGARDING BATTERERS

The statutes governing the arrest of batterers are expanding as well, particularly those governing arrest even in cases where the police have not witnessed the crime. In many jurisdictions, warrants are no longer required to arrest a batterer. In 15 states, codes *require* police to make an arrest when they have determined that battering has occurred. In 13 states, the police are required to make a warrantless arrest when a protection order is violated, and in 25 states, police are permitted to make such an arrest without a warrant when a protection order has been violated.

LAWS REGARDING CHILDREN

Laws governing the treatment of children in homes where battering is occurring are also changing. One-third of the states require the courts to consider domestic violence in making custody decisions. Others states suggest supervised visitation when there is a finding of domestic violence.

Victims of battering appear to be better protected by adversarial rather than mediated divorce proceedings, because of the nature of spouse abuse and the fear and intimidation that battered women feel in the face of their abusers. In particular, custody mediation does not appear to enhance the likelihood of battered women's being awarded custody. Several factors are against the women in this decision. First, historically, children have been considered to be the property of the father. Second, women are at a considerable disadvantage economically every time they enter court, and therefore they are at a disadvantage in obtaining custody of the children. Third, a victim's psychological status at the time of court proceedings is likely to be similar to that of a trauma victim—intimidated and terrified. She may even see herself as responsible for the battering and therefore may not present as a very credible witness or custodial parent. Her psychological state is particularly unfortunate, as battering cases are more likely to include custody disputes than are divorces where no violence has occurred. It has been estimated that women lose custody up to 70% of the time to men who are abusive (Chesler, 1986). A dramatic example of an abusive father obtaining custody comes from the case that served as vignette for Hansen et al.'s (1991) study of therapists' awareness of violence. In this case, the batterer served only a year in jail for the murder of his wife and, after his release, fought for and was granted custody of the children who previously had been placed with their maternal grandparents.

One consequence of custody battles is the battered woman's fear of reprisals for her testimony in court, a fear that is often justified. Protection orders issued by the courts are time limited. Even during the effective time of a protection order, the woman and her children may still be in substantial danger from the batterer, who may ignore the legal document and attempt to harm them. The woman and her children may be at substantial risk, as violence often increases following the dissolution of the marriage, especially if there are children involved. Divorces in which children are involved have other consequences in addition to the emotional pain of custody hearings. Of particular note is that the abuser is likely to remain in contact with the woman he has abused and thus may have continued opportunities to abuse her.

As Liss and Stahly point out in Chapter 14, courts tend to ignore violence in their consideration of visitation, perhaps viewing the battering as a spousal rather than a parenting concern. When supervised visitation is mandated, finding a trustworthy and acceptable monitor may not be feasible owing to such factors as cost and the father's ability to veto recommended monitors. However, courts are changing; they are starting to pay more attention to the issue of abuse in making custody and visitation decisions.

Even if she has lost custody, a battered woman can file for a change of custody, in particular if violence has been visited upon the children. However, experts indicate that filing for change of custody may count against the battered mother, especially where information about the battering has not been entered into court records. For example, if the mother has never filed a battery charge or had police intervention but brings battering up in a custody trial, these accusations may be seen as a trial strategy to gain custody of the children, rather than as facts (J. Bray, personal communication, February 1992). Similarly, a trial strategy will be perceived by the opposition if the children have been hurt and a custody filing precedes a child abuse report.

LAWS REGARDING PRACTITIONERS

Legal and ethical practices governing therapists are changing as well. Not all of the legal and ethical consequences are yet clear: The precedent has been set in the medical field that if an assessment question is not asked and then a negative outcome prevails, the practitioner is still responsible (see Cervantes, Chapter 12). Psychotherapists may be held similarly accountable if they fail to assess for violence in the family and someone is later hurt. As yet, there are no legal mandates requiring the reporting of spousal abuse. However, in California and a few other states, duty to warn the potential victim may apply in cases of spouse abuse when the client is the batterer. The same does not hold true when the client is the victim, except when the victim makes threats to retaliate against the batterer. When the batterer is the client, the therapist may be required to warn the victim when specific threats of abuse toward the "clearly identified" victim are expressed by the batterer during therapy. Clearly, the question of duty becomes more confusing when the therapist is treating the couple, but under these conditions the victim is likely to hear the threat as it is expressed.

The standards for providing ethical treatment when battering is present are changing as well. Currently, the therapist is expected to provide an accurate assessment of the client (including identifying the existence of battering), recognize the needs of the client, and address those needs. The therapist is expected to develop a treatment plan consistent with the standards of the profession and to implement the treatment through appropriate interventions. Some have argued that therapists have an ethical responsibility to ensure the safety of clients (Margolin, 1982). It seems clear to us that therapists have an ethical responsibility to protect victims of spousal violence even though precedents for standards of care for the profession remain unclear.

Current Status of Assessment

Historically, spouse abuse has been underassessed and underreported. Psychotherapists may be at least partly at fault: Goodstein and Page (1981) report that among a sample of battered women who were seen by the police, 65% had sought out mental health help, but most did not return for a second visit because the practitioner never asked about the abuse. How many other battered women who did not come the attention of police may also have had one session of therapy and not returned when the violence was not addressed? Our research also points to therapists' difficulty in recognizing the seriousness of battering and their tendency to minimize violence as contributing to the underrepresentation (Hansen, Harway, & Cervantes, 1991). Why therapists experience such difficulty in identification of violence has yet to be determined. Possible explanations for the minimization are many. One explanation comes from the just world hypothesis (Perloff, 1983). According to this belief, therapists (and others) may hold fast to the notion that, because the world is fair, bad things happen only to bad people and not to good people. A therapist holding this belief might fail to spot that the "bad outcome" of being abused might happen to a client who appears to be a quite likable individual. Another explanation for therapists' failure to spot cases of violence may be that making an assessment of violence in a family requires some type of immediate action. As our latest research shows, therapists do not seem to know what to do to intervene appropriately even when it is very clear to them that battering is occurring (see Harway & Hansen, Chapter 4). Given that assessment of abuse requires being prepared to intervene, and that most therapists have not been trained to provide the proper kind of intervention, it is possible that therapists simply do not see the violence.

Still another explanation for therapists' not identifying existing violence more often has been proposed by Root (1992) and others (see

Harway's discussion in Chapter 3). According to this argument, the very nature of private psychotherapeutic practice encourages using DSM-III-R diagnostic codes for insurance billing purposes. The tendency to provide this type of diagnosis may encourage even a highly ethical therapist to focus on pathological behaviors (which are billable) rather than situational events (such as being battered by a mate).

Assessment of violence in couples is difficult. Often only the woman seeks help, and when she attends therapy with her spouse she may minimize the violence from fear of reprisal or because she has colluded with her spouse in believing she is responsible for her own victimization. In addition, many batterers are reluctant to attend therapy and the woman may seek intervention in the form of individual support. As battering has long been viewed as a private concern, the battered woman is unlikely to volunteer information about her victimization. Batterers are unlikely to present for individual therapy; when they do consent to treatment, they often minimize their aggression and present the wife as responsible for the couple's problems.

Current Status of Approaches to Treatment

TREATMENT GOALS IN WORKING WITH BATTERED WOMEN

Currently recommended professional standards for providing individual therapy to victims of battering focus on ensuring the safety of the battered woman before attempting any other intervention. Second, treatment needs to address issues of empowerment, normalization, social networking, and long-term protection (see Register, Chapter 8). Battered women are survivors of trauma and should be treated as such. In addition, therapists need to incorporate outside agencies in providing social support and referrals. In working with battered women, therapists may find that economic concerns and protection issues may be more pressing to the woman and that considering these may be as stressful as dealing with the psychological consequences of the battering. In considering treatment issues with this population, it becomes clear that the role of the therapist is to be much more than a neutral, disengaged third party (the traditional stance of family therapy in particular and psychotherapy in general), but that in fact the therapist must act as a political change agent in ensuring that the client survives. Moreover, because the client's presenting issues do not happen in a vacuum, but in a context (here the context of the mate's violence), the context must be acknowledged and acted upon. This renders therapist neutrality an untenable position.

Feminist approaches to therapy in general, and with this population in particular, consider the context of the problem as equally important as (and in some cases more important than) the behavior of the recipient of the problem. Feminist therapists therefore would see the role of the therapist working with individuals affected by violence as that of a change agent rather than a neutral, disengaged expert. New models of intervention (to be described in more detail below) consider the client to be the expert on her situation, rather than see the therapist as the expert. The client's ability, in this paradigm, to legitimate her own experience and her own sense of reality serves to empower her. Of course, there is much controversy over this position, and many respondents to our surveys of therapists indicated some confusion about exactly what their role should be when confronted with family violence. Some more traditional therapists felt that their role was restricted to the four walls of their office, to helping the client clarify her interpersonal perceptions, obtain insight, and work on her interpersonal interaction. Other therapists indicated that their role should encompass becoming an advocate for the client.

COUPLES TREATMENT GOALS

In cases of battering, the treatment of the couple in therapy has been widely criticized. As noted in Chapter 6 (Hansen), the perspective presented by the couple to the therapist may lead the therapist to perceive the victim as responsible for her own victimization and may lead to interventions that result in victim blaming. Further, many approaches to family therapy focus on the examination of transactions and reciprocal interactions among family members. This approach can result in therapy that attributes "coresponsibility" for the violence to both partners when applied to couples where battering is occurring. In addition, many family therapists, in an effort to avoid blame and focus on systemic concerns, may advocate "no responsibility" for the violence and not address the aggressive actions at all.

However, there are situations, as Hansen and Goldenberg note in Chapter 7, in which working with the couple is indicated. This is especially true when the couple is able to conquer and overcome the violence in their relationship. For these couples, where neither member suffers from a serious mental illness, couples therapy may be advocated, but only when the safety of the clients has been ensured. Such therapy can assist the victim in learning to protect herself while in the relationship and assist the batterer in finding other, more productive, ways to experience his feelings. For some couples, in conjoint counseling the positive characteristics of the relationship can be addressed as well as the battering, and treatment has a greater likelihood of success. However, when working conjointly with a couple for whom violence has been a factor, a therapist must proceed with extreme caution, (a) to avoid perpetuation of the behavior through reinforcement of already existing perceptions of victim responsibility or coresponsibility, and (b) to ensure that, though he or she may continue to remain detached and nonblaming, the therapist becomes involved to ensure the safety of the clients through addressing the aggression directly in the therapy session.

Therapy with couples who have experienced violence but who now *can control their violence* can be empowering for both the woman and the abuser. Such therapy, if carefully monitored, can provide the couple with an in vivo experience of alternative interaction. In addition, the positive qualities of the relationship can be highlighted in therapy and can continue to be incorporated into the therapeutic process. Women who have been victimized by abuse are strengthened as they are able to retain their relationships without experiencing the continued trauma of ongoing battering and the new stresses that separation would bring. Batterers learn alternative ways of getting their needs met without having to choose between the false dichotomy of ignoring their emotional needs and meeting their emotional needs through violence.

Battering exists in the lesbian community also. Although estimates vary, it appears to be occurring at rates similar to those in the heterosexual population (Renzetti, Chapter 15). Therapists working with lesbian couples need to be prepared to assess for abuse and to intervene appropriately. Battered lesbians are likely to have even greater problems than heterosexual women in discussing battering with therapists, because the social unacceptability of battering is compounded by the social unacceptability of being gay and the political unacceptability in the gay community of acknowledging the existence of battering. Lesbians' exacerbated needs for privacy and secrecy are strong social concerns that restrict the likelihood that these women will receive services.

There are special social, economic, and racial contributing factors in many cases of domestic violence involving people of color; thus a multicultural perspective is important in viewing domestic violence. Such a perspective can be defined as the ability to relate to, assess, and evaluate the presentation of clinical symptoms from a framework that views the person and family within a cultural context. The therapist with a multicultural perspective is able to distinguish beneficial cultural elements from pathological contributions to family functioning. Emphasis is placed on the therapist's need to understand his or her own cultural postures and the assumptions of his or her own therapeutic orientation. The therapist must be careful not to confuse societal factors that contribute to domestic violence with societal or cultural expectations. As more multicultural and multiracial families are seeking therapy, practitioners are being challenged to broaden their frameworks to incorporate a multicultural perspective in their professional practice.

TREATMENT GOALS IN WORKING WITH THE BATTERER

Treatment of the batterer has most often taken place in groups that focus on anger management, sex role socialization, and individual responsibility for the violence (see Gondolf, Chapter 9). Research has not supported the effective use of insight in therapy with batterers. Sociopathic and antisocial personalities who batter and may be referred for therapy appear to need more restrictive and comprehensive interventions that specifically address their serious problems. Men who have drug and alcohol problems, too, have more acute issues that must be addressed simultaneously in treatment. Drugs and alcohol loosen inhibitions, but they are neither the "cause" of nor an excuse for abuse. Batterers' programs need to address the "dangerousness" of their population and the high client dropout rate. Clients who have not been ordered into treatment by the courts frequently stop attending when their own objectives—most often the return of their spouses—have been met. Further, psychotherapy as the sole intervention in cases of battering sends an implicit message to the batterer that wife assault is a "psychological problem" but not necessarily a crime. That battering is in fact a crime must be made clear to the batterer.

Men who abuse alcohol are more frequently violent and more severely abusive than batterers who are not substance abusers (see Cooley, Chapter 17). However, it is noteworthy that these men tend to abuse their spouses both when drunk and when sober. When these men present for treatment in the context of drug and alcohol abuse programs, the language they learn may suggest that their victims are in fact to blame for the abuse. Acquiring such a perspective could be seriously detrimental to these men's treatment for battering. Concepts such as codependence, when applied to the partners of men who abuse both substances and women, may imply that a woman is coresponsible for the abuse. Moreover, specialists in substance abuse treatment may prioritize the goals of intervention so that the focus is on becoming sober, with spouse abuse a secondary consideration. Such prioritizing can seriously endanger the safety of the wife; in addition, it diminishes the significance of her trauma, fails to acknowledge the likelihood that battering is occurring while the abuser is sober, and may perpetuate for the batterer the myth of no responsibility for the violence because "the alcohol made me do it."

TREATMENT GOALS IN WORKING WITH CHILDREN OF VIOLENT FAMILIES

Children of violent couples require special consideration. First and foremost, their safety must be ensured. Children's understanding of marital discord varies with their developmental age and becomes increasingly less egocentric in older children. The amount of exposure that children have to violence in the home (as witnesses, covictims, or confidants) affects their emotional experience and understanding of the events (see Berman, Chapter 11). The emotional trauma and resulting emotional unavailability of both parents also affects the children. Often, children in violent families function as emotional orphans, attending to their own emotional needs as if they were raising themselves. Older children may take on the responsibility for younger ones, with sons sometimes taking on the role of emotional caretaker for their mothers. Moreover, children's attitudes toward the appropriateness of battering are formed by what they have witnessed, and most batterers (though not necessarily victims) report coming from such homes. Psychotherapeutic treatment of children from violent homes can involve all family members, with the exception of the father who continues to batter. However, special consideration must be given to the children's possible unspoken fear of the abuser. Recovery from trauma may be hampered by his presence. In addition, the battered woman may need psychological support to shore up her effectiveness as a parent, because she may continue to see herself as ineffective and powerless. Such a perspective will undoubtedly interfere with her ability to parent, especially if she has sons.

Current Status of Research and Training

The future of intervention with violent families rests in part on the contributions of those training new therapists and those contributing to the research literature.

IMPLICATIONS FOR TRAINING

Because of the high incidence of family violence in our society, all therapists must be prepared to provide proper assessment and intervention for their affected clients. This includes both therapists who bill themselves as specializing in domestic violence and those who do not but who will almost certainly encounter such cases in their practice.

The data presented in Chapter 4 (Harway & Hansen) suggest the following:

1. Therapists as a group are not all sufficiently knowledgeable about how to identify violence in families and would benefit from additional special training in working with violent families.
2. Even when therapists are able to spot violence, half do not respond in an appropriate crisis intervention mode to ensure the safety of their clients.

We recommend that training in these areas begin with new therapists in master's and doctoral programs. This training might include special courses in the identification of violence, including awareness of the prevalence of violence in American families, recognition of the existence of violence in a particular client family, recognition of the seriousness of the violence (until proven otherwise, all domestic violence must be considered serious), understanding of and proper attribution of the psychological basis for the violence, and knowledge of appropriate interventions in cases of violence. Supervisors, too must be sensitized to these issues so that they may properly monitor trainees' ability to apply their knowledge (see Goodwin, Chapter 10, for more on the supervision process).

Therapists who are already practicing also need special training in the area of domestic violence. We strongly recommend continuing education programs for practicing therapists, including those who plan to provide supervision to others. However, our data also suggest that not every therapist needs the same kind of training, as certain people have certain styles of therapeutic response that may be damaging to their clients. For example, nondirective therapy, or any therapeutic approach that is cautious and thorough in providing assessment to the exclusion of immediate intervention, may be contraindicated in cases of extreme violence. Knowledge of legal protections for battered women is particular vital. We believe that training should include consideration of the role of the therapist in the case of violent families, extending beyond simply counseling and psychotherapy into more active interventions, including advocacy. Among the fields in which such training is needed are psychology, marriage and family therapy, family medicine, family law, mediation, public health, social work, sociology, and psychiatric nursing. Although not all of the people trained in these fields are therapists (many are), it is likely that professionals in each of these areas will encounter domestic violence in the course of their work.

CONTENTS OF SPECIAL DOMESTIC VIOLENCE TRAINING COURSES

The following are some special topics we would suggest for inclusion in a generic course on domestic violence (which could then be tailored for different therapist subgroups). The list is based upon the recommendations stated within the individual chapters of this volume:

1. All courses must address the definitions of violence and include the full spectrum of battering, from psychological to extreme forms of physical abuse (McHugh, Chapter 5).
2. All courses need to address the existing myths about violence in families. Prevalence statistics, including cultural and ethnic diversity of prevalence, must be presented (Harway & Hansen, Chapter 1; Cervantes & Cervantes, Chapter 13).
3. Courses designed to train professionals in the field need to include a component that directs the trainee toward self-examination of personal attitudes about family violence that might inadvertently affect the process of therapy (Hansen, Chapter 6; Goodwin, Chapter 10).
4. Courses need to explore the complex dynamics of battering, from both individual and family perspectives (Harway, Chapter 3; Hansen, Chapter 6).
5. The effects of victimization on women and children must be addressed from both dynamic and legal perspectives (Berman, Chapter 11; Liss & Stahly, Chapter 14).
6. Detailed information on perpetrators is needed in any training program (McHugh, Chapter 5; Gondolf, Chapter 9).
7. Courses need to help professionals learn to recognize the existence of violence in particular client families (Harway & Hansen, Chapter 4).
8. Professionals need training in assessing the safety of clients when battering is occurring (Harway & Hansen, Chapter 4; Register, Chapter 8).
9. Courses must provide training in crisis intervention techniques, including safety and safety planning (Harway & Hansen, Chapter 4; Register, Chapter 8).
10. Professionals need to learn about services available to battered women and violent families, including (but not limited to) law enforcement agencies; victim assistance and victim compensation programs; legal, medical, and financial assistance programs; educational and training programs; housing and employment assistance; substance abuse programs; and agencies for special needs of women facing multiple oppressions (Register, Chapter 8; Cooley, Chapter 17).
11. Professionals also need to have knowledge of how to work with any community agencies that may interact with the families of batterers and their victims (Register, Chapter 8).
12. Professionals must learn appropriate interventions to use in cases of violence, including (but not limited to) the following:
    a. assessment: safety assessment, identifying client's coping skills, historical issues (e.g., Is there child abuse in the woman's history?), and assessment of multiple problems (e.g., sexuality issues, drugs and alcohol, eating disorders) (Register, Chapter 8; Renzetti, Chapter 15; Cooley, Chapter 17)
    b. crisis intervention: providing protection to the victim (Harway & Hansen, Chapter 4; Register, Chapter 8)

c. education: battering education and information about the effects of victimization, parenting, health care, and skills development (Register, Chapter 8; Liss & Stahly, Chapter 14)
d. referrals: advocacy referrals and referrals to other needed services (Register, Chapter 8)
e. psychotherapy for individual victims: providing emotional support, validation of feelings and experiences, anger and rage work, self-esteem and self-nurturing work, development of assertiveness skills, grief and loss work, exploring options and choices for life-styles, gathering information about healthy nonviolent relationships and feeling deserving of these, exploring termination issues (to learn about positive ways of leaving) (although some of these issues appear elsewhere in this list, they are mentioned here within the specific context of focusing interventions around them) (Register, Chapter 8)
f. modalities of intervention: learning how and when to refer to specific forms of treatment for batterers, victims, and children of batterers (Hansen & Goldenberg, Chapter 7; Register, Chapter 8; Gondolf, Chapter 9; Berman, Chapter 11)

This extensive list of areas to be covered underlines one important reality of working with violent families: that such work often goes beyond the purely psychotherapeutic into many other arenas. Psychotherapists working with violent families cannot afford to be the neutral third party for which their training prepares them; rather, they need to assume a more active stance. Consequently, we must adequately prepare therapists to ensure protection for battered clients and batterers who present for therapy. It is time for educators to begin to implement such training programs and for licensing boards to require their licentiates to be prepared to protect their clients who come from violent families.

Current research about spouse abuse has been described as influenced by societal assumptions, by priorities of funding sources, by accessibility and accuracy of respondents, and by the researchers' personal biases (McHugh, Chapter 5). Researchers need to develop studies that focus on the questions battered women might ask and to design research that can be immediately applied toward more effective interventions. Particular efforts should be directed toward the evaluation of programs for batterers, shelters for battered women, and "societal transformations" (see McHugh, Chapter 5). In addition, research is needed that will provide information to be used in designing effective interventions focusing on predictors of battering, on the relationship between abuse and alcohol (Cooley, Chapter 17), on nonmarital dyad battering, and on battering that occurs in the gay and lesbian community (Renzetti, Chapter 15).

New Treatment Models

In reviewing the contributions of this volume on battering and family violence, we would be remiss if we did not look to the future to identify and describe here new theoretical explanations of violence and new models for treating family members.

A THEORY ABOUT TRAUMA: A NEW APPROACH TO VICTIMS

Among the more exciting new models that we encountered in preparing this book was one we found in the work of Maria Root, who presents a theory that provides explanatory power to the symptoms exhibited by women survivors of battering (as well as by survivors of both sexes of all forms of trauma) and suggests a model for treatment that makes clear to the battered woman that her symptoms are the result of, rather than the cause of, battering. It is beyond the scope of this volume to describe Root's theory on trauma in detail, but we want to discuss her work briefly here, especially as it relates to battering (see Root, 1992, for a more complete picture).

Root's formulations of trauma and the effects of trauma on those who experience it are predicated on the belief that trauma permanently changes an individual's personal construction of reality: To the victim of trauma, "people may begin to appear less benevolent, events less random, and living more encumbered" (Root, 1992, p. 229). Root distinguishes trauma from stress. Stress is recognized as inconveniencing and upsetting, and reactions to it are relieved when the stressor is removed. Trauma, however, leaves permanent marks and destroys basic "organizing principles by which we come to know self, others and the environment" (p. 229). The work that therapists must do to help clients heal from battering and other trauma, therefore, is to help them inject their lives with new meaning, with new organizing principles to replace those that have been destroyed, to make the world once again a safe place to be.

Another key premise of Root's theory of trauma is that what is viewed as traumatic is determined by the person experiencing the event, and not by the observer—even if the observer is the traumatized person's therapist. Root indicates that one of the difficulties in working with a traumatized individual is that as time passes after the original trauma, the effects of the event are obscured by daily crises that require immediate resolution. Therapists thus may have great difficulty in relating symptoms to the original trauma. It is likely that the mental health practitioner will overlook the behaviors that are most likely to be the direct results of the traumatic experience of being battered, and so a variety of daily crises may become the focus of therapy. Moreover, it is also highly likely that, to the therapist, the traumatogenic root of the symptoms will remain diffuse, so that he or she sees these symptoms as the cause, rather than the result, of battering.

Root's theory has additional implications for mental health practitioners' treatment of battered women and may in fact help explain the empirical findings we reported in Chapter 4. The "just world hypothesis" (Perloff, 1983) can be used to explain the belief (or defense) of most persons that bad things happen only to bad people, that "you get what you deserve." As therapists are continually exposed to the horrors of others' lives (including secrets of abuse and betrayal of loved ones), they have a variety of defenses available to them. Specifically, therapists can believe their clients and become indirectly traumatized themselves, or they can convince themselves that the clients must be to blame for their experiences, because bad things do not happen to good people. This conceptualization serves to maintain the therapist's sense of invulnerability and results in the classic victim-blaming stance. It is easy to find examples of victim blame in our society: the rape victim who "asked for it," the battered wife whose batterer uses the highly effective legal defense that "the bitch deserved it," the client who is "seductive" and whose therapist (violating all ethical codes) consequently engages in a sexual relationship with her.

One consequence of adopting the second of these conceptualizations is that, in addition to being blamed for her victimization, the victim is blamed for the symptoms she develops in reaction to her trauma. Moreover, these symptoms are pathologized rather than seen as perfectly normal coping reactions to abnormal events. Battered women and other trauma survivors exhibit behaviors that are often "viewed as regressive behaviors, signs of instability, or impaired emotional functioning" (Root, 1992, p. 248) but may be "survival behaviors." Root suggests reconceptualizing these behaviors as indications that the woman "has the capacity for self-preservation" (p. 248). These behaviors include egocentrism and self-referencing behaviors that serve to protect the battered woman from being caught unaware; perseveration, which may overshadow the handling of any other information as the survivor experiences memories of the trauma in visual, motor, and cognitive channels, perhaps simultaneously; anger, a fighting behavior that protects from attack; withdrawal and shutting down, flight responses that allow the person to reenergize to fight again; and splitting, which allows for the separation of threatening from safe cues.

Root has further enhanced our understanding of the sequelae of battering. She indicates that trauma inflicted by another human being has an especially potent role in influencing the survivor to reconceptualize her worldview. "Woman battering," she says, "is a direct trauma that in chronic patterns also entails a form of insidious trauma, psychological threat" (p. 242). She also points out that a child who views his or her mother being battered is damaged in multiple ways: The child (a) sustains indirect trauma from seeing the event, (b) fears the loss of the mother, and (c) when old enough to take the mother's perspective, may even feel that he or she too has been beaten.

The final area we want to introduce from Root's work concerns the use of the DSM-III-R (American Psychiatric Association, 1987). Post-traumatic stress disorder (PTSD) is the DSM-III-R diagnosis originally given to a constellation of symptoms manifested by certain distressed war veterans and later expanded to include other trauma survivors. In critiquing the use of this diagnosis, Root suggests that "no matter how sensitively proposed an individual theory is, it still tends to talk about the victim's characteristics in a way that lends itself to blaming the survivor of trauma" (p. 238). Moreover, she also indicates that responses of individuals to trauma take on a variety of forms, not always fitting within the criteria for PTSD of DSM-III-R. At the same time, many clients require insurance reimbursement for their therapy. Many mental health practitioners have a dilemma brought on by their desire to help clients obtain reimbursement, which may require a PTSD diagnosis even though different forms of post-trauma responding are present for particular clients. However, some practitioners may want to avoid stigmatizing diagnoses entirely. Other practitioners may provide a DSM-III-R diagnosis and desire to continue to behave ethically. To resolve the cognitive dissonance thus generated, the therapist may then see the client as to blame for the symptoms, which then "become" the individual's pathology. This type of reframing on the part of the therapist may leave him or her confused about appropriate treatment. In any case, the therapist will undoubtedly intervene differently than if the behaviors were seen as simply coping behaviors in the face of trauma once the client's behavior has been labeled as symptomatic of PTSD or some other diagnosis. DSM-IV, currently being prepared, may include a category of stress-related disorders and some relational disorders; however, the underlying tenet of DSM pathologizes behaviors we are likely to see in trauma survivors. The DSM indicates that the response of the victim to trauma is a personality disorder and as such does not consider the impact of the environment on the individual.

A NEW MODEL FOR TREATING BATTERERS

Segel-Evans (personal communication, August 1989) recently described a model for working with batterers that has proven to be extremely effective in the treatment of violent men. The cycle of violence and control is an elaboration of the cycle of violence described by Walker (1984a). Walker's three phases of violence include a stage in which tension rises, followed by the battering stage, followed by a period of tension relief and/or remorse, which she calls the "honeymoon" period. Segel-Evans contributes to our understanding of the cycle by positing that tensions rise in response to personal triggers, such as past trauma. The feelings that arise in response to the personal triggers (such as vulnerability, fear, hurt, shame, helplessness, guilt, rejection, loneliness) are defended against by calling into play blame, anger, projection, self-righteousness, and attack because of male sex role socialization. These behaviors usually lead to escalation, with the partner being seen as the enemy, and are accompanied by a belief that attack or violence is appropriate. Escalation is rapidly followed by the battering, which may include emotional, verbal, economic, sexual, or physical violence or a combination of all of these. This physical discharge seems to bring relief of the tension buildup, but along with it comes remorse (usually at a superficial level), accompanied perhaps by justification, blame, denial, rationalization, and minimization. The relief and the experience of renewed control that is the immediate result make escalation and violence likely to reoccur in spite of the ultimate cost.

During this cycle, the commitment of the batterer is to control his partner and to control his own feelings of vulnerability. Battering serves to defend the batterer against his feelings, as is the case with most addictions, where the addictive substance is ingested to ward off or numb against feelings. This ingestion is followed, as is battering, by a phase of remorse accompanied by justification, denial, rationalization, and so on. Segel-Evans's focus on battering as a defense against feelings helps explain why alcoholics also often batter and why treating the alcohol abuse without treating the battering does not cure the underlying malady.

Segel-Evans's treatment involves a cycle of resolution and problem solving. With treatment, the rise in tension reported above is followed by recognition of the feelings and problem solving in lieu of violence, followed by a true resolution. The commitment becomes a commitment to partnership rather than to control.

A CURRENT MODEL OF FAMILY

Family therapy in the 1980s and 1990s has generated increased attention to brief or solution-oriented therapy (de Shazer, 1990; White & Epston, 1990). These approaches, as their name implies, are typically brief, solution focused, intent on the individual and family context of the presenting problem, and operate from an entirely different philosophical underpinning from that of more long-term therapies. This new approach to family therapy comes from a constructivist perspective, where the focus is not on understanding the truth of a phenomenon, largely because of the belief that there is no single underlying truth. Instead, truth is understood to be constructed by the individual and can be considered only in the context in which the phenomenon occurs.

A constructivist therapist thus would work with the client in eliciting the client's own self-narratives. The meanings the client ascribes to his or her actions are what are important, and the frame within which the actions take place must be considered so that the action can be placed within its context. The most influential frame is the client's narrative about his or her life and relationships. This narrative, constructed by the client, shapes his or her life. Thus, according to this approach, it is the meaning the individual makes of the things he or she has experienced that affect what that person does, and it is at the level of meaning that interventions must be made. A constructivist therapist would ask the client, "What does this mean to you?" In working with couples or families, the constructivist therapist would look to the stories they tell about their experience. Through these stories, the therapist can discern which aspects of their lives the clients select to express and which are most meaningful to them. Conflicted couples or families may be those who enter therapy with different stories or different interpretations of the same stories to share.

Michael White (1988-1989), a respected constructivist therapist, originated the notion of externalizing the problem, that is, the objectification of the problem for which the person seeks therapy. He encourages clients to describe how problems have affected their lives, their relationships, or their views of themselves, putting the problems as something outside of, rather than a shameful part of, the clients. He further encourages clients to disown the problems, making the problems something that no longer speak to the clients as the truth of their identity (e.g., "What is this having to do with your relationship that goes against your better judgment?"). This approach is one that White applies to work with batterers. The externalizing conversation is one that shakes the client out of the settled certainty of his identity in the relationship. Through the steps of deconstruction—identifying the influence of the problem on the person's life—White is able to help clients change in rapid order. He indicates that since we are multistoried (even about the same event), the therapist needs a point of entry into these multiple stories. This White identifies as the unique outcome—what we take to be essential to our nature that is part of our story. He also indicates that there are multiple ways to look at a story. The first way is through what he calls the landscape of action: events that are described in highly specific and particular sequences arranged through linear time through the past, present, and future according to particular plots. Second, he describes the landscape of consciousness or the landscape of meaning. In helping the client to deconstruct and reconstruct his or her story, the role of the therapist is to formulate questions to guide the client in understanding the landscapes of action and of consciousness. The goal is the reconstruction of the story, the reauthoring of the client's story.

White claims to be extremely effective in using this approach with violent men. The situation described below applies to those situations in which the man has ended the violence and the woman wants to continue the relationship. Elsewhere, White (1986) describes other approaches to working with men who continue their violence and their wives who continue to receive the violence.

When the violence has ceased, White is an advocate of working conjointly. Since safety is no longer an issue, he operates to analyze the violence in the context of patriarchal ideology. He believes strongly that a conjoint approach is most effective because then the therapist can emphasize the man's responsibility for his violent acts, counter beliefs about the woman's provocation of the violence, and help the woman to separate from the relationship if she should become aware of her desire to do so. Conjoint interviewing, he indicates, allows the woman to become empowered and to reauthor her story. The therapist can examine with the client the appropriateness of various patriarchal beliefs, such as the following:

> the notion that women are the property of men and, flowing from this, the idea that men have the right to do with their property what they wish; . . . the notion of hierarchy as the natural order, of man's unquestionable entitlement to assume the superior position in this natural order, accompanied by a very great emphasis on control of those less entitled beings (women) by "power-over" tactics. (White, 1988-1989, p. 102)

Conjoint therapy, according to White's model, would entail eliciting the couple's theory about men's aggression in general and why the specific instances of violence occurred when they did; summarizing the couple's account of their view of violence to indicate familiarity with this view; and informing the couple about a new account of men's violence, one at odds with that presented by the couple. The therapist paradoxically encourages the clients to incorporate the new teachings into their world by presenting the new view of violence as one that conflicts so much with the couple's view that they might find it disturbing. The therapist also emphasizes that coping with the new account could be so disturbing that it will precipitate deep changes in the couple's relationship, with the man perhaps even feeling compelled to defend his own account in the face of the one proposed by the therapist. When the therapist is female, White proposes suggesting that the new account may be even more threatening coming from a woman. The therapist continues by ascertaining whether the couple is ready to hear the new account (the therapist may even suggest that the couple may want to maintain a skeptical attitude about the new account until they have heard the complete story), describing patriarchal ideology as the context of violence of men toward women (examining the media, historical events, theories of biology and genetics, ejaculatory theories about anger, the woman's experience of oppression, and so on), and asking the man or woman, "Do you think you should comply with these impoverishing instructions relating to the idea of power over others, or does the idea of a growing appreciation of personal resourcefulness and empowerment seem more attractive?" (White, 1988-1989, p. 103). Next steps involve identifying occasions when violence should have been expected but did not occur and asking the couple how they might handle the ways in which breaking free of societal constraints might set them apart from others, such as, "If you oppose these ideas about men's supremacy, this could set you apart from other men. How would you cope with this?"

The work of White and his colleagues has recently been critiqued by Crudgington and Brennan (1992) for emphasizing cognition (a male approach to knowing) to the exclusion of female knowledge, which they call "the landscape of emotion," which they say "is significantly constituted by the feelings of the characters in the story, and also by those of the reader as s/he enters, at the invitation of the writer. It features the emotional response by characters and readers through a feeling response to the events and plots as they unfold through the landscape of action" (p. 3).

Traditional models in working with batterers and/or battered women have focused on cognitive approaches, often to the exclusion of the emotional aspects of intervention. Therapy that relies on accurate and clear thinking to work may not be as effective because cognitive distortion is common with both perpetrators and battered women. Moreover, approaches that are more societally focused may be required, as battering occurs within a social context that perpetuates the social acceptability of violence (see Hansen, Chapter 6). Jenkins's (1990) approach to working with violent men may be such a model in that it incorporates White's notions within a systemic sociocultural context. The core of his model is to help the abuser accept responsibility for his behavior.

A NEW MODEL FOR ADDRESSING CONCERNS OF SOCIETY

Feminist theory identifies societal tolerance of spouse abuse as a major obstacle facing efforts to reduce battering. The social context surrounding the family needs to exert social sanctions against battering for domestic violence to decrease significantly. Theorists have recommended unified and coordinated multidimensional social efforts that will have an impact on social and public policy (Gelles & Straus, 1989). A new approach has been generated from the social policies implemented in Duluth, Minnesota. The Duluth model advocates, first and foremost, that the community be responsible for imposing sanctions on violence. No longer is it the individual battered woman's responsibility to bring action against her assailant; instead, actions and sanctions against spousal violence are societal responsibilities. The woman's actions are, therefore, separated from the control imposed upon her by the batterer. He can no longer influence her to drop charges or to assist him in avoiding the consequences for his actions. Instead, the community assumes direct responsibility for prohibiting the violence and applying consequences for violation of sanctions. Second, the Duluth model advocates interagency coordination of policy and action. The coordination of services among the various agencies encompassing police, prosecutors, judges, probation department, and mental health services is advocated to ensure the optimal and consistent implementation of consequences and follow-through with treatment programs. All agencies and programs provide the same consistent message: "Domestic violence is a crime that a community will not tolerate" (Hoffman, 1992).

The Duluth project began in 1981, when the city's judges and police chief agreed to take on an ambitious new program. The cornerstone of the project is the Domestic Abuse Intervention Project (DAIP), the umbrella agency that oversees the coordination and implementation of services. Duluth has implemented a mandatory arrest policy for misdemeanor assaults. Batterers are arrested regardless of the expressed desires of their victims. The police are not required to witness an assault in order to make an arrest. However, they are required to make an arrest based on "probable cause," such as visible injury. The DAIP follows the abuser from the time he is arrested. An abuser is prosecuted with or without the testimony of his victim, and a victim's original statement to police is used as testimony if the victim refuses to testify. Judges may delay the trial if the woman refuses to testify, reflecting an awareness on the part of the courts that the woman might be frightened of retaliation by her spouse. If the batterer denies abuse, the court holds a civil trial (this occurs in approximately 20% of cases); this practice has resulted in a high finding of abuse (as high as 98%) (Pence, Duprey, Paymar, & McDonnell, 1989). Typically, the court orders "counseling" for the batterer, which is provided by the DAIP (in 89% of all cases); incarceration is ordered for a smaller proportion (3.5%).

Counseling consists of an educational program provided by the DAIP that includes up to 24 weeks of systematic intervention. The program, which is broken up into 3-week modules, focuses on the education of the batterer. Each module helps the batterer to identify abusive behavior, recognize his own emotional responses and connection to the abusive behavior, and learn new behavior. In addition, the abuser may be referred for separate therapeutic counseling that is offered in conjunction with the educational program. Current literature produced by the Duluth project suggests that the educational model alone may be as effective an intervention and more cost-effective. Intervention programs are also coordinated for the victims of abuse, both spouses and children. Such programs focus on empowerment and development of self-esteem, education in legal rights, and victim advocacy. Again, a critical component is the monitoring of all interventions by the DAIP, both of the batterer and the battered.

Reports from Duluth indicate that in the more than 10 years since implementation, not one woman has died as a result of domestic violence. In addition, the chief prosecutor reports losing only three cases of spouse abuse in her 9 years as prosecutor. Problems in the program appear with the evidence of repeat offenders (upward of 40%), the constant number of cases that have appeared before the courts (about 450 a year), and the appearance of sons in the program whose fathers were also abusers. Such data suggest that the program is not yet acting as a social deterrent to abuse but may at this time provide a consistent statement of community values that abuse is not acceptable. Changes in behavioral and familial demonstration of social attitudes may take longer.

Efforts to implement similar programs elsewhere have met with varied success. A primary difficulty may be that efforts elsewhere have consisted solely of the educational program for batterers rather than the systematic implementation of a program that includes the removal of responsibility for the prosecution of the batterer from the battered woman and the coordination of services by an umbrella agency such as the DAIP. These two components appear to be critical elements in efforts to implement social change.

Another community program that has been developed is the Jurismonitor project in Boulder, Colorado. One aspect of this program is the use of electronic ankle bracelets, which are worn by recognized batterers; when a perpetrator approaches a battered woman's home, the device activates a communication unit to alert authorities. Additional components of this program include treatment for batterers and support groups for battered women. Although this program is too new to have been properly assessed, it shows a great deal of promise.

Looking Toward the Future

Gelles and Straus (1989) have written, "Our examination of family violence over the years has consistently found that socially structured inequality is a prime contributor to violence in the home" (p. 203). Following the preparation of this volume, we too are left with specific concerns and a recognition of the need for social change.

At the legal level, we have documented the progress being made to treat spouse abuse as a crime and to provide victims with the protection they need. By documenting this progress, we have highlighted where continued change is needed. We have noted the need for changes in the law in jurisdictions that still require the act of violence to be witnessed by the arresting officer for an arrest to be made. Changes are also needed where laws still require the battered woman to testify and where the batterer is allowed to use his influence upon her to prevent the implementation of the law. In states and jurisdictions that do not adequately address the issue of spouse abuse in custody decisions, change must also come. Data overwhelmingly support the traumatic impact on children of spouse abuse, and document that as many as 70% of spouse abusers abuse their children as well. These findings must be taken into consideration in custody battles.

At the treatment level, we are aware that therapists continue to fail to recognize the seriousness of violence and fail to recognize appropriate and effective ways of intervening in cases when violence is present. We have put forth specific cautions for attending to the social context of established inequality, attending to the therapeutic potential for victim blaming, and attending to the potential for serious harm when the violence is not addressed or is addressed inappropriately. We have also discussed the specific care that needs to be taken in treating the battered woman while not blaming her for her victimization; in treating the batterer, while continuing to recognize the criminal component of his actions; in treating the couple who may want to continue as a couple; and in treating the children who themselves have been victimized by the experience but who are the children of the batterer as well. We have also addressed training needs by presenting a model curriculum and describing who might best be prepared for working with violent families.

We have highlighted the treatment needs of less recognized populations as well. Services and sensitivity are needed in the treatment of abuse for members of the gay and lesbian communities, who must overcome the social stigma of sexual preference as well as the stigma of battering. Special services and sensitivity are also needed in providing treatment for members of identifiable ethnic communities who must address their own cultural expectations as well as those of the dominant culture in learning that spouse abuse is no longer condoned by this society and is a crime. In addition, special services are needed for batterers who have addictions as well as the propensity to abuse their spouses; both problems must be addressed.

At the social level, we have demonstrated the need for the coordination of efforts. The Duluth model supports the argument that a united front and continued focus are essential. Only with repeated efforts at all levels can social change be expected or even hoped for. The difficulty and deep entrenchment of the problem are illustrated by frightening data indicating that, even with the best efforts, abusers continue to abuse. We need to continue our efforts, and not allow ourselves to become discouraged. We need to promote legal change and mandatory arrest policies. We need to work toward coordination of efforts and consistent implementation of consequences for family violence. We need to educate therapists in the recognition of battering and appropriate therapeutic interventions for victims, families, and batterers. We need to support existing efforts to coordinate services provided by state battered women's coalitions (see the appendix to this volume for a listing). Such changes are taking place, and it is our hope that the next review will document even further progress.

Appendix

State Coalitions Against Domestic Violence

Alabama Coalition Against Domestic Violence
P.O. Box 4762
Montgomery, AL 36101

Contact: Carol Gundlach
(205) 832-4842
(205) 832-4803 (fax)

Alaska Network on Domestic Violence and Sexual Assault
419 6th Street, No. 116
Juneau, AK 99801

Contact: Cindy Smith
(907) 586-3650
(907) 463-4493 (fax)

Arizona Coalition Against Domestic Violence
301 West Hatcher Road
Phoenix, AZ 85201

Contact: Jeanne McCleod
(602) 371-8505

Arkansas Coalition Against Violence to Women & Children
7509 Cantrell, No. 213
Little Rock, AR 72207

Contact: Lydia Walker
(501) 663-4668

Central California Coalition on Domestic Violence
219 McHenry Avenue
Modesto, CA 95354

Contact: Irene Westbury
(209) 524-1888/4331
(209) 524-2045 (fax)

Southern California Coalition Against Domestic Violence
California Women's Law Center
11852 Santa Monica Boulevard
Suite 5
Los Angeles, CA 90025

Contact: Sheila Kuehl
(310) 447-3639

Northern California Coalition Against Domestic Violence
1717 5th Avenue
San Rafael, CA 94901

Contact: Donna Garske
(415) 457-2464
(415) 457-6457 (fax)

Colorado Coalition Against Domestic Violence
P.O. Box 18902
Denver, CO 80218

Contact: Jan Mickish
(303) 573-9018

Connecticut Coalition Against Domestic Violence
22 Maple Avenue
Hartford, CT 06114

Contact: Anne Menard
(203) 524-5890

D.C. Coalition Against Domestic Violence
P.O. Box 76069
Washington, DC 20013

Contact: Joanne Tulonen
(202) 857-0216

Florida Coalition Against Domestic Violence
1177 Louisiana Avenue, Suite 213
Winter Park, FL 32789
or
P.O. Box 1201
Winter Park, FL 32790-1201

Contact: Sue Armstrong
(407) 628-3885

Georgia Network Against Domestic Violence
250 Georgia Avenue, SE, Suite 365
Atlanta, GA 30312

Contact: Cathy Beam
(404) 524-3847
(404) 594-7738 (fax)

Hawaii State Committee on Family Violence
P.O. Box 31107
Honolulu, HI 96820-1107

Contact: Carol Lee
(808) 532-3800
(808) 532-3804 (fax)

Idaho Network to Stop Violence Against Women
1415 Camelback Lane, Apt. B103
Boise, ID 83702

Contact: Rose Moore
(208) 384-5121

Illinois Coalition Against Domestic Violence
937 South 4th Street
Springfield, IL 62703

Contact: Joyce Pruitt
(217) 789-2830

Indiana Coalition Against Domestic Violence
c/o YWCA Women's Shelter
605 North 6th Street
Lafayette, IN 47901

Contact: Sheri Kilty
(317) 742-0075
or
c/o Center for Women & Family
P.O. Box 2048
Louisville, KY 40201

Contact: Leslie Hamelman
(502) 581-7231
(502) 581-7204 (fax)

Iowa Coalition Against Domestic Violence
Lucas Building, Ground Floor
Des Moines, IA 50319

Contact: Dianne Fagner
(515) 281-7284
(515) 242-6119 (fax)

Kansas Coalition Against Sexual & Domestic Violence
P.O. Box 1341
Pittsburg, KS 66762
or
c/o SAFEHOUSE
101 East 4th Street, Suite 214
Pittsburg, KS 66762

Contact: Dorothy Miller
(316) 232-2757
(316) 232-1564 (fax)

Kentucky Domestic Violence Association
P.O. Box 356
Frankfort, KY 40602

Contact: Sherry Currens
(502) 875-4132

Louisiana Coalition Against Domestic Violence
P.O. Box 2133
Baton Rouge, LA 70821

Contact: Meg Ross
(504) 389-301
(504) 358-3444 (fax)

Maine Coalition for Family Crisis Services
P.O. Box 590
Sanford, ME 04073

Contact: Kim Sherburne
(207) 324-1957

Maryland Network Against Domestic Violence
167 Duke of Gloucester Street
Annapolis, MD 21401

Contact: Kinaya Sokoya
(301) 839-5815
(301) 779-2100 (fax)
or
Heartly House, Inc.
P.O. Box 831
Fredrick, MD 21701

Contact: Sue Hecht
(301) 662-8800
(301) 663-4334 (fax)

Massachusetts Coalition of Battered Women's Services
107 South Street, 5th Floor
Boston, MA 02111

Contact: Carolyn Ramsey
(617) 426-8492

Michigan Coalition Against Domestic Violence
P.O. Box 16009
Lansing, MI 48901

Contact: Joan Dauphine/Carol Sullivan
(616) 484-2924
(313) 954-1199 (fax)

Minnesota Coalition for Battered Women
Physician's Plaza, Suite 201
570 Asbury Street
St. Paul, MN 55104

Contact: Marsha Frey
(612) 646-6177
(612) 646-1527 (fax)

Mississippi Coalition Against Battered Women
P.O. Box 333
Biloxi, MS 39533

Contact: Jane Philo
(601) 435-1968
(601) 435-0513 (fax)

Missouri Coalition Against Domestic Violence
311 East McCarty, No. 34
Jefferson City, MO 65101

Contact: Colleen Coble
(314) 634-4161

Montana Coalition Against Domestic Violence
104 North Broadway, No. 406
Billings, MT 59101

Contact: Jackie Garcia
(406) 252-0133
(406) 252-1092 (fax)

Nebraska Domestic Violence and Sexual Assault Coalition
1630 K Street, Suite H
Lincoln, NE 68508

Contact: Sarah O'Shea
(402) 476-6256
(402) 477-0837 (fax)

Nevada Network Against Domestic Violence
2100 Capurro Way, Suite 21-I
Sparks, NV 89431

Contact: Sue Meushke
(702) 358-1171
(702) 358-0616 (fax)

New Hampshire Coalition Against Domestic and Sexual Violence
P.O. Box 353
Concord, NH 03302-0353

Contact: Grace Mattern
(603) 224-8893
(603) 226-1831 (fax)

New Jersey Coalition for Battered Women
2620 Whitehurst/Hamilton Square Road
Trenton, NJ 08690-2718

Contact: Sandy Clark
(609) 584-8107

New Mexico State Coalition Against Domestic Violence
c/o La Casa, Inc.
P.O. Box 2463
Las Cruces, NM 88044

Contact: Susan Gonzales
(505) 526-2819
(505) 525-3792 (fax)

New York State Coalition Against Domestic Violence
79 Central Avenue
Albany, NY 12206

Contact: Gwen Wright
(518) 432-4864

North Carolina Coalition Against Domestic Violence
P.O. Box 51875
Durham, NC 27717-1875

Contact: Diane Hall
(704) 885-7233

North Dakota Council on Abused Women's Services
State Networking Office
418 East Rosser Avenue, Suite 310
Bismarck, ND 58501

Contact: Bonnie Palecek
(701) 255-6240
(701) 255-2411 (fax)

Ohio Domestic Violence Network
P.O. 1433
Marion, OH 43301-1433
or
Templum House
P.O. Box 5466
Cleveland, OH 44101

Contact: Nancy Neylon
(216) 634-7501

Oklahoma Coalition on Domestic Violence and Sexual Assault
P.O. Box 5089
Norman, OK 73070

Contact: Shari Ford
(405) 360-7125

Oregon Coalition Against Domestic and Sexual Violence
2336 Southeast Belmont Street
Portland, OR 97214

Contact: Judith Armatta
(503) 239-4486/4487
(503) 287-5130 (fax) (Kinko's)

Pennsylvania Coalition Against Domestic Violence
2505 North Front Street
Harrisburg, PA 17110-1111

Contact: Susan Kelly-Dreiss/Bonnie Fowler
(717) 234-7353
(717) 234-7428 (fax)

Rhode Island Council on Domestic Violence
324 Broad Street
Central Falls, RI 02863

Contact: Donna Nesselbush
(401) 723-3051

South Carolina Against Domestic Violence and Sexual Assault
P.O. Box 7776
Columbia, SC 29202

Contact: Vicki Ernest
(803) 232-1339
(803) 242-9489 (fax)

South Dakota Coalition Against Domestic Violence/Sexual Assault
P.O. Box 595
Agency Village, SD 57262

Contact: Brenda Hill
(605) 624-5311

Tennessee Task Force Against Domestic Violence
P.O. Box 120972
Nashville, TN 37212-0972

Contact: Kathy England/ Elizabeth Barger
(615) 242-8288
(615) 244-4920 (fax)

Texas Council on Family Violence
3415 Greystone, Suite 220
Austin, TX 78731

Contact: Debby Tucker
(512) 794-1133
(512) 794-1199 (fax)

Citizens Against Physical and Sexual Abuse
P.O. Box 3617
Logan, UT 84321

Contact: Diane Stuart
(801) 752-4493
(801) 753-0372 (fax)

Vermont Network Against Domestic Violence and Sexual Assault
P.O. Box 405
Montpelier, VT 05602

Contact: Judy Rex
(802) 223-1302

Virginians Against Domestic Violence
P.O. Box 5692
Richmond, VA 23220

Contact: Christie Van Audenhove
(804) 780-3505

Washington State Coalition Against Domestic Violence
200 W Street, SE, Suite B
Tumwater, WA 98501

Contact: Mary Pontarolo
(206) 352-4029
(206) 352-4078 (fax)
or
B. J. Cooper, President WCADV
c/o RR 1, Box 232B
Valley, WA 99181
(509) 233-2088
(509) 684-3796

West Virginia Coalition Against Domestic Violence
P.O. Box 85
Sutton, WV 26601

Contact: Sue Julian/Dianne Reese
(304) 765-2250

Wisconsin Coalition Against Domestic Violence
1051 Williamson Street
Madison, WI 53703

Contact: Kathleen Krenek
(608) 255-0539

Wyoming Self Help Center
341 East E Street, Suite 135A
Casper, WY 82601
(307) 235-2814
(307) 266-4105 (fax)
or
Crisis Intervention Services
P.O. Box 1127
Riverton, WY 82501

Contact: Rosemary Bratten
(307) 587-3545

Note: Delaware has no state domestic violence coalition.

References

Achenbach, T. M., & Edelbrock, C. S. (1981). Behavioral problems and competencies reported by parents of normal and disturbed children aged 4 through 16. *Monographs of the Society for Research in Child Development, 46* (Serial No. 188).

Adams, D. (1988). Treatment models of men who batter: A profeminist analysis. In K. Yllö & M. Bograd (Eds.), *Feminist perspectives on wife abuse* (pp. 176-199). Newbury Park, CA: Sage.

Adams, D. (1989). Feminist-based interventions for battering men. In P. L. Caesar & L. K. Hamberger (Eds.), *Treating men who batter: Theory, practice, and programs* (pp. 3-23). New York: Springer.

Aguirre, B. E. (1985). Why do they return? Abused wives in shelters. *Social Work, 30,* 350-354.

Alessi, J. J., & Hearn, K. (1984). Group treatment of children in shelters for battered women. In A. R. Roberts (Ed.), *Battered women and their families: Intervention strategies and treatment programs* (pp. 49-61). New York: Springer.

Alonso, A. (1985). *The quiet profession.* New York: Macmillan.

American Psychiatric Association. (1980). *Diagnostic and statistical manual of mental disorders* (3rd ed.). Washington, DC: Author.

American Psychiatric Association. (1987). *Diagnostic and statistical manual of mental disorders* (3rd ed., rev.). Washington, DC: Author.

American Psychological Association. (1992). Ethical principles of psychologists and code of conduct. *American Psychologist, 47,* 1597-1611.

American Psychological Association. (1990). *Guidelines for providers of psychological services to ethnic, linguistic, and culturally diverse populations.* Washington, DC.

Amsel, A. (1958). Role of frustrative non-reward in non-continuous reward situation. *Psychological Bulletin, 55,* 102-119.

Archer, N. H. (1989). Battered women and the legal system: Past, present, and future. *Law and Psychology Review, 13,* 145-163.

Aries, P. (1970). *Centuries of childhood: A social history of family life.* New York: Knopf.

Armstrong, K. (1986). *The gospel according to woman.* Garden City, NY: Doubleday.

Attneave, C. (1982). American Indian and Alaska Native families: Emigrants in their own homeland. In M. McGoldrick, J. K. Pearce, & J. Giordano (Eds.), *Ethnicity and family therapy* (pp. 55-82). New York: Guilford.

Attorney General's Family Violence Task Force of Pennsylvania. (1989). *Domestic violence: A model protocol for police response.* Harrisburg, PA: Office of the Attorney General.

Avis, J. M. (1988). Deepening awareness: A private study guide to feminism and family therapy. *Psychotherapy and the Family, 3,* 15-46.

Bagarozzi, D. A., & Giddings, C. W. (1983). Conjugal violence: A critical review of current research and clinical practices. *American Journal of Family Therapy, 11*(1), 3-15.

Ball, P. G., & Wyman, E. (1977-1978). Battered wives and powerlessness: What can counselors do? *Victimology, 2*(3-4).

Bandura, A. (1973). *Aggression: A social learning analysis.* Englewood Cliffs, NJ: Prentice-Hall.

Barnett, E. R., Pittman, C. B., Ragan, C. K., & Salus, M. K. (1980). *Family violence: Intervention strategies* (Publication No. [OHDS] 80-30258). Washington, DC: U.S. Department of Health and Human Services.

Barron v. Barron, 445 A.2d 1182 (1982).

Basta, J. M. (1990, August). *The behavioral adjustment of battered women's children: An empirical investigation.* Paper presented at the annual meeting of the American Psychological Association, Boston.

Bates v. Bates, 793 S.W.2d 788 (1990).

Bateson, G. (1972). *Steps to an ecology of mind.* New York: Ballantine.

Bell, C. C. (1991). *Impact of violence on African American children.* Paper presented at the Fifth Annual Multicultural Mental Health Conference on Families and Children: The Different Faces of Violence, University of New Mexico School of Medicine, Albuquerque.

Bell, C. C., & Chance-Hill, N. (1991). Treatment of violent families. *Journal of the National Medical Association, 183,* 203-208.

Bent, R. J., Schindler, N., & Dobbins, J. E. (1992). Management and supervision competency. In R. L. Peterson, J. D. McHolland, R. J. Bent, E. Davis-Russell, G. E. Edwall, K. Polite, D. L. Singer, & G. Stricker (Eds.), *The core curriculum in professional psychology* (pp. 121-126). Washington, DC: National Council of Schools of Professional Psychology and American Psychological Association.

Bepko, C., & Krestan, J. (1985). *The responsibility trap: A blueprint for treating the alcoholic family.* New York: Free Press.

Bepko, C., & Krestan, J. (1990). *Too good for her own good.* New York: Harper & Row.

Berger, K. S. (1991). *The developing person through childhood and adolescence.* New York: Worth.

Berlin, I. N. (1987). Effects of changing Native American cultures on child development. *Journal of Community Psychology, 15,* 299-306.

Berlin, I. N. (1991). *Violence related to acculturation among Southwest Indian adolescents: Implications to prevention and treatment.* Paper presented at the Fifth Annual Multicultural Mental Health Conference on Families and Children: The Different Faces of Violence, University of New Mexico School of Medicine, Albuquerque.

Berman, P. (1989). Professional women, paraprofessional women, and victimized women: A multisystem empowerment approach. *Journal of Politics, Economics, Psychology, Sociology, & Culture, 6-7,* 95-113.

Bernard, G. W., Vera, H., Vera, M. I., & Newman, G. (1982). Till death do us part: A study of spouse murder. *Bulletin of the American Academy of Psychiatry and the Law, 10,* 271ff.

Bernard, J. (1982). *The future of marriage* (2nd ed.). New Haven, CT: Yale University Press.

Bernard, J. L., & Bernard, M. L. (1984). The abusive male seeking treatment: Jekyll and Hyde. *Family Relations, 33,* 543-547.

Bessenyey, I. M. (1989). Visitation in the domestic violence context: Problems and recommendations. *Vermont Law Review, 14,* 57-78.

Bettelheim, B. (1943). Individual and mass behavior in extreme situations. *Journal of Abnormal and Social Psychology, 38,* 417-452.

Billings-Beck, G. (1991). *Philosophy and treatment of battered women.* California: Haven Hills Shelter.

Blackman, J. (1986). Potential uses for expert testimony: Ideas toward the representation of battered women who kill. *Women's Rights Law Reporter, 9,* 227-238.

Blackman, J. (1989). *Intimate violence: A study of injustice.* New York: Columbia University Press.

Blum, H. P. (1982). Psychoanalytic reflections on the "beaten wife syndrome." In M. Kirkpatrick (Ed.), *Women's sexual experience: The dark continent* (pp. 263-267). New York: Plenum.

Bly, R. (1990). *Iron John: A book about men.* Reading, MA: Addison-Wesley.

Bochnak, E. (Ed.). (1981). *Women's self-defense cases: Theory and practice.* Charlotte, VA: Michie.

Bograd, M. (1984). Family systems approaches to wife battering: A feminist critique. *American Journal of Orthopsychiatry, 54,* 558-568.

Bograd, M. (1986). Lifting the shade on family violence. *Family Therapy Networker, 10*(4).

Bograd, M. (1988a). Feminist perspectives on wife abuse: An introduction. In K. Yllö & M. Bograd (Eds.), *Feminist perspectives on wife abuse* (pp. 11-26). Newbury Park, CA: Sage.

Bograd, M. (1988b). Power, gender and the family: Feminist perspectives on family systems theory. In M. A. Dutton-Douglas & L. E. A. Walker (Eds.), *Feminist psychotherapies: Integration of therapeutic and feminist systems* (pp. 118-133). Norwood, NJ: Ablex.

Bologna, H. J., Waterman, C. K., & Dawson, C. J. (1987, July). *Violence in gay male and lesbian relationships: Implications for practitioners and policy makers.* Paper presented at the Third National Conference for Family Violence Researchers, Durham, NH.

Borkowski, M., Murch, M., & Walker, V. (1983). *Marital violence: The community response.* London: Tavistock.

Bowen, M. (1966). *Family systems theory* (Videotapes). Washington, DC: Georgetown University Family Center.

Bowen, M. (1974). Alcoholism as viewed through family systems theory and family psychotherapy. *Annals of the New York Academy of Sciences, 233,* 115-122.

Bowen, M. (1978). *Family therapy in clinical practice.* New York: Jason Aronson.

Bowker, L. H. (1983). *Beating wife-beating.* Lexington, MA: Lexington.

Bowker, L. H. (1984). Coping with wife abuse: Personal and social networks. In A. R. Roberts (Ed.), *Battered women and their families: Intervention strategies and treatment programs.* New York: Springer.

Bowker, L. H. (1986). *Ending the violence.* Holmes Beach, FL: Learning Publications.

Bowker, L. H., Arbitell, M., & McFerron, J. R. (1988). On the relationship between wife beating and child abuse. In K. Yllö & M. Bograd (Eds.), *Feminist perspectives on wife abuse* (pp. 158-174). Newbury Park, CA: Sage.

Boyd-Franklin, N. (1989). *Black families in therapy: A multi-systems approach.* New York: Guilford.

Brand, P. A., & Kidd, A. H. (1986). Frequency of physical aggression in heterosexual and female homosexual dyads. *Psychological Reports, 59,* 1307-1313.

Breines, W., & Gordon, L. (1983). The new scholarship on family violence. *Signs, 8,* 490-531.

Breuer, J., & Freud, A. (1964). Studies in hysteria (A. Brill, Trans.). In J. Strachey (Ed.), *The standard edition of the complete psychological works of Sigmund Freud* (Vol. 2). London: Hogarth. (Original work published 1895)

Brodsky, A., & Hare-Mustin, R. (1980). *Women and psychotherapy: An assessment of research and practice.* New York: Guilford.

Brooks, G. R. (1990). Traditional men in marital and family therapy. *Journal of Feminist Family Therapy, 2,* 51-74.
Brown, L. S. (1990). Taking account of gender in the clinical assessment interview. *Professional Psychology: Research and Practice, 21,* 12-17.
Brown, L. S. (1991). Diagnosis and dialogue. *Canadian Psychology, 32,* 142-144.
Brown, L. S. (1992). Personality disorders. In L. S. Brown & M. S. Ballou (Eds.), *Personality and psychopathology: Feminist reappraisals.* New York: Guilford.
Brown, L. S., & Ballou, M. S. (Eds.). (1992). *Personality and psychopathology: Feminist reappraisals.* New York: Guilford.
Brown, L. S., & Root, M. P. P. (1990). *Diversity and complexity in feminist therapy.* Binghamton, NY: Harrington Park.
Brown, S. (1985). *Treating the alcoholic: A developmental model of recovery.* New York: John Wiley.
Brown, S. L. (1991). *Counseling victims of violence.* Alexandria, VA: American Association for Counseling and Development.
Browne, A. (1987). *When battered women kill.* New York: Free Press.
Browne, A. (1989). *Are women as violent as men?* Commentary presented at the annual meeting of the American Society of Criminology, Reno, NV.
Browne, A. (1991, July 9). Testimony before the Senate Subcommittee on Children, Family, Drugs and Alcoholism.
Browne, A., & Dutton, D. G. (1990). Escape from violence: Risks and alternatives for abused women. In R. Roesch, D. G. Dutton, & V. F. Sacco (Eds.), *Family violence: Perspectives in research and practice.* Burnaby, BC: Simon Fraser University Press.
Browne, A., & Williams, K. R. (1989). Exploring the effect of resource availability and the likelihood of female-perpetrated homicides. *Law and Society Review, 23*(1), 75-94.
Bruch, C. S. (1988). And how are the children? The effects of ideology and mediation on child custody law and children's well-being in the United States. *International Journal of Law and the Family, 2*(1).
Brush, L. D. (1990). Violent acts and injurious outcomes in married couples: Methodological issues in the National Survey of Families and Households. *Gender and Society, 4,* 56-67.
Brygger, M. P., & Edleson, J. L. (1985). *The Domestic Abuse Project: A multi-systems intervention.* Duluth, MN: Domestic Abuse Intervention Project.
Brygger, M. P., & Edleson, J. L. (1987). The Domestic Abuse Project: A multisystems intervention in woman battering. *Journal of Interpersonal Violence, 2,* 324-326.
Burch, B. (1987). Barriers to intimacy: Conflicts over power, dependency, and nurturing in lesbian relationships. In Boston Lesbian Psychologies Collective (Ed.), *Lesbian psychologies* (pp. 126-141). Urbana: University of Illinois Press.
Burt, M. R. (1980). Cultural myths and supports for rape. *Journal of Personality and Social Psychology, 38,* 217-230.
Caesar, P. L. (1988). Exposure to violence in the family-of-origin among wife abusers and maritally nonviolent men. *Violence and Victims, 3,* 49-64.
Caesar, P. L., & Hamberger, L. K. (Eds.). (1989). *Treating men who batter: Theory, practice, and programs.* New York: Springer.
Campbell, J. C. (1985). Beating of wives: A cross-cultural perspective. *Victimology, 10,* 174-185.
Caplan, P. J. (1985). *The myth of women's masochism.* New York: NAL-Dutton.
Caplan, P. J. (1991). How do they decide what is normal? The bizarre, but true, tale of the DSM process. *Canadian Psychology, 32,* 162-170.
Caplan, P. J., & Hall-McCorquodale, I. (1985). Mother-blaming in major clinical journals. *American Journal of Orthopsychiatry, 55,* 345-353.

Caringella-MacDonald, S. (1988). Parallels and pitfalls: The aftermath of legal reform for sexual assault, marital rape, and domestic violence victims. *Journal of Interpersonal Violence, 3,* 174-189.

Carlson, B. E. (1984). Children's observations of interparental violence. In A. R. Roberts (Ed.), *Battered women and their families: Intervention strategies and treatment programs* (pp. 147-167). New York: Springer.

Carlson, C. (Ed.). (1990). *Perspectives on the family: History, class, and feminism.* Belmont, CA: Wadsworth.

Carmen, E. H., Rieker, P. P., & Mills, T. (1984). Victims of violence and psychiatric illness. *American Journal of Psychiatry, 141,* 378-383.

Carmody, D. C., & Williams, K. R. (1987). Wife assault and perceptions of sanctions. *Violence and Victims, 2*(1).

Carrington, F. (1989, September). Avoiding liability for police failure to protect. *Police Chief.*

Carter, B., & McGoldrick, M. (Eds.). (1989). *The changing family life cycle: A framework for family therapy* (2nd ed.). Needham, MA: Allyn & Bacon.

Carter, E. (1989). Everything I do is for the family. In M. McGoldrick, C. M. Anderson, & F. Walsh (Eds.), *Women in families: A framework for family therapy.* New York: W. W. Norton.

Carver, C. S., & Scheier, M. F. (1992). *Perspectives on personality* (2nd ed.). Boston: Allyn & Bacon.

Cervantes, J. M., & Ramirez, O. (1992). Between spirituality and family therapy with Latino children and their families: A conceptual exploration. In L. Valdez & J. Koss-Chionio (Eds.), *Working with culture: Psychotherapeutic interventions with ethnic minority children* (pp. 103-128). San Francisco: Jossey-Bass.

Cervantes, J. M., & Romero, D. (1983, August). *Hispanic mental health clinicians: Personal and professional development issues.* Paper presented at the annual meeting of the American Psychological Association, Anaheim, CA.

Chambers, D. L. (1984). Rethinking the substantive rules for custody disputes in divorce. *Michigan Law Review, 833,* 477-569.

Chandler, S. (1986). *The psychology of the battered woman.* Unpublished doctoral dissertation, University of California, Berkeley, Department of Education.

Cheney, A. B., & Bleker, E. G. (1982, August). *Internal-external locus of control and repression-sensitization in battered women.* Paper presented at the annual meeting of the American Psychological Association, Washington, DC.

Chesler, P. (1986). *Mothers on trial.* New York: McGraw-Hill.

Chesler, P. (1989). *Women and madness.* New York: Harcourt Brace Jovanovich. (Original work published 1972)

Cocozzelli, C., & Hudson, C. (1989). Recent advances in alcoholism diagnosis and treatment assessment research: Implications for practice. *Social Service Review, 37,* 533-552.

Coleman, D., & Straus, M. A. (1986). Marital power, conflict and violence. *Violence and Victims, 1,* 139-153.

Coleman, K. H. (1980). Conjugal violence: What 33 men report. *Journal of Marital and Family Therapy, 6,* 207-213.

Coley, S. M., & Beckett, J. O. (1988). Black battered women: A review of empirical literature. *Journal of Counseling and Development, 66,* 266-270.

Comas-Diaz, L., & Griffith, E. H. (1988). *Clinical guidelines in cross cultural mental health.* New York: John Wiley.

Combahee River Collective. (1989). Black feminism. In S. Ware (Ed.), *Modern American women: A documentary history* (pp. 354-364). Belmont, CA: Wadsworth.

Cook, D. R., & Frantz-Cook, A. (1984). A systemic treatment approach to wife battering. *Journal of Marital and Family Therapy, 10,* 83-93.

Corenblum, B. (1983). Reactions to alcohol-related marital violence: Effects of one's own abuse experience and alcohol problems on causal attribution. *Journal of Studies on Alcohol, 44,* 665-674.

Crudgington, G., & Brennan, E. (1992). [Letter to Michael White]. Unpublished manuscript.

Cummings, E. M., Vogel, D., Cummings, J. S., & El-Sheikh, M. (1989). Children's responses to different forms of expression of anger between adults. *Child Development, 60,* 1392-1404.

Cummings, E. M., Zahn-Waxler, C., & Radke-Yarrow, M. (1981). Young children's responses to expressions of anger and affection by others in the family. *Child Development, 52,* 1274-1282.

Cummings, E. M., Zahn-Waxler, C., & Radke-Yarrow, M. (1984). Developmental changes in children's reactions to anger in the home. *Journal of Child Psychology and Psychiatry, 25,* 63-74.

Cummings, J. S., Pellegrini, D. S., Notarius, C. I., & Cummings, E. M. (1989). Children's responses to angry adult behavior as a function of marital distress and history of interparent hostility. *Child Development, 60,* 1035-1043.

Davidson, T. (1977). Wife beating: A recurring phenomenon throughout history. In M. Roy (Ed.), *Battered women: A psychosocial study of domestic violence.* New York: Nostrand Reinhold.

Davidson, T. (1978). *Conjugal crime: Understanding and changing the wife beating pattern.* New York: Hawthorne.

Davis, E. G. (1972). *The first sex.* Baltimore: Penguin.

Deal, J. E., & Wampler, K. S. (1986). Dating violence: The primacy of previous experience. *Journal of Social and Personal Relationships, 3,* 457-471.

Deed, M. (1991). Court-ordered child custody evaluations: Helping or victimizing vulnerable families? *Psychotherapy, 11,* 76-84.

Dell, P. (1989). Violence and the systemic view: The problem of power. *Family Process, 28,* 1-14.

Demaris, A. (1989). Attrition in batterers counseling: The role of social and demographic factors. *Social Service Review, 63,* 142-154.

Demaris, A., & Jackson, J. D. (1987). Batterers' reports of recidivism after counseling. *Social Casework, 68,* 458-465.

Dena Lynn F. v. Harvey H. F., 419 A.2d 1374 (1980).

Deschner, J. P. (1984). *The hitting habit: Anger control for battering couples.* New York: Free Press.

de Shazer, S. (1990). What is it about brief therapy that works? In J. K. Zweig & S. G. Gilligan (Eds.), *Brief therapy: Myths, methods and metaphors* (pp. 90-99). New York: Brunner/Mazel.

Devine v. Devine, 398 So.2d 686 (1981).

Dienhart, A., & Avis, J. A. (1990). Men in therapy: Exploring feminist-informed alternatives. *Journal of Feminist Family Therapy, 2,* 25-49.

Dobash, R. E., & Dobash, R. P. (1977-1978). Wives: The "appropriate" victims of marital violence. *Victimology, 2,* 426-442.

Dobash, R. E., & Dobash, R. P. (1979). *Violence against wives: A case against the patriarchy.* New York: Free Press.

Dobash, R. E., & Dobash, R. P. (1983). Unmasking the provocation excuse. *Aegis, 37,* 67-68.

Dobash, R. E., Dobash, R. P., & Cavanaugh, K. (1985). The contact between battered women and social and medical agencies. In J. Pahl (Ed.), *Private violence and public policy* (pp. 142-165). London: Routledge & Kegan Paul.

Dodge, K. A., Bates, J. E., & Pettit, G. S. (1990). Mechanisms in the cycle of violence. *Science, 250,* 1678-1683.

Donat, P. L. N., & D'Emilio, J. (1992). A feminist redefinition of rape and sexual assault: Historical foundations and change. *Journal of Social Issues, 48,* 9-22.

Douglas, M. A. (1982, August). *Behavioral assessment with battered women.* Paper presented at the annual meeting of the American Psychological Association, Washington, DC.

Douglas, M. A. (1985). The role of power in feminist therapy: A reformulation. In L. B. Rosewater & L. E. A. Walker (Eds.), *Handbook of feminist therapy: Women's issues in psychotherapy* (pp. 241-249). New York: Springer.

Duran, A. (1990). Cross-gender supervision problems: Reality, social fictions or unconscious processes? In R. C. Lane (Ed.), *Psychoanalytic approaches to supervision* (pp. 128-131). New York: Brunner/Mazel.

Dutton, D. G. (1986). The outcome of court-mandated treatment for wife assault: A quasi-experimental evaluation. *Violence and Victims, 1,* 163-175.

Dutton, D. G. (1987). The criminal justice response to wife assault. *Law and Human Behavior, 2,* 189-206.

Dutton, D. G. (1988a). *The domestic assault of women: Psychological and criminal justice perspective.* Boston: Allyn & Bacon.

Dutton, D. G. (1988b). Profiling of wife assaulters: Preliminary evidence for a trimodal analysis. *Violence and Victims, 3,* 5-30.

Dutton, D. G., & Painter, S. L. (1981). Traumatic bonding: The development of emotional attachments in battered women and other relationships of intermittent abuse. *Victimology, 6,* 139-155.

Dutton, M. A. (in press). *Healing the trauma of woman battering: Assessment and intervention.* New York: Springer.

Dutton-Douglas, M. A., & Walker, L. E. A. (Eds.). (1988). *Feminist psychotherapies: An integration of feminist and therapeutic systems.* Norwood, NJ: Ablex.

Dutton, M. A., Chrestman, K. R., & Gold, S. (1991). *Comparison of traumatic effects across trauma groups.* Paper submitted for the poster session of the Seventh Annual Meeting of the International Society for Traumatic Stress Studies, Washington, DC.

Edleson, J. L., Eisikovits, Z. C., & Guttman, E. (1985). Men who batter women: A critical review of the evidence. *Journal of Family Issues, 6,* 229-247.

Edleson, J. L., & Grusznski, R. (1988). Treating men who batter: Four years of outcome data from the Domestic Abuse Project. *Journal of Social Service Research, 12,* 3-22.

Edleson, J. L., & Syers, M. (1990). The relative effectiveness of group treatments for men who batter. *Social Work Research and Abstracts, 26,* 10-17.

Edleson, J. L., Syers, M., & Brygger, M. P. (1987, July). *Comparative effectiveness of group treatment for men who batter.* Paper presented at the Third National Conference for Family Violence Researchers, Durham, NH.

Egeland, B., Jacobvitz, D., & Sroufe, L. A. (1988). Breaking the cycle of abuse: Relationship predictors. *Child Development, 59,* 1080-1088.

Eisikovits, Z. C., & Edleson, J. L. (1989). Intervening with men who batter: A critical review of the literature. *Social Service Review, 37,* 385-414.

Elliott, P. (1990). Introduction. In P. Elliott (Ed.), *Confronting lesbian battering.* St. Paul: Minnesota Coalition for Battered Women.

Ellis, D. (1987). Post-separation woman abuse: The contribution of lawyers as "barracudas," "advocates" and "counselors." *International Journal of Law and Psychiatry, 10,* 403ff.

Ellis, D. (1989). Marital conflict mediation and postseparation wife abuse. *Law and Inequality, 8,* 317-339.

Ellis, D., & Wight-Peasley, L. (1986). *Wife abuse among separated women: The impact of lawyering styles.* Paper presented at the meeting of the International Association for the Study of Aggression, Chicago.

Emery, R. (1982). Interparental conflict and the children of discord and divorce. *Psychological Bulletin, 92,* 310-330.

Eron, L. D. (1987). The development of aggressive behavior from the perspective of a developing behaviorism. *American Psychologist, 42,* 435-442.

Everett, F., Proctor, N., & Cartmell, B. (1983). Providing psychological services to American Indian children and families. *Professional Psychology: Research and Practice, 14,* 588-603.

Ewing, C. (1987). *Battered women who kill.* Lexington, MA: Lexington.

Fagan, J. (1989). Cessation of family violence: Deterrence and dissuasion. In L. Ohlin & M. Tonry (Eds.), *Family violence.* Chicago: University of Chicago Press.

Falicov, C. (1982). Mexican families. In M. McGoldrick, J. K. Pearce, & J. Giordano (Eds.), *Ethnicity and family therapy* (pp. 134-163). New York: Guilford.

Fantuzzo, J. W., DePaola, L. M., Lambert, L., Martino, T., Anderson, G., & Sutton, S. (1991). Effects of interparental violence on the psychological adjustment and competencies of young children. *Journal of Consulting and Clinical Psychology, 59,* 1-8.

Fantuzzo, J. W., & Lindquist, C. U. (1989). The effects of observing conjugal violence on children: A review and analysis of research methodology. *Journal of Family Violence, 4,* 77-94.

Farrington, K. M. (1980). Stress and family violence. In M. A. Straus & G. T. Hotaling (Eds.), *The social causes of husband-wife violence* (pp. 94-114). Minneapolis: University of Minnesota Press.

Faunce, P. A. (1985). A feminist philosophy of treatment. In L. B. Rosewater & L. E. A. Walker (Eds.), *Handbook of feminist therapy: Women's issues in psychotherapy* (pp. 1-4). New York: Springer.

Feazell, C. S., Mayers, R., & Deschner, J. (1984). Services for men who batter: Implications for programs and policies. *Family Relations, 33,* 217-223.

Feldman, S. E. (1983). Battered women: Psychological correlates of the victimization process. *Dissertation Abstracts International, 44,* 1221-B.

Ferrant, S. (1992). *Cognitive processing in battered women: Identification of and relationship to severity of violence.* Unpublished doctoral dissertation, Fielding Institute, CA.

Ferraro, K. J., & Johnson, J. M. (1983). How women experience battering: The process of victimization. *Social Problems, 30,* 325-339.

Fields, M. D. (1978a). *Battered women: Issues of public policy* (Statement to the U.S. Commission on Civil Rights). Washington, DC: U.S. Commission on Civil Rights.

Fields, M. D. (1978b). Does this vow include wife beating? *Human Rights, 7,* 40-45.

Finesmith. (1983). Police response to battered women: A critique and proposal for reform. *Seton Hall Law Review, 14,* 74ff.

Finkelhor, D., Gelles, R. J., Hotaling, G. T., & Straus, M. A. (Eds.). (1983). *The dark side of families: Current family violence research.* Beverly Hills, CA: Sage.

Finkelhor, D., Hotaling, G. T., & Sedlak, A. (1990). *Missing, abducted, runaway, and thrownaway children in America: National incidence study.* Washington, DC: Office of Juvenile Justice and Delinquency Prevention.

Finkelhor, D., Hotaling, G. T., & Yllö, K. (1988). *Stopping family violence: Research priorities for the coming decade.* Newbury Park, CA: Sage.

Finn, P., & Colson, S. (1990). *Civil protection orders: Legislation, current court practice, and enforcement.* Washington, DC: National Institute of Justice.

Fiora-Gormally, N. (1978). Battered women who kill: Double standard out of court, single standard in? *Law and Human Behavior, 2,* 133-165.

FireThunder, C. (1991). *Empowering communities to address violence: The role of mental health providers and educators.* Paper presented at the Fifth Annual Multicultural Mental Health Conference on Families and Children: The Different Faces of Violence, University of New Mexico School of Medicine, Albuquerque.

Fiske, S., & Taylor, S. E. (1984). *Social cognition.* Reading, MA: Addison-Wesley.

Fleming, J. B. (1979). *Stopping wife abuse: A guide to the emotional, psychological, and legal implications for the abused woman and those helping her.* Garden City, NY: Anchor.

Flemons, D. G. (1989). An ecosystemic view of family violence. *Family Therapy, 16,* 1-10.

Follingstad, D. R., Neckerman, A. P., & Vormbrock, J. (1988). Reactions to victimization and coping strategies of battered women: The ties that bind. *Clinical Psychology Review, 8,* 373-390.

Fortune, M. (1981). *Family violence: A workshop manual for clergy and other service providers.* Rockville, MD: National Clearinghouse on Domestic Violence.

Freud, S. (1964). An outline of psychoanalysis. In J. Strachey (Ed.), *The standard edition of the complete psychological works of Sigmund Freud* (Vol. 23). London: Hogarth. (Original work published 1940)

Frieze, I. H. (1979). Perceptions of battered wives. In I. H. Frieze, D. Bar-Tal, & J. S. Carroll (Eds.), *New approaches to social problems: Applications of attribution theory.* San Francisco: Jossey-Bass.

Frieze, I. H. (1987). The female victim: Rape, wife-beating, and incest. In G. VandenBos & B. Bryant (Eds.), *Cataclysms, crises, and catastrophes: Psychology in action.* Washington, DC: American Psychological Association.

Frieze, I. H., & Knoble, J. (1980, September). *The effects of alcohol on marital violence.* Paper presented at the annual meeting of the American Psychological Association, Montreal.

Frieze, I. H., Knoble, J., Washburn, C., & Zomnir, G. (1980). *Types of battered women.* Paper presented at the meeting of the Association for Women in Psychology, Santa Monica, CA.

Frieze, I. H., & McHugh, M. C. (in press). Power and influence strategies in violent and nonviolent marriages. *Psychology of Women Quarterly.*

Frieze, I. H., Parsons, J. E., Johnson, P. B., Ruble, D. N., & Zellman, G. L. (1978). *Women and sex roles: A social psychological perspective.* New York: W. W. Norton.

Fromm-Reichman, F. (1948). Notes on the development of treatment of schizophrenics by psychoanalytic psychotherapy. *Psychiatry, 11,* 263-273.

Ganley, A. L. (1981). *Court-mandated counseling for men who batter: A three-day workshop for mental health professionals* (Participants' manual). Washington, DC: Center for Women's Policy Studies.

Ganley, A. L. (1987). Perpetrators of domestic violence: An overview of counseling the court-mandated client. In D. J. Sonkin (Ed.), *Domestic violence on trial: Psychological and legal dimensions of family violence* (pp. 155-173). New York: Springer.

Ganley, A. L. (1990). Feminist therapy with male clients. *Journal of Feminist Family Therapy, 2,* 1-23.

Gaquin, D. A. (1977-1978). Spouse abuse: Data from the National Crime Survey. *Victimology, 2,* 632-642.

Garbarino, J. (1990, August). *What children can tell us about living in danger.* Paper presented at the annual meeting of the American Psychological Association, Boston.

Garbarino, J., Dubrow, N., Kostelny, K., & Pardo, C. (1992). *Children in danger: Coping with the consequences of community violence.* San Francisco: Jossey-Bass.

Gardner, R. A. (1989). *The parental alienation syndrome and the differentiation between fabricated and genuine child sex abuse.* Cresskill, NJ: Creative Therapeutics.

Gayford, J. J. (1975). Wife battering: A preliminary survey of 100 cases. *British Medical Journal, 1,* 194-197.

Gayford, J. J. (1978). Battered wives. In J. P. Martin (Ed.), *Violence and the family.* New York: John Wiley.

Geffner, R. (1990). Family abuse and ethical issues, *Family Violence Bulletin, 6*(4), 1.

Geller, J. A., & Wasserstrom, J. (1984). Conjoint therapy for the treatment of domestic violence. In A. R. Roberts (Ed.), *Battered women and their families: Intervention strategies and treatment programs* (pp. 383-348). New York: Springer.

Gelles, R. J. (1974). *The violent home: A study of physical aggression between husbands and wives.* Beverly Hills, CA: Sage.

Gelles, R. J. (1979). *Family violence.* Beverly Hills, CA: Sage.

Gelles, R. J. (1980). Violence in the family: A review of research in the seventies. *Journal of Marriage and the Family, 42,* 873-885.

Gelles, R. J., & Straus, M. R. (1989). *Intimate violence: The causes and consequences of abuse in the American family.* New York: Simon & Schuster.

Gentemann, K. M. (1984). Wife beating: Attitudes of a non-clinical population. *Victimology, 9,* 109-119.

Gentry, C. E., & Eaddy, V. B. (1982). Treatment of children in spouse abusive families. *Victimology, 7,* 240-250.

Giles-Sims, J. (1983). *Wife battering: A systems theory approach.* New York: Guilford.

Gillespie, C. K. (1989). *Justifiable homicide.* Columbus: Ohio State University Press.

Gillespie, D. (1971). Who has the power? The marital struggle. *Journal of Marriage and the Family, 33,* 445-458.

Gilligan, C. (1982). *In a different voice: Psychological theory and women's development.* Cambridge, MA: Harvard University Press.

Goldner, V. (1985a). Feminism and family therapy. *Family Process, 24,* 31-47.

Goldner, V. (1985b). Warning: Family therapy may be hazardous to your health. *Family Therapy Networker, 9*(6), 19-23.

Goldner, V. (1992). Making room for both/and. *Family Therapy Networker, 16*(2), 54-61.

Goldner, V., Penn, P., Sheinberg, M., & Walker, G. (1990). Love and violence: Gender paradoxes in volatile attachments. *Family Process, 29,* 343-364.

Goldstein, R. K., & Page, A. W. (1981). Battered wife syndrome: Overview of dynamics and treatment, *American Journal of Psychiatry, 138,* 1036-1044.

Gondolf, E. W. (1985a). Anger and oppression in men who batter: Empiricist and feminist perspectives and their implications for research. *Victimology, 10,* 311-324.

Gondolf, E. W. (1985b). *Men who batter: An integrated approach for stopping wife abuse.* Holmes Beach, FL: Learning Publications.

Gondolf, E. W. (1987a). Changing men who batter: A developmental model of integrated interventions. *Journal of Family Violence, 2,* 345-369.

Gondolf, E. W. (1987b). Evaluating programs for men who batter: Problems and prospects. *Journal of Family Violence, 2,* 95-108.

Gondolf, E. W. (1987c). Seeing through smoke and mirrors: A guide to batterer program evaluations. *Response to Victimization of Women and Children, 10,* 16-19.

Gondolf, E. W. (1988a). The effect of batterer counseling on shelter outcome. *Journal of Interpersonal Violence, 3,* 275-289.

Gondolf, E. W. (1988b). The state of the debate: A review essay on woman battering. *Response to Victimization of Women and Children, 11*, 3-8.

Gondolf, E. W. (1988c). Who are those guys? Towards a behavioral typology of men who batter. *Violence and Victims, 3*, 187-203.

Gondolf, E. W. (1990a). An exploratory survey of court-mandated batterer programs. *Response to Victimization of Women and Children, 13*(3), 7-11.

Gondolf, E. W. (1990b). *Psychiatric response to family violence: Identifying and confronting neglected danger.* Lexington, MA: Lexington.

Gondolf, E. W. (1991). A victim-based assessment of court-mandated counseling for batterers. *Criminal Justice Review, 16*, 214-226.

Gondolf, E. W., & Fisher, E. R. (1988). *Battered women as survivors: An alternative to treating learned helplessness.* Lexington, MA: Lexington.

Gondolf, E. W., Fisher, E. R., & McFerron, J. R. (1988). Racial differences among shelter residents: A comparison of Anglo, Black and Hispanic battered women. *Journal of Family Violence, 3*, 39-51.

Gondolf, E. W., & Foster, R. A. (1990). Wife assault among V.A. alcohol rehabilitation patients. *Hospital and Community Psychiatry, 21*, 17-79.

Gondolf, E. W., & Foster, R. A. (1991). Preprogram attrition in batterer programs. *Journal of Family Violence, 6*, 337-349.

Gondolf, E. W., & Russell, D. E. H. (1986). The case against anger control for treatment programs for batterers. *Response to Victimization of Women and Children, 9*(3), 2-5.

Goode, W. J. (1971). Force and violence in the family. *Journal of Marriage and the Family, 33*, 624-636.

Goodman, E. (1989, May 23). Curtains for the "bitch-deserved-it" defense. *Boston Globe.*

Goodman, G. S., Bottoms, B. L., Herscovici, B. B., & Shaver, P. (1989). Determinants of the child victim's perceived credibility. In S. J. Ceci, D. F. Ross, & M. P. Toglia (Eds.), *Perspectives on the child witness.* New York: Springer-Verlag.

Goodman, M. S. (1990). Pattern changing: An approach to the abused woman's problem. *Family Violence Bulletin, 6*(4), 14-15.

Goodrich, T. J. (Ed.). (1991). *Women and power: Perspectives for family therapy.* New York: W. W. Norton.

Goodrich, T. J., Rampage, C., Ellman, B., & Halstead, K. (1985). Feminism: Shedding new light on the family. *Family Therapy Networker, 9*(6).

Goodstein, R. K., & Page, A. W. (1981). Battered wife syndrome: Overview of dynamics and treatment. *American Journal of Psychiatry, 138*, 1036-1044.

Goodwin, B. J. (1990, August). *Training therapists to recognize family violence.* Paper presented at the annual meeting of the American Psychological Association, Boston.

Goodwin, B. J. (1991, March). *Victims and violence: Some of us are still silent and black and blue.* Paper presented at the midwinter meeting of the National Council of Schools of Professional Psychology, Tucson, AZ.

Goodwin, B. J., & McHugh, M. C. (1990). *Termination terrorism.* Panel presented at the meeting of the Association for Women in Psychology, Tempe, AZ.

Goodwin, B. J., & McHugh, M. C. (1991). The battered woman: Theoretical, empirical, and clinical considerations. In *Proceedings of the National Council of Schools of Professional Psychology.* Washington, DC: National Council of Schools of Professional Psychology.

Goolkasian, G. A. (1986). *Confronting domestic violence: A guide for criminal justice agencies.* Washington, DC: U.S. Department of Justice, National Institute of Justice.

Graham, D. L. R., Rawlings, E., & Rimini, N. (1988). Survivors of terror: Battered women, hostages, and the Stockholm syndrome. In K. Yllö & M. Bograd (Eds.), *Feminist perspectives on wife abuse* (pp. 217-233). Newbury Park, CA: Sage.

Green, A. H. (1986). True and false allegations of sexual abuse in child custody disputes. *Journal of the American Academy of Child Psychiatry, 25,* 449-456.

Grusznski, R. J., Brink, J. C., & Edleson, J. L. (1988). Support and education groups for children of battered women. *Child Welfare, 67,* 431-444.

Grusznski, R. J., & Carrillo, T. P. (1988). Who completes batterer's treatment groups? An empirical investigation. *Journal of Family Violence, 3,* 141-150.

Halle, P. M., Burghardt, K. J., Dutton, M. A., & Perrin, S. (1991, August). *The effects of sexual abuse on women in battering relationships.* Paper submitted for the student poster session at the annual meeting of the American Psychological Association, San Francisco.

Hamberger, L. K., & Hastings, J. E. (1986). Personality correlates of men who abuse their partners: A cross-validation study. *Journal of Family Violence, 1,* 37-49.

Hamberger, L. K., & Hastings, J. E. (1988). Skills training for treatment of spouse abusers: An outcome study. *Journal of Family Violence, 3,* 121-130.

Hamberger, L. K., & Hastings, J. E. (1989). Counseling male spouse abusers: Characteristics of treatment completers and dropouts. *Violence and Victims, 4,* 275-286.

Hamberger, L. K., & Hastings, J. E. (1991). Personality correlates of men who batter and nonviolent men: Some continuities and discontinuities. *Journal of Family Violence, 6,* 131-148.

Hammond, N. (1989). Lesbian victims of relationship violence. *Women and Therapy, 8,* 89-105.

Hanks, S. E., & Rosenbaum, C. P. (1977). Battered women: A study of women who live with violent alcohol-abusing men. *American Journal of Orthopsychiatry, 47,* 291-306.

Hansen, M., Harway, M., & Cervantes, N. (1990). *Curtains for "the bitch deserved it" defense.* Paper presented at the midwinter meeting of the Division of Family Therapy, American Psychological Association.

Hansen, M., Harway, M., & Cervantes, N. (1991). Therapists' perceptions of severity in cases of family violence. *Violence and Victims, 6,* 225-235.

Hare-Mustin, R. T. (1978). A feminist approach to family therapy. *Family Process, 17,* 181-194.

Harlow, H., & Harlow, M. (1971). Psychopathology in monkeys. In H. D. Kimmel (Ed.), *Experimental psychopathology* (pp. 203-229). New York: Academic Press.

Hart, B. (1986a). Lesbian battering: An examination. In R. Lobel (Ed.), *Naming the violence* (pp. 173-189). Seattle, WA: Seal.

Hart, B. (1986b). Preface. In K. Lobel (Ed.), *Naming the violence* (pp. 9-16). Seattle, WA: Seal.

Hart, B. (1988a). Beyond the "duty to warn": A therapist's "duty to protect" battered women and children. In K. Yllö & M. Bograd (Eds.), *Feminist perspectives on wife abuse* (pp. 234-248). Newbury Park, CA: Sage.

Hart, B. (1988b). *Safety for women: Monitoring batterers' programs.* Harrisburg: Pennsylvania Coalition Against Domestic Violence.

Hart, B. (1990a). Gentle jeopardy. *Mediation Quarterly, 7*(4), 317-330.

Hart, B. (1990b). *Violent no more: Intervention against wife abuse in Ohio.* Columbus: Ohio Domestic Violence Network.

Hart, B. (1991a). *Clippings research on domestic homicide in Pennsylvania, 1990-91.* Harrisburg: Pennsylvania Coalition Against Domestic Violence.

Hart, B. (1991b). *Costs of domestic violence.* Harrisburg: Pennsylvania Coalition Against Domestic Violence.

Hart, B. (1991c). Safety planning for children: Strategizing for unsupervised visits with batterers. In B. Hart (Ed.), *Battering and addiction: Consciousness-raising for battered women and advocates* (pp. 24-33). Harrisburg: Pennsylvania Coalition Against Domestic Violence IV.

Hart, B., Stubbling, E., & Stuehling, J. (1990). *Confronting domestic violence: Effective police response.* Harrisburg: Pennsylvania Coalition Against Domestic Violence.

Hartnett, O., & Bradley, J. (1987). Sex roles and work. In D. Hargreaves & A. Colley (Eds.), *The psychology of sex roles* (pp. 215-232). Cambridge: Hemisphere.
Harway, M., & Hansen, M. (1990a, August). *Family violence: Issues of concern in therapeutic practice.* Paper presented at the annual meeting of the American Psychological Association, Boston.
Harway, M., & Hansen, M. (1990b). Therapists' recognition of wife battering: Some empirical evidence. *Family Violence Bulletin, 6*(3), 16-18.
Harway, M., Hansen, M., & Cervantes, N. (in press). Therapist awareness of appropriate intervention in treatment of domestic violence. In R. Geffner (Ed.), *Research and treatment in family violence: Practical implications.* Binghamton, NY: Haworth.
Heilbrun, C. G. (1988). *Writing a woman's life.* New York: Random House.
Hendricks-Matthews, M. (1982). The battered woman: Is she ready for help? *Social Casework, 63,* 131-137.
Henninger, T. (1986, March). The American family. *Harrisburg Area Women's News.*
Herrell, S. B., & Hofford, M. (1990). *Family violence: Improving court practice.* Reno, NV: National Council of Juvenile and Family Court Judges.
Hetherington, E. M. (1979). Divorce: A child's perspective. *American Psychologist, 34,* 851-858.
Hilberman, E. (1980). Overview: The "wife-beater's wife" reconsidered. *American Journal of Psychiatry, 137,* 1336-1347.
Hilberman, E., & Munson, K. (1977-1978). Sixty battered women. *Victimology, 2,* 460-471.
Hilton, N. Z. (1989). One in ten: The struggle and disempowerment of the battered women's movement. *Canadian Journal of Family Law, 7,* 313-335.
Hinchey, F. S., & Gavalek, J. R. (1982). Empathic responding in children of battered mothers. *Child Abuse and Neglect, 6,* 395-401.
Hines, P. M. (1989). The family life cycle of poor black families. In B. Carter & M. McGoldrick (Eds.), *The changing family life cycle: A framework for family therapy* (2nd ed., pp. 513-544). Needham, MA: Allyn & Bacon.
Hjelle, L. A., & Ziegler, D. J. (1992). *Personality theories: Basic assumptions, research, and applications* (3rd ed.). New York: McGraw-Hill.
Hoagland, S. L. (1988). *Lesbian ethics: Toward new value.* Palo Alto, CA: Institute of Lesbian Studies.
Hoffman, J. (1992, February 2). When men hit women. *New York Times Magazine,* pp. 23-27, 64-66, 72.
Hoffman, L. W. (1981). *Foundations of family therapy.* New York: Basic Books.
Hoffman, L. W. (1990). *Old scapes, new maps: A training program for psychotherapy supervisors.* Cambridge, MA: Milusik.
Hornstein, S. J. (1985). Domestic violence by and against women: An interview about lesbian violence. *Western Center of Domestic Violence Review, 10,* 3-11.
Hornung, C. A., McCullough, B. C., & Sugimoto, T. (1981). Status relationships in marriage: Risk factors in spouse abuse. *Journal of Marriage and the Family, 43,* 675-692.
Hotaling, G. T., & Sugarman, D. B. (1986). An analysis of risk markers in husband to wife violence: The current state of knowledge. *Violence and Victims, 1,* 101-124.
Hudson, P. S. (1984). The crime victim and the criminal justice system: Time for a change. *Pepperdine Law Review, 11,* 23-62.
Hughes v. Hughes, 463 A.2d 478 (1983).
Hughes, H. M. (1982). Brief interventions with children in a battered women's shelter: A model preventive program. *Family Relations, 31,* 495-502.
Hughes, H. M. (1986). Research with children in shelters: Implications for clinical services. *Children Today, 15*(2), 21-25.

Hughes, H. M. (1988). Psychological and behavioral correlates of family violence in child witnesses and victims. *American Journal of Orthopsychiatry, 18,* 77-90.

Hughes, H. M., Parkinson, D., & Vargo, M. (1989). Witnessing spouse abuse and experiencing physical abuse: A "double whammy"? *Journal of Family Violence, 4,* 197-209.

Hutchinson, E. D. (1987). Use of authority in direct social work practice with mandated clients. *Social Service Review, 37,* 580-598.

Jacob, T. (1975). Family interaction in disturbed and normal families: A methodological and substantive review. *Psychological Bulletin, 82,* 35-65.

Jaffe, P. G., Wolfe, D. A., & Wilson, S. K. (1990). *Children of battered women: Issues in child development and intervention planning.* Newbury Park, CA: Sage.

Jaffe, P. G., Wolfe, D. A., Telford, A., & Austin, G. (1986). The impact of police charges in incidents of wife abuse. *Journal of Family Violence, 1*(1).

James, K., & McIntyre, D. (1983). The reproduction of families: The social role of family therapy? *Journal of Marital and Family Therapy, 9,* 119-129.

James, K., & McIntyre, D. (1989). "A momentary gleam of enlightenment": Towards a model of feminist family therapy. *Journal of Feminist Family Therapy, 1,* 3-24.

Janoff-Bulman, R., & Frieze, I. H. (1983). A theoretical perspective for understanding reactions to victimization. *Journal of Social Issues, 39,* 1-17.

Jenkins, A. (1990). *Invitations to responsibility.* Adelaide, SA, Australia: Dulwich Centre Publications.

Jones, A. (1981). *Women who kill.* New York: Holt, Rinehart & Winston.

Jones, J. M. (1988). Racism in black and white: A bicultural model of reaction and evolution. In P. A. Katz & D. A. Taylor (Eds.), *Eliminating racism: Profiles in controversy* (pp. 117-136). New York: Plenum.

Judicial Council Advisory Committee on Gender Bias in the Courts. (1990). *Achieving equal justice for women and men in the courts.* Sacramento, CA: Author.

Kagan, J. (1989). *Unstable ideas: Temperament, cognition, and self.* Cambridge, MA: Harvard University Press.

Kalmuss, D. S. (1984). The intergenerational transmission of marital aggression. *Journal of Marriage and the Family, 46,* 11-19.

Kalmuss, D. S., & Seltzer, J. A. (1986). Continuity of marital behavior in remarriage: Case of spouse abuse. *Journal of Marriage and the Family, 48,* 113-120.

Kanuha, V. (1990). Compounding the triple jeopardy: Battering in lesbians of color relationships. *Women and Therapy, 9,* 169-184.

Kass, F., Spitzer, R. L., Williams, J. B., & Widiger, T. (1989). Self-defeating personality disorder and DSM III R: Development of diagnostic criteria. *American Journal of Psychiatry, 146,* 1022-1026.

Kaufman, E., & Kaufman, P. N. (1979). *Family therapy of drug and alcohol abuse.* New York: Gardner.

Kaufman, J., & Zigler, E. (1987). Do abused children become abusive parents? *American Journal of Orthopsychiatry, 57,* 186-192.

Keen, S. (1991). *Fire in the belly: On being a man.* New York: Bantam.

Keller, M. (Ed.). (1974). Trends in treatment of alcoholism. In *Second special report to the U.S. Congress on alcohol and health* (pp. 145-167). Washington, DC: U.S. Department of Health, Education and Welfare.

Kelly, E. E., & Warshafsky, L. (1987, July). *Partner abuse in gay male and lesbian couples.* Paper presented at the Third National Conference for Family Violence Researchers, Durham, NH.

Kelly, J. B., & Wallerstein, J. S. (1982). *Surviving the breakup: How parents and children cope with divorce.* New York: Basic Books.

Kelly, L. (1988). How women define their experiences of violence. In K. Yllö & M. Bograd (Eds.), *Feminist perspectives on wife abuse* (pp. 114-132). Newbury Park, CA: Sage.

Kim, S. C. (1985). Family therapy for Asian Americans: A strategic-structural framework. *Psychotherapy, 22,* 342-348.

Kimmel v. Kimmel, 392 N.W.2d 904 (1986).

Klein, D. (1992, February 9). "Domestic" violence isn't tame—it's wild, ugly crime. *Los Angeles Times,* Sect. E, p. 1.

Koestner, R., Weinberger, J., & Franz, C. (1990). The family origins of empathic concern: A 26-year longitudinal study. *Journal of Personality and Social Psychology, 58,* 709-717.

Koop, C. E. (1989, January 3). [Comments to the American College of Obstetricians and Gynecologists].

Koss, M. P. (1990). The women's mental health research agenda: Violence against women. *American Psychologist, 45,* 374-380.

Koss, M. P., & Dinero, T. E. (1988). Predictors of sexual aggression among a national sample of male college students. In R. A. Prentky & V. L. Quinsey (Eds.), Human sexual aggression: Current perspectives [Special issue]. *Annals of the New York Academy of Sciences, 528,* 133-146.

Krestan, J. (1991). The baby and the bathwater. In T. J. Goodrich (Ed.), *Women and power: Perspectives for family therapy* (pp. 229-233). New York: W. W. Norton.

Krestan, J., & Bepko, C. S. (1980). The problem of fusion in the lesbian relationship. *Family Process, 19,* 277-289.

Kurz, D. (1987). Emergency department responses to battered women: Resistance to medicalization. *Social Problems, 34,* 69-81.

Kurz, D., & Coughey, K. (1989, August 9). *The effects of marital violence on the divorce process.* Paper presented at the annual meeting of the American Sociological Association.

Lamb, S. (1991). Acts without agents: An analysis of linguistic avoidance in journal articles on men who batter women. *American Journal of Orthopsychiatry, 61,* 250-257.

Leeder, E. (1988). Enmeshed in pain: Counseling the lesbian battering couple. *Women & Therapy, 1,* 81-99.

Lefcourt, C. (1989). Mediation. In C. Lefcourt (Ed.), *Women and the law* (p. 7A, 2-44). New York: Clark Boardman.

Lentzer, H. R. (1980). *Intimate victims: A study of violence among friends and relatives.* Washington, DC: U.S. Department of Justice, Bureau of Justice Standards.

Leonard, K., & Jacob, T. (1988). Alcohol, alcoholism, and family violence. In V. B. Van Hasselt, R. L. Morrison, A. S. Bellack, & M. Hersen (Eds.), *Handbook of family violence* (p. 389). New York: Plenum.

Lerman, L. G., & Livingston, F. (1983, September/October). State legislation on domestic violence. *Response to Victimization of Women and Children, 6.*

Lerner, H. (1984). Female dependency in context: Some theoretical and technical considerations. In P. Rieker & E. Carmen (Hilberman) (Eds.), *The gender gap in psychotherapy: Social realities and psychological processes.* New York: Plenum.

Lerner, H. (1985a). *The dance of anger.* New York: Harper.

Lerner, H. (1985b). Putting feminism into practice: 5 case studies. *Family Therapy Networker, 9*(6), 36-39.

Leslie, R. S. (1990, March-April). The dangerous patient: Tarasoff revisited. *California Therapist,* pp. 11-14.

Leventhal, B. (1990). Considerations in starting a support group for battered lesbians. In P. Elliott (Ed.), *Confronting lesbian battering* (pp. 81-87). St. Paul: Minnesota Coalition for Battered Women.

Lewis, D. O., Shanok, S. S., Pincus, J. H., & Glaser, G. H. (1979). Violent juvenile delinquents: Psychiatric, neurological, psychological, and abuse factors. *Journal of the American Academy of Child Psychiatry, 18,* 307-319.

Lie, G., & Gentlewarrior, S. (1991). Intimate violence in lesbian relationships: Discussion of survey findings and practice implications. *Journal of Social Service Research, 15,* 41-49.

Lindenbaum, J. P. (1985). The shattering of an illusion: The problem of competition in lesbian relationships. *Feminist studies, 11,* 85-103.

Lopez, S. R., Grover, K. P., Holland, D., Johnson, M. J., Kain, C. D., Kanel, K., Mellins, C. A., & Rhyne, M. C. (1989). Development of culturally sensitive psychotherapists. *Professional Psychology: Research and Practice, 20,* 369-376.

Loseke, D. R., & Cahill, S. E. (1984). The social construction of deviance: Experts on battered women. *Social Problems, 31,* 296-310.

Loulan, J. (1988). Research on the sex practices of 1566 lesbians and the clinical applications. In E. Cole & E. D. Rothblum (Eds.), *Women and sex therapy.* New York: Haworth.

Luepnitz, D. A. (1988). *The family interpreted: Feminist theory in clinical practice.* New York: Basic Books.

Lynch, C. G., & Norris, T. L. (1977-1978). Services for battered women: Looking for a perspective. *Victimology, 2,* 553-562.

Maccoby, E. E. (1990). Gender and relationships: A developmental account. *American Psychologist, 45,* 513-520.

Maccoby, E. E., & Jacklin, J. A. (1974). *The psychology of sex differences.* Stanford, CA: Stanford University Press.

MacKinnon, L. K., & Miller, D. (1987). The new epistemology and the Milan approach: Feminist and sociopolitical considerations. *Journal of Marital and Family Therapy, 13,* 139-155.

Madanes, C. (1990). *Sex, love, and violence.* New York: W. W. Norton.

Magill, J. (1989). Family therapy: An approach to the treatment of wife assault. In B. Pressman, G. Cameron, & M. Rothery (Eds.), *Intervening with assaulted women: Current theory, research, and practice* (pp. 47-56). Hillsdale, NJ: Lawrence Erlbaum.

Main, M., & George, C. (1985). Response of abused and disadvantaged toddlers to distress in agemates: A study in the day care setting. *Developmental Psychology, 21,* 407-412.

Makepeace, J. M. (1983). Life events stress and courtship violence. *Family Relations, 32,* 101-109.

Marecek, J., & Hare-Mustin, R. T. (1991). A short history of the future: Feminism and clinical psychology. *Psychology of Women Quarterly, 15,* 521-536.

Margolin, G. (1982). Ethical and legal considerations in marital and family therapy. *American Psychologist, 37,* 788-801.

Margolin, G. (1988). Interpersonal and intrapersonal factors associated with marital violence. In G. T. Hotaling, D. Finkelhor, J. T. Kirkpatrick, & M. A. Straus (Eds.). *Family abuse and its consequences: New directions in research* (pp. 203-217). Newbury Park, CA: Sage.

Marks, L. (1986). *Protecting confidentiality: A legal manual for battered women's programs.* New York: National Center on Women and Family Law.

Martin, D. (1976). *Battered wives.* San Francisco: Glide.

Masten, A. S., Best, K. M., & Garmezy, N. (1990). Resilience and development: Contributions from the study of children who overcome adversity. *Development and Psychopathology, 2,* 425-444.

McAndrew, R. (1985, April). Battering in lesbian relationships. *Labyrinth,* p. 5.

McGoldrick, M., Pearce, J. K., & Giordano, J. (Eds.). (1982). *Ethnicity and family therapy.* New York: Guilford.

McHugh, M. C. (1987, June). *Woman blaming.* Paper presented at the annual meeting of the National Women's Studies Association, Baltimore.
McHugh, M. C. (1990, August). *Gender issues in psychotherapy: Victim blame/woman blame.* Invited address presented at the annual meeting of the American Psychological Association, Boston.
McHugh, M. C., Frieze, I. H., & Browne, A. (1992). Research on battered women and their assailants. In M. Paludi & F. Denmark (Eds.), *Handbook on the psychology of women.* Westport, CT: Greenwood.
Meier, J. (1987, May). Battered justice. *Washington Monthly,* pp. 37-45.
Miller, E. T., & Porter, C. A. (1983). Self-blame in victims of violence. *Journal of Social Issues, 39,* 139-152.
Mills, M. J., Sullivan, G., & Eth, S. (1987). Protecting third parties: A decade after "Tarasoff." *American Journal of Psychiatry, 144,* 68-74.
Mills, T. (1985). The assault on the self: Stages in coping with battering husbands. *Qualitative Sociology, 8,* 103-123.
Mintz, J., Mintz, L., & Goldstein, M. (1987). Expressed emotion and relapse in first episodes of schizophrenia. *British Journal of Psychiatry, 151,* 314-320.
Minuchin, S. (1984). *Family kaleidoscope.* Cambridge, MA: Harvard University Press.
Minuchin, S., & Fishman, H. C. (1981). *Family therapy techniques.* Cambridge, MA: Harvard University Press.
Mio, J. S. (1989). Experiential involvement as an adjunct to teaching cultural sensitivity. *Journal of Multicultural Counseling and Development, 17,* 38-46.
Money, J., & Ehrhardt, A. A. (1972). *Man and woman, boy and girl: Differentiation and dimorphism of gender identity from conception to maturity.* Baltimore: Johns Hopkins University Press.
Moore, D. M. (Ed.). (1979). *Battered women.* Beverly Hills, CA: Sage.
Moore, R., & Gillette, D. (1990). *King, warrior, magician, lover: Rediscovering the archetypes of the mature masculine.* New York: HarperCollins.
Morrow, S. L., & Hawxhurst, D. M. (1989). Lesbian partner abuse: Implications for therapists. *Journal of Counseling and Development, 68,* 58-62.
Mowbray, C. T., Herman, S. E., & Hazel, K. L. (1992). Gender and serious mental illness. *Psychology of Women Quarterly, 16,* 107-126.
Mugford, J., Mugford, S., & Easteal, P. W. (1989). Social justice, public perceptions, and spouse assault in Australia. *Social Justice, 3,* 103-123.
Murillo, N. (1971). The Mexican American family. In N. W. Wagner & M. J. Hang (Eds.), *Chicanos: Social and psychological perspectives.* St. Louis: C. V. Mosby.
Myers, B. A. (1989). *Lesbian battering: An analysis of power, inequality and conflict in lesbian relationships.* Unpublished doctoral dissertation, Indiana University of Pennsylvania, Department of Psychology.
Myers, S., Gelles, G., Hanson, R., & Keilitz, S. (1988). Divorce mediation in the states: Institutionalization, use and assessment. *State Court Journal, 12*(4).
National Organization for Victim Assistance. (1987). Crime victim compensation. In *1987 NOVA legislative directory.* Washington, DC: Author.
Neidig, P. H., & Friedman, O. H. (1984). *Spouse abuse: A treatment program for couples.* Champaign, IL: Research Press.
New York Task Force on Women in the Courts. (1987). Report of the New York Task Force on Women in the Courts. *Fordham Urban Law Journal, 15*(1).
NiCarthy, G. (1982). *Getting free: A handbook for women in abusive relationships.* Seattle, WA: Seal.

Nichols, M. P., & Schwartz, R. C. (1991). *Family therapy: Concepts and methods.* Boston: Allyn & Bacon.

Nicoloff, L. K., & Stiglitz, E. A. (1987). Lesbian alcoholism: Etiology, treatment, and recovery. In Boston Lesbian Psychologies Collective (Ed.), *Lesbian psychologies* (pp. 283-293). Urbana: University of Illinois Press.

Nobles, W. (1980). African philosophy: Foundations for black psychology. In R. Jones (Ed.), *Black psychology* (2nd ed., pp. 53-70). New York: Harper & Row.

Ochberg, F. M. (1980). Victims of terrorism. *Journal of Clinical Psychiatry, 41,* 73-74.

Okun, B. F. (1992). *Effective helping: Interviewing and counseling techniques* (4th ed). Pacific Grove, CA: Brooks/Cole.

Okun, L. (1986). *Woman abuse: Facts replacing myths.* Albany: State University of New York Press.

O'Leary, K. D., Barling, J., Arias, I., Rosenbaum, A., Malone, J., & Tyree, A. (1989). Prevalence and stability of physical aggression between spouses: A longitudinal analysis. *Journal of Consulting and Clinical Psychology, 57,* 263-268.

Pagelow, M. D. (1981a). Factors affecting women's decision to leave violent relationships. *Journal of Family Issues, 2,* 391-414.

Pagelow, M. D. (1981b). *Woman-battering: Victims and their experiences.* Beverly Hills, CA: Sage.

Pagelow, M. D. (1989). *The forgotten victims: Children of domestic violence.* Paper prepared for presentation at the Domestic Violence Seminar of the Los Angeles County Domestic Violence Council.

Pagelow, M. D. (1990). Effects of domestic violence on children and their consequences for custody and visitation agreements. *Mediation Quarterly, 7*(4), 347-363.

Painter, S. L., & Dutton, D. (1985). Patterns of emotional bonding in battered women: Traumatic bonding. *International Journal of Women's Studies, 8,* 363-375.

Pantony, K., & Caplan, P. J. (1991). Delusional dominating personality disorder: A modest proposal for identifying some consequences of rigid masculine socialization. *Canadian Psychology, 32,* 120-133.

Pence, E. (1989). Batterer programs: Shifting from community collusion to community confrontation. In P. L. Caesar & L. K. Hamberger (Eds.), *Treating men who batter: Theory, practice, and programs* (pp. 24-50). New York: Springer.

Pence, E., Duprey, M., Paymar, M., & McDonnell, C. (1989). *The justice system's response to domestic assault cases: A guide for policy development.* Duluth: Minnesota Program Development.

Pence, E., & Paymar, M. (1986). *Power and control: Tactics of men who batter.* Duluth: Minnesota Program Development.

Perloff, L. S. (1983). Perceptions of vulnerability to victimization. *Journal of Social Issues, 39,* 41-62.

Pfouts, J. H. (1978). Violent families: Coping responses of abused wives. *Child Welfare, 57,* 101-111.

Pharr, S. (1986). Two workshops on homophobia. In K. Lobel (Ed.), *Naming the violence* (pp. 202-222). Seattle, WA: Seal.

Phillips, H. V. (1974). *Essentials of social group work skills.* New York: Association.

Pillemer, K. (1985). The dangers of dependency: New findings on domestic violence against the elderly. *Social Problems, 33,* 146-158.

Pinderhughes, E. (1989). *Understanding race, ethnicity and power.* New York: Free Press.

Pirog-Good, M., & Stets, J. (1985). Male batterers and battering prevention programs: A national survey. *Response to Victimization of Women and Children, 8,* 8-12.

Pirog-Good, M., & Stets, J. (1986). Programs for abusers: Who drops out and what can be done. *Response to Victimization of Women and Children, 9,* 17-19.

Pittman, F. S. (1987). *Turning points.* New York: W. W. Norton.

Pizzey, E. (1974). *Scream quietly or the neighbors will hear.* Short Hills: Ridley Enslow.

Pizzey, E. (1975). Chiswick Women's Aid: A refuge from violence. *Royal Society of Health Journal.*

Pope, K. S., & Vasquez, M. J. T. (1991). *Ethics in psychotherapy and counseling.* San Francisco: Jossey-Bass.

Porat, N. (1986). Support groups for battered lesbians. In K. Lobel (Ed.), *Naming the violence* (pp. 80-87). Seattle, WA: Seal.

Porter, N. (1985). New perspectives on therapy supervision. In L. B. Rosewater & L. E. A. Walker (Eds.), *Handbook of feminist therapy: Women's issues in psychotherapy* (pp. 332-343). New York: Springer.

Post, D. (1991). Protecting domestic violence shelters' records (with forms). *Practical Lawyer, 37*(1).

Pressman, B. (1989). Wife-abused couples: The need for comprehensive theoretical perspectives and integrated treatment models. *Journal of Feminist Family Therapy, 1,* 23-43.

Pressman, B., Cameron G., & Rothery, M. (Eds.). (1989). *Intervening with assaulted women: Current theory, research, and practice.* Hillsdale, NJ: Lawrence Erlbaum.

Ptacek, J. (1984, August). *The clinical literature on men who batter: A review and critique.* Paper presented at the Second National Conference for Family Violence Researchers, Durham, NH.

Ptacek, J. (1988). Why do men batter their wives? In K. Yllö & M. Bograd (Eds.), *Feminist perspectives on wife abuse* (pp. 133-157). Newbury Park, CA: Sage.

Ramirez, M., III. (1983). *Psychology of the Americas.* New York: Pergamon.

Ramirez, M., III. (1991). *Psychotherapy and counseling with minorities.* New York: Pergamon.

Ramirez, O. (1989). Mexican American children and adolescents. In J. T. Gibbs, L. N. Huang, & Associates, *Children of color: Psychological interventions with minority youth* (pp. 224-250). San Francisco: Jossey-Bass.

Renzetti, C. M. (1988). Violence in lesbian relationships: A preliminary analysis of causal factors. *Journal of Interpersonal Violence, 3,* 381-399.

Renzetti, C. M. (1989). Building a second closet: Third party responses to victims of lesbian partner abuse. *Family Relations, 38,* 157-163.

Renzetti, C. M. (1992). *Violent betrayal: Partner abuse in lesbian relationships.* Newbury Park, CA: Sage.

Rich, A. (1979). *On lies, secrets, and silence: Selected prose, 1966-1979.* New York: W. W. Norton.

Richardson, A. (1990). *The effects of the presence of female batterers on male batterers.* Unpublished master's paper, California Family Study Center, North Hollywood.

Richardson, D. C., & Campbell, J. L. (1980). Alcohol and wife abuse: The effects of alcohol on attributions of blame for wife abuse. *Personality and Social Psychology Bulletin, 6,* 51-56.

Riche, M. (1984). The systemic feminist. *Family Therapy Networker, 8,* 43-44.

Ridington, J. (1978). The transition process: A feminist environment as reconstructive milieu. *Victimology, 3,* 563-575.

Roberts, A. (Ed.). (1984). *Battered women and their families: Intervention strategies and treatment programs.* New York: Springer.

Roff, J. D., & Knight, R. (1981). Family characteristics of childhood symptoms, and adult outcome in schizophrenia. *Journal of Abnormal Psychology, 90,* 510-520.

Romero, M. (1985). A comparison between strategies used on prisoners of war and battered women. *Sex Roles, 13,* 537-547.

Root, M. P. P. (1992). Reconstructing the impact of trauma on personality. In L. S. Brown & M. S. Ballou (Eds.), *Personality and psychopathology: Feminist reappraisals* (pp. 229-265). New York: Guilford.

Rosenbaum, A., & O'Leary, K. D. (1981). Marital violence: Characteristics of abusive couples. *Journal of Consulting and Clinical Psychology, 49,* 63-71.

Rosenbaum, A., & O'Leary, K. D. (1986). The treatment of marital violence. In N. S. Jacobson & A. Gurman (Eds.), *Clinical handbook of marital therapy* (pp. 385-405). New York: Guilford.

Rosewater, L. B. (1985). Schizophrenic, borderline or battered? In L. B. Rosewater & L. E. A. Walker (Eds.), *Handbook of feminist therapy: Women's issues in psychotherapy* (pp. 215-225). New York: Springer.

Rosewater, L. B. (1987). A critical analysis of the proposed self-defeating personality disorder. *Journal of Personality Disorders, 1,* 190-195.

Rosewater, L. B., & Walker, L. E. A. (Eds.). (1985). *Handbook of feminist therapy: Women's issues in psychotherapy.* New York: Springer.

Rounsaville, B. (1978). Theories in marital violence: Evidence from a study of battered women. *Victimology, 3,* 11-31.

Roy, M. (1977). A current survey of 150 cases. In M. Roy (Ed.), *Battered women: A psychosocial study of domestic violence* (pp. 25-44). New York: Van Nostrand Reinhold.

Roy, M. (1982). *The abusive partner: An analysis of domestic battering.* New York: Van Nostrand Reinhold.

Rubin, L. (1979). *Women of a certain age: The midlife search for self.* New York: Harper & Row.

Rubin, L. (1983). *Intimate strangers: Men and women together.* San Francisco: Harper Colophon.

Russell, D. E. H. (1982). *Rape in marriage.* New York: Macmillan.

Russell, M. (1988). Wife assault theory, research and treatment: A literature review. *Journal of Family Violence, 3,* 193-208.

Rutter, M., & Giller, H. (1983). *Juvenile delinquency: Trends and perspectives.* New York: Guilford.

Sade, J. E., & Notarius, C. I. (1985). Emotional expression in marital and family relationships. In L. L'Abate (Ed.), *The handbook of family psychology and therapy* (pp. 378-401). Monterey, CA: Brooks/Cole.

Sanders v. Sanders. (1982). 420 So. 2d 790.

Saunders, D. G. (1977). Marital violence: Dimensions of the problem and modes of intervention. *Journal of Marriage and Family Counseling, 3*(1), 43-52.

Saunders, D. G. (1984). Helping husbands who batter. *Social Casework, 65,* 347-353.

Saunders, D. G., & Browne, A. (1990). Domestic homicide. In R. T. Ammerman & M. Herson (Eds.), *Case studies in family violence* (pp. 379-402). New York: Plenum.

Saunders, D. G., & Hanusa, D. R. (1984, August). *Cognitive behavioral treatment for abusive husbands: The short-term effects of group therapy.* Paper presented at the Second National Conference for Family Violence Researchers, Durham, NH.

Saunders, D. G., & Parker, J. C. (1989). Legal sanctions and treatment follow-through among men who batter: A multivariate analysis. *Social Work Research and Abstracts, 25,* 21-29.

Saunders, D. G., & Size, P. B. (1986). Attitudes about woman abuse among police officers, victims, and victim advocates. *Journal of Interpersonal Violence, 1,* 25-42.

Schaef, A. (1986). *Codependence: Misunderstood, mistreated.* New York: Harper & Row.

Schechter, S. (1982). *Women and male violence.* Boston: South End.

Schlesinger, A. M., Jr. (1992). *The disuniting of America: Reflections on a multicultural society.* New York: W. W. Norton.

Schneider, E. M. (1986). Describing and changing: Women's self-defense work and the problem of expert testimony on battering. *Women's Rights Law Reporter, 9,* 195-222.

Schur, E. M. (1984). *Labeling women deviant.* New York: Random House.

Schutte, N. S., Bouleige, L., Fix, J. L., & Malouff, J. M. (1986). Returning to a partner after leaving a crisis shelter: A decision faced by battered women. *Journal of Social Behavior and Personality, 1,* 295-298.

Schutte, N. S., Malouff, J. M., & Doyle, J. S. (1988). The relationship between characteristics of the victim, persuasive techniques of the batterer and returning to the battering relationship. *Journal of Social Psychology, 128,* 605-610.

Scott, J. P. (1963). The process of primary socialization in canine and human infants. *Monographs of the Society for Research in Child Development, 28*(1), 1-47.

Seagull, E. A., & Seagull, A. A. (1991). Healing the wound that must not heal: Psychotherapy with survivors of domestic violence. *Psychotherapy, 28,* 16-20.

Seligman, M. E. P. (1975). *Helplessness: On depression, development and death.* San Francisco: Freeman.

Selzer, M. L. (1971). The Michigan Alcoholism Screening Test: The quest for a new diagnostic instrument. *American Journal of Psychiatry, 127,* 1653-1658.

Shanley, K. (1989). Thoughts on Indian feminism. In S. Ware (Ed.), *Modern American women: A documentary history* (pp. 349-352). Belmont, CA: Wadsworth.

Sherman, L. W., & Berk, R. A. (1984). The specific deterrent effect of arrest for domestic assault. *American Sociological Review, 49,* 261-272.

Silverstein, L., & Taffel, R. (1991). *Feminist theory and family therapy: An empirical study.* Paper presented at the Twenty-second Annual Midwinter Meeting of the American Psychological Association, San Antonio, TX.

Skolnick, J. H., & Bayley, D. H. (1986). *The new blue line.* New York: Free Press.

Smith, A. J., & Siegel, R. F. (1985). Feminist therapy: Redefining power for the powerless. In L. B. Rosewater & L. E. A. Walker (Eds.), *Handbook of feminist therapy: Women's issues in psychotherapy* (pp. 13-21). New York: Springer.

Smith, S. (1984). The battered woman: A consequence of female development. *Women and Therapy, 3*(2), 3-10.

Snell, J., Rosenwald, R., & Robey, A. (1964). The wife-beater's wife: A study of family interaction. *Archives of General Psychiatry, 11,* 107-112.

Soler, E. (1987). Domestic violence is a crime: A case study of the San Francisco family violence project. In D. J. Sonkin (Ed.), *Domestic violence on trial: Psychological and legal dimensions of family violence* (pp. 21-38). New York: Springer.

Sonkin, D. J. (1986). Clairvoyance as common sense: Therapist's duty to warn and protect. *Violence and Victims, 1,* 7-21.

Sonkin, D. J. (1987). The assessment of court-mandated male batterers. In D. J. Sonkin (Ed.), *Domestic violence on trial: Psychological and legal dimensions of family violence* (pp. 174-196). New York: Springer.

Sonkin, D. J., & Durphy, M. (1985). *Learning to live without violence: A handbook for men* (2nd ed.). San Francisco: Volcano.

Sonkin, D. J., & Dutton, D. G. (Eds.). (1988). Wife assaulters [Special issue]. *Violence and Victims, 3*(1).

Sonkin, D. J., & Ellison, J. E. (1986). The therapist's duty to protect victims of domestic violence: Where we have been and where we are going. *Violence and Victims, 1,* 205-213.

Sonkin, D. J., Martin, D., & Walker, L. E. A. (1985). *The male batterer: A treatment approach.* New York: Springer.

Stahly, G. B. (1983). *Victim derogation of the battered woman, the just world and observer's past history of victimization.* Unpublished doctoral dissertation, University of California, Riverside.

Stahly, G. B. (1990, April). Battered women's problems with child custody. In G. B. Stahly (Chair), *New directions in domestic violence research.* Symposium conducted at the annual meeting of the Western Psychological Association, Los Angeles.

Stahly, G. B. (1991, August). *Custody issues for women* (Task Force Report, Division 35 Executive Committee Meeting, Boston). Washington, DC: American Psychological Association.

Stahly, G. B., Oursler, A., & Takano, J. (1988, April). *Family violence and child custody: A survey of battered women's fear and experiences.* Paper presented at the annual meeting of the Western Psychological Association, San Francisco.

Staples, R. (1990). Changes in black family structure: The conflict between family ideology and structural conditions. In C. Carlson (Ed.), *Perspectives on the family: History, class, and feminism* (pp. 281-293). Belmont, CA: Wadsworth.

Star, B. (1983). *Helping the abuser: Intervening effectively in family violence.* New York: Family Service Association.

Stark, E., & Flitcraft, A. (1981). Psychiatric perspectives on the abuse of women: A critical approach. In A. Lurie & E. Quitkin (Eds.), *Identification and treatment of spouse abuse: Health and mental health agency roles* (pp. 9-33). New York: Long Island Jewish-Hillside Hospital.

Stark, E., & Flitcraft, A. (1985). Women-battering, child abuse and social heredity: What is the relationship? In N. Johnson (Ed.), *Marital violence.* New York: Routledge & Kegan Paul.

Stark, E., & Flitcraft, A. (1988a). Personal power and institutional victimization: Treating the dual trauma of woman battering. In F. M. Ochberg (Ed.), *Post-traumatic therapy and victims of violence* (pp. 115-151). New York: Brunner/Mazel.

Stark, E., & Flitcraft, A. (1988b). Women and children at risk: A feminist perspective on child abuse. *International Journal of Health Services, 18*(1), 97-118.

Stark, E., Flitcraft, A., & Frazier, W. (1979). Medicine and patriarchal violence: The social construction of a private event. *International Journal of Health Services, 9,* 461-493.

Stark, E., Flitcraft, A., Zuckerman, D., Grey, A., Robison, J., & Frazier, W. (1981). *Wife abuse in the medical setting: An introduction for health personnel.* Rockville, MD: National Clearinghouse on Domestic Violence.

Steinglass, P. (1979). Alcoholism and the family: A review. *Marriage and the Family Review, 2,* 12-19.

Steinglass, P., Bennett, L., Wolin, S., & Reiss, D. (1987). *The alcoholic family.* New York: Basic Books.

Steinmetz, S. (1977). Wife-beating, husband-beating: A comparison of the use of physical violence between spouses to resolve marital fights. In M. Roy (Ed.), *Battered women: A psychosocial study of domestic violence* (pp. 63-67). New York: Van Nostrand Reinhold.

Sternbach, J. (1990). *Humanity vs. domination.* Workshop presented at the meeting of the American Association for Marriage and Family Therapy, Washington, DC.

Stets, J. E., & Pirog-Good, M. A. (1989). Sexual aggression and control in dating relationships. *Journal of Applied Social Psychology, 19,* 1392-1412.

Stordeur, R. A., & Stille, R. (1989). *Ending men's violence against their partners: One road to peace.* Newbury Park, CA: Sage.

Straus, M. A. (1974). Cultural and social organizational influences on violence between family members. In R. Prince & D. Barrier (Eds.), *Configurations: Biological and cultural factors in sexuality and family life* (pp. 53-69). Lexington, MA: D. C. Heath.

Straus, M. A. (1977-1978). Wife-beating: How common and why? *Victimology, 2,* 443-458.

Straus, M. A. (1979). Measuring intrafamily conflict and violence: The Conflict Tactics (CT) Scale. *Journal of Marriage and the Family, 41,* 75-88.

Straus, M. A. (1980). The marriage license as hitting license: Evidence from popular culture, law, and social science. In M. A. Straus & G. T. Hotaling (Eds.), *The social causes of husband-wife violence* (pp. 39-50). Minneapolis: University of Minnesota Press.

Straus, M. A. (1987). The costs of family violence. *Public Health Reports, 102*(6), 638-640.

Straus, M. A., & Gelles, R. J. (1986). Societal change and change in family violence from 1975 to 1985 as revealed by two national surveys. *Journal of Marriage and the Family, 48,* 465-479.

Straus, M. A., & Gelles, R. J. (1988). How violent are American families? Estimates from the National Family Violence Resurvey and other studies. In G. T. Hotaling, D. Finkelhor, J. T. Kirkpatrick, & M. A. Straus (Eds.), *Family abuse and its consequences: New directions in research* (pp. 14-36). Newbury Park, CA: Sage.

Straus, M. A., & Gelles, R. J. (1989). How violent are American families? Estimates from the National Family Violence Resurvey and other studies. In M. A. Strauss & R. J. Gelles (Eds.), *Physical violence in American families* (pp. 95-132). New Brunswick, NJ: Transaction.

Straus, M. A., Gelles, R. J., & Steinmetz, S. K. (1980). *Behind closed doors: Violence in the American family.* Garden City, NY: Anchor/Doubleday.

Straus, M. A., & Steinmetz, S. K. (1974). *Violence in the family.* New York: Harper & Row.

Strube, M. J., & Barbour, L. S. (1983). The decision to leave an abusive relationship: Economic dependence and psychological commitment. *Journal of Marriage and the Family, 45,* 785-793.

Stump, J. B. (1985). *What's the difference?* New York: Morrow.

Suchanek, J., & Stahly, G. B. (1991, April). *The relationship between domestic violence and paternal custody in divorce.* Paper presented at the annual meeting of the Western Psychological Association, San Francisco.

Sue, D. W. (1990). Culture-specific strategies in counseling: A conceptual framework. *Professional Psychology: Research and Practice, 21,* 424-433.

Sue, D. W., & Sue, S. (1990). *Counseling the culturally different: Theory and practice* (2nd ed.). New York: John Wiley.

Sue, S., & Zane, N. (1987). The role of culture and cultural techniques in psychotherapy: A critique and reformulation. *American Psychologist, 42,* 37-45.

Sun, M., & Thomas, E. (1987). *Custody litigation on behalf of battered women.* New York: National Center on Women and Family Law.

Symonds, A. (1979). Violence against women: The myth of masochism. *American Journal of Psychotherapy, 33,* 161-173.

Taggart, M. (1985). The feminist critique in epistemological perspective: Questions of context in family therapy. *Journal of Marital and Family Therapy, 11,* 113-126.

Tarasoff v. Regents of the University of California, 17 Cal 3rd 425 (1976).

Taubman, S. (1986). Beyond the bravado: Sex roles and the exploitive male. *Social Work, 31,* 12-18.

Teichman, M., & Teichman, Y. (1989). Violence in the family: An analysis in terms of interpersonal resource-exchange. *Journal of Family Violence, 4,* 127-142.

Teyber, E. C., & Hoffman, C. D. (1989). Missing fathers. In O. Pocs (Ed.), *Annual editions: Marriage and family* (15th ed.). Guilford, CT: Dushkin.

Thaxton, L. (1985). Wife abuse. In L. L'Abate (Ed.), *The handbook of family psychology and therapy* (pp. 878-899). Monterey, CA: Brooks/Cole.

The way we were: Looking back at 10 years of the family therapy newsletter. (1992, January/February). *The Family Therapy Newsletter,* 30-79.

Thoennes, N., & Tjaden, P. G. (1990). The extent, nature and validity of sexual abuse allegations in custody visitation disputes. *Child Abuse and Neglect, 14,* 151-163.

Tolman, R. M., & Bennett, L. W. (1990). A review of quantitative research on men who batter. *Journal of Interpersonal Violence, 5,* 87-118.

Tolman, R. M., & Bhosley, G. (1989). A comparison of two types of pregroup preparation for men who batter. *Journal of Social Science Research, 13,* 33-43.

Tolman, R. M., & Bhosley, G. (1990). The outcome of participation in a shelter-sponsored program for men who batter. In D. Knudsen & J. Miller (Eds.), *Abused and battered: Social and legal responses.* New York: Aldine de Gruyter.

Trankina, F. (1983). Clinical issues and techniques in working with Hispanic children and their families. In G. Powell, J. Yamamoto, A. Romero, & A. Morales (Eds.), *The psychosocial development of minority group children.* New York: Brunner/Mazel.

Treadway, D. (1989). *Before it's too late: Working with substance abuse in the family.* New York: W. W. Norton.

U.S. Commission on Civil Rights. (1982). *Under the rule of thumb: Battered women and the administration of justice.* Washington, DC: Government Printing Office.

U.S. Department of Commerce, Bureau of the Census. (1987). *Child support and alimony: 1987* (Current Population Reports, Special Studies Series, P-23, No. 167, 1). Washington, DC: Government Printing Office.

U.S. Department of Justice, Bureau of Justice Statistics. (1983). *Report to the nation on crime and justice: The data.* Washington, DC: Government Printing Office.

U.S. Department of Justice, Bureau of Justice Statistics. (1986). *Report to the nation on crime and justice: The data.* Washington, DC: Government Printing Office.

VandeCreek, L., & Merrill, W. (1990). Mental health services for the culturally different. In G. Stricker, E. Davis-Russell, E. Bourg, E. Duran, W. R. Hammond, J. McHolland, K. Polite, & B. E. Vaughn (Eds.), *Toward ethnic diversification in psychology, education and training* (pp. 195-201). Washington, DC: National Council of Schools of Professional Psychology and American Psychological Association.

Van der Kolk, B. A. (1987). The psychological consequences of overwhelming life experiences. In B. A. Van der Kolk (Ed.), *Psychological trauma* (pp. 1-30). Washington, DC: American Psychiatric Press.

von Erden, J., & Goodwin, B. J. (1992). *The unidentified battered woman: The importance of the intake interview.* Paper presented at the meeting of the Association for Women in Psychology, Long Beach, CA.

Waldo, M. (1987). Also victims: Understanding and treating men arrested for spouse abuse. *Journal of Counseling and Development, 65,* 385-388.

Walker, G. A. (1990). *Family violence and the women's movement: The conceptual politics of struggle.* Toronto: University of Toronto Press.

Walker, L. E. A. (1977). Battered women and learned helplessness. *Victimology, 2,* 252-354.

Walker, L. E. A. (1979). *The battered woman.* New York: Harper & Row.

Walker, L. E. A. (1981). Battered women: Sex roles and clinical issues. *Professional Psychology: Research and Practice, 12*(1), 84-94.

Walker, L. E. A. (1982). Beyond the juror's ken: Battered women. *Vermont Law Review, 7,* 1ff.

Walker, L. E. A. (1983). The battered woman syndrome study. In D. Finkelhor, R. J. Gelles, G. T. Hotaling, & M. A. Straus (Eds.), *The dark side of families: Current family violence research* (pp. 31-47). Beverly Hills, CA: Sage.

Walker, L. E. A. (1984a). *The battered woman syndrome.* New York: Springer.

Walker, L. E. A. (1984b, August). *The battered woman syndrome study: Psychological profiles.* Paper presented at the Second National Conference for Family Violence Researchers, Durham, NH.

Walker, L. E. A. (1984c). Battered women, psychology, and public policy. *American Psychologist, 29,* 1178-1182.

Walker, L. E. A. (1984d). *Women and mental health policy.* Beverly Hills, CA: Sage.

Walker, L. E. A. (1987). Inadequacies of the masochistic personality disorder diagnosis for women. *Journal of Personality Disorders, 1,* 183-189.

Walker, L. E. A. (1989a). Psychology and violence against women. *American Psychologist, 44,* 695-702.

Walker, L. E. A. (1989b). *Terrifying love: Why battered women kill and how society responds.* New York: HarperCollins.

Walker, L. E. A. (1991). Post-traumatic stress disorder in women: Diagnosis and treatment of battered woman syndrome. *Psychotherapy, 28,* 21-29.

Walker, L. E. A., & Browne, A. (1985). Gender and victimization by intimates. *Journal of Personality, 53,* 179-195.

Walker, L. E. A., & Edwall, G. E. (1987). Domestic violence and determination of visitation and custody in divorce. In D. J. Sonkin (Ed.), *Domestic violence on trial: Psychological and legal dimensions of family violence* (pp. 127-152). New York: Springer.

Wallerstein, J., & Blakeslee, S. (1989). *Second chances.* New York: Tichnor & Fields.

Warburton, J., Newberry, A., & Alexander, J. (1989). Women as therapists, trainees, and supervisors. In M. McGoldrick, C. M. Anderson, & F. Walsh (Eds.), *Women in families: A framework for family therapy* (pp. 152-165). New York: W. W. Norton.

Ware, S. (Ed.). (1989). *Modern American women: A documentary history.* Belmont, CA: Wadsworth.

The way we were: Looking back at ten years of the *Family Therapy Networker.* (1992). *Family Therapy Networker, 16*(1), 30-49.

Weiner, J. P., & Boss, P. (1985). Exploring gender bias against women: Ethic for marriage and family therapy. *Counseling and Values, 30,* 9-23.

Weitzman, J., & Dreen, K. (1982). Wife beating: A view of the marital dyad. *Social Casework, 63,* 259-265.

Weitzman, L. (1985). *The divorce revolution: The unexpected social and economic consequences for women and children in America.* New York: Free Press.

Wendorf, D. J., & Wendorf, R. J. (1985). A systemic view of family therapy ethics. *Family Process, 24,* 443-460.

Wheeler, D. (1985). The fear of feminism in family therapy: The risks of making waves. *Family Therapy Networker, 9*(6), 53-55.

Wheeler, D., Avis, J. M., Miller, L. A., & Chaney, S. (1989). Rethinking family therapy training and supervision: A feminist model. In M. McGoldrick, C. M. Anderson, & F. Walsh (Eds.), *Women in families: A framework for family therapy* (pp. 135-151). New York: W. W. Norton.

White, M. (1986, Spring). The conjoint therapy of men who are violent and the women with whom they live. *Dulwich Centre Newsletter.* In M. White (1989) *Selected Papers* (pp. 101-105). Adelaide, Australia: Dulwich Centre.

White, M. (1988-1989, Summer). The externalizing of the problem and the reauthoring of lives and relationships. *Dulwich Centre Newsletter* (pp. 5-28).

White, M., & Epston, D. (1990). *Narrative means to therapeutic ends.* New York: W. W. Norton.

Whitehurst, R. N. (1974). Violence in husband-wife interactions. In S. R. Steinmetz & M. A. Straus (Eds.), *Violence in the family* (pp. 75-82). New York: Dodd, Mead.

Willbach, D. (1989). Ethics and family therapy: The case management of family violence. *Journal of Marital and Family Therapy, 15,* 43-52.

Wilner, D. M., Freeman, H. E., Surber, M., & Goldstein, M. S. (1985). Success in mental health treatment interventions: A review of 211 random assignment studies. *Journal of Social Service Research, 8,* 1-21.

Wilson, S. K., Cameron, S., Jaffe, P. G., & Wolfe, D. A. (1989). Children exposed to wife abuse: An intervention model. *Social Casework, 70,* 180-184.

Woodruff, R. A., Gruze, S. B., Clayton, P. J., & Carr, D. (1973). Alcoholism and depression. *Archives of General Psychiatry, 28,* 97-100.

Woody, R. H. (1988). *Protecting your mental health practice: How to minimize legal and financial risk.* San Francisco: Jossey-Bass.

Wyatt, G. E. (1992). The sociocultural context of African American and white American women's rape. *Journal of Social Issues, 48,* 77-91.

Yates, A. (1987). Current status and future directions of research on the American Indian child. *American Journal of Psychiatry, 144,* 1135-1142.

Yllö, K. (1984). The status of women, marital equality and violence against wives: A contextual analysis. *Journal of Family Issues, 5,* 307-320.

Yllö, K. (1988). Political and methodological debates in wife abuse research. In K. Yllö & M. Bograd (Eds.), *Feminist perspectives on wife abuse* (pp. 28-50). Newbury Park, CA: Sage.

Yllö, K., & Bograd, M. (Eds.). (1988). *Feminist perspectives on wife abuse.* Newbury Park, CA: Sage.

Zammuner, V. L. (1987). Children's sex-role stereotypes: A cross-cultural analysis. In P. Shaver & C. Hendrick (Eds.), *Sex and gender.* Newbury Park, CA: Sage.

Zimbardo, P. G., Haney, C., & Banks, W. C. (1973, April 8). A Pirandellian prison: The mind is a formidable jailer. *New York Times Magazine,* pp. 38-60.

Zorza, J. (1991). *Mandatory arrest summary chart.* New York: National Center on Women and Family Law.

Author Index

Subject Index

About the Authors

Pearl S. Berman, Ph.D., is currently an Associate Professor of Psychology at Indiana University of Pennsylvania and a Child and Family Clinic Supervisor for the Center for Applied Psychology. Her training is in clinical psychology, with special interests in the areas of child physical and sexual abuse and neglect, and spousal violence. She has published repeatedly in these areas. The intent of her research and clinical work is to facilitate the recovery and empowerment of victims.

Joseph M. Cervantes, Ph.D., has a diplomate in clinical psychology from the American Board of Professional Psychology. He received his Ph.D. from the University of Nebraska, Lincoln. He is currently Codirector of Cervantes Institute, an outpatient child/adolescent mental health practice specializing in the treatment of multicultural families and school/community consultation. His research interests include multiethnic/multicultural theories of practice, the role of spirituality in psychotherapy, and consultation to ethnic minority communities.

Nancyann N. Cervantes, Ph.D., J.D., received her Ph.D. from Emory University and is a clinical psychologist with a specialty in child/family mental health practice and law. Her law degree from the University of Arizona has added further refinement to her integration of both disciplines. She is currently Codirector of Cervantes Institute, an outpatient child/adolescent mental health practice specializing in the treatment of multicultural families and school/community consultation. Her research interests include ethics in professional practice and mental health policy development.

Cynthia S. Cooley, M.A., is a therapist in private practice in Seattle, Washington. She is on the faculty of the Marriage and Family Therapy Program at Presbyterian Counseling Center and at the Montlake Institute. She founded the Chemical Dependency Studies Program at the California Family Study Center in 1984 and served as its Director for seven years. She remains on the center's adjunct faculty. Her current interests include a feminist application of Bowen family systems theory for issues of grief and loss for recovering individuals and families.

Irene Goldenberg is Acting Head of Medical Psychology at the University of California, Los Angeles, in the Department of Psychiatry, where she teaches family therapy. She is coauthor (with Herbert Goldenberg) of *Family Therapy: An Overview,* which is used throughout the United States. She is currently working on a revision of her book *Today's Families,* which she also coauthored with her husband.

Edward W. Gondolf, Ed.D., M.P.H., is a Professor of Sociology in the Graduate Human Service Program at Indiana University of Pennsylvania. He is Research Director of the Mid-Atlantic Addiction Training Institute and an Adjunct Professor at Western Psychiatric Institute and Clinic, University of Pittsburgh Medical School. He is also affiliated with the Domestic Abuse Counseling Center for men who batter in Pittsburgh and is a consultant to the batterers clinic of the Veterans Affairs Medical Center, Pittsburgh. He is the author of several books on domestic violence and community development issues, including *Men Who Batter* (1985), *Battered Women as Survivors* (with E. R. Fisher; 1988), and *Psychiatric Response to Family Violence* (1990).

Beverly J. Goodwin, Ph.D., is currently an Assistant Professor of Psychology at Indiana University of Pennsylvania, where she teaches both undergraduate and graduate courses. She also is associated with Alma Illery Medical Center in Pittsburgh, Pennsylvania, where she specializes in providing services to a culturally diverse clientele. She received her doctorate from the University of Pittsburgh Clinical Psychology Program. Her specialty areas are personality theory, psychopathology, supervision and training issues, curriculum transformation, and relationship violence. She has published numerous articles and has presented papers on these topics at national conferences.

Marsali Hansen is an Assistant Professor of Psychology at Indiana University of Pennsylvania. She received her Ph.D. in psychology from Peabody College of Vanderbilt University in 1980. She specializes in providing family psychology training to doctoral students and in introducing family psychology to undergraduates. She has published and presented on the topic of therapist perceptions of spouse abuse, and she maintains a part-time private practice with a special focus on children and family concerns.

Barbara J. Hart, Esq., is Staff Counsel for the Pennsylvania Coalition Against Domestic Violence. Her work for the coalition focuses on public policy-making, training, and technical assistance on myriad issues related to domestic violence. She is coauthor (with E. Stubbling and J. Stuehling) of *Confronting Domestic Violence: Effective Police Response,* a training manual for law enforcement response to domestic violence. She is also author of *Safety for Women: Monitoring Batterers' Programs,* a manual that seeks to describe how batterers' treatment programs can be accountable to battered women survivors, and *Domestic Violence Protection Orders: Handbook for District Court Administrators, Prothonotaries, and Special Court Administrators.* She is the editor of *Battering and Addiction: Consciousness-Raising for Battered Women and Advocates.*

Michèle Harway, Ph.D., is Director of Research and Professor at the California Family Study Center in North Hollywood. In addition to conducting research on women and women's issues, she trains master's-level clinicians and sees individuals, families, and couples in psychotherapy. She is coauthor (with Helen S. Astin) of *Sex Discrimination in Career Counseling and Education* and coeditor (with S. Mednick and K. Finello) of *Handbook of Longitudinal Research,* Volumes I and II. In addition, she has published several dozen articles on family violence, sex differences, sex bias and stereotyping, and other topics. She is concurrently completing a book on professional women and child care.

Mary P. Koss is a Professor of Family and Community Medicine, Psychiatry, and Psychology at the University of Arizona in Tucson. With Dr. Mary Harvey, she is coauthor of *The Rape Victim: Clinical and Community Interventions.* She is Cochair of the American Psychological Association Task Force on Violence Against Women and a member of the National Institute of Mental Health Working Group on Violence. She is an Associate Editor of both *Psychology of Women Quarterly* and *Violence and Victims,* and is a Consulting Editor for the *Journal of Interpersonal Violence, Violence Update,* and the *Journal of Child Sexual Abuse.* She is the recipient of the Stephen Schaefer Award for Outstanding Research Contributions to the Victim's Assistance Field given by the National Organization for Victim's Assistance and the Brotherpeace Award for Academic Contributions to Activism by the National Organization of Men Against Sexism.

Marsha B. Liss is a developmental psychologist (Ph.D., SUNY Stony Brook) and an attorney (J.D., UCLA). She is Professor of Psychology and Human Development at California State University, San Bernardino. In 1991-1992, she was a Fellow of the Society for Research in Child Development at the National Center on Child Abuse and Neglect. She is remaining at the National Center on Child Abuse and Neglect for 1992-1993 as the Special Assistant to the Director. She has written on the effects of television, development of sex roles, legal and policy issues involving children's rights, and domestic violence and custody. As a volunteer attorney at the Harriet Buhai Center for Family Law, she assisted indigent clients with custody, guardianship, and paternity cases. She is the editor of *Social and Cognitive Skills: Sex Roles and Children's Play* (1983).

Maureen C. McHugh, Ph.D., is the Director of Women's Studies and Associate Professor of Psychology at Indiana University of Pennsylvania. She is active in Division 35 (Psychology of Women) of the American Psychological Association, and is the Membership Chair of the Association for Women in Psychology. She received her doctorate from the University of Pittsburgh in 1983. A social psychologist by training, she specializes in gender issues in psychology. She has published and presented papers in the areas of sex differences in attributions, gender bias in psychology, and victim blame. She is currently working on a series of papers on relationship violence.

Elizabeth Register, M.A., is retired from the faculty of the California Family Study Center, where she taught courses in human sexuality, women's studies, and domestic violence. She is currently in private practice in Toluca Lake, California, as a licensed marriage and family therapist and a certified sex therapist. She also serves as clinical supervisor and trainer at Discovery House in La Crescenta, California. She is approved as a supervisor by the American Association of Marriage and Family Therapists and the American Association of Sex Educators, Counselors and Therapists. She is the author of "Gender Issues in Supervision" in the California Association of Marriage and Family Therapists volume *Practical Applications in Supervision* (1990). Her current research interests are focused on aging parents and families.

Claire M. Renzetti is Professor of Sociology at St. Joseph's University, Philadelphia, Pennsylvania. She is author of *Violent Betrayal: Partner Abuse in Lesbian Relationships* (1992) and coauthor of *Women, Men, and Society*; *Social Problems: Society in Crisis*; and *Criminology*. In addition, she is coeditor of a volume on researching sensitive topics and a forthcoming collection of articles on social problems. Her research on domestic violence, the women's movement, and women and economic development has appeared in various scholarly journals, including the *Journal of Interpersonal Violence, Family Relations, Sex Roles,* and *Contemporary Crises.*

Kathleen Severson is a therapist in private practice in Seattle, Washington. She holds a master's degree in counseling from Seattle University and is a Ph.D. candidate in counseling psychology at the University of Washington. She is an adjunct faculty member at Seattle Central Community College and serves as a consultant to other therapists. Her current interests include the application of environmental perspectives to healing from abuse and the effects of major life changes on women's sense of self.

Geraldine Butts Stahly completed her doctorate in psychology at the University of California, Riverside, and is currently an Associate Professor in the Psychology Department at California State University, San Bernardino. She is an applied social psychologist with numerous publications on the topics of victimology and family violence. She has worked extensively in the criminal justice system, conducting training on domestic violence for prosecutors and judges and giving expert testimony in criminal and civil trials. One of her current research interests is the area of custody issues in violent families, and she recently chaired the Task Force on Child Custody Issues for Division 35 of the American Psychological Association.

Lenore E. A. Walker, Ed.D., is a licensed psychologist in independent practice with Walker & Associates in Denver, Colorado, and Executive Director of the Domestic Violence Institute. A diplomate in clinical psychology from the American Board of Professional Psychology, she has pioneered the introduction of expert witness testimony on "battered woman self-defense" in U.S. courts. Her research on the psychological effects of battering on women and the dynamics of the battering relationship began in the 1970s with research funded by the National Institute of Mental Health. Her psychology interests have concentrated on women's mental health issues and on stopping all forms of violence against women and children. She has published widely on these topics, and her books include *The Battered Woman* (1979), *Women and Mental Health Policy* (1984), *The Battered Woman Syndrome* (1984), *Feminist Psychotherapies* (with M. A. Dutton, 1988), *Handbook on Sexually Abused Children* (1988), and *Terrifying Love: Why Battered Women Kill and How Society Responds* (1989).